THE WEST YORKS... W...

Part 1: Th...

by Christopher Goddard

Alfie and the squirrel,
a perennial stand-off

For the wild men of the woods

Published by Christopher Goddard

www.christophergoddard.net

Amended First Edition – 2017

Printed in Bradford by Kiss Graphics

Text and images © Christopher Goddard 2017

ISBN 978-0-9954502-0-2

ACKNOWLEDGEMENTS

With thanks to everyone who helped make this book possible:

Amanda Batty, Rob Blake, Roger Burnett, David Cant, Jamie Cook,
Gill Corteen, Robin Dalton, Pete Gierth, Nick Goddard, Roger
Goddard, Claire Godden, Robin Gray and Pennine Prospects, Rosie
Holdsworth, Janina Holubecki, Christina Hooley, Heather Ibbetson,
Hywel Lewis, Drew Marsh, Philip Marshall, Diana Monaghan and the
Hebden Bridge Local History Society, Richard Robson and the
Greater Elland Historical Society, Mark Simmonds, Dave Smalley,
Nigel Smith, Matt Taylor, Frank Woolrych and Tony Wright.

And of course my wonderfully supportive partner Caroline.

THE WEST YORKSHIRE WOODS: Part 1

CONTENTS

Introduction

i   Overview Map
iii   The West Yorkshire Woods
vii   How Trees Work
ix   History of the Woodlands of the Calder Valley
xxxi   List of Ancient Woodlands
xxxv   Woodland Glossary

1   **Chapter 1 – Norwood Green & Shelf**
       Route 1: Judy & Shelf Woods from Shelf

9   **Chapter 2 – Shibden Dale**
       Route 2: Shibden Dale from Northowram
       Route 3: Beacon Hill, Shibden Park, Sunny Vale & Chelsea Valley from Halifax

23   **Chapter 3 – Brighouse & Elland**
       Route 4: Elland Park, Cromwell & Strangstry Woods from Elland or Brighouse

33   **Chapter 4 – Halifax & Copley**
       Route 5: North Dean Wood, Wainhouse Tower & Wood House Scar from
          West Vale or Copley
       Route 6: Wheatley Valley & Mixenden from Halifax

47   **Chapter 5 – Blackburn & Holywell Valleys**
       Route 7: Blackburn Valley from Barkisland
       Route 8: Holywell Brook from Stainland

57   **Chapter 6 – Ryburn Valley**
       Route 9: Lower Ryburn Valley from Sowerby Bridge
       Route 10: Upper Ryburn Valley from Ripponden

71   **Chapter 7 – Luddenden Dean**
       Route 11: Luddenden Dean from Luddenden Foot

79   **Chapter 8 – Mytholmroyd & Cragg Vale**
       Route 12: Redacre Wood, Brearley Wood & Scout Rock from Mytholmroyd
       Route 13: Cragg Vale from Mytholmroyd

95   **Chapter 9 – Hebden Dale**
       Route 14: Crimsworth Dean & Lumb Falls from Hebden Bridge
       Route 15: Hardcastle Crags & Hebden Dale from Midgehole

113   **Chapter 10 – Hebden Bridge to Todmorden**
       Route 16: Colden Clough & Eaves Wood from Hebden Bridge
       Route 17: Jumble Hole, Rawtonstall Wood & Horsehold Scout from Hebden
          Bridge
       Route 18: Lumbutts, Shaw & Ingham Cloughs from Todmorden

137   **Chapter 11 – Todmorden & Walsden**
       Route 19: The Woods of Todmorden
       Route 20: The Cliviger Gorge from Lydgate or Cornholme
       Route 21: Gorpley & Ramsden Cloughs from Walsden

153   **Bibliography**

158   **Index / Gazetteer**

THE WOODS OF THE CALDER

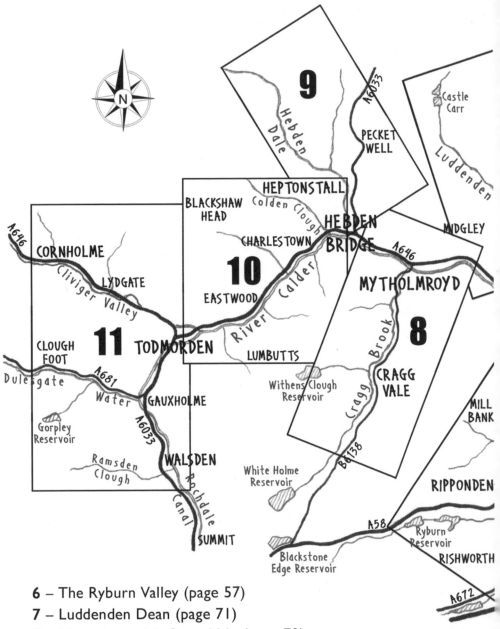

6 – The Ryburn Valley (page 57)

7 – Luddenden Dean (page 71)

8 – Mytholmroyd & Cragg Vale (page 79)

9 – Hebden Dale (page 95)

10 – Hebden Bridge to Todmorden (page 113)

11 – Todmorden & Walsden (page 137)

VALLEY - Overview Map

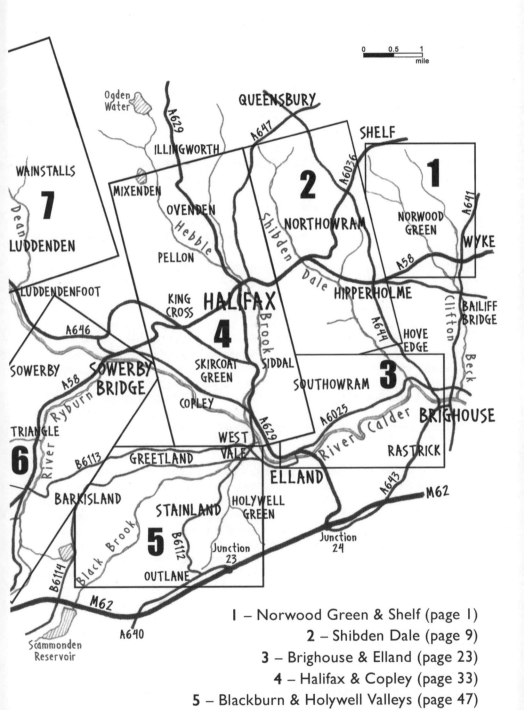

1 – Norwood Green & Shelf (page 1)
2 – Shibden Dale (page 9)
3 – Brighouse & Elland (page 23)
4 – Halifax & Copley (page 33)
5 – Blackburn & Holywell Valleys (page 47)

MY WEST YORKSHIRE WOODS

"One more thing: I grew up in the woods. I understand many things because of the woods. Trees standing together, growing alongside one another, providing so much."

(The Log Lady, from *Twin Peaks*)

Tinker Bank Wood is much like any other pocket of woodland in the Calder Valley – it is steep, muddy and littered with rocks – yet it is endlessly fascinating. I visit it several times a week to walk the dog and see it in all seasons and all weathers, and I never tire of it.

The way to Tinker Bank Wood is along Dark Lane, a narrow old path lined with some veteran ash and sycamores. The bark of some of the sycamores is like a map, its contour lines picked out where the bark has peeled off. At the end of the lane, The Hollings is a romantic-looking terrace of cottages climbing up the hillside. Flowers spill out of the gardens into the path and I have always thought this would be a great place to live – though in truth I know it to be dark and dank beneath the Heptonstall hillside. There is a brief tunnel beneath the rhododendrons beyond, that forms the gateway into Tinker Bank Wood and you emerge in its midst at a junction of four paths. Several public footpaths cross the wood, many of them age-old routes, so you can vary your walk through it each day. Even then, there are still hidden corners in between that I stumble across with surprise now and then.

The first part of the wood is dominated by mature sycamore trees. It is the least interesting area, in spite of the few twisted oaks that wind like corkscrews towards the light. The leaves here are mulched up and broken only by the bluebells that will herald the spring with their bright clarion colours. Higher up, there are a couple of stately horse chestnut trees along the Hebden Hey track. They are the finest single trees in the wood and their huge leaf paws dominate the ground in autumn, a richer orange even than the beech beyond. Beech trees take over above the track, a bank of 19th-century plantings that are now at maturity and liable to fall in every storm. Throughout the wood, there are the shallow feet and broken-up trunks of fallen beech. At the top, there are so few left that light pours in where normally the beech canopy provides the densest shade.

Moving into the wood, the ground gets rougher, with lumps of gritstone scattered liberally across the slope. One is a curious mossy bowl balanced precariously on its side, others look like miniature versions of the great crags on the Heptonstall hillside above. This is now ancient semi-natural woodland and a true mix of trees; oak is more dominant, joined by the frail silver birch, and there is a thicker covering of ferns and brambles across the woodland floor. The grace of the birch is somewhat besmirched by lichen and pollution, but its bark peels off in satisfying paper-like sheets and there are huge polypores clinging to many of the trunks. Beech and ash saplings grow beneath the canopy, though few seem to last into maturity, and fallen trees block the way at every turn. You can see less in here and, as you pick your way between the trees, you are liable to come across the unmistakeable flattened circle of a hearth once used for charcoal burning or a curious circular pit lined with stone, whose historical significance has long since become indecipherable. At the bottom of the wood, the slope drops very steeply down to the old bowling club and allotments along Hebden Water. It steepens into a rocky scout further along, where a large boulder provides a good vantage point and place to relax in the summer.

The far end of the wood is my favourite, beyond the line of an old wall that once divided Tinker Bank Wood from Lee Wood. It is now identifiable only by the tall stoops along the bottom path, where holly closes in around the feet of the oak trees. Paths meander through these dark bowers to emerge in small clearings of oak, birch and rowan, one of which houses an early charcoal hearth, and another an area rich in russula mushrooms as well as the bones and feathers of a dead heron. In the middle of the densest holly tree, which bears the finest of berries in the winter, is a small tarpaulin shelter that is almost invisible from the path ten feet away. At the edge of the wood, you can gaze over the dry stone wall to a bright open field and the wooded slopes of Galstones Bank and Crimsworth Wood, at the top of which is the striking war memorial. There is even a small plantation of spruce trees beyond the wall, one of which has escaped some distance into the wood, a surreal three-foot miniature dwarfed by oaks.

Yet this is only part of Tinker Bank Wood, which blends seamlessly into Lee Wood and extends along the Hebden Hey track for another half a mile to lead into the Hardcastle Crags woodland, but that is another country. My corner of Tinker Bank Wood is just 300m long and less than 200m wide, yet there is a whole world to discover in it. There are at least four charcoal hearths, the site of a former hut perhaps used by someone working in the wood, the well-defined line of a level or trackway above the existing track, and the remains of a stone cross inscribed with lettering I am yet to decipher. The trees are full of the sounds of woodpeckers, tits, thrushes, magpies, warblers and robins, while there are plenty of squirrels that Alfie loves to chase, as well as inquisitive deer who come down from the woods around Hardcastle Crags. The wood changes at every turn, in every light, and with every season. And the most remarkable thing is that this is not a particularly remarkable piece of woodland; I could be describing any corner of woodland on any doorstep. While the moors inspire with their vast empty swathes and open vistas, it is the ever-changing intricacy of the woodlands that makes us return time after time. There is something simultaneously reassuring and unsettling about the familiarity of woods that are different every time you look at them.

a path through Tinker Bank Wood

THE WEST YORKSHIRE WOODS

You may not immediately think of woodland when you think of West Yorkshire – indeed the county has only approximately 4% woodland cover, which is well below the national average. Yet there are many of its valleys where the rich woodland clinging to the steep slopes below the moors and developed hillsides forms one of the defining elements of the landscape. Often these are thin strips of woodland that barely show up on maps, but they have a striking visual impact. It is hard to ignore in places like Hebden Bridge or Copley in the Calder Valley, Bingley or Newlay on the Aire Valley, or Honley in the Holme Valley. I have begun with the Calder Valley[1] for Part 1, as it is most local to me, but the pattern is repeated to a greater or lesser degree in the Aire, Holme and Wharfe Valleys.

For the purposes of this book, I have focused on the woods that line the River Calder and its tributaries between Brighouse and the county boundary beyond Todmorden. This is the borough now known as Calderdale, though I have occasionally gone over the borough border where it cuts off the head of Clifton Brook and Shibden Dale. The area contains several significant tributaries to the main river – Shibden Dale, Hebble Brook, Black Brook, the Ryburn Valley, Luddenden Dean, Cragg Vale, Hebden Dale, each following a similar landscape pattern. Large-scale industrial development along the streams has now either been converted into modern housing or industrial estates, or else abandoned to nature. A thick cloak of woodland then reaches up the steep valley sides and, where it levels out, fields, farms and older settlements take over, before finally the moorland wastes are reached. Although there is only 14km² of woodland in Calderdale, over half of it is considered ancient woodland in one form or another, meaning it has been continuously wooded since 1600. As well as water, wood was one of the great natural resources of the Upper Calder Valley – it was used for fuel (both as firewood and charcoal), and to build houses, furniture and machinery. Though the woodlands are old, the trees in them rarely are, largely due to the ravages of industrial development – the oldest trees here are mostly sycamores planted over 200 years ago, though there are some other ancient beeches and limes. For more detail on how the woodland landscape in the valley was shaped, see the following History section.

There are various definitions of woodland, but the definition used in UK forestry statistics is 'land under stands of trees with a canopy cover of at least 20% (or having the potential to achieve this), including integral open space, and including felled areas that are awaiting re-stocking'. There is no minimum size for a woodland, nor minimum height of tree, so the definition includes woodland scrub but not areas solely consisting of gorse, rhododendron or other bushes. Internationally the definition usually uses a figure of 10% canopy cover but includes a minimum height at maturity of 5m. What is interesting about these definitions is just how little canopy cover is required for an area to be considered woodland, when generally we think it having almost complete cover (which says a lot about the sort of woodland we have encouraged). Thus, there are many more wooded areas than simply those mapped in green on OS maps, which don't include scrub or younger woodland.

In this book, I have mapped nearly all of the woodlands in these valleys, as well as the often treeless areas in between. I hope to have captured the feel of these landscapes and the sense that, even in places with relatively little woodland, trees play a huge part in imbuing them with character. I decided to map the different trees with different symbols to give a better impression of the character of each area. Although I have not plotted every single tree, it has still taken plenty of time to record the dominant tree types in every corner of woodland, as well as along green lanes or around old farmsteads. Oak,

---

[1] Local historian Jack Uttley stressed that this has always been the Calder Valley (an Anglian name) rather than Calderdale (a Danish/Viking name) as this was part of the Anglo-Saxon kingdom that stretched as far north as the Craven Gap. *Calder* itself is a Celtic word, usually taken to mean 'violent stream', though others have suggested it translates as 'wooded water'.

birch, beech and sycamore are the most predominant, and there are enough ash, chestnut, willow, lime, holly and conifers to justify their inclusion. For others, like elm, cherry, hazel, elder and rowan, there are either not enough or they are too small to warrant a symbol. The distinction between trees and shrubs is not entirely clear – we often think of trees as those with one main stem rather than a cluster of stems, but coppicing produces trees that blur the definition. So, for the purposes of this book, woody shrubs like hazel, elder, willow and holly are considered trees.

Putting names to woodland areas is not always easy. Often various names have existed for the same wood; in other cases there is none recorded. Tinker Bank Wood is a case in point. The name now appears to refer to a small area of wood above Lee Wood Road, with the whole area below the road shown on maps as Lee Wood. However, the name undoubtedly predates the 1793 road, and the old walls in the lower part of the wood neatly divide it into three; Slater Bank Wood at the south end, Tinker Bank Wood in the middle and Lee Wood beginning only near the north end.

There are 21 suggested routes in this book, which are all of a similar technical difficulty. These routes are not wooded throughout – this in itself would be rather dull – but provide as full an exploration of the Calder Valley's wooded landscape as possible. You may at times think I am stretching the woodland point a little, but they remain lovely walks and it is partly the variety of landscape that makes them so appealing. The natural distribution of trees gives distinctive character and identity to different places and, the closer you look at them, the more this character will reveal itself. I began this book with a passing layman's interest in trees and have finished it with a completely new outlook on the endless variety of these familiar and reassuring embodiments of nature.

Access to the Woods

Access to the woods is not as straightforward as the moors. Where woods are owned by the local council (e.g. North Dean Wood, Elland Park Wood, Centre Vale Park, Eaves Wood and Colden Clough) or a body like the National Trust (e.g. Hardcastle Crags), they are Open Access and you can walk anywhere. Others are very definitely private (e.g. those in the Castle Carr Estate and below Hathershelf Scout) and there is no access to several appealing-looking chunks of woodland, some of which have been included in the book for the sake of completeness. However, the bulk of the Calder Valley's woodlands fall between these two extremes. Even in 1904, W.B. Crump remarked on the open nature of many of the valley's woods, particularly those around Hebden Bridge, which have traditionally been considered accessible even where there are no Public Rights of Way. You'll find various paths into and through areas of woodland that are not legally enshrined as Public Rights of Way, but which are obviously well used. Often these are on the edge of urban areas and used by local dog walkers, but on the whole there is little issue with their use, even where the wood is privately owned.

As a result, it can often be hard to tell where you are or are not supposed to be in the woods. The best response, as ever, is common sense. Follow local signage, don't damage walls or fences, and don't interfere with any management practices (like stacks of logs or equipment) within the woods. Exploring the woods off its paths can be interesting but is often very precarious in this area, so steep and loose are the slopes, and you often end up sliding inevitably into the stream at the bottom of a clough. Be warned and take care.

There is also a degree of misinformation about your rights in woodland. While you do have a right to forage for leaves, berries, and mushrooms along paths and other legally accessible ground, there is no right to gather firewood here. Those commoners' rights are usually long gone, traded away for tiny parcels of land during the Enclosure Acts. Where they do remain, it is for local commoners only. Common Woods, like those in Hipperholme, Cragg Vale and Eastwood, are remnants of this past, when woodlands were a community resource for more than leisurely strolls.

HOW TREES WORK

We tend to take it for granted that we know how trees work, but there is actually a lot I learned during the writing of this book, so here's a little refresher.

A tree is made up of crown, trunk and roots – each serving a different purpose. The crown is composed of hundreds of thousands of leaves, which are the tree's boiler room. Here, the green chlorophyll allows the tree to absorb energy from sunlight, which is then converted into sugars by using water from the roots and carbon dioxide from the air. Oxygen is released as a by-product, an evolutionary fluke that is one of the reasons that our planet is hospitable. An acre of trees absorbs the equivalent amount of carbon dioxide as that produced by driving 26,000 miles, and produces enough oxygen for eighteen people to breathe.

The trunk acts as both the tree's joist and its plumbing system, and is formed of a number of different concentric layers. The outer bark is made of cork and protects it from the ravages of the elements and disease, as well as preventing water loss. Though it is regenerated regularly, many trees (particularly saplings) struggle to survive when their bark is stripped by the likes of squirrels and deer. The distinctive outer part of the bark is actually dead cork cells, which vary in appearance and thickness between different species, but give trees much of their character. Underneath, the inner bark (or phloem)

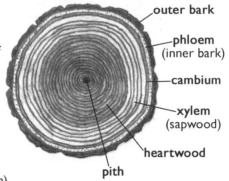

outer bark

phloem (inner bark)

cambium

xylem (sapwood)

heartwood

pith

is made up of vessels that allow the sugars produced in the leaves to be transported around the tree, essentially feeding its roots and branches. These sugars are dissolved in water and form the sap we are familiar with oozing from a damaged or cut tree. If you were to cut a ring around the tree through this layer, the tree would almost certainly die.

Beneath the bark, sapwood is a thicker woody layer of tissue, composed of xylem vessels that transport water and minerals from the roots to the leaves, as well as storing them. These cells are continually refreshed by a layer called the cambium, which lays down new wood each year and causes the tree to grow. All of a tree's trunk, roots and branches thus expand outwards and it is this growth that produces the rings on trees and allows us to age them. The thickness of the ring depends upon the size of the tree's trunk and the amount of leaves it has in its crown to produce sugars, as well as other environmental factors like light intensity and pollution.[2] As a general rule, the trunk of a tree in a wood grows by half an inch a year, though this will be more rapid in its early years and diminish as it nears maturity (when it has a greater surface area to cover and often a reduced crown). Often the trees that grow to live the oldest are those which have suffered most during their lifetime, whether by regular cutting, growing on poor soil or suffering environmental hardship, all of which lead to it reaching maturity later.

Sapwood has to be grown afresh as it steadily fills with resin and forms heartwood, the older dead wood at the centre of the trunk. In most trees, this is significantly darker than its sapwood and the division is clear in any cross section. The heartwood gives the tree its strength, though in older trees its core may rot away to leave it hollow.

Trees do not grow steadily, but in spurts when conditions are right, largely in the warmer months. Deciduous trees shed their leaves in the winter for various reasons; to conserve water and nutrients, and to prevent damage during winter storms; the effect of both high winds and snow is limited by removing the large surface area created by its

---

[2] In industrial areas like the Calder Valley, you often find older trees have a whole section of densely packed rings that correspond to the era when smoke clogged the valleys and limited the tree's ability to photosynthesise fully.

leaves. They do this by a process called abscission, whereby anything useful is retrieved from the leaves before the supply to them is sealed off. As chlorophyll is one of the first parts of the leaves to be broken down and re-absorbed, they discolour first before falling to the ground when cut off. Interestingly, green leaves would naturally all fade through yellow to brown, but as this yellow colour is so attractive to aphids, many species inject a form of red pigment into their leaves during the process to produce the array of autumnal oranges and reds we enjoy.

Trees are also very susceptible to injury as they cannot heal themselves. Instead they seal off the damaged area, meaning it will never be productive again. Many older trees bear the scars of these hardships and are covered in knots and burrs, with little in the way of productive living branches (i.e. the oak on p129). A knot is formed where a branch has fallen off or a bud is dormant, each being subsequently swallowed up by the growing trunk, and often ending up preserved deep inside the rings of older trees. A burr is a large bark-covered outgrowth filled with the knots of dormant buds, and often forms as a result of an infestation.

The roots provide water, minerals and stability to the tree, the latter particularly important on steep Pennine hillsides. The depth they reach varies greatly between species; a beech's roots are slight while an oak may send down tap roots for several metres (though generally this only occurs where it needs to seek moisture on well-drained soil). Roots tend to extend well beyond the range of the branches, ending in tiny rootlets covered in fine hairs that can absorb water and minerals. The end of most roots are remarkably close to the surface (usually within three inches), as this is where most water and nutrients are found. As a result, they are very vulnerable to changes in soil depth or composition caused by human interference or natural run-off.

Trees have several ways of reproducing: self-seeding, suckering and planting. Suckers are shoots that grow from the roots of an existing tree, often some distance from its parent, and it is the only way some species can reproduce, particularly at the edge of their climatic range (e.g. the English elm, lime and sweet chestnut). Suckering is the most common form of reproduction and can lead to groves of genetically identical trees all from the same original growth. Indeed many of our oldest living things take this form, including the ancient yews of Fortingall and Llangernyw.

A tree that has grown from seed is known as a maiden, but the ability to do this is dependent on a number of things. Firstly trees generally produce viable seed only when they have reached maturity (anything from twenty to over a hundred years),[4] and even then they produce seeds only occasionally. When environmental conditions are right, often following a hot summer, all the mature trees of a given species are likely to seed in the same season. On these occasions, vast quantities of seed are produced and the woodland floor is covered in acorns, mast or keys; otherwise they produce nothing. Even having done this, they are reliant on not having squirrels run off with everything, or having it washed away by run-off, a particular problem in this area. Of the seed that does survive and develop into seedlings, most will be killed by further predation or bark-stripping. Also, in Britain, many seedlings struggle to establish themselves or die out after a couple of years because the trees are at the edge of their climatic range, something that is being slowly altered by climate change.

So much about trees is still not well understood. Trees are now known to 'talk' to each other by emitting chemical pheromones when being attacked to alert other trees nearby, or to help weak trees recover or seedlings to establish themselves by providing for them through micorrhizal networks (fungal threads that physically link the roots of different trees). Yet this theory was considered lunatic just twenty years ago, suggesting these remarkable life-giving organisms are far more refined than we ever thought.

---

[4] Oak trees never produce seed until they are at least forty years old, and often far longer in poorer growing conditions.

A HISTORY OF THE WOODLANDS
OF THE CALDER VALLEY

*"Truly the waste and destruction of our woods has been so universal
that I conceive nothing less than an universal plantation of all sorts of
trees will supply and will counter the defect"*
(John Evelyn, *Sylva*)

These words, written in 1664, show that Britain's woodlands have been under threat for a
long time. The eminent woodland historian Oliver Rackham suggests we have been
managing our woods since 1300, as so much had been felled by then that it had become a
necessity. Acts to prevent the felling of woodland were passed in the reigns of Henry VIII
in 1543, Elizabeth I in 1558 (*An Act that Timber shall not be Felled to make Coals for the
burning of Iron*) and Charles II (which precipitated John Evelyn's paper on the subject of
good forestry). These measures were often precipitated by a lack of oak timber for
building Navy ships, which tended to be a problem after wars; in Charles' case the Civil
War. Much later, both World Wars took a toll on our woodlands, the first leading directly
to the formation of the Forestry Commission. In addition, there were plenty of local
regulations, often preventing mature wood from being used for making charcoal, and
Furness even suppressed all its iron bloomeries for a time in the 16th century to allow
the woodland to recover. Woodland paranoia is nothing new.

I have heard it said by many people that the Calder Valley was densely wooded until
the Middle Ages, since when its woodland has been steadily consumed to meet increasing
industrial demands. However, I tend to buy into Oliver Rackham's notion that the chief
destroyer of woodland has always been agriculture and any industry's reliance on trees
actually causes them to be preserved. The voracious demand for timber, charcoal and
other woodland products that has led many to observe that we were essentially a wood
culture until the industrial revolution is ultimately likely to have preserved our ancient
woodland. Otherwise what we have remaining might also have been cleared. The
industrial revolution continued that trend, preserving woods precisely because it relied
upon them in so many ways.

That being said, the history of our woods is particularly hard to untangle. Other than
the royal estates, few records were kept beyond incidental details, like the records of
woodland or timber sales, and as a result much conjecture arises. From these scraps, we
have some idea of local woodland history, but so much of it is based on more broadly
observed patterns. Given that each area and woodland is different from the next, there is
much we don't know and large gaps in the summary that follows. In it I will attempt to
explain at least partially the complicated picture that leaves us with the curious piecemeal
woodlands we have today.

The Prehistoric Wildwood and its Demise

During the last Ice Age, the Calder Valley was never glaciated, though its waters were
interrupted to the east by the Vale of York glacier near Horbury, creating a vast Lake
Calderdale which covered much of Dewsbury, Brighouse and Huddersfield. Large glacier
lakes formed to the west of the Pennines and it was these that breached the ridge in
several places when the glaciers began to melt, scouring the deep valleys that we know
today. The previous level of the valley can be clearly seen in the shelf of flatter ground and
the series of hanging valleys above the woods in the Upper Calder Valley. Many of the
valleys are now overhung by crags of Kinderscout Grit that are underlain by softer shale
beds. This caused a series of subsequent landslips forming features like Hardcastle

Crags, Hathershelf Scout in Mytholmroyd and Robin Hood's Scar in Elland Park Wood.

After the Ice Age, the alpine climate quickly changed and Britain (then a peninsula of the continent) became far warmer and drier during the Boreal Period (from cl1,000BC). Forests developed, initially composed of the more arctic trees of birch, aspen and sallow, but soon incorporating colonising trees from the warmer climates to the south; first hazel and pine, then oak and alder, followed by lime and elm, and finally ash, beech, holly and hornbeam. These began as sparse forests with heather and heath flora underneath, but developed into what we know as the wildwood that preceded man's arrival on these shores.

We think of this as a dense impassable cloak of trees and bushes full of wild animals, and the wildwood is often seen as our own Garden of Eden, a longed for romantic vision of a natural world forever lost. But, writing about the wildwood of lowland Europe, Frans Vera has suggested this vision never existed, envisaging more of an open wood pasture like that of the New Forest. Natural woodlands are very dynamic, shifting continuously and having significant open areas. Indeed most native British trees don't like being shaded and prefer to establish on liminal areas. Grazing by wild herbivores was an important natural check on the woodland's growth, preventing it from becoming a closed canopy and allowing plenty of variety to develop, including lower areas of thorns, fruit bushes and scrub. However, more inaccessible places like the steep cloughs of the Pennines may have been naturally denser.

The earliest evidence of Mesolithic activity in the South Pennines are flints dating from around 8000BC, when the few people were primitive hunter-gatherers. They possessed stone axes, but probably only felled a few trees around their temporary homes, and were present in Britain in such small numbers that their impact on the wildwood would have been minimal. Around 6000BC, movements of the plates around the North Sea caused Britain to be separated from Europe, marooning its plant species almost entirely until the arrival of the Romans. Any trees that were established by this time are considered native to Britain; of over 80,000 different types of trees discovered on earth, we have just 33 native species.

By 4500BC, while the south-east was dominated by lime, the upland areas of northern England were characterised by oak, hazel and alder woodlands, the birch having entirely disappeared and the alder found only in wetter areas. This marked the beginning of the Neolithic Era, when small-scale agricultural practices began to be developed. Trees were felled to create open areas of heath, which may have been preserved by burning (although it should be noted that, of Britain's native trees, only pine is susceptible to this). Cultivation and clearance of woodland areas continued throughout the Bronze Age (c2500-800BC) and subsequent Iron Age (c800-50BC), by which time metal axes and ploughs made the work easier to undertake. Oliver Rackham estimated that half of England's wildwood would have been cut down by 500BC, with most of the damage done in the early Iron Age. In West Yorkshire, the Elmet Project has projected the woodland cover may have been as low as 30% by this time. It is thought that much of the wildwood was considered useless, maybe simply being burned, because coppiced poles rather than large unmanageable timber were necessary for almost everything. It is thought that some degree of coppicing had been introduced by the Neolithic Era, which some have suggested could equally have been called the Wood Age. Highly specialised woodwork has been found from this era, and woodland crafts like joinery and wheelwrighting are thought to have been fully developed by the Iron Age.

The archaeological ages covered so far are defined by the materials that have best survived in the archaeological record – stone, bronze, iron – but the most important material to all of them was wood. The problem is that wooden objects tend not to survive in the archaeological record and therefore its importance is often under-estimated. We are now uncovering prehistoric features like the timber Sea Henges off the coast of Norfolk, the four-acre raised island of Flag Fen near Peterborough, and the wooden Sweet Track across the Somerset levels – all mighty undertakings that relied on a ready source of the appropriate wood (often coppiced for the purpose). It is no surprise that trees were worshipped by the early inhabitants of Britain and many trees were considered sacred; yew, hazel, elder, alder, holly, ash and oak. The Druids are most associated with pagan tree worship, though doubtless this grew out of earlier traditions. During the Iron Age, the Druids were a class of learned Celtic people that included the religious leaders. Very little is actually recorded about them, but their veneration of sacred oak groves and the mistletoe that grew there was recorded by Pliny the Elder. The word *druid* itself is thought to translate as 'oak-knower'.

The original wild animals of the forest – the auroch (wild cattle), boar (wild pig) and tarpan (wild horse) – were steadily domesticated as agriculture developed, while those that remained wild were extensively hunted. The tarpan was extinct in the Neolithic Age and the auroch in the Bronze Age, though the boar survived until the Middle Ages. The deer, wolves and bears remained wild, the latter eventually being intentionally hunted to extinction by the Vikings. Agriculture (as opposed to a nomadic existence) began the division between areas of wood and pasture, with forms of basic enclosure ending the fluid lines between the two that were characteristic of areas of natural wood pasture. Woodland becomes naturally denser when it is enclosed from livestock, particularly once the natural herbivores have been hunted to extinction. Thus begins the process of creating the defined pattern of woodland shapes that we are familiar with today.

a wild boar

The climate also steadily deteriorated after 1500BC, becoming wetter and cooler during the second of two Atlantic Periods to resemble more closely that of today. As the soil became wetter and more acidic, peat formed on the high ground, and species like the pine and elm quickly disappeared. In the South Pennines, the pollen grains of oak, hazel and alder, as well as a number of stumps, have been found at the base of the dark layer of peat that reflects this change in climate – before this, the soil formed was pinkish and not black. Where trees had been cleared, nutrients were washed out of the previously rich soil and cotton-grass and blanket bog took over. Some of the lower heaths would still have been covered in sparse oak-heath woodland that was considered pasturable, but people started to settle further down the hillsides, clearing new areas of trees as they went. The valley bottoms would have remained damp swamps covered in alder and willow, and little clearance of these areas would have taken place except at fords – all of the tracks kept to the drier high ground.

When the Romans arrived, Julius Caesar described Britain as being 'one horrible forest' and its people as 'a true forest people', who fled into the woods when under threat. Even so, by that time a lot of the wildwood is thought to have gone and agriculture was well-developed throughout the country, suggesting that it could not have been that widely forested. The Romans cut down further trees when building roads and settlements, but introduced many others; poplar, plane, walnut and sweet chestnut. As well as for edible nuts, the chestnut was probably introduced as a form of coppice crop, a practice that was widespread in Italy; the Romans recognised the value of a reliable source of useful wood.

The population of the country was about 5 million when the Romans left at the beginning of the 5th century, and yet had dwindled to just 1.5 million within three centuries, possibly due to plague. In this dark age, secondary woodland is thought to have re-established in many parts of the country, although the Domesday Book of 1086 records limited woodland cover over much of the country (approximately 15% cover in England). However, its rough and steep terrain meant the Calder Valley (along with those of the Colne and Holme) was still more extensively wooded than the rest of West Yorkshire. On more fertile agricultural land in the east of the county, often no woodland remained in a parish. Settlement of the upper shelves, and to a lesser extent the swampy valleys, continued in Anglian times with many of our Anglo-Saxon placenames dominated by reference to woodlands (i.e. wood, shaw, grove, hagg, copse, firth, greave, storth, birks and carr) or the clearings in woodlands (i.e. ley, royd, field, stubbing, hey and hurst). The ending '-royd' is most common in this area, derived from the Old English *rod*, which meant land cleared for cultivation. However, many of these names may refer to older clearings or names previously inherited, and do not necessarily signify a land that was as wooded as you might think.

The Norman Forests & their Legacy

Until the 18th century, the word afforest meant to designate an area as forest under Forest Law. Only later did it become associated with planting an area with trees. Woodland and forest were always very different things; the latter, derived from the Latin *foris* meaning 'outside', referred to an area of land outside the law of the land, one instead governed by Forest Law and over which deer were allowed to roam freely. Forests contained areas of woodland, but were by no means covered in trees. Much of the forest would be pasture or arable land, with foresters employed to keep deer from destroying crops among other duties.

Forests were common across Europe before they were introduced to England by the Normans after 1066. Until then the king was just another noble, but William the Conqueror introduced the idea that all land ultimately belonged to the Crown and that he had the right to keep and hunt deer on land belonging to anyone. A forest always belonged to the king, otherwise it was merely a chase, park (if enclosed) or warren (where it housed only small game). In the forest, you tended to find red deer, wolves and boar, whereas the chase had just fallow and roe deer and wild fox. Many of these areas were already established as chases by the Saxon overlords, having previously been common hunting grounds.

The strict rule of Forest Law introduced by the Normans sought to preserve the chases and their privileges upon them. A litany of fines were imposed for minor offences, with mutilation and death being meted out for more serious breaches (like poaching). Though Forest Law was created by the Normans, they attributed it to King Canute in 1016 to try to give precedence and justify the harshness of the laws they were introducing. Forest Law was a complicated bureaucratic system with nearly as many officials as deer. Each forest was looked after by a keeper, beneath which served verderers (legal officials), foresters (who looked after game in the forest), woodwards (who looked after the timber itself), regarders (surveyors of the forest) and agisters (in charge of the pasturage of cattle). Beneath the officials of the forest served several local graves, who collected rents and generally acted as the eyes of the lords on the ground. Men were required to take this responsibility on for a year for limited remuneration; as a result, it was undesirable and unpopular work and many paid significant amounts to avoid having to take up office.

The Domesday Book mentions 25 forests in 1086, but this system grew subsequently under William II, Henry I, Richard I and John to reach a peak of about 143 forests in England and another 100 or so in Wales. The Forest Laws also became progressively more severe, with even the clergy becoming subject to them under Henry II. Only with the *Carta de Foresta* in 1217, did Henry III relax the Forest Laws, vowing that henceforth no one should be killed for these misdemeanours. It complemented the *Magna Carta* two years earlier and reintroduced rights for free men to access the royal forests and develop their own land within the forest. Some of its clauses remained in place until 1971, and it is still used by the special courts of the New Forest and Forest of Dean.

During the 13th century, bands of outlaws developed in some of the royal forests and the woods became a dangerous place. In Sherwood Forest, there was no new planting of trees recorded for nearly a century, and it was only with the subsequent sell off of royal forests that it is thought law, order and good woodland practice were restored. The legend of Robin Hood was born out of this dark period, and there are plenty of historians who link the original legend more with Yorkshire than Nottinghamshire. He is likely to have been one or several men of the backwoods living off hunted animals and there are suggestions that he resided in the forests of the Manor of Wakefield. Certainly there is no shortage of sites in the Calder Valley with claimed associations with the outlaw, including Robin Hood Rocks in Cragg Vale, Robin Hood's Penny Stone on Midgley Moor, and Robin Hood's Grave at Kirklees Priory near Brighouse.

After the *Carta de Foresta*, tenants of the royal forests were allowed to gather limited amounts of dry firewood, cut holly for winter feed, pasture pigs and cattle at certain times of year, and fell occasional trees under supervision for building or repairing their house. This was as compensation for the other restrictions imposed on them. There were fines for trespasses against the venison (i.e. poaching deer), trespasses against the vert (i.e. stealing wood), and assarting (clearing trees), with all disputes and punishments settled through the manorial courts. They were not allowed to cut down trees, drive off deer from their crops, erect fences, keep dogs, set snares, or even collect honey. No new houses were permitted to be built in the forests. Despite the harsh nature of these laws, those in wooded areas often suffered less poverty than elsewhere because of their few privileges. The Lord of the Manor was required to provide accommodation for his tenants, thus granting them timber from which to build their houses (in the case of the lower classes this was likely elm or ash rather than oak). The walls were made of either bound wattle from the underwood (usually hazel) or split timber planks. Until the 17th century, the only stone was for the slates used in roofing and early delfs were quarried for stone largely for this purpose.

After the Norman Conquest, much of the land in the Calder Valley became the possession of the king as part of the Manor of Wakefield. In 1088, the manor was granted to the first Earl of Warren by William II in return for his loyalty. Covering most of the parish of Halifax from the Hebble Brook to Todmorden, the Forest of Sowerbyshire[5]

---

[5] It is often referred to as the Forest of Hardwick, but it would appear this never existed and was based on a misinterpretation of a 16th century document which distinguished between 'hardwicke' and 'out of hardwicke'. A.H. Smith says this related to the sheep-farming areas in the Manor of Wakefield and those beyond, the former roughly correlating with the upland areas of the Forest of Sowerbyshire.

was one of the Manor's hunting grounds. It was widely used by the Earls of Warren through the 12th and 13th centuries, although in 1277 the tenants of the forest disputed their obligation to be beaters for forest hunts unless the earl was present in person.

The parishes of Elland-cum-Greetland and Southowram (and later Todmorden) formed an island within the Manor of Wakefield that was instead part of the Honour of Pontefract. Centred around Pontefract Castle, this land was granted to the De Lacy family soon after the Norman Conquest for their involvement in the Harrying of the North, in which the north was conquered once and for all. This area ultimately became the sub-Manor of Elland that was the possession of the Eland family and subsequently the Saviles. Within the Forest of Sowerbyshire, the Earls of Warren enclosed a large deer park some time in the 12th century in what is now Erringden Parish. Erringden Deer Park is thought to have provided deer not only for hunting within the Forest of Hardwick but for restocking the lords' other forests and parks in the manor. Cattle and sheep would also have been kept in the deer park, probably associated with the vaccary at Cruttonstall – names ending in '-tonstall' are almost unique to this area and indicate the existence of a former vaccary (a large medieval ranch). The whole park was enclosed within nearly twelve miles of wooden palings, whose upkeep was the job of the palisser (from whose house is derived Palace House in Hebden Bridge[6]). Palings were made of good oak timber and were expensive to maintain.

There were three species of deer that were hunted; roe, fallow and red. Only the fallow wasn't native, possibly introduced by the Romans but more likely by the Normans themselves. This became the Norman hunt of choice because it could be most easily confined in deer parks. The fallow and roe deer are known as bucks (male) and does (females), while the red deer are known as stags and hinds. Venison originally referred to the meat of the red deer, fallow deer and wild boar. Each had their own season during which they were hunted, as did the boar, between them covering most of the year. Despite the severity of punishment, poaching was commonplace, people always

roe deer

being known to 'indulge in a little uncanonical hunting'. There are plenty of fines recorded for poaching, even by Sirs and Reverends, as well as allowing cattle into the park, taking too much wood, brush, ferns, rushes or acorns, or even simply for cursing the forester.

The wild boar is thought to have been hunted to extinction by the 1260s, although 'a ravenous boar of a most enormous size' was known to live in Cliffe Wood near Bradford in the 14th century. Attempts had been made to reintroduce them, but this boar had possibly escaped from captivity and a reward was eventually offered for its head. It can still be seen on the city's coat of arms. Wolves were present in Britain throughout the Middle Ages, although attempts were made to eradicate them (Edward I in particular demanded this), and the last wolf killed in Yorkshire was recorded in 1369. Beavers were hunted to extinction in England by the 12th century. Pheasants were only introduced by the Normans, who hunted both these and woodcocks in their woods.

From the 13th century, the Earls of Warren were granted baronial jurisdiction over the Manor of Wakefield, meaning they could introduce and enforce their own law. Out of this came Halifax's notorious Gibbet Law, which was exercised for the whole bailiwick of Sowerbyshire and by which anyone found guilty of stealing anything (usually cloth hanging on tenters) worth more than 13½d. was executed. The gibbet was located out near the

---

[6] There is also a Palace Holme along the former deer park boundary near Burnt Acres Bridge.

forest rather than in the capital of Wakefield so as to deter the local tenants, who were referred to as being 'savage and thievish'. The judge and jury who enforced the law were the foresters and other burghers of the forest. Many similar gibbets existed, but none lasted as long as Halifax. Despite the *Carta de Foresta*, Gibbet Law prevailed until 1650, when it was ended by Oliver Cromwell.

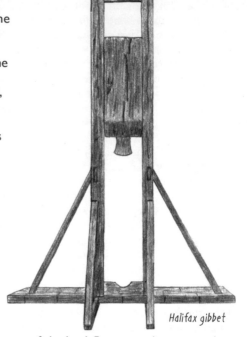

Halifax gibbet

The population doubled in the century and a half following the Domesday Book. As the population grew, so more land was assarted[7] and the woodland that remained was defined more clearly as wood pasture or coppice. Almost none of it was virgin wildwood, but was owned by a community or landowner. By the late 12th century, the population was large enough that some of the steep wooded slopes in this area began to be felled for farming, as land was steadily cleared downwards away from the population centres on higher ground.

Much of the land in the Calder Valley remained demesne holdings, meaning they remained under the ownership and management of the lord. Peasants who managed to save some money would apply to the manorial court to assart some land, and this would generally be approved on payment of an entry fine (fee) and an annual rent. In the north, the word *rod* was used instead of *assart* and this became corrupted to royd, indicating land won from the woodland. And won it was, by hard graft; to clear a royd trees were felled, bushes uprooted, and the ground graved (dug over with a graving spade), limed and manured. A royd by law had to be enclosed, usually by a ditch and hedge or wooden fence – stone walling only began in the 17th century, by which time there was a more plentiful supply of stone than wood. These early enclosures were generally small and with irregular shapes. The fields between Bank Top and Priestley Ing (Cragg Vale) are of this type, so too those at Wood Houses (Sutcliffe Wood) and Daisy Bank (Mytholmroyd). A newly created royd may have been good for growing only potatoes at first, then oats[8] and finally grazing meadow, once the soil had been enriched enough. But it wouldn't take too many years before it returned to its natural state if not looked after, and bracken often grows many years later in places where this occurred.

At the beginning of the 14th century, the lords of the manor released further areas of preserved woodland for clearance to allow cultivation, thus increasing their rents on the land. Areas like Warley Wood, Sowerby Wood and Blackwood were cleared at this time and are preserved only in names like Warley Wood Lane and Blackwood Common. The Manor of Wakefield was divided into several graveships, each of which usually had its own common wood, over which commoners held rights of pannage and for the gathering of wood for fuel and hedging. Pannage was the right to allow pigs to graze on uncultivated land, usually on the fruits of the woodland floor, which included worms, insects and a variety of mast from the trees, the most plentiful and important being

---

[7] Assarting was the clearance of trees to make way for enclosures for agriculture or settlement.
[8] Oats were a dominant crop in this area as it was better suited to the damp and cool conditions. It was made into porridge and havercake, and often fed to horses and cattle.

acorns. Away from common woods, this was often a useful supplementary source of income for the Lord of the Manor. The name Wood Lane (and sometimes Fall Lane) often refers to the routes taken by commoners to these areas of woodland, as it does in Hipperholme. Stephen Welsh suggests Blackwood Common may have been the graveship of Sowerby's common wood. Each parish was also likely to have its own hollings, where holly was farmed to provide winter feed for livestock. It is thought more of the woods in the deer park itself were reserved for timber, and there is likely to have been a carpentry workshop, where many of the estate's timber buildings were prefabricated on site.

The population and pressure on woods grew until the Black Death, which arrived in Yorkshire in 1349. Initial assarts granted by the Manor of Wakefield in the 12th century were up to two acres, but by the intense period of clearance in the early 14th century this was reduced to half an acre. With the Black Death, up to 50% of the land was vacated by death (i.e. whole families dying) and further plagues throughout the latter half of the 14th century resulted in many farms lying abandoned and royds being abandoned to nature. The population of the Forest of Sowerbyshire is thought to have reached a low of about a thousand around 1400. Assarting all but disappeared until the middle of the 15th century, at which time the Erringden Deer Park (now under the ownership of Richard Duke of York) was dispaled. The fences were torn down with glee by those who had been living under the repressive Forest Laws for so long. The park was opened up to eight tenants initially, but within a hundred years had some 62 tenants and sub-tenants farming the land.

In Scotland, many of the forests remained and were even added to, but in England and Wales Forest Law became irrelevant except to protect the king's timber. A few remained quite untouched, largely because they were quite so wooded, like the Forest of Dean and the New Forest, but many others are left as simply confusing names on the map where there is little woodland remaining (e.g. the Forests of Needwood, Duffield, Inglewood, and Clarendon). Charles I removed lots of the royal forests for farmland during his reign, including the Forest of Galtres in the Vale of York.

Charles I attempted to restore Forest Law in the 16th century to the few royal forests that remained, but there were riots over common rights and they became the realm of the criminal again. Though forests declined, parks (originally enclosed hunting grounds) remained part of the landscape in Tudor, Stuart, Georgian and Victorian times, with changing fashions reflecting each different period. Only Shibden Park can be considered part of this tradition locally, though a number of grand houses had gardens laid out in which trees were a large part of the appeal. To them we owe some of our more exotic ornamental species, and in some cases the preservation of ancient features and areas of woodland.

Hunting continued long after the Forest Laws, with poaching punishable by transportation or death until 1830. Hawking (the hunting of hares with birds of prey) became very fashionable, and only aristocrats were allowed to keep hawks. Fox hunting developed from the 17th century,[9] before which time foxes were simply killed as vermine. Organised hunts began in the 18th century, for which packs of hounds were kept – that at Howroyde in Barkisland was formed in the 1750s. Northowram Hunt took place across the Shibden Estate, Halifax Hunt met at both Stainland and Causeway Foot, Halifax and Calder Vale Hunt met at both Midgley and Warley, Todmorden Hunt near the Hare and Hounds, and Portsmouth Hunt at the head of the valley. Harriers, a term now widely used by cross-country and fell runners, were those who followed the hunt on foot. Deer were rarely seen or hunted, so when one was set loose on Skircoat Moor in 1827, 300 horsemen and 3000 harriers are reported to have turned out to chase it.

---

[9] The mural above the doorway to Scout Hall in Shibden Dale is one of the earliest depictions of fox hunting, dating from 1680.

Woodland Folklore

The dark forest has always been associated with the unknown; throughout the Middle Ages the woods were wild places full of danger, beasts and wrong-doing. The wodewose was a Celtic personification of the wildwood – a wild man who was honoured in ancient rituals but feared like a beast. In local folklore, we find Tom Bell in Hardcastle Crags, along with stories of witches and 'wild men of the woods'. In truth many of these would simply have been charcoal-burners or woodsmen who were often thought of as strange.

The medieval forests of England were also favourite haunts of the numerous hermits who lived countrywide, especially where there were caves. In Sanskrit they are known as *vanaprasthas* (meaning forest dwellers). In Norland, a Hermitroyd was recorded in 1460, with other hermitages mentioned in Elland and Halifax parishes. There was also a cave associated with St Toby in Eaves Wood. They were not complete recluses, but were often seen as sages and served to help travellers by watching roads and bridges. The Victorians came to romanticise these figures, so much so that local people were sometimes hired to pose as hermits by a cave in the woods as a form of tourist attraction.

It is a tradition that continues to this day, with numerous people having lived for a time in crude shelters in the woods of the valley. A friend recalls how he and another friend spent separate seasons in a basic hut they'd constructed in Eaves Wood after the end of relationships. Other signs can be found, crumbling and moss-covered, of these temporary abodes, testament to our strong bond with the woods around us.

There are also many positive associations with the woods in folklore. The Green Man was a romantic pagan figure, probably either a forester or an ordinary man taking refuge in the woods. It was said his head, if cut off, would grow back like a tree, and he symbolised the spring and rebirth. Trees were heavily involved in spring fertility rituals; in the Middle Ages greenwood marriages often took place on May Eve and resulted in many a pregnancy. The following day a birch maypole was fetched from the woods and placed at an important junction, usually one with three exits. Maypole dancing was a later addition, with ceremonies originally associated with the renewal of the maypole. Branches were cut from it and attached to each house to bless them with the tree spirit.

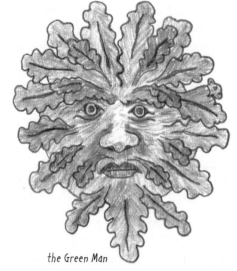

the Green Man

A Woodland Economy

The woodland economy existed since Neolithic man first started coppicing trees, but it was probably between the late 15th and 18th centuries that our woods were worked hardest, and all of the associated woodland crafts were at their peak. A small-scale non-agricultural landscape can be identified during this era in most of the rural valleys of south-west Yorkshire. It was an industry based entirely around the value of the woodland and the charcoal it produced.

The population steadily grew through the 15th and 16th centuries and the woollen industry took over much of the Calder Valley by the Tudor period. This, along with the parallel development of the iron industry, placed great pressure on the woodland resources that remained. Iron smelting relied on a steady stream of charcoal and most bloomeries were located close to the source of charcoal, often established by those who owned the woods to work alongside their coppices. Woodland was seen as a good source of income for the Lords of the Manor and there would hardly have been a wood that wasn't coppiced in some way, even on the steep slopes of the South Pennines. Every wood was managed sustainably with a view to living off its resources in the long term and tenants were appointed every year to oversee the woodland.

By the 17th century, the Manor of Wakefield became broken up, becoming largely the property of the Lacy family in Midgley, the Savile family in Wadsworth, Heptonstall and Stansfield, the land of the Crown in Sowerby and Warley, and entirely freehold in the cases of Langfield and Erringden, where rights were bought by the freeholders in 1592. There was a steady rise of yeoman clothiers, wealthier peasants who had been able to buy up property and become upwardly mobile. A yeoman was a freeman who owned his land, which entitled him to a certain status; though they remained below gentlemen, they were allowed to serve on juries and vote locally. These were usually the clothiers who had made good of the new woollen industry and, from the 17th century onwards, they built many of the grand stone houses that line the hillsides of the Calder Valley. These were some of the first stone houses in the area as stone had become cheaper, and subsequently the older wooden houses were either replaced or encased with stone.

Through the 17th and 18th centuries, Parliamentary Enclosure Acts took place to all farming land, with a consequent loss of common rights. Although many of these rights were of limited use by the 18th century, the rights to collect fuel in the common woods and pasture animals there were lost forever. After the Napoleonic Wars, the 1830s and 1840s was the greatest period of enclosure, with large fields enclosed by long straight dry-stone walls and numerous farms springing up on the least fertile hillsides. Yet many of the woods were preserved throughout this period, probably because of their importance for industrial charcoal manufacture and domestic fuel. The Little Ice Age reached its height in the 17th century, further increasing the demand for domestic fuel. Thus we owe the survival of many of our ancient woods to the demands of the textile industry. At the same time though, that industry changed the make-up of the woodlands greatly, including altering the soil and hydrology. As a result there was a lack of dead wood and limited ground flora in woods that had their turfs removed regularly to cover charcoal hearths.

There would have been many structures in the woods over the years, with some of the scattered remains and flattened areas still discernable today. Bark, carpentered planks, seasoning wood and winter feed were among the things that would have been stored in the woods at times, so there would have been crude barns, carpenters' workshops and the temporary abodes of various craftsmen.

Coppicing

It is important to note the traditional distinction between wood and timber; timber refers to large trees that have grown to maturity, while wood is the underwood (thin younger poles, brush, etc). In any deed of sale for a woodland each type of wood is listed separately as trees (timber) and poles (underwood). On the whole, large trees were of more limited use; they were hard to fell, extract and work, and necessary only for large-scale building projects. Many of the great halls were built using jointed timber of medium-sized trees, not the giant two hundred year old oaks that we often envisage.[10] It is very unlikely that any wood from this area would have been used for such grand purposes as building the Navy's ships; we are so far from the coast and oak trees can be grown for the purpose in Herefordshire much faster due to the warmer climate there. In any case, most areas where there was good timber (e.g. flatter areas) would have been cleared by the Middle Ages, leaving the steep, inaccessible slopes to produce the sort of woodland that could only ever be used for fuel, whether as charcoal or domestic firewood. Small managed trees were of far more use, and indeed value, so coppicing was big business.

Coppicing relies on the capacity of most trees to produce multiple new shoots from a single cut stem – the word coppice comes from the Old French *copeiz*, meaning 'to cut'. An oak pole can grow 7ft a year and a willow pole up to 11ft, and these young shoots tend to grow straight up towards the light for the first few years. Thus, within ten years, the coppicer could produce from a single stool (or stoven) dozens of long straight poles that could be easily cut and removed, and had many more uses. Often coppice cycles were longer, particularly where it was closely associated with charcoal burning.

Coppices were divided into hags (the northern equivalent of cants), each representing an area to be cut in one season, and the hag-men were responsible for cutting the coppiced poles. A coppiced wood usually had a boundary of a combined bank and ditch, often with a stock-proof hedge or fence that had to be carefully maintained. Any route through the wood would have had barriers across its entrance stoops to control access, particularly by animals, and there were fines for trespass or damaging the coppice boundary. As late as 1855, a labourer John Wardle was convicted of trespass in Elland Park Wood and fined £2 (approximately £1500 today). Grazing in coppiced woodland was rarely permitted, apart from occasionally towards the end of the coppice cycle. Rabbits and squirrels were the scourge of the forester and coppiced woods suffered particularly. Rabbits had been introduced to Britain around the 13th century as a delicacy and most manors had breeding warrens of the type that can be seen at Coneygarth above Mytholmroyd. There were also Coney Woods in Ripponden and Shibden whose name likely relates to the same practice.

Pollarding was a similar practice that involved cutting a tree above the grazing height of animals to leave a thick trunk about six feet high (known as the bolling) and numerous sprouting shoots above that can be harvested in the same way as a coppice. An oft-pollarded tree is usually hollow, but said to be stronger as it can move with the elements, and ultimately only the outer living wood is important to the tree. A pollarded tree may also be known as a dodderel, doddle or dodder. Many common woods were used for producing underwood in this way, with commoners and tenants allowed to gather the poles from pollarded trees. In fact, in these woods young trees were often topped illegally to create pollards that would then provide poles that could be legally collected subsequently. Pollarding was common in the Lake District, where it was a necessity to graze sheep on the same ground where trees were cultivated, and it is a practice that

---

[10] Houses in Britain were not built like the log cabins of the continent that suited long straight pines, but rather evolved a form of their own. Uneven timbers from the twisted oaks of Britain formed a frame between which wattle and daub panels created walls.

would have made sense in parts of the upper Calder Valley. The large deer population in the Calder Valley means that coppicing is now more difficult, and it has been suggested that pollarding would be far more suitable; indeed, it has been practised on oak and ash in part of Hall Wood, Todmorden.

Initially coppices were a mix of various trees because their main uses, as firewood and fencing, could make use of most types of wood. Oak found particular favour in the Pennines, though, and Heather Ibbetson has suggested that the woods of Luddenden Dean were managed for almost monocultural coppicing of oak from the 13th to early 19th centuries. This provided fuel for small-scale iron bloomeries and charcoal burning hearths, and may well have been typical of the whole of the Upper Calder Valley. Little changed in the coppicing of woods throughout this period, other than slightly longer coppice rotations and the growing of a wider variety of trees for particular uses. Trees were generally slower growing on these soils, so the coppiced poles were cut on rotations of up to fifteen years, lengthening to as much as twenty years by the mid-17th century. This may be due to the Little Ice Age, which is thought to have further slowed the growth of trees, or changing demands for poles. It has been estimated that, in West Yorkshire, for every 180 trees cut on a single coppice cycle, another 10 were left for two cycles and 10 left until the third cycle or beyond.

At the end of a wood's use for coppicing, trees were often singled in this area, reducing it back to a single stump from which a normal-looking tree would grow. Thus, we find there is often little sign of coppicing in trees we know were used for that purpose for centuries. A former coppice can most easily be identified from trees with a number of main trunks growing from the ground level, sometimes with a gap between them (though hazel and willow tend to grow in this manner naturally). Even where they were singled, the evidence of coppicing may remain around the base of the trees. The best examples of oak coppicing locally include Scarr and Long Woods near Skircoat Green, Knotts Wood above Cornholme and Well Holme Park in Brighouse. The oak, though, struggled with pollution and so many of these suffered during the 19th century and many oak woods were abandoned in favour of less intensive and more ornamental species like beech. Former coppices can often be identified by names like Coppy and Spring Wood (a reference to the tendency of the new growth to spring up), both of which are common in the Calder Valley, many of the Coppys being a long way above the present wood line.

an example of a formerly coppiced stool that has been allowed to grow out

Charcoal Burning and Iron Blooming

Charcoal burning is generally thought of as the oldest recorded woodland industry and has taken place with similar methods across the world since metals were first smelted in around 3000BC. In Sweden rectangular kilns were used and in China the wood was burnt in a pit, but these variations in method are minimal.

Charcoal burning hearths (also known as stances or pits) are found throughout the British Isles, and typically form circular platforms anything between six and thirteen metres in diameter. They generally face southwest or south due to the wind direction, though this is not necessarily true in the Calder Valley, where the steepness of the valleys means that choice of aspect is often limited. However, it does mean the platforms stand out very clearly on the otherwise steep ground. They were also often located near streams and trackways. Sometimes a separate area above, below or to the side was also levelled for living and working during the burn, though these may not have been as necessary for the relatively small operations carried out locally. Be careful not to confuse charcoal hearths with landslips, which are common on steep wooded slopes where layers of clay are lubricated by springs, but there are hundreds to be found in the Calder Valley. Over forty have been identified in Hardcastle Crags, but the best examples are probably those along the bottom of Burnt Acres Wood (its name, like Burnt Wood in Cragg Vale, relating to its use for charcoal production). If you were to dig beneath the surface, particularly on the downhill side, you are likely to find accumulations of charcoal and burnt wood in all of these sites.

Having gained a licence for the coaling of the underwood, the production of charcoal was a lengthy process. The charcoal burner (or wood collier) first had to carefully select and fell the underwood within an area of the coppice – oak, ash, hazel, alder and birch were most commonly used – before allowing the wood to season until the following year. The wood (approximately two tons in total) was cut into four-foot lengths (billets) and stacked in piles known as cords. Each charcoal hearth would likely have been reused on a cycle every number of years when the coppiced wood was ready to be re-felled.

Once the wood was ready to be burnt, the turf[11] was removed from the hearth and the stack carefully built over a number of weeks, with the billets built up around a central flue or pole. The stack was surrounded by grass, bracken and turf, gathered both within the wood and from surrounding commons, then covered in fine dust to prevent any air getting in. The charcoal burner had a sieve for riddling the dust that covered the stacks, as well as long poles for allowing ventilation where necessary. In the Pennines, the usual method was to have a central pole that would be removed once the stack was built and

a charcoal stack before it is covered with turf and dust

---

[11] Interestingly, this highlights how much more shaded our woodlands have become as it is hard to find grassy areas within the woods today. There would be no turf to remove now, and most of the charcoal hearths you find have little or no grass on them.

burning charcoal dropped down in its place to light the whole thing. The top was then quickly sealed to prevent complete combustion of the wood; the intent was to heat the wood just enough to drive off first moisture, then tar and creosote, and leave only pure carbon. The stacks burned first with thick white smoke, then feint blue, and finally nothing, at which point it could be opened and allowed to cool.

Wind could very quickly cause the whole thing to burn and undo months of work, so charcoal burners had to be in attendance throughout the burn, which could take anything from two to ten days. They erected and moved hurdles as the wind changed and filled gaps in the outside of the stack as they appeared. A charcoal burner's stool was said to be one-legged to ensure they couldn't fall asleep at any point during the burn. During the coaling season (April to November), charcoal burners often lived with their families in primitive wigwam-style huts with wattle walls and tiled turf and brushwood roofs, a form of temporary family dwelling with some basic furniture. Some were burnt or asphyxiated as they slept if the wind suddenly changed. Charcoal burners often had alternative seasonal employment, such as haymaking or harvesting, and many turned to weaving during the winter to earn an income. Some sold their own produce directly, others used a middle man. Charcoal burners were unpopular because of the unpleasant smoke they produced and are often presented in literature as being somewhat strange; they were treated as a separate community, rather like gypsies. James Broadbent, the Judas of the Cragg Vale Coiners, who betrayed his cohorts, was probably the most famous charcoal burner in the area, but I like William Dearden's reference to Old Ned, who sat guard in Rawtonstall Wood communing with the fairies of Turret crags.

Charcoal hearths are often found near the sites of early iron bloomeries, which needed charcoal to smelt iron because it gave a longer more intense heat than timber or peat (it was similarly associated with baking). The charcoal was also used in brass making, copper-smelting, glass manufacture, gunpowder factories, pencils, shoe blacking and medieval soap (which used beech wood charcoal). Large flat irons were also filled with charcoal for ironing sheets, while woolcombers used it for heating their combs. It was also used for domestic fuel locally, but it is likely that while there was such a high demand for charcoal for smelting iron, peat would have been far more cost-effective for domestic use.

Early iron bloomeries used a primitive method of heating ironstone in an open circular stone bank, fed with air largely by the wind (or occasionally makeshift bellows). The slag melted at around 900°C and ran off via a channel, after which other impurities were hammered out of the 'bloom' of softened ironstone that was produced. The wrought iron was then forged on site using a stone anvil, before being finished at a blacksmith's workshop, but the quality of the iron depended entirely on the local stone. This form of iron ore extraction in crude kilns is thought to have taken place since the Iron Age around 1200BC and very little changed for over two and a half millennia. The whole process was very inefficient, though; producing just two tons of iron required charcoal from approximately an acre of woodland. Each furnace could be used only once, and though the hearth could be reused, this required heating the whole thing from scratch again. It was also very difficult to transport charcoal because a lot of it was needed and it broke up easily, so forges were usually within a few miles of a charcoal burning area.

Little tends to remain of these kilns, but bloomery sites have been located by the slag left behind, which ran down the hillside or was channelled into a ditch for cooling. It is usually beneath the topsoil and turf, but iron slag has been found in Walshaw Wood, Hebden Dale (the track to Overwood cuts through an area of slag, which covers the surface and can be clearly seen in the bank above), Horsehold Wood (Beaumont Clough), Rawtonstall Wood, Luddenden Dean, Gorpley Clough, and Birks Wood (Walsden) among many other places in Calderdale. Several lumps of cast iron were also found at Furnace during the construction of Ramsden Reservoir, and deep beneath the gravel by

Widdop Reservoir. Bloomeries were recorded in the early 14th century, when smiths were employed in working iron across various parts of the Forest of Sowerby. The first known reference to a mechanically operated forge hammer to shape the iron was in Warley in 1350. There are also Cinder Hills in Todmorden, Southowram and Norwood Green that often indicate the sites of early furnaces.

Ironstone was present throughout the area in glacial drift deposits (like Jackson Rock) and small localised seams (like those that have been recorded in Luddenden Dean and Hebden Dale). Many of these would have been worked out long before the 19th century, originally by quarrying and later by digging angled tunnels (or adits)[12] along the shallow seams. There was also a large-scale iron furnace at Holme Chapel in Cliviger, often associated with a significant source of crude clay ironstone at nearby Ruddle Scout, its name taken from the red colour of the ironstone. However, it is thought unlikely this would have been the main source of ironstone for the whole Upper Calder Valley. Instead packhorses would have brought high-quality ore down from Furness (another place-name derived from its iron heritage) in Cumbria, as has been recorded in parts of Rossendale. Often it was far cheaper to move a ton of iron than it was 6 tons of charcoal.

Bloomeries were encouraged by the Norman earls in the 13th century, but took off particularly after the Civil War, when iron was in demand everywhere and there was likely to be a bloomery in every parish. By then enclosed blast furnaces had been developed, heating the ironstone within a dome to far higher temperatures, thus melting the iron as well as the slag. The latter floated on top, so the molten iron was run off as liquid into casts, producing cast iron rather than wrought iron. It also enabled the furnace to be reloaded until the charcoal ran out, but it was still reliant entirely on a ready supply of charcoal until the late 18th century, when coke and limestone began to be used instead. This resulted in a dramatic reduction in the number of small local furnaces in charcoal-producing woodlands like those of the Upper Calder Valley, which were replaced by the likes of Low Moor Ironworks, which were established in 1788 to produce wrought iron on a far larger scale. Charcoal continued to be used in some industries during the 19th century, such as woolcombing for the manufacture of worsted, but the last charcoal burners in the area were recorded in Crimsworth Dean in 1903.

Whitecoal was a distinct fuel associated with the smelting of lead ore, and was usually found in oak woods where there were coal measures. Short lengths of oak were dried in whitecoal kilns about 5m diameter, and used to mix with charcoal for smelting lead. They can now be identified by a distinct depression known as a Q-pit (a Q-shaped hollow) with a spout pointing downhill. They are usually found on dry steep slopes near to streams and some have been identified in Hardcastle Crags.

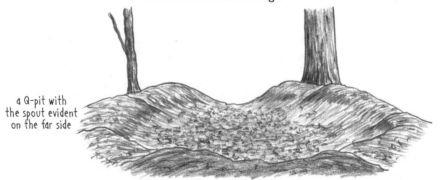

a Q-pit with the spout evident on the far side

---

[12] This sort of mining was only known from the 16th century. Any earlier mining beneath the surface used bellpits, where a vertical shaft was sunk into the seam and then worked horizontally. Similar processes were used in the area for extracting both ironstone and coal.

Traditional Woodland Crafts

Charcoal burning was just one of the many woodland crafts that relied on a supply of coppiced wood. Many of our traditional surnames are related to woodland crafts, including Sawyer, Cleaver, Cooper, Carpenter, Barker, Tanner, Bowyer, Fletcher, Wainwright, Cartwright, Hooper, Turner, Joiner, Arkwright, Boardman, Cole, Collier and Coleman (the latter three are found far from the coalfields, as collier originally referred to someone involved in the charcoal industry). Many of these crafts persisted until the early 20th century, when the last few craftsmen died, though some have been rekindled in recent years.

Saws have been used since the 15th century, **sawyers** traditionally using large two-person 7ft blades to cut the timber. Even when saws were introduced, they were outlawed by some landowners, who wanted axe cuts that could be angled downwards to leave a concave stump in which water would gather and thereby rot the stump. Lengthwise sawing (known as ripping) required the use of a saw pit; these were usually rectangular, the size of a grave and some six feet deep to allow a man (the under-dog, from which we get the common phrase) to stand underneath with one end of the saw while the top-dog stood above. They were usually located in the wood in a place that would not fill with water.

Barkers stripped the bark off trees, largely for use in the tanning industry, a process known as bark peeling (or pilling). Oak bark has the highest tannin content and so was most commonly sought, but birch, larch and rowan were also used. Bark peelers often lived like charcoal burners in temporary huts in the woods during the summer. Larger trees were stripped of bark where they stood, often in spring, then left to stand before felling in winter. Often this was done by women using mallets, a peeling iron and a barking bill (also known as a spud), the latter to cut the bark into short lengths. The rough outer bark of older trees was of no use as it contained little tannin, but that from branches and dead trees was collected diligently. Strips of bark were then dried in stacks for two to three weeks, before being ground finely in a bark mill (powered either by a waterwheel or horse gin). The ground bark was then used to produce tanning liquor, into which suspended hides were dunked. Tannic acid in the bark seeped slowly into pores in the hide, both drying it out, colouring it and preserving it. Eventually after a number of weeks soaking they were layered in the tan pit and covered with water, before being dried, oiled and finished by the currier and then cut to shape by the bender.

Tanning was big business from the late 17th to the mid 19th century, as leather straps were widely used in the mills as well as in clothing. Indeed it was said to be the second largest industry in the country after textiles, and oak became as highly sought for its bark as its renowned timber. Even at a time when the size of the British shipping fleet was growing at its fastest,[13] it is said shipbuilders still could often not compete with the tanneries for procuring oak. It is particularly relevant in this area, which never had a relationship with shipbuilding industry (neither providing timber nor salvaging ships' timbers for use in cottages) but whose burgeoning textile industry created a massive demand for leather belts and straps. Around Todmorden and Eastwood, the UK's picker making[14] capital, several picker works imported tough buffalo hide for use in the picker straps that drove the shuttles over the looms.

Although many of the local woods would have supplied oak bark to the mills, the demand was so high it would have been imported in large quantities too. There are places where there were tan pits in the woods themselves, but most of the tanning was done in-house by mills (e.g. the tan pits for Croft Mill in Hebden Bridge, whose well is still visible

---

13 It is estimated the British fleet more than doubled in size between 1780 and 1860.
14 Crude pickers were originally hand-made from flexible lengths of hazel, holly or birch, and indeed Todmorden's James Fielden is credited with making the first of these in the 19th century.

below Commercial Street) or by dedicated tanneries. There was a tannery at Hipperholme owned by Robert Taylor, another in Sowerby Bridge operated by George Thompson & Son, and large tanneries at White Lee in Mytholmroyd, Bridge Royd in Eastwood and Crown Works in Northowram. The smell of the tanneries was notorious, so they would often be located on the edge of a settlement. The popularity of the name Barker (which was often used for tanners as well as bark-peelers) around Hebden Bridge and the presence of Barkers Terrace is also testament to the importance of the tanning industry.

Clog sole cutters also often worked in the wood itself, living in rude shelters usually made with turf walls and a bracken roof. A clogger is recorded living and working in Bradley Wood near Rastrick until the 1920s. They cut rough blocks from the wood that could then be brought into the workshop to be trimmed and hollowed by the clog-makers themselves. Alder was the most popular clog wood, as it is easy to work and water resistant, but birch, sycamore and beech were also used (the latter particularly once clogs were mass-produced). Clogs were common traditional footwear but became particularly popular locally for mill-workers, whose feet they raised from the wet floor. The most well-known clog-maker was Maude's (later Walkley's) in Mytholmroyd, who made the famous Maude clog sole and are still trading to this day. By the time they were making 120,000 pairs a year, most of the wood was imported from Scandinavia, but a shortage of leather in World War II meant clogs were suddenly in demand again and a number of local woods were clear-felled partly to provide beech for clog soles.

the Maude sole clog

Once the wood was removed from the woodland and sold, there were endless possible uses for it. Many **carpenters** worked in the wood where the timber fell, constructing substantial items like waterwheels and building frames at semi-permanent workshops. Among the broad array of carpenters, boardwrights (or boardmen) were table-makers and arkwrights made wooden chests or coffers. **Coopers** used to make churns, butter bowls, wash tubs and dye vats, as well as barrels, but it was the latter that required particular skill and could be made using only the highest quality oak. **Turners** made wooden dishes, plates and other domestic utensils, usually from sycamore, ash or beech whose sap didn't taint the food, on a basic pole lathe. There are plenty of records of turners and coopers being fined for having stolen wood to make their wares. Bobbin turners were particularly plentiful in this area, but this basic operation was replaced by large bobbin mills, like Cornholme Mill and Cote Hill Bobbin Works on the edge of Halifax, which developed to supply the mills. Though initially they used timber from the adjacent woods, mainly beech, sycamore and holly, such was the demand that timber soon had to be imported from Staffordshire and eventually Ireland. **Bodgers** were turners who made chairs using a pole lathe and green wood, most often beech; as a consequence, they were more populous in the south of the country where they often worked at huts in the woods. **Wheelwrights** (or wainwrights) used local seasoned timber, the hub (or naft) usually cut from elm, the spokes made of riven oak and the felloes (of the rim) from ash. **Bowyers** and **fletchers** made bows and arrows respectively. There were even **grainers**, who painted wood to make it more aesthetically pleasing.

The thinner brash and underwood was used for hedgelaying and wicker baskets. **Basket-makers** used willow and hazel rods which they soaked in small ponds in the wood before weaving baskets from them. It was particularly common in the osier beds around Elland from the 18th century, providing heavy-duty skeps for transporting woollen textiles in the mills. **Besom-makers** (or broom squires) mostly used birch brash to make brooms and brushes, but it was little more than a side business for older men and women who could do little else. The long handles of these brooms, and similar for pitchforks, rakes and hoes, were also made from local trees and were known as stails. **Birch wine-making** was even more of a part-time craft, but rights for birch sap still had to be leased for a few shillings a year. The wine was usually collected in spring while the sap was rising and then mixed with honey, cloves, lemon peel and even ale.

The Industrial Revolution

In local tradition it was said a squirrel could travel from Royds Hall to Shibden Hall without touching the ground and, even in 1700 we find the whole of the Shore hillside described as being covered in fine timber trees with only occasional clearings. Yet looking through so many of the photos from the turn of the 20th century one is struck by how few trees there were on the hillsides. There was not a tree on Beacon Hill, Horsehold Scout, Heptonstall Eaves, Bank Top Wood, Rud Clough and many more places where now there are many. In that intervening period of the 18th and 19th centuries, the industrial revolution undoubtedly left its sooty mark on the woodlands of the Calder Valley. The earliest textile mills relied on a steady supply of water and were often built on the tributary valleys (Colden Clough, Cragg Vale, Luddenden, Hebden Water). From the 13th and 14th centuries, these had been the sites of the earliest corn and fulling[15] mills in the area. Weaving had taken place in the area since Anglian times, but as the industry developed, most of the wool was brought into the area from North Yorkshire and Lincolnshire, as sheep farming locally was only done on a relatively small scale and the wool it produced was often too coarse. But what the area did have was good water for washing the wool, then driving the fulling and dyeing process. In much of the Calder Valley, they produced kersey, a coarse cloth, but later moved to the production of worsted, which did not need to be fulled.

The fulling process was quickly mechanised, with hammers powered by a waterwheel. Different types of overtop waterwheels were developed for the mills on these steep streams, which had less flow but a far greater drop. This allowed mills to be clustered much closer together, but necessitated the construction of large numbers of dams and goits to keep them running in dry weather. The local woods around these mills provided oak bark for leather tanning, alder and birch for clog soles, holly and beech for bobbins, and sycamore for rollers and shuttles.

Although there were initially strong links between the textile industry and the local woodland, the pace of the industrial revolution quickly outstripped the ability of the local woods to supply it. The arrival of the canals – the Calder and Hebble Navigation in the 1770s and the Rochdale Canal in the 1790s – had a profound impact on the way the local woodlands were managed. Instead of looking locally for resources, it was suddenly much easier to move wood, stone and coal far greater distances. Coal was immediately a cheaper fuel than charcoal, with a result that charcoal burning and much of the associated coppicing declined rapidly during the 19th century. Most industries became reliant on imports from Scandinavia and Ireland. Bobbins were no longer made from local beech but holly from Staffordshire and sycamore from Ireland, and clogs from alder and birch from Norway.

---

[15] Fulling mills were known as walk mills and fullers were therefore known as walkers, while weavers were known as websters and dyers as listers. However, although the fulling process originally involved people walking on the cloth in a trough of water to thicken and felt the wool after weaving, the term is actually derived from a Norse word *wauk* used by sheep farmers to refer to the process of thickening the cloth. Fulling comes from a French word *fouler*, meaning to tread things, whether cloth, corn or grapes.

Driven by this supply of cheap coal brought in by canal, steam power largely replaced water power in the early 19th century and mills (with their new tower chimneys) began to concentrate in the main valley bottom close to the canal. The railway opened in 1840, further facilitating the rapid movement of resources, and large towns quickly developed. By the end of the century, every stone in the valley was turned black with soot, and the trees around them suffered similarly.

Pollution was a significant inhibitor of woodland growth and propagation for centuries, changing the soil profile greatly. It is estimated that each day anything up to three tons of soot was deposited on each square mile of an industrial town like those in the Calder Valley.[16] This artificially lowered the pH of the soil, making it more acidic and limiting the activity of soil organisms. Before the Clean Air Act of 1956, many trees struggled to self-seed and plenty were killed or stunted by the thick smoke that hung over the valleys. Sunlight to the trees was reduced, as was their ability to photosynthesise and grow properly. One of the best examples of this is at Scarr Wood near Halifax, where the stunted and twisted trunks of the oak coppice is the direct result of industrial pollution – you can even see at the top where the trees have started to grow straighter over the last fifty years. If you look at the rings of many trees that survived through the industrial era, it can be striking how closely packed their rings were during that time. Sycamore was a survivor,[17] but the ash, elm, and pine slowly disappeared.[18] Mosses and lichens also changed, with those that were sulphur dioxide tolerant coming to dominate the area, while the wild flowers of the woodland floor were greatly diminished. In 1910, Charles Crosland lamented the changes he'd observed in Elland Park Wood, once described as being covered with woodruff, forget-me-not, primrose and wild hyacinth.

a twisted oak in Scarr Wood stunted by pollution

Although the trees themselves suffered greatly, the woodland cover of the Calder Valley was also subject to wholesale changes. With the decline of traditional coppicing practices, clear-felling became more prevalent in the 19th century, along with the fashion for replanting with large stands of similar trees. Although plantation had taken place on a small scale since the 13th century, it was relatively rare and large plantations did not exist until the 18th century, when trees began to be grown exclusively as timber. Stands of just one or two species of tree were planted, often according to the fashion of the time: wych-elm, hornbeam, beech, larch and various conifers have been in vogue at different times.

The romantic landscaping movement, as practised by Capability Brown and other landscape gardeners of the late 18th century, also changed the way we look at trees, from pure productivity to including consideration of aesthetic beauty. As a consequence, estates like the Saviles' land at Hardcastle Crags were planted with a wide range of fashionable and ornamental trees in the latter half of the 19th century. Many of these ornamental forests were kept 'tidy' to satisfy what its Victorian visitors expected; dead wood was

---

[16] From a 1956 article by the Socialist Medical Association, *Death in the Air! The Menace of Air Pollution.*

[17] There have been studies that have shown sycamore trees even thriving on carbon-filtered air and growing 25% taller in these conditions than clean air.

[18] Kew Gardens was so concerned about the effect of pollution on its trees, particularly the conifers, that a National Pinetum was established at Bedgebury near Tunbridge Wells in 1925.

often removed and so hindered the soil's development. You could argue that this view of trees is one still in vogue today.

A particularly damaging Victorian fashion was to clear-fell and replant existing ancient woodland with these new plantations. In the Calder Valley, it was the beech tree that seems to have been most fashionable and, for a period in the mid- to late-19th century, nearly every cleared hillside was planted wholesale with beech and sycamore.[19] Whether it was intended to supply the area's mills with bobbins, shuttles and clogs, we are not sure, but the beech was seen as a fast-growing replacement for those trees that had been felled. In many cases it would simply have been ornamental, associated with the vogue for manufacturers to improve their newly acquired estates. However, the beech did not thrive on the steep hills and thin soil of the Pennines, growing too slowly and irregularly to be of much use. There are records of it being used for chockwood in propping up mines, as well as being chopped down during the two World Wars (Callis Wood, Spa Wood in Luddenden and Sutcliffe Wood in Cragg Vale are exampled), but otherwise these plantations have remain largely untouched to this day. Yet, perhaps we should consider it fortunate that the fate of the similarly industrial valleys of South Wales didn't befall West Yorkshire's woods. Hitherto some of the most wooded parts of the country, the Welsh Valleys were subject to wholesale plantation in the 19th century, virtually none of which survived, leaving a barren wasteland that gave way to the vast conifer plantations that cloak them today.

By the end of World War I the traditional forestry industry was dead in Britain; the last charcoal burning in the area was recorded in Crimsworth Dean in 1903. Forestry had long been the preserve of the aristocracy rather than the common man,[20] and a lack of men and the possibility of relatively cheap imports from the empire meant that woodland management was almost completely abandoned. But a new forestry industry replaced it, that of the Forestry Commission, which planted quick-growing high-yield spruce and larch. It was seen as the most cost-effective way of using the land, particularly after both World Wars, when there was a drive to bring all available land into production. This included ancient but unproductive woodland, which was literally blown up,[21] bulldozed or even sprayed by helicopter, and replaced wholesale with conifers or turned into farmland. It is estimated that anything up to a half of Britain's remaining ancient woodland was lost in this way between 1945 and 1975. It is fortunate that the Calder Valley escaped this, with conifers only planted on previously open ground. Even now, around Baitings and Ogden Reservoirs, broadleaves are being planted where the old conifers fall.

Many of the trends of the industrial era are being reversed following the decline in the traditional industries of the area. The Clean Air Acts of 1956 and 1968 helped remove the sooty smog that hung over the valley for years and, as the soil became less acidic again, so other trees returned to our slopes. Ash is the most noticeable; once almost alien to the Upper Valley, its saplings seem to be replacing sycamore everywhere and are every gardener's menace. We have also seen flora returning to the woodland floor that was not present for over a hundred years, with bluebells particularly flourishing throughout the valley.

A number of roe deer were released onto the moors above Cragg Vale in the 1970s to help repopulate the valley and are now seen all over the Upper Valley, though it took

---

[19] It was likely that these plantations were originally slightly more mixed than they are today. Scotsman's Mixture, which included pine and larch trees as well as beech and sycamore, was widely planted around the north-west by Scottish foresters in the mid-19th century, but the conifers didn't survive. Likewise most of the elm and ash trees that were planted failed to thrive at a time of such high pollution.
[20] As opposed to France, where the traditional forestry industry has survived, even thrived, to this day. Every town has its own saw mill and a bag of charcoal will invariably be locally produced.
[21] The Forestry Commission is supposed to have dynamited a number of ancient oaks in their efforts to plant lines of what they considered practical Norway spruce trees in the 1920s.

them a number of years to reach Todmorden. They are a wonderful and common sight, though they are the bane of woodland managers for their penchant for eating new shoots and stripping bark. Because they have no natural predator, it is estimated there are now more roe deer in the country than at any time in history.

Tree-planting has taken over from felling; in this area alone, we have seen council-led plantations by White Rose Forest (originally by the Calder Civic Trust in the 1970s), Calderdale's Million Tree Campaign, Pennine Edge Forest, and the Forest of Burnley, as well as community reforestation groups like Treesponsibility (formed in 1998 and planting 5ha of new woodland every year since). From the 1950s, Calderdale Council bought up lots of old mill and slum sites and planted a variety of trees across these slopes. These areas, at sites such as Southowram Bank, Brackenbeds, Lobb Mill, Tod Bottom and Exley Bank are still not marked as woodland on OS maps, but they are now covered in reasonably mature trees. New stands are emerging all the time, while so many of those denuded scrub slopes of the 1900s have seen birch and oak re-establish young heath woodland. From a low point of 5% at the turn of the 20th century, 8.5% of England is now wooded – things are starting to move in the right direction. However, as the recent floods demonstrate, there is still far more that can be done. With increasing climatic uncertainty, there are loud calls for more trees to be planted throughout the valley. It is not a time to rest on our laurels.

Ancient Woodland – taking stock

So what are we now left with after the wildwood has steadily been denuded, coppiced, and replanted over millennia because of our incessant demand for wood?

Although 12% of the UK is covered by woodland, it is still one of the least wooded countries in Europe, and if England is taken on its own that figure drops to just 8.5%. Only 2% of the UK is covered by what is termed 'ancient woodland', and only half of that is considered semi-natural (rather than cleared and replanted). Ancient woodland is defined as those areas that have been continuously wooded since 1600. Even if it has been clear-felled some time during that period, it can still be considered a plantation on an ancient woodland site (PAWS) providing it has never had another land use. If it is interplanted (i.e. replanted among existing trees) then it can still be termed ancient semi-natural woodland (ASNW).[22]

In marked contrast to the uniformity of more recent plantations, ancient woods change considerably as you move through them in response to soil conditions, changes which often appear inexplicable on first glance. Many wild-flowers are also very good indicators of ancient woodland, as they take a long time to establish and require undisturbed areas of soil to be able to spread. When its trees are felled, an ancient wood tend to spring into life with a carpet of flowers for the first few years; this is even possible where a plantation has existed for over a hundred years. It is simply impossible to replicate what is in these soils. However, it should be noted that an absence of these flowers in a wood does not mean it can't be ancient; centuries of charcoal burning (with its turf removal and soil scraping) and industrial pollution have also left their mark on the soil of this area.

the wood anemone, a good indicator species of ancient woodland

---

[22] It is referred to as semi-natural because any notion of completely natural woodland disappeared with the wildwood.

Ancient woodland is important for many reasons, one being that older trees fix significantly more carbon than younger trees. However, there are not that many really old trees in the Upper Calder Valley, due to both the demand for timber and the high levels of pollution. People tend to associate ancient woods with large old trees, when in fact many of them remained as coppices and so have few of this type of tree. Most truly old trees tend to be found in parks or gardens, where they have been planted and preserved for their aesthetic beauty, including a number of limes and sycamores thought to be planted around two hundred years ago.

Our natural woodland at this climate is birch-oak-rowan upland oak woodland. Of course, the climate of the Calder Valley is different to the east of Halifax than it is in the hills of the upper valley. Todmorden gets twice as much annual rainfall as Brighouse, and is different even from the area around Hebden Bridge. The wetter and more acid soils of the Pennines support different trees (for example, the silver birch largely being replaced by downy birch by the head of the valley).

Amongst the best ancient woodland indicator species are wood anemone, yellow archangel, wood sorrel and sweet woodruff. Common species like ramsons (wild garlic), bluebells, dogs mercury, common violet and wild strawberry can also be good indicators of the origin of a wood, but you have to be careful as these vary across the country; for example, wild garlic is far more common in the north and so is not necessarily indicative of ancient woodland. Ivy is the opposite, tending to be found only in secondary woodland rather than colonising existing woodland.

Ancient woods only tend to be located on poor ground that was not useful for other purposes, often at the far corners of parishes. In the Pennines, that meant the steep, rough and inaccessible cloughs that were not suitable for agriculture or intensive grazing. They are rarely along main roads, which under a statute of 1284 had to be free of woods and trees for 200ft either side, to prevent highwaymen from hiding there. Many have woodbanks around them constructed any time from the dark ages to the 19th century and now characterised by a low earth bank similar to ancient earthworks. In this area, the stone walls that surround most of our woods may have been constructed on top of these earlier banks, as stone was not widely used for building until the 17th century. There would also have been internal earth banks (and later walls), marking sub-divisions of the wood. As manors were split, so too were their woodlands, thus an old wall in a wood is not necessarily evidence that the area was once open fields. These banks, and even the walls that followed, took some effort to build and show the value of the woods to those who built them.

What we are left with are quite random parcels of ancient woodland; often the odd shapes of woodland that doesn't mirror the underlying ground is an indication of the antiquity of the wood. It is often hard to say why one wood has survived and another has not. Usually it was at the mercy of chance factors; someone's personal preference, the sheer cost and effort of grubbing out the trees, a government subsidy to improve the land, etc.

Only 4% of the borough of Calderdale is now wooded (well below the national average), representing just 14km², yet of it over 50% is recorded as ancient woodland. There are over ninety different ancient woodlands recorded on the Ancient Woodland Inventory in Calderdale, covering some 755 hectares *(see full list and details on page xxxi)*. Of these, well over half are defined as being ancient semi-natural woodland. Some of the best examples of ancient woodland can be found at the far west end of Elland Park Wood or in Brandy Hole Wood in Greetland. The latter woodland has been cut off by several housing estates and so has remained undisturbed by deer and non-native species. There is a great array of regenerated sessile oak of different ages and native ground flora species, but interestingly this wood is not included on the Ancient Woodland Inventory, evidence that it is still an incomplete record.

LIST OF CALDERDALE'S ANCIENT WOODLANDS

These details are taken from Natural England's Ancient Woodland Inventory, which was originally compiled in the 1980s and is being updated by the Woodland Trust. It still cannot be considered a complete record of our ancient woods, but gives a reasonable picture, particularly for the larger woodlands. The results are arranged (like the rest of the book) from east to west.

Woodland Name	Area	Type
Judy Woods (Norwood Green)	64.0ha	Both
Sun Wood/North Wood (Shelf)	15.5ha	ASNW
Wood Fall (Shelf)	5.5ha	PAWS
Henacre Wood (Queensbury)	4.8ha	ASNW
Howcans Wood (Stump Cross)	1.8ha	ASNW
Common Wood (Hipperholme)	4.3ha	PAWS
Freeman's Wood (Brighouse)	3.3ha	PAWS
Cromwell Wood (Brighouse)	5.2ha	ASNW
Binns Wood (Elland)	4.2ha	PAWS
Elland Park Wood (Elland)	32.0ha	Both
Strangstry Wood (Rastrick)	13.9ha	ASNW
Clifton Wood (Brighouse)	10.7ha	PAWS
Long Wood (Halifax)	8.7ha	ASNW
Scar Wood (Halifax)	10.0ha	ASNW
North Dean Wood (Copley)	26.0ha	Both
Crawstone Hall Wood (Greetland)	3.9ha	ASNW
Zachariah Wood (Greetland)	1.5ha	ASNW
Stubbings Wood (Stainland)	4.1ha	ASNW
Fall Spring Wood (Stainland)	2.1ha	ASNW
Beestones Wood/Beestonley Wood (Stainland)	6.9ha	ASNW
Whittle Wood (Stainland)	2.3ha	ASNW
Bottomley Wood (Barkisland)	3.7ha	ASNW
Barkisland Clough (Barkisland)	3.2ha	ASNW
Back Wood/Lee Wood (Outlane)	5.7ha	ASNW
Heys Wood (Outlane)	1.8ha	ASNW
Red Dike Plantation (Outlane)	4.6ha	PAWS
Rough Hey Wood (Triangle)	13.1ha	Both
Cheetham Wood/Rishworth Hall Wood (Rishworth)	9.4ha	Both
Turner Wood (Rishworth)	18.1ha	Both
Hanson Wood (western part) (Rishworth)	0.3ha	ASNW
Brearley Wood (Midgley)	9.8ha	ASNW
Han Royd Bank (Midgley)	4.4ha	ASNW
Scout Wood (Mytholmroyd)	4.4ha	PAWS
Hollin Hey Wood/Holderness Wood (Cragg Vale)	14.4ha	ASNW
Sutcliffe Wood (Cragg Vale)	6.0ha	PAWS
Parrock Clough (Cragg Vale)	5.9ha	ASNW
Broadhead Clough (Cragg Vale)	13.6ha	ASNW
Lord Wood (Cragg Vale)	7.0ha	PAWS
Whams Wood/Paper Mill Wood (Cragg Vale)	7.7ha	ASNW
Deacon Hill Wood (Cragg Vale)	4.8ha	ASNW
Bank Top Wood (Cragg Vale)	5.3ha	ASNW
Higher House Wood/Knowl Wood (Cragg Vale)	10.3ha	ASNW
Hove Yard Wood (Cragg Vale)	7.3ha	PAWS
Redacre Wood/Hill House Wood (Mytholmroyd)	6.1ha	ASNW
Burlees Wood (Mytholmroyd)	2.9ha	ASNW

Woodland Name	Area	Type
Higher Mayroyd Wood (Hebden Bridge)	4.1ha	ASNW
Common Bank Wood (Hebden Bridge)	1.9ha	PAWS
Spring Wood (Hebden Bridge)	15.4ha	ASNW
Tinker Bank Wood (Hebden Bridge)	2.9ha	ASNW
Middle Dean Wood/Crimsworth Wood/Purprise Wood (Hebden Bridge)	11.0ha	ASNW
Horse Hey Wood/Helliwell Wood (Hebden Bridge)	2.1ha	ASNW
Abel Cote Wood/Green Hirst Wood (Hebden Bridge)	6.9ha	ASNW
Hollin Hall Wood (Hebden Bridge)	6.7ha	ASNW
Foul Scout Wood (Hebden Bridge)	24.5ha	ASNW
Hebden Wood/Lee Wood (Hebden Bridge)	24.4ha	PAWS
Shackleton Wood (southern part) (Hebden Bridge)	10.8ha	PAWS
Shackleton Wood (northern part) (Hebden Bridge)	17.7ha	ASNW
Walshaw Wood/Over Wood (Hebden Bridge)	19.7ha	PAWS
High Greenwood Wood (Hebden Bridge)	13.3ha	Both
Ingham Wood (Hebden Bridge)	7.3ha	PAWS
Greenwood Lee Wood (Hebden Bridge)	8.3ha	Both
Mould Grain Wood (Hebden Bridge)	4.4ha	PAWS
Crow Nest Wood (Hebden Bridge)	11.3ha	PAWS
Hebble End Wood (Hebden Bridge)	6.1ha	Both
Eaves Wood (Hebden Bridge)	17.4ha	ASNW
Colden Clough (Hebden Bridge)	25.6ha	PAWS
Rawtonstall Wood (Hebden Bridge)	15.0ha	ASNW
Horsehold Wood (Hebden Bridge)	14.8ha	PAWS
Knott Wood (Charlestown)	7.5ha	PAWS
Callis Wood (Charlestown)	25.8ha	ASNW
Beverley Wood (Charlestown)	3.7ha	PAWS
Cowbridge Wood (Charlestown)	1.6ha	PAWS
Common Bank Wood (Eastwood)	6.1ha	ASNW
Lodge Wood (Eastwood)	3.1ha	ASNW
Burnt Acres Wood/Height Wood (Eastwood)	12.4ha	ASNW
Lower East Lee Wood (Eastwood)	2.7ha	ASNW
Back Wood (Eastwood)	1.7ha	Both
Gut Royd Wood (Eastwood)	2.2ha	ASNW
Shaw Wood/Haugh Wood (Eastwood)	5.7ha	PAWS
Causeway Wood/Ingham Wood (Todmorden)	4.5ha	ASNW
Longfield Wood (Todmorden)	5.1ha	ASNW
Robin Wood/Barewise Wood (Todmorden)	16.1ha	PAWS
Stannally Wood/Well Wood (Todmorden)	5.1ha	ASNW
Hartley Royd Wood (Todmorden)	3.5ha	ASNW
Knotts Wood (Todmorden)	1.1ha	ASNW
Back Wood (Cornholme)	0.8ha	ASNW
Dawk Hole Wood (Cornholme)	5.7ha	ASNW
Stones Wood (Todmorden)	9.0ha	Both
Gorpley Wood (Todmorden)	7.4ha	ASNW
Pasture Side Wood/Fir Wood (Walsden)	1.5ha	ASNW
Henshaw Wood/Spring Wood (Walsden)	7.8ha	Both
Ramsden Wood/Jack Wood (Walsden)	7.5ha	PAWS
Moorhey Wood/Clunter Wood (Walsden)	4.4ha	PAWS

ASNW = Ancient Semi-Natural Woodland
PAWS = Plantation on Ancient Woodland Site
Both = Combination of ASNW and PAWS

The Future

On the surface, it is very easy to look at the woodland cloak along the valley and all the new woodland planting schemes, and imagine that the outlook is pretty good for the woodland of the Calder Valley at the moment. But things are never that simple. What is easy to view as beautiful, rambling, natural woodland is actually ecologically and silviculturally barren. Most of the oak clough woodlands are now in poor condition due to years of neglect and overgrazing. Many of our ancient woodlands are under threat from invasive non-native species, whether the grey squirrel,[23] sycamore or the plague of Himalayan balsam that has taken to the Calder Valley's sodden hollows. Changes in drainage have resulted in a loss of most of our wet woodland, so examples like Broadhead Clough are rare and protected as nature reserves. The 19th-century beech plantations have largely been left unmanaged for over a hundred years, with most of the trees having developed well beyond maturity without being felled or thinned.[24] Their dense canopy restricts the development of saplings other than beech, which themselves are increasingly spreading into oak woodland and shading out the other seedlings there. Then there is disease, with a number of pandemics spreading alarmingly across the country; ash dieback, bleeding canker (which has decimated the country's horse chestnut trees) and Ramorum disease (the cause of sudden oak death among other things) have all now reached the Calder Valley.

A traditional woodsman from the Middle Ages would probably not recognise our woodland as it is today; they would wonder at all the large trees and why there was so little new growth, variety and, above all, light. It has been suggested by Frans Vera that woodlands are now the darkest they've ever been; we're not talking about dense conifer plantations, just regular broadleaf woods like those up and down the Calder Valley. Much is revealed by the traditional use of the terms 'closewoods' for the sort of plantation that we are now accustomed to in most woodland, and 'weeding' to refer to the thinning of trees (i.e. to weed out).

In 1988, Calderdale Council commissioned a woodland management plan that stressed the urgent need to manage what had become derelict woods. Very little has changed in the intervening years, only the need has become more desperate than ever. At the time, the council owned 33% of all the borough's woodland, but have disposed of a number of these assets in the intervening years, further restricting their ability to enact the changes they recommended. A new woodland plan has just been produced, outlining the council's approach to managing the 700 hectares of woodland they still own, which includes Colden Clough, Shelf Woods, Rough Hey Wood, Elland Park Wood and North Dean Wood.

But fortunately the council is no longer alone in looking after our woods. In recent years, numerous smaller organisations have sprung up, recognising the potential economic and environmental value of these woodlands. Some woods are now being managed by organisations like Black Bark and Knott Wood Coppicers. Black Bark have planted hazel coppicing and areas of mixed woodland to provide an array of woodland products – firewood, charcoal, bean poles, hedging stakes, chair sticks, timber and fascines (bundles of brash used for slowing down the erosion of gulleys on peat moorland). Community groups are being further encouraged by Forest Culture to manage their own woodlands, increasing the benefits it can bring them while developing a community who cares for and about each woodland. The other side of this is

---

[23] The prevalence of grey squirrels results in large-scale bark stripping, which can seriously damage mature trees and entirely destroy many young saplings.
[24] In every storm in recent years, large numbers of these beech trees are toppled. Very few naturally-seeding trees have been damaged as they are more suited to recovering naturally than those that have been planted, which can often be taken out wholesale.

educating landowners, many of whom have no idea what to do with their woodland, so that it can be productive and financially beneficial, even if it is only providing firewood.[25] At the heart of this is a need to change the culture in terms of the way we look at woodland – it is a working landscape not a wasteland or natural wilderness. Part of this education is provided by enterprises like Black Bark and Tinderwood Trust, who offer forest schools and woodland education activities for the next generation.

As well as identifying ancient woodland sites, the Woodland Trust is encouraging the Ancient Woodlands Restoration Project, with a particular focus on bringing PAWS (Plantations on Ancient Woodland Sites) back into line. Though dormant, these ancient woods can be rejuvenated by careful management because the soil and flora within them often have long memories. Bulbs of plants like bluebells and wood sorrel that have been dormant for decades often suddenly return to life when the shading trees are removed, and it is hoped this will occur where some of the 19th-century beech and sycamore is cleared (as has already happened at Rough Hey Wood in the Ryburn Valley). It is felt the thinning of unmanaged woods and careful management thereafter can also provide substantial forestry by-products that can be used for biomass production.

Pennine Prospects are also currently looking into woodland archaeology in the South Pennines, so much of which is still unknown, unrecorded or not understood beneath the dense cloak of leaves, moss and Himalayan balsam in Calderdale. Using LIDAR (a satellite image that shows a landscape without its vegetation), they are hoping to reveal many more sites of Q pits, charcoal hearths, woodland boundaries and ancient trackways in the area. There are also people looking into food as part of the history of managing woods, by focusing on old orchards and nut woods.

Meanwhile, further woodland creation has proven benefits for improving water quality and biodiversity, protecting the soil, providing carbon storage and mitigating flood risk. The latter is particularly relevant after all the flooding in the Calder Valley in recent years. The South Pennines Local Nature Partnership estimate that we have the potential to double our woodland cover in the South Pennines by 2060, with clough woodland a priority. Working alongside Moors for the Future, 600 hectares of clough woodland were planted in the Upper Derwent Valley in Derbyshire, and similar is thought possible within the catchment of the River Calder. Planting around urban areas is also important for short-term flood prevention. But all of this remains dependent on government subsidy and so far consists of local groups like Treesponsibility working on small sites.

However, we are still planting trees much as we did after World War I. Though conifers have been replaced by a mix of native species (oak, birch, rowan, hazel, hawthorn, fruit trees and the like), they are still planted close together in a way that will need ongoing management. Though it serves some of the purposes of a wood – landscape amelioration and flood prevention – there are many others these plantations don't. Woodlands work best when they are managed and profitable, or when they are naturally formed. Planted trees always have more of a struggle to settle and survive challenges like storms, disease, and changing climate. Even genetically superior super-trees are fallible to these factors, as well as lacking the natural variation that make woodlands so magical.

Ultimately the most important question is whether we can bring woodland back into active management. There is an availability of money for increasing forestry productivity, but most people don't want to manage woodland for silvicultural practices – they just want to enjoy it as a leisure amenity and for the wildlife it shelters. If we have no intention of managing these woods we are trying to create, aren't we just creating the derelict woods of the future?

---

[25] Though it should be noted that coppiced hazel poles grow faster and sell higher than simple firewood.

A WOODLAND GLOSSARY

booth (or **butt**) = shelter on summer grazing grounds

brier = rose

carr = wooded marshland (Old Norse), often where alders grow

chet, cet = wood (from the Celtic *coed*)

dob = local dialect for a robin

firth (or **frith**) = wood (Old English)

grove (or **grave**) = suggests a plantation

hag = portion of a coppice wood (Saxon), or referring to haws (though largely out of use by 18th century)

heps = rosehips

hollin = place where holly was grown

holt = small wood or grove of trees

hurst = copse or wooded hill (Old English)

imbers = raspberries

ing = clearing (Saxon)

laverock = wood sorrel

lund (or **lound**) = a glade (Old Norse), from which we get the modern form lawn

lumb = wooded section of a valley

manwood (or **meanwood**) = common or boundary wood (so too mangrove)

owler (or **oller/eller**) = alder

royd (or **ridding**) = land cleared of trees

scholes = shelter on summer grazing grounds

shaw = small wood (Old English), often as narrow strip

shroggs = scrubland, often covered in heather and gorse

slade = woodland clearing or green road

snedding = cutting away of the side branches after a tree is felled

snigging = a method for removing felled trees in which the tree is drawn butt-end first by horse or tractor. Sometimes it is lifted off the ground by a timber bob with wheels and attached to the back of a horse, occasionally on a sleigh with chains.

spinney = plantation (or wood) of thorns

spring = coppice wood

stocks = the stumps or coppice stool of a tree

storth (or **storrs**) = coppice wood (Old Norse)

stub (noun) = the stump of a tree, but may originally have referred to pollarded trees

stub (verb) = to grub up the stump of trees

stubbing = area of woodland cleared but for stumps (stubs)

thwaite = open space or clearing in the wood

tod = a pollard or tree stump

vert = any woodland cover in which game could shelter

wicken = rowan

withen = willow

CHAPTER 1 - NORWOOD GREEN & SHELF

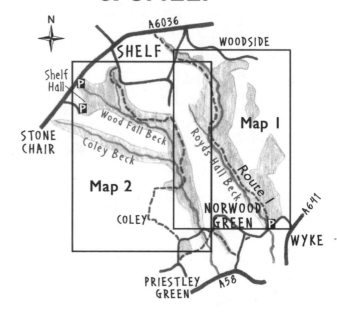

Map Sheet: Explorer 288 (Bradford & Huddersfield)

Public Transport: Buses 681/2 run regularly through Shelf between Halifax and Bradford. Bus 226 runs from Halifax to Norwood Green twice daily.

Parking: Free car parks at Shelf Hall Park and layby along Station Road in Norwood Green.

Here, on Calderdale's north-eastern corner, we find a remarkable green oasis. With the urban sprawl of **Shelf**, Buttershaw, Low Moor and Wyke on all sides, **Norwood Green** and Coley have managed to retain a bucolic 19th-century air. The great estates of Coley, Rookes and Royds Halls doubtless played their part, but so too the steepness of the land in an area where settlements generally stuck to the broad reaches of high ground. The river that ends its course lined with industry as Clifton Beck in Brighouse, forks upstream into two charming dingles, Coley Beck and Royds Hall Beck. The latter forms the boundary between Calderdale and Bradford boroughs, but I have included all of the wonderful Judy Woods that straddle the stream here.

These woodlands' existence was preserved by a particular pattern of ownership; first by private estate (Royds Hall), then industry (the Low Moor Company, for whom the woods provided charcoal, ironstone, and coal) and later by the local council. As such, it is an area rich with historic features, particularly the series of remarkably preserved 18th-century bell pits in Royds Hall Great Wood. The woods are best explored from the timeless village of Norwood Green, but equally Shelf Hall and Shelf village give great access to the woods.

the Clapping Tree in Judy Woods

1

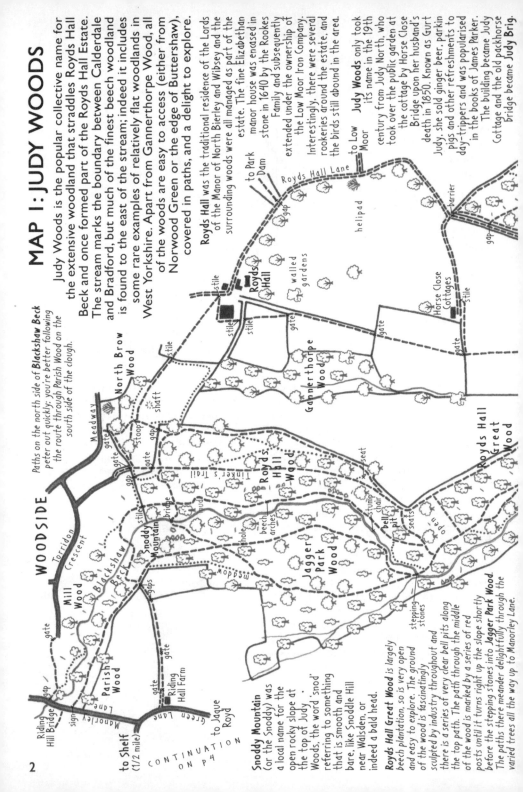

MAP 1: JUDY WOODS

Judy Woods is the popular collective name for the extensive woodland that straddles Royds Hall Beck and once formed part of the Royds Hall Estate. The stream marks the boundary between Calderdale and Bradford, but much of the finest beech woodland is found to the east of the stream; indeed it includes some rare examples of relatively flat woodlands in West Yorkshire. Apart from Gannerthorpe Wood, all of the woods are easy to access (either from Norwood Green or the edge of Buttershaw), covered in paths, and a delight to explore.

Royds Hall was the traditional residence of the Lords of the Manor of North Bierley and Wibsey and the surrounding woods were all managed as part of the estate. The fine Elizabethan manor house was encased in stone in 1640 by the Rookes Family and subsequently extended under the ownership of the Low Moor Iron Company. Interestingly, there were several rookeries around the estate, and the birds still abound in the area.

Judy Woods only took its name in the 19th century from Judy North, who took over the public garden at the cottage by Horse Close Bridge upon her husband's death in 1850. Known as Gurt Judy, she sold ginger beer, parkin pigs and other refreshments to day-trippers and was popularised in the books of James Parker. The building became Judy Cottage and the old packhorse bridge became Judy Brig.

WOODSIDE

Paths on the north side of *Blackshaw Beck* peter out quickly; you're better following the route through Parish Wood on the south side of the clough.

Snoddy Mountain (or the Snoddy) was a local name for the open rocky slope at the top of Judy Woods, the word 'snod' referring to something that is smooth and bare, like Snoddle Hill near Walsden, or indeed a bald head.

Royds Hall Great Wood is largely beech plantation, so is very open and easy to explore. The ground of the wood is fascinatingly sculpted by industry throughout and there is a series of very clear bell pits along the top path. The path through the middle of the wood is marked by a series of red posts until it turns right up the slope shortly before the stepping stones into *Jagger Park Wood*. The paths there meander delightfully through the varied trees all the way up to Manorley Lane.

CONTINUATION ON P4

to Shelf (1/2 mile)

Coal and ironstone seams beneath the whole area are recorded as having been worked from as early as the 12th century. The earliest shafts took the form of **bell pits** (also known as beehive pits), of which there are several in **Royds Hall Great Wood**, identifiable by the depression left after the material used to fill in the shaft compacted down. Larger shafts were sunk by William Rookes and the whole area extensively worked in the 18th century; these can be seen in Low Wood, Old Hanna Wood and near North Brow Wood, as well as by various sinkholes where the tunnels collapsed. In 1789, the estate was bought by the recently formed Low Moor Iron Company, which was to become one of the world's largest producers of iron. However, mining in the woods themselves is thought to have ended by the 1820s, when much of the beech here was planted, replacing oak felled during the Napoleonic Wars. The last of the nearby pits to close was **Norwood Green Colliery** (or Flathers Pit) in 1960, from which a mineral railway ran across Low Wood to the main ironworks in Low Moor.

The **Old White Beare** is named after a ship that fought against the Spanish Armada. The White Bear was one of the Navy's great man o' wars at the time and its timbers were used to rebuild the pub when it burnt down in 1646.

to Ox Heys
stile
Birks Close
gap
gate
gate
gate
sign
sign
Ellis Memorial Clock Tower
P
B
village hall
gate
stile
Croft Top Farm
gate
gap
Sowden Lane
Royds Hall Beck
trial hole
steps
bell pits
bell pits
gate
stile
stile
steps
bridge
Judy Cottage (site)
gate
gap
Judy Wood
gap
steps
Judy Brig
gap
Sheep Hole
gap
Old Hanna Wood
trial hole
gaps
gaps
bollards
gap
High Fernley Road
bridge
sinkholes
bridges
shafts
steps
Low Wood
post
mud
falls
bridge
seat
bridge
sinkholes
mineral trackway
stile
Turnip Hill
Doctor Wood
gate
to Wyke (1/2 mile)
P
railway
stile
John Wood
Norwood Green Colliery (site)
Pickle Bridge
Norwood Green Mill
Station Road
Pear Tree Inn
War Memorial
B
Rookes Lane
B
stile
gap
NORWOOD GREEN
Old White Beare
Village Street
to Rookes Wood
gap

CONTINUATION ON P5

It is possible to follow **Royds Hall Beck** through Low Wood, a faint path continuing near the right bank until a fence cuts it off below Judy Brig and the steepness of the ground beyond prevents further progress. The relatively-open wood above is covered in paths.

Norwood Green was originally North Wood Green, a name dating back to the 13th century. At one time it was thought to rival Halifax, but never grew into the town that was imagined and was left to become a quiet backwater.

Pickle Bridge was the original name of Wyke & Norwood Green Station and gave its name to a branch line running from here down to Brighouse.

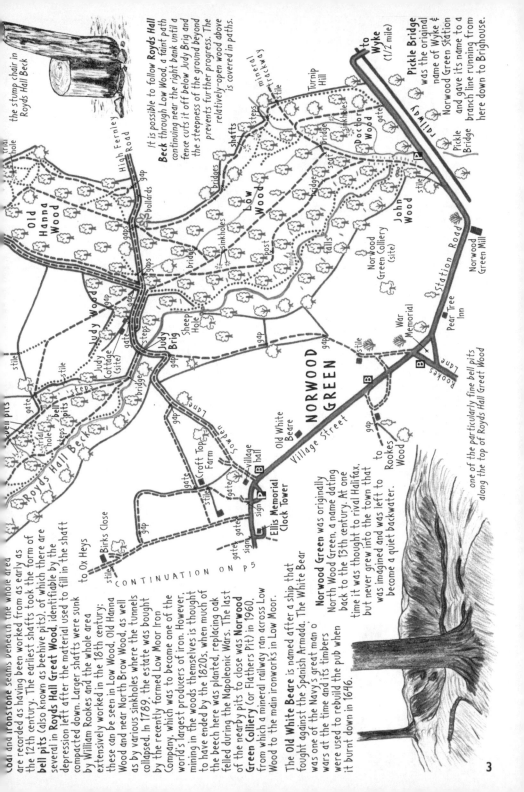

the stump chair in Royds Hall Beck

one of the particularly fine bell pits along the top of Royds Hall Great Wood

MAP 2: SHELF WOODS & COLEY BECK

Shelf was once renowned for its large areas of woodland, providing timber and charcoal across the region, yet only its clough woods remain today. The broad term Shelf Woods now tends to refer to the parish council-owned woods of Wood Fall, Sun Wood and North Wood. Other than the top end of Coley Beck, they are largely accessible from Shelf and provide a verdant oasis in this area.

Shelf New Hall was built in 1861 by Samuel Bottomley as a Victorian version of an old manor house. Its substantial grounds were used as Shelf Hall Pleasure Gardens in the 1890s, and the house as a prisoner-of-war camp during World War II. The council acquired it as a park and demolished the house in 1951, leaving only the stable block alongside Shelf Hall Cottage. The 17th century **Shelf Old Hall** was located where Shelf Village Hall now stands, but was never as important as the name suggests.

Wood Fall is an ancient woodland with some fine sessile oak, as well as plantations of sycamore and beech, particularly around the 99 Steps and an avenue leading below Shelf Hall.

There are no paths along the south side of **Wood Fall Beck**, but plenty along the north side from the 99 Steps (of which there are now well over 100). Nearing Brow Lane on the edge of Shelf, a path continues down to the waterfall at *Annet Hole* and on through the thin trees to **Shelf Hall Park**.

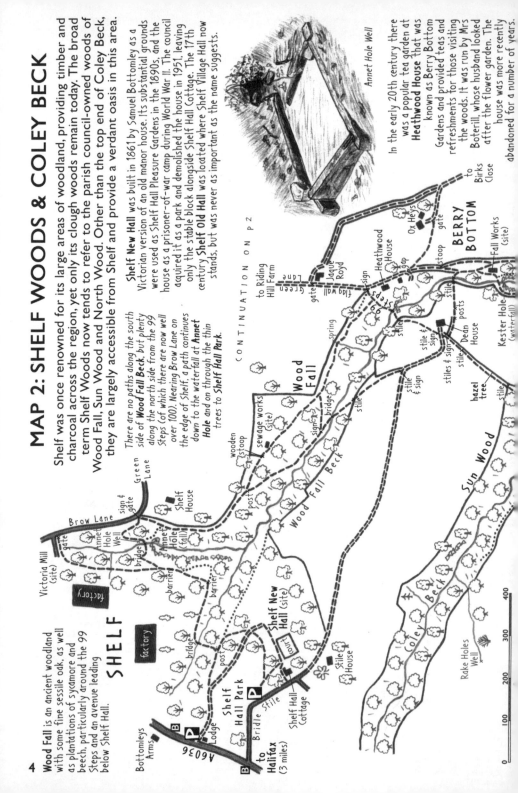

Annet Hole Well

In the early 20th century there was a popular tea garden at **Heathwood House** that was known as Berry Bottom Gardens and provided teas and refreshments for those visiting the woods. It was run by Mrs Boterill, whose husband looked after the flower garden. The house was more recently abandoned for a number of years.

CONTINUATION ON P 2

to Riding Hill Farm

Jaque Royd

flag wall

Jaque Green Lane

gate

sign

spring

Steps
99
Steps

stile

Heathwood House

gap

stoop

gate

to Birks Close

Ox Heys

BERRY BOTTOM

Fall Works (site)

stile

stile

stile & sign

Dean House

stiles & sign

stile

Kester Hole (waterfall)

hazel tree

stile

Sun Wood

Wood Fall

Wood Fall Beck

sign

bridge

stile

sewage works (site)

wooden stoop

to Riding Hill Farm

Green Lane

sign & gate

gate

Brow Lane

sign & gate

Annet Hole Well

Victoria Mill (site)

factory

Shelf House

post

Annet Hole (fall)

bridge

barrier

barrier

barrier

SHELF

factory

Shelf New Hall (site)

bridge

post

court

Stile House

Shelf Park

Shelf Hall Park

Lodge

B

P

Bottomleys Arms

P

to Bridle Stile

Shelf Hall Cottage

to Halifax (3 miles)

A6036

B

Rake Holes Well

Coley Beck

0 100 200 300 400

4

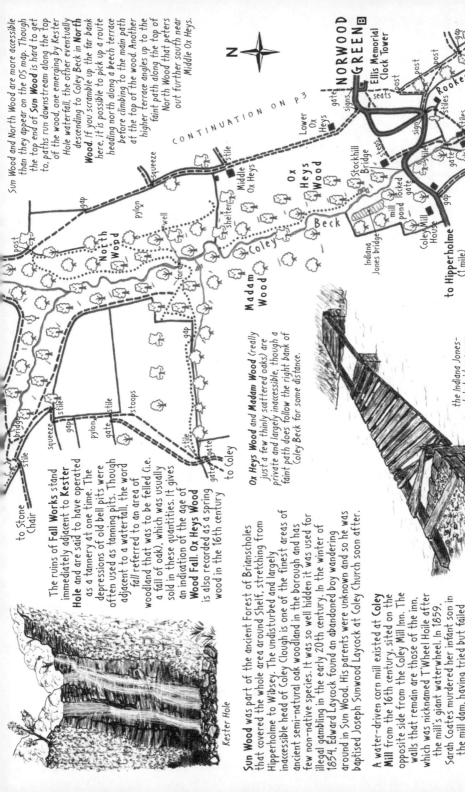

CONTINUATION ON P3

N

NORWOOD GREEN B

Ellis Memorial Clock Tower

Rookes Wood

Coley Mill Inn (site)

gap

post

post

signs

seats

sign

gate

gate

stiles

stiles

stile

stile

Lower Ox Heys

steps

Stockhill Bridge

gate

locked gate

Ox Heys Wood

Coley Mill House

mill pond

Indiana Jones bridge

gap

Beck

(Coley)

to Hipperholme (1 mile)

Middle Ox Heys

stile

squeeze

shelter

well

ford

Madam Wood

gap

North Wood

pylon

post

gap

stile

pylon

gate

squeeze

stoops

stile

gap

bridge

stile

stile

gate

gate

stile

to Coley

to Stone Chair

Sun Wood and North Wood are more accessible than they appear on the OS map. Though the top end of **Sun Wood** is hard to get to, paths run downstream along the top of the wood, one emerging by Kester Hole waterfall, the other eventually descending to Coley Beck in **North Wood**. If you scramble up the far bank here, it is possible to pick up a route heading north along a beech terrace before climbing to the main path at the top of the wood. Another higher terrace angles up to the top of faint path along the top of North Wood that peters out further south near Middle Ox Heys.

Ox Heys Wood and *Madam Wood* (really just a few thinly scattered oaks) are private and largely inaccessible, though a faint path does follow the right bank of Coley Beck for some distance.

the Indiana Jones-style bridge across Coley Mill pond

Kester Hole

The ruins of **Fall Works** stand immediately adjacent to **Kester Hole** and are said to have operated as a tannery at one time. The depressions of old bell pits were often used as tanning pits. Though adjacent to a waterfall, the word *fall* referred to an area of woodland that was to be felled (i.e. a fall of oak), which was usually sold in these quantities. It gives an indication of the age of **Wood Fall**. **Ox Heys Wood** is also recorded as a spring wood in the 16th century

Sun Wood was part of the ancient Forest of Briansholes that covered the whole area around Shelf, stretching from Hipperholme to Wibsey. The undisturbed and largely inaccessible head of Coley Clough is one of the finest areas of ancient semi-natural oak woodland in the borough and has few non-native species. It was so well hidden it was used for illegal gambling in the early 20th century. In the winter of 1854, Edward Laycock found an abandoned boy wandering around in Sun Wood. His parents were unknown and so he was baptised Joseph Sunwood Laycock at Coley Church soon after.

A water-driven corn mill existed at **Coley Mill** from the 16th century, sited on the opposite side from the Coley Mill Inn. The walls that remain are those of the inn, which was nicknamed T'Wheel Hoile after the mill's giant waterwheel. In 1859, Sarah Coates murdered her infant son in the mill dam, having tried but failed to kill herself in the process. The mill was demolished in the 1940s.

5

ROUTE I: JUDY & SHELF WOODS FROM SHELF

Distance: 6 miles (10km)

Ascent: 230m

Parking: Free street parking on A6036 in Shelf and Station Road in Norwood Green.

Public Transport: Shelf is on the 681/682 bus routes between Halifax and Bradford.

Character: A true woodland walk in the main, descending the length of the delightful Judy Woods to Norwood Green, before returning via Coley Beck and Shelf Woods. It is easy walking and there are waterfalls, bell pits and ancient halls to see. If driving, it is as easy to start the route in Norwood Green. After heavy rain some of the stream crossings may be awkward.

Bethel Chapel in Shelf was built in 139 days in 1853 and has a tradition of relying on lay preachers, on whom it is believed the Holy Spirit has conferred divine authority. Surrounded by railings is the grave of Joseph Jagger who travelled to Monte Carlo in 1875 and won 2 million Francs in eight days by applying knowledge of the spindles on roulette machines gleaned from working in local mills. It has been suggested he was the inspiration for the music hall song *The Man Who Broke the Bank at Monte Carlo*, but this was actually the confidence trickster Charles Wells, who repeated the feat in 1891.

2 The path continues along the top of **Parish Wood** and across the open heath at the top of Snoddy Mountain. Carry straight on through the ancient **Jagger Park Wood** until it descends towards Blackshaw Beck. Stay on the right side of the stream until you join another path to cross some stepping stones. There are various paths through **Royds Hall Great Wood**, all leading down to Judy Brig, the easiest following the faded red waymarkers along the bottom of the slope. To find the bell pits, head up to the top of the wood.

Russula (or brittle-gills) form a family of similar mushrooms with white gills and stems, but a whole variety of cap colours (mainly yellows, greys and reds). They can be identified by the fact that gills break readily when squashed. Most are edible, though the bright red sickener has given rise to the rest of the clan a bad name.

6 There were windmills in both Shelf and Northowram that were rarities in this area and are remembered in the names of pubs. Shelf's fine **pinfold** can be found along a footpath between Brow Lane and some steps beside the Duke William pub.

1 From the row of shops in the middle of **Shelf**, follow the A6036 east towards Bradford. Opposite the Prince of Orange, turn right down some steps before **St Michael's Church** and follow the left edge of the field to reach a gap into the woods above Blackshaw Beck. Where the narrow path reaches a road, turn right then immediately left into **Parish Wood**.

The beautiful **Ellis Memorial Clock Tower** in Norwood Green was erected on Queen Victoria's Jubilee in 1897 in memory of Ephraim Ellis. It can be seen by heading 200m off the route into the village along the top of Rookes Wood.

Jagger Park Wood refers to coal-jaggers, who carried coal away from the pits here by packhorse train.

8 Turn left beyond Heathwood House and start down the **99 Steps**, but turn right off them at a waymark post to skirt along the top of **Wood Fall**. You can go either way where the path forks, but I prefer bearing left down to follow **Wood Fall Beck** for a bit. Nearing the first buildings of Shelf, bear left down a steep path above **Annet Hole** waterfall and cross the stream. At the top of the far slope, double back sharply to the right on a path that soon emerges on Brow Lane. Turn left to return to the main road through **Shelf**.

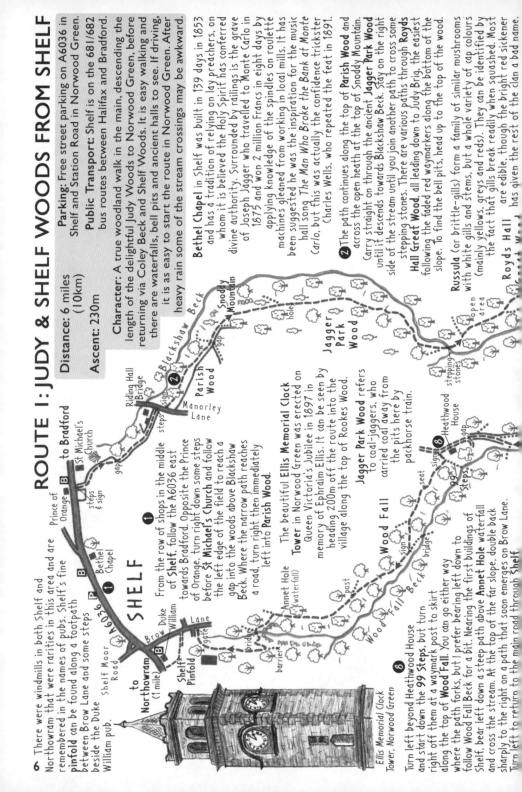

Ellis Memorial Clock Tower, Norwood Green

SHELF

A6036 Shelf Moor Road

to Northowram (1 mile)

to Bradford

St Michael's Church

Prince of Orange

Bethel Chapel

Duke William

Brow Lane

Shelf Pinfold

Blackshaw Beck

Riding Hall Bridge

Manorley Lane

Parish Wood

Snoddy Mountain

Jagger Park Wood

stepping stones

Heathwood House

Royds Hall Great Wood

open area

Wood Fall

Wood Fall Beck

Annet Hole (waterfall)

barrier

99 Steps

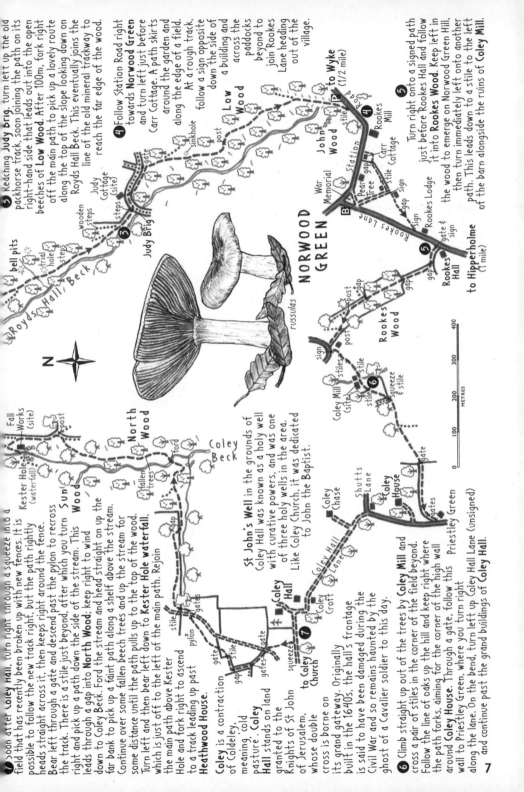

1 Soon after **Coley Hall**, turn right through a squeeze into a field that has recently been broken up with new fences. It is possible to follow the new track right, but the path rightly heads straight across it, then keeps right around the fence. Bear left through a gate and descend past the pylon to recross the track. There is a stile just beyond, after which you turn right and pick up a path down the side of the stream. This leads through a gap into **North Wood**; keep right to wind down to **Coley Beck**. Ford the stream and head straight on up the far bank to pick up a faint path along a shelf above the stream. Continue over some fallen beech trees and up the stream for some distance until the path pulls up to the top of the wood. Turn left and then bear left down to **Kester Hole waterfall**, which is just off to the left of the main path. Rejoin the main path above Kester Hole and fork right to ascend to a track leading up past **Heathwood House**.

Coley is a contraction of Coldeley, meaning 'cold pasture'. **Coley Hall** stands on land granted to the Knights of St John of Jerusalem, whose double cross is borne on its grand gateway. Originally built in the 1640s, the hall's frontage is said to have been damaged during the Civil War and so remains haunted by the ghost of a Cavalier soldier to this day.

St John's Well in the grounds of Coley Hall was known as a holy well with curative powers, and was one of three holy wells in the area. Like Coley Church, it was dedicated to John the Baptist.

2 Reaching **Judy Brig**, turn left up the old packhorse track, soon joining the path on its right-hand side that leads out into the open beeches of **Low Wood**. After 100m, fork right off the main path to pick up a lovely route along the top of the slope looking down on Royds Hall Beck. This eventually joins the line of the old mineral trackway to reach the far edge of the wood.

4 Follow Station Road right towards **Norwood Green** and turn left just before Carr Cottage. A path skirts around the garden and along the edge of a field. At a rough track, follow a sign opposite down the side of a building and across the paddocks beyond to join Rookes Lane heading out of the village.

5 Turn right onto a signed path just before Rookes Hall and follow it into **Rookes Wood**. Keep left in the wood to emerge on Norwood Green Hill, then turn immediately left onto another path. This leads down to a stile to the left of the barn alongside the ruins of **Coley Mill**.

6 Climb straight up out of the trees by **Coley Mill** and cross a pair of stiles in the corner of the field beyond. Follow the line of oaks up the hill and keep right where the path forks, aiming for the corner of the high wall around **Coley House**. Through a gate, follow this wall to **Priestley Green**, where you turn right along the lane. On the bend, turn left up Coley Hall Lane (unsigned) and continue past the grand buildings of **Coley Hall**.

N

bell pits
trial hole
Royds Hall Beck
wooden steps
steps
3 Judy Brig
Judy Cottage (site)
steps
sinkhole
post
gate
Low Wood
John Wood
War Memorial
Station
Pear Tree
Carr Cottage
Rookes Mill
stile
gap / sign
Rookes Lodge
Rookes Lane
gate & sign
P to Wyke (1/2 mile)
Wyke Road
5 Rookes Hall
to Hipperholme (1 mile)

NORWOOD GREEN

russulas

Fall Works (site)
post
North Wood
Kester Hole (waterfall)
fallen trees
Sun Wood
ford
Coley Beck
gap
stile
pylon
gates
gate
gap
stile
gates
squeeze
gates
7 Coley Hall
Coley Croft
to Coley Church
Coley Hall Lane
Coley Chase
Shutts Lane
Coley House
gates
Priestley Green

gap / post
Rookes Wood
sign
Coley Mill stiles (site)
stile
squeeze & stile **6**
gate
gate
sign

0 100 200 300 400
METRES

THE BEECH

It is hard to mistake the beech, which is derived from the Anglo-Saxon word *boc* that originated from its use in book covers. When its leaves come out in spring they are a lurid lime green that often seems unreal, especially when set against the dark trunks and ground beneath the canopy. In autumn the leaves turn the sort of orange we expect all leaves to turn, crisp and bright, the perfect fall through which to kick one's feet. But in between, the beech has a dense, dark canopy all summer; great for cool shade on a hot day, but devoid of life but for the grey squirrels bounding around among the beech masts of the open woodland floor.

The beech is considered native to southern England and was probably the last tree to colonise Britain before it was separated from mainland Europe. It is recognisable by its its fine reddish buds and smooth grey bark, in which are often seen eye-shaped markings thought to be the Evil Eye. It produces seed infrequently and its mast (beech nuts) doesn't spread far from the parent tree. It doesn't like being exposed to the wind or particularly dry or wet soil as it is so shallow rooting. Yet it is very tolerant of shade, so its seedlings grow well under the sort of dense canopies beech woods possess. The bare ground devoid of wild flowers underneath the trees is a result of the lack of light from early in the season and the fact that its dense leaf matter is so slow to rot away, as well as an enzyme produced by beech which further inhibits growth. Regeneration is further limited by soil erosion on the bare, steep slopes which means that all the seed on the woodland floor is washed away.

Beech is strong and even-grained, so was the most popular wood for turning and making furniture. Medieval soap also used beech-wood charcoal. It was used for hedging from the 19th century because it retains many of its copper leaves through the winter – the largest hedge in the world is beech and lines the A93 in Perthshire. In this area, bobbins and shuttles for the mills were all initially made from imported beech; as supplies dwindled in the latter half of the 19th century, so many mill-owners planted large swathes of beech across the hillsides to provide a local supply, often clear-felling ancient oak coppices to do so. On some of the wealthier estates it was also planted as a fashionable ornamental tree for its autumnal fire.

However, beech was unsuited to the soil, steep slopes and shaded valleys of the Pennines and so grew slowly and irregularly. Consequently it was never much used and instead left to grow old in great stands all across the hillsides. It was later used as chockwood in mines right up to the 1980s, as well as for clog soles, particularly during the war, when manufacturers were forced to source their wood locally again. Most of these local beech trees are now nearing the end of their natural 180-year lifespan, hence many of them come down in every new storm. A good mature beech woodland would generally be expected to have about 40% beech in it, rather than the 95% we find in this area, so many are now being thinned. Beech seedlings, though, thrive as the tree's natural range moves slowly north with the effect of climate change. Only the grey squirrel appears to be able to slow it down, as it loves to strip the bark of beech seedlings above all others.

CHAPTER 2 - SHIBDEN DALE

Map Sheet: Explorer 288 (Bradford & Huddersfield)

Public Transport: Stump Cross and Northowram are on the 681/682 bus routes between Halifax and Bradford and 533 from Halifax. Hipperholme is on the 548/549 bus routes between Halifax and Brighouse. Queensbury is on the 576 bus route between Halifax and Bradford.

Parking: Pay car parks in Shibden Park, small free parking area by the sports pitches in Northowram, and various street parking elsewhere.

tall stoop in Henacre Wood

This long and very rural valley immediately east of Halifax is a surprisingly green enclave in the heart of West Yorkshire. I have called the whole chapter Shibden Dale, though in fact it becomes the Walterclough Valley below the confluence with Jum Hole Beck, which itself flows through the Chelsea Valley. At the same point, Shibden Brook becomes Red Beck, as if it now has sufficient iron oxide pollution to warrant this name. The name Shibden itself is a corruption of 'Sheep Dene'.

Shibden Wood was a considerable tract in the Middle Ages, as was Hipperholme Wood, but both are thought to have been gradually eaten into by large medieval populations in both Northowram and Hipperholme. The ancient Forest of Brian Scholes also covered a large part of this region and remnants of it can be found in the Chelsea Valley, Shelf and Judy Woods (see Chapter 1). Shibden Dale itself was full of medieval settlements, many of the grand houses now standing as arresting ruins or, in the case of Shibden Hall, as a fascinating museum.

Though industry inevitably filled the valley, with some of its mines only very recently closed, Shibden Dale has managed to retain its rural air and avoid being developed. Settlements crowd the hilltops above, where Elland flags were quarried on a large scale, but all you see from below are the charming castellations of the judd walls formed from the quarry waste. It is a wonderful escape.

MAP 3: SHIBDEN DALE NORTH

The head of Shibden Dale, most easily accessed from the edge of Queensbury, may be just in Bradford, but is a beautiful wooded culmination of this long valley. The steep slopes are crowned by great judd walls, looking like the ramparts of old forts, and lost in the trees are a number of crumbling old halls, former sewage works and colliery sites. It is a favourite area of mine, yet one that is difficult to explore since many of the Public Rights of Way are unusable, while various other unofficial paths exist, especially around Henacre Wood.

Shibden Head Brewery was established in the 18th century by the Stocks family of Upper Shibden Hall. Joseph Stocks & Company came to own some 56 pubs in the area until they were eventually bought by Websters in 1932.

Queensbury was only named at a meeting in 1863, prior to which it was known by the name of the Queen's Head pub. The hamlet of **Ambler Thorn** is far older and Ambler is a common local name.

There are various unofficial paths around the old sewage works. The main track runs down from Hanging Royd, with another traceable from near Lower Shibden Hall. A path continues past the works down to Shibden Brook; stepping over a gap in the wall to the left leads into Henacre Wood with paths heading up both sides of the stream.

The top of Shibden Dale is littered with the ruins of grand houses. The Italianate mansion at **Upper Shibden Hall** dates from the 1830s, when Michael Stocks built what he called Catherine House on the site of a much earlier hall, at which Sir Thomas Browne was staying when he wrote *Religio Medici* in 1643. Houses were also recorded at Nether Shibden (now **Lower Shibden Hall**) and **Hanging Royd** in 1306 and Hanging Royd in 1309. The latter's barn was used for toss ha'penny games in the 1960s. **Water Scout** was built in 1618 but has been left to crumble since the 1930s. Even the sewage works at Shibden Head contained a private house for its manager

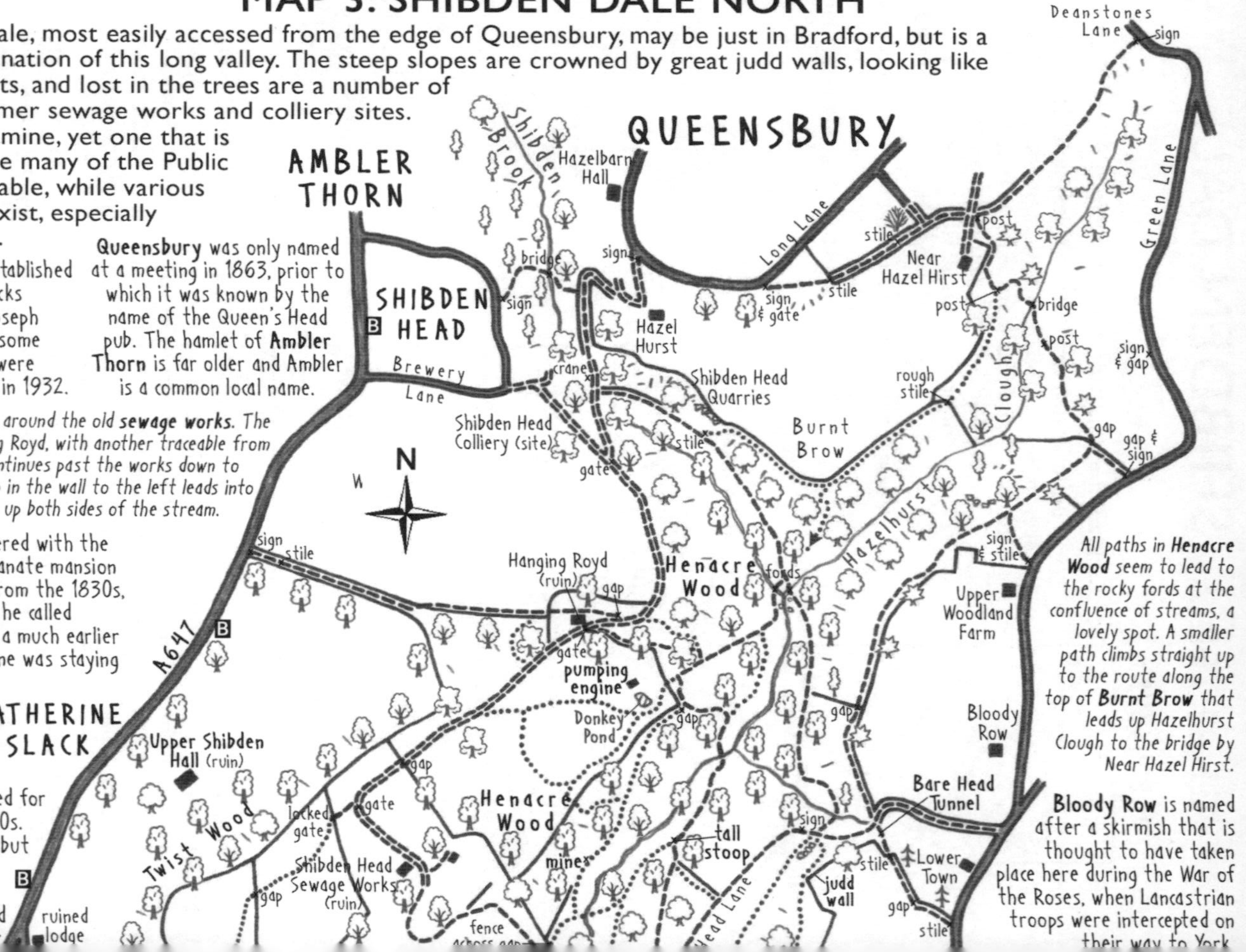

All paths in **Henacre Wood** seem to lead to the rocky fords at the confluence of streams, a lovely spot. A smaller path climbs straight up to the route along the top of **Burnt Brow** that leads up Hazelhurst Clough to the bridge by Near Hazel Hirst.

Bloody Row is named after a skirmish that is thought to have taken place here during the War of the Roses, when Lanastrian troops were intercepted on their way to York

QUEENSBURY

AMBLER THORN

SHIBDEN HEAD

CATHERINE SLACK

Deanstones Lane sign

Green Lane

Long Lane

Shibden Brook

Hazelbarn Hall

Near Hazel Hirst

Hazel Hirst

Shibden Head Quarries

Burnt Brow

Hazlehurst

Henacre Wood

Upper Woodland Farm

Bloody Row

Bare Head Tunnel

Lower Town

Judd wall

Hanging Royd (ruin)

Pumping engine

Donkey Pond

Shibden Head Colliery (site)

Shibden Head Sewage Works (ruin)

Head Lane

Brewery Lane

Upper Shibden Hall (ruin)

A647

Twisel Bottom

ruined lodge

N

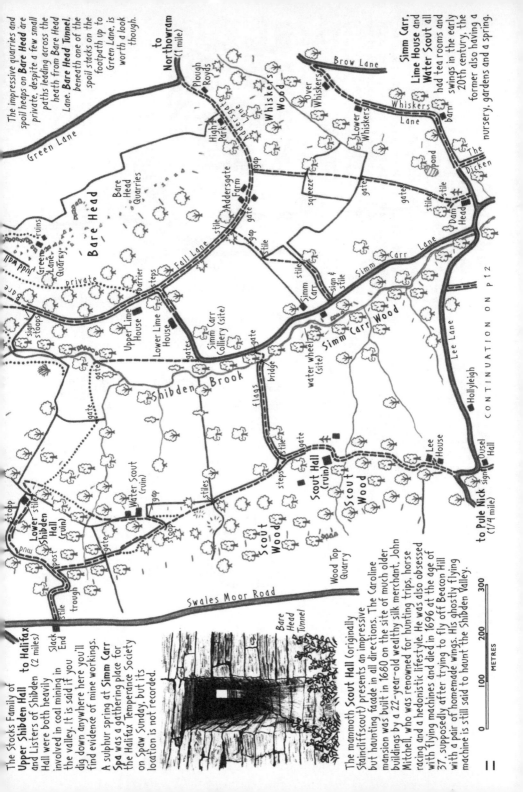

The impressive quarries and spoil heaps on **Bare Head** are private, despite a few small paths leading across the heath from Bare Head Lane. **Bare Head Tunnel**, beneath one of the spoil stacks on the footpath up to Green Lane, is worth a look though.

Simm Carr, Lime House and **Water Scout** all had tea rooms and swings in the early 20th century, the former also having a nursery, gardens and a spring.

The Stocks Family of **Upper Shibden Hall** and Listers of Shibden Hall were both heavily involved in coal mining in the valley. It is said if you dig down anywhere here you'll find evidence of mine workings.

A sulphur spring at **Simm Carr Spa** was a gathering place for the Halifax Temperance Society on Spaw Sunday, but its location is not recorded.

The mammoth **Scout Hall** (originally Stainliffscout) presents an impressive but haunting facade in all directions. The Caroline mansion was built in 1680 on the site of much older buildings by a 22-year-old wealthy silk merchant, John Mitchell, who was renowned for hunting trips, horse racing and a hedonistic lifestyle. He was also obsessed with flying machines and died in 1696 at the age of 37, supposedly after trying to fly off Beacon Hill with a pair of homemade wings. His ghostly flying machine is still said to haunt the Shibden Valley.

to **Northowram** (1 mile)

Brow Lane

Whiskers Lane

Whiskers Wood

Over Whiskers

Lower Whiskers

barn

The Dicken

pond

Dam Head

stile

gate

Green Lane

Plough Royds

High Park

Addersgate Lane

squeeze

gate

Bare Head

Bare Head Quarries

Green Lane Quarry

ruins

Bare Head Pond

private

Addersgate Farm

stile

Fall Lane

gap

stile

stile

Simm Carr

sign & stile

Carr Lane

Simm

Simm Carr Wood

Lee Lane

Hollyleigh

barrier

steps

sign & stoops

Upper Lime House

Lower Lime House

Simm Carr Colliery (Site)

gate

gates

Shibden Brook

water wheel (site)

bridge

flags

steps

stile

gate

Scout Wood

Scout Hall (ruin)

Lee House

Dusel Hall

sign

to **Pule Nick** (1/4 mile)

CONTINUATION ON P12

gate

gate

Water Scout (ruin)

gap

stoops

stiles

gate

Lower Shibden Hall (ruin)

stile

Slack End

post

trough

stile

to **Halifax** (2 miles)

mud

mud

stoop

Swales Moor Road

Wood Top Quarry

Bare Head Tunnel

METRES
0   100   200   300

11

MAP 4: SHIBDEN DALE SOUTH & SHIBDEN PARK

This lush section of **Shibden Dale** is crossed by the busy A58, but retains its quiet charm elsewhere. To the south is Shibden Hall and Park, a popular and easily accessed country park. To the north there are the dense slopes of Staups Common and several smaller areas of woodland linked by an often frustrating network of paths, especially above Shibden Mill Inn.

Although **Springfield Mine No. 1** closed in 1991, Parkinsons' **Springfield Mine No. 2** operated as recently as 2012, the last in a valley that was once covered in drift mines, works and quarries. A small family-run mine, fireclay was extracted from narrow 3-foot high tunnels into the hillside and supplied refractories in Halifax. The fireclay in this area east of Halifax could withstand particularly high temperatures and so has long been used to make glasshouse pots for the manufacture of Waterford glass.

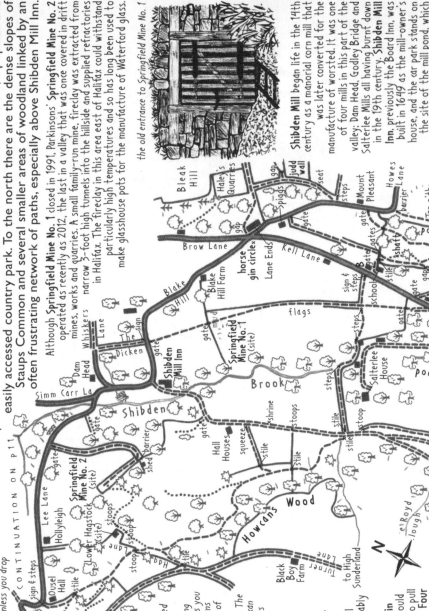

the old entrance to Springfield Mine No. 1

Shibden Mill began life in the 14th century as a manorial corn mill that was later converted for the manufacture of worsted. It was one of four mills in this part of the valley; Dam Head, Godley Bridge and Salterlee Mills all having burnt down in the 19th century. **Shibden Mill Inn**, previously the Board Inn, was built in 1649 as the mill-owner's house, and the car park stands on the site of the mill pond, which was later used as a boating lake.

The only satisfactory path off Lee Lane climbs above **Ousel Hall** to cross Hag Lane and skirt along the foot of **Howans Wood**. The steps off the lane higher up lead only to a fenced field unless you drop right down the slope to the stile above Ousel Hall.

The hillside between Lee Lane and Upper Lane is crossed by Rights of Way but impossible to access without climbing some of the myriad barbed wire fences in between. A fenced track leads up from **Lee Lane**, but abandons you near a small shed. Heading straight on over the barrier here leads you across the slope to the foot of Howans Wood, or up to the right to the ruins of **Lower Hagstock** (its name probably relating to the practice of pollarding). The old Hag Lane, now densely overgrown, can be traced here, a path continuing up its left side to reach **Upper Lane**.

The name of **Howans Wood** is thought to be of Celtic origin, a corruption of a word similar to Oliana, the Roman name for Ilkley.

Black Boy Farm (then Black Boy House) was the birthplace of serial killer John Christie, having remarkably also been the home of Dr Crippen.

There is a well-preserved **horse gin circle** opposite Lane Ends, which would have been used to enable horses to pull coal up the adjacent mine shaft of **Four Lane End Colliery**, a small family-run mine.

to **Boothtown** (1/2 mile)

ski slope

Upper Hagstock Upper Lane

Pule Nick

Ousel Hall

Hollyleigh

Lee Lane

Lower Hagstock (site)

Hag Lane

stoops

stoops

Springfield Mine No. 2 (site)

Simm Carr La

Dam Head

Dicken

Whiskers Lane

Shibden Mill Inn

Shibden

Brook

Hall Houses

squeeze

shrine

stoop

shed

barrier

Black Boy Farm

Turner Lane

to High Sunderland

Howans Wood

elRoyd Clough

Wood

Salterlee House

Springfield Mine No. 1 (site)

flags

Blake Hill Farm

Blake Hill

Brow Lane

Bleak Hill

Haley's Quarries

Judd Wall

Spriggs

Mount Pleasant

Kell Lane

Lane Ends

horse gin circle

school

sign & steps

Top o'th' Hill Delf

Howes Lane

Wood

N

CONTINUATION ON P.11

CONTINUATION ON P.11

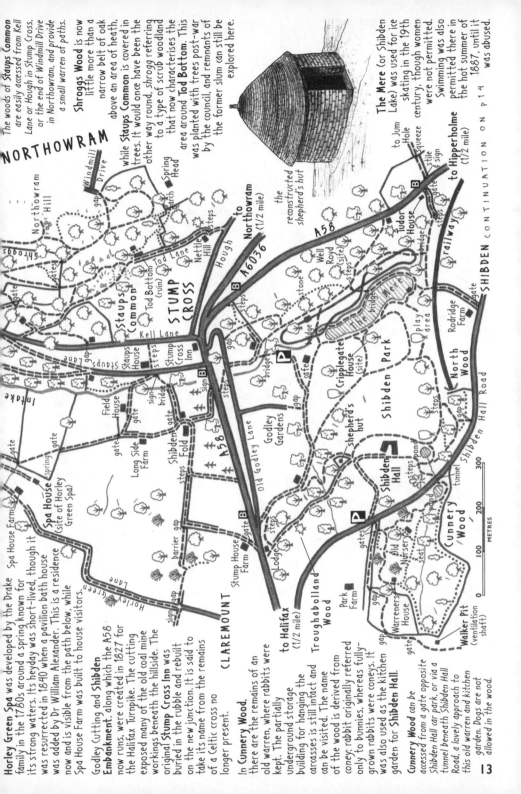

The woods of **Staups Common** are easily accessed from Kell Lane or Hough in Stump Cross, or the end of Windmill Drive in Northowram, and provide a small warren of paths.

Shroggs Wood is now little more than a narrow belt of oak above an area of heath. **Staups Common** is covered in trees, it would once have been the other way round, shrogg referring to a type of scrub woodland that now characterises the area around **Tod Bottom**. This area was planted with trees post-war by the council, and remnants of the former slum can still be explored here.

The Mere (or Shibden Lake) was used for ice skating in the 19th century, though women were not permitted. Swimming was also permitted there in the hot summer of 1887, until it was abused.

NORTHOWRAM

SHIBDEN CONTINUATION ON P14

Northowram Hill

Windmill Drive

Spring Head

the reconstructed shepherd's hut

to Jum Hole

squeeze

Tudor House

stile & sign

steps

to Hipperholme (1/2 mile)

gate

railway

A58

Shroggs

gates

Staups Common

Tod Bottom (ruin)

Tod Lane

Nettle Hill

steps

to Northowram (1/2 mile)

A6036

Hough

STUMP CROSS

Kell Lane

Staups House

Stump Cross Inn

Staups Lane

gap

steps

gap

Stump Cross

Well Royd (site)

stone

bridge

bridge

The Mere

bridge

bridge

play area

North Wood

Rodridge Farm

Field House

sign

gate

bridge

sign

Shibden Fold

gate

steps

A58

café

Cripplegate House (site)

Shibden Park

Shibden Hall Road

Intake

Long Side Farm

gap

gate

Godley Gardens

shepherd's hut

Shibden Hall

steps

pond

gate

Spring gate

Old Godley Lane

CLAREMOUNT

Horley Green Lane

sign

gap

barrier

gap

Lodge

Stump House Farm

gate

steps

tunnel

road

Cunnery Wood

Old Nursery

seat

300

Spa House (site of Horley Green Spa)

Horley Green Spa was developed by the Drake family in the 1780s around a spring known for its strong waters. Its heyday was short-lived, though it was resurrected in 1840 when a pavilion bath house was added by Dr William Alexander. This is a residence now and is visible from the path below, while Spa House Farm was built to house visitors.

to Halifax (1/2 mile)

Troughaboland Wood

Park Farm

gap

Warreners House

Walker Pit (ventilation shaft)

gate

gap

200

100

METRES

0

Godley Cutting and Shibden Embankment, along which the A58 now runs, were created in 1827 for the Halifax Turnpike. The cutting exposed many of the old coal mine workings beneath the hillside. The original **Stump Cross Inn** was buried in the rubble and rebuilt on the new junction. It is said to take its name from the remains of a Celtic cross no longer present.

In **Cunnery Wood**, there are the remains of an old warren, where rabbits were kept. The partially underground storage building for hanging the carcasses is still intact and can be visited. The name of the wood is derived from coney; rabbit originally referred only to bunnies, whereas fully-grown rabbits were coneys. It was also used as the kitchen garden for **Shibden Hall**.

Cunnery Wood can be accessed from a gate opposite Shibden Hall car park, or via a tunnel beneath Shibden Hall Road. A lovely approach to this old warren and kitchen garden. Dogs are not allowed in the wood.

13

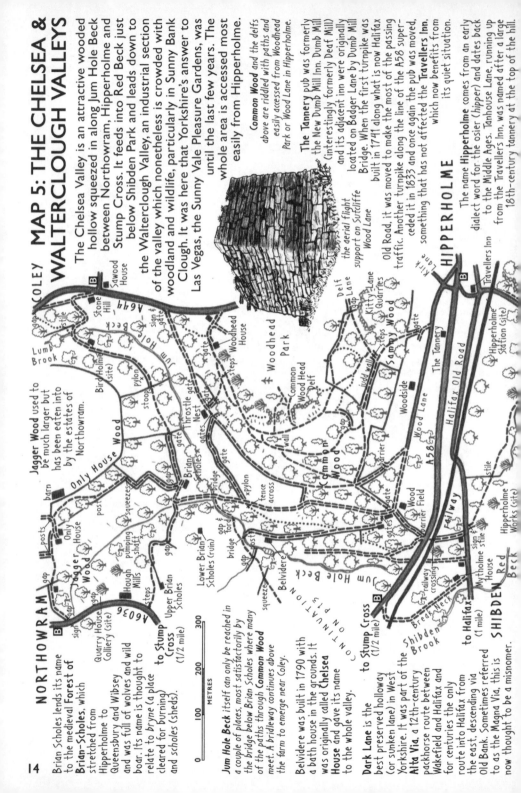

COLEY MAP 5: THE CHELSEA & WALTERCLOUGH VALLEYS

The Chelsea Valley is an attractive wooded hollow squeezed in along Jum Hole Beck between Northowram, Hipperholme and Stump Cross. It feeds into Red Beck just below Shibden Park and leads down to the Walterclough Valley, an industrial section of the valley which nonetheless is crowded with woodland and wildlife, particularly in Sunny Bank Clough. It was here that Yorkshire's answer to Las Vegas, the Sunny Vale Pleasure Gardens, was until the last few years. The whole area is accessed most easily from Hipperholme.

Common Wood and the delfs above are riddled with paths and easily accessed from Woodhead Park or Wood Lane in Hipperholme.

The **Tannery** pub was formerly the New Dumb Mill Inn. Dumb Mill (interestingly formerly Deaf Mill) and its adjacent inn were originally located on Badger Lane by Dumb Mill Bridge. When the first turnpike was built in 1741 along what is now Halifax Old Road, it was moved to make the most of the passing traffic. Another turnpike along the line of the A58 superceded it in 1833 and once again the pub was moved, something that has not affected the **Travellers Inn**, which now benefits from its quiet situation.

HIPPERHOLME

The name **Hipperholme** comes from an early dialect word for the osier (*hipper*) and dates back to the Middle Ages. Tanhouse Lane, running up from the Travellers Inn, was named after a large 18th-century tannery at the top of the hill.

NORTHOWRAM

Brian Scholes lends its name to the medieval Forest of **Brian-Scholes**, which stretched from Hipperholme to Queensbury and Wibsey and was full of wolves and wild boar. Its name is thought to relate to *bryne* (a place cleared for burning) and *scholes* (sheds).

Jagger Wood used to be much larger but has been eaten into by the estates of Northowram.

Jum Hole Beck itself can only be reached in a couple of places, most satisfactorily by the bridge below Brian Scholes where many of the paths through *Common Wood* meet. A bridleway continues above the farm to emerge near Coley.

Belvidere was built in 1790 with a bath house in the grounds. It was originally called **Chelsea House** and gave its name to the whole valley.

Dark Lane is the best preserved holloway (or sunken lane) in West Yorkshire. It was part of the **Alta Via**, a 12th-century packhorse route between Wakefield and Halifax and for centuries the only route into Halifax from the east, descending via Old Bank. Sometimes referred to as the Magna Via, this is now thought to be a misnomer.

0 100 200 300
METRES

14

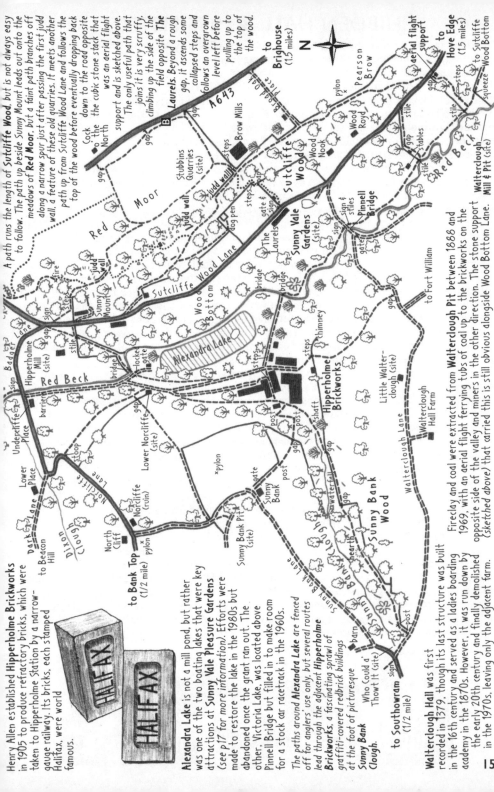

CONTINUATION ON pp24-25

A path runs the length of **Sutliffe Wood**, but is not always easy to follow. The path up beside Sunny Mount leads out onto the meadows of **Red Moor**, but a faint path branches off along a narrow spur just after passing the first judd wall, a feature of these old quarries. It meets another path up from Sutliffe Wood Lane and follows the top of the wood before eventually dropping back down to the road opposite the cubic stone stack that was an aerial flight support and is sketched above. The only useful path that joins it is very scruffy, climbing up the side of the field opposite **The Laurels**. Beyond a rough gap, it ascends some collapsed steps and follows an overgrown level left before pulling up to the top of the wood.

Henry Allen established **Hipperholme Brickworks** in 1905 to produce refractory bricks, which were taken to Hipperholme Station by a narrow-gauge railway. Its bricks, each stamped Halifax, were world famous.

Alexandra Lake is not a mill pond, but rather was one of the two boating lakes that were key attractions at **Sunny Vale Pleasure Gardens** (see p17 for more information). Efforts were made to restore the lake in the 1980s but abandoned once the grant ran out. The other, Victoria Lake, was located above Pinnell Bridge but filled in to make room for a stock car racetrack in the 1960s.

The paths around **Alexandra Lake** are fenced off for anglers' use only, but several routes lead through the adjacent **Hipperholme Brickworks**, a fascinating sprawl of graffiti-covered redbrick buildings at the foot of picturesque **Sunny Bank Clough**.

Walterclough Hall was first recorded in 1379, though its last structure was built in the 16th century and served as a ladies boarding academy in the 1870s. However, it was run down by the early 20th century and finally demolished in the 1970s, leaving only the adjacent farm.

Fireclay and coal were extracted from **Walterclough Pit** between 1888 and 1969, with an aerial flight ferrying tubs of coal up to the brickworks on the opposite side of the valley and miners in the other direction. The stone support (sketched above) that carried this is still obvious alongside Wood Bottom Lane.

15

SHIBDEN HALL & MISS LISTER

Shibden Hall was originally a timber-framed house built by William Otes in the early 15th century using huge oak beams and posts from local trees. It faced south and was located just off the old Wakefield Gate. It was modified and encased with stone in both the 16th and 17th centuries, before having its Gothic tower and library added later by Miss Lister. Having been briefly occupied by the Saviles, it was held by the Waterhouse family, the last of whom was knighted by King James as Lord of the sub-Manor of Halifax-cum-Heptonstall. After he was outlawed for bankruptcy, the Lister family inherited the hall by marriage around 1619 and held it until 1923.

Shibden Hall's most famous inhabitant was Miss Lister, whose prodigious journals, travels and correspondence made her renowned as an independent woman far ahead of her time. Anne Lister was born in 1791 in the East Riding and regularly visited her uncle and aunt at Shibden Hall before moving in with them at 16, as she preferred living with them than her own parents. She assisted her uncle with the management of the estate, encouraging him to buy up property that had previously been part of the estate, totalling some 400 acres. She was known as Gentleman Jack among local people and essentially viewed as a man. She particularly looked after the tenant farms and extensive coal mines on the estate, which were at their peak at this time.

Following her uncle's death in 1826, Miss Lister ran the estate and inherited it in entirely in 1836. She remodelled much of the estate, making it more open and in keeping with the Capability Brown era in which she lived. She built a new entrance to the hall from the new turnpike road through Godley Cutting, constructing the lodge there in 1837. A tunnel was dug beneath the older road, which allowed a stream to run into the gardens. She converted the house into a traditional baronial residence and had planned further extensions and courtyards had she lived.

She and her partner, Ann Walker, a wealthy neighbour, had their marriage solemnised by a priest in York in 1834, which allowed Anne the funds to develop the estate and ended with Ms Walker briefly inheriting the estate. The union was disapproved of by her neighbour, Christopher Rawson, who burnt effigies of the lesbians. Lister also claimed he stole coal from her and smoked her workers out of the pit by burning dung. She died while travelling through Georgia in 1840, leaving the code in which the intimate parts of her journals were written a mystery, until John Lister cracked the cryptic alphabet in the early 20th century.

John Lister was Shibden Hall's last resident, restoring the hall and thoroughly researching its history. In the 1870s, he rescued Cripplegate House from demolition in the centre of Halifax and re-erected the medieval timer-framed house in Shibden Park near the shore of the Mere. Shibden Estate was presented to the town of Halifax in 1923 and opened as a museum following John Lister's death ten years later. Despite being part of the open-air Folk Museum of West Yorkshire, Cripplegate House was allowed to fall into disrepair and consequently was pulled down in 1971. Another house rescued by John Lister can be seen on the A58 near Stump Cross. Now Tudor House, it began life as the House at the Maypole, a fine pre-Tudor merchant's house that was then renamed Daisy Bank when it was re-erected on the Shibden Estate. The hall has recently been restored and is open to the public, along with the Folk Museum, which houses a fine collection of horse-drawn vehicles in the 17th-century barn behind.

Shibden Hall

SUNNY VALE PLEASURE GARDENS

Located in a quiet corner of the Walterclough Valley, 'The Playground of the North' was Yorkshire's answer to Las Vegas, an extravagant array of amusements and rides arranged around a 40-acre theme park. It was immensely popular for annual excursions from across the north, with many special trains having to be laid on during the season. Visitors alighted at Hipperholme, where they were met by a one-legged hurdy-gurdy player who only knew one tune, before walking down Sutcliffe Wood Lane to the turnstiles. An avenue of rhododenrons led to the cottages, where they collected pre-ordered teas before dropping into a magical world.

Joseph Bunce was a market gardener from London who moved to the area in 1874. He started a smallholding at Wood Bottom Farm in the Walterclough Valley, but soon saw its potential, as the valley was a popular place to ramble and take the country air. Sunny Vale Pleasure Gardens (or Sunny Bunces as it was often known) officially opened on May 1st 1880 and had only a few hundred visitors in its first season. But it gradually grew, with ever-increasing attractions, and eventually hosted over 100,000 visitors a year.

Victoria Lake (or Lower Lake), which is no longer present, was constructed in 1883 below the gardens and was used for rowing. The far larger Alexandra Lake followed and had a promenade all the way round – this remains as the private fishing pond of Upper Lake. There were rowing boats, hand-powered pedalos and a steam launch on the lakes, which were also often used for ice skating when they froze in winter. Various amusements and rides were laid out around the lakes; the helter-skelter, swing boats, flying chair, roller rink, go-karts, open-air theatre and donkey rides. There was also a maze based on that at Hampton Court; local Southowram kids knew a back way in through the maze without paying. A miniature railway ran through the site, an early switchback railway being replaced by the Baby Bunce in 1922, a train that had previously served at Blackpool Pleasure Beach and Halifax Zoo. It was renamed after Joseph's grand-daughter and is still in service at Lightwater Valley.

Baby Bunce, the Sunny Vale Miniature Railway

Joseph Bunce died in 1918, but the business was carried on by his sons. Despite the war and the rise of seaside resorts, the Bunces kept introducing novel features and remained popular throughout the 1930s. Water cycling, swan boats, the Automatic Café (with very early self-service machines), a Palace of Illusion, seasonal shows and re-enactments (like that of the Titanic sinking), speed boat testing and outdoor dancing were all introduced, along with new rides – the Aerial Glider, the Flyer, Gallopers Roundabout and the Glacier (the latter a long slide considered to be the most terrifying). There were even early illuminations carnivals before those at Blackpool.

In 1945, the estate was sold to Fred Thompson for £20,000, but its success wasn't sustainable and it was soon on sale again. Eventually its contents were sold off and attempts were made to turn it into an exclusive club, Sunny Vale Country Club, or run it as a roller rink. In 1958 it was bought by Bert Myers and a go-karting track laid, with fortnightly races held on Sunday afternoons. The Lower Lake was filled in to build a larger track for stock car and banger racing and demolition derbies. These events were very popular until the 1980s, when the track area was used for landfill; this area and the donkey stables can still be traced, but vegetation has returned to much of the site, covering the tracks of its fascinating history.

ROUTE 2: SHIBDEN DALE FROM NORTHOWRAM

Distance: 8 miles (12.5km)

Ascent: 430m

Parking: Free car park by the sports pitches on Hough (a continuation of Town Gate) in Northowram.

Public Transport: Northowram and Stump Cross are on the 681/682 bus routes between Halifax and Bradford, as well as the 534 circular from Halifax.

Character: A thorough exploration of Shibden Dale, from Shibden Park all the way up to Shibden Head via Scout Hall, Shibden Mill Inn and Chelsea Valley. This area is rarely densely wooded and so mixes open fields, rough heath and country lanes with the pockets of charming woodland.

5 A rough path created by bikers leads straight up the bank, but if you bear left there is a gentler path up the side of the wall. Emerging on a track at the top, turn right then immediately left through a gap by the ruins of **Hanging Royd.** A path leads on across the fields, following the side of an old wall before climbing steeply up a lonnin to the A647. Follow the road left past the ivy-shrouded ruins of **Upper Shibden Hall,** then fork left onto Swales Moor Road. Opposite the house at Slack End, turn left over a stile and follow another lonnin down into the beech woods. Turn sharp right at a waymark post and then descend steadily below **Scout Wood,** keeping straight on by a stoop to reach a stile amid the hollies.

6 A narrow fenced path leads down to join the top of the shortcut and pick up a track by the grand ruins of **Scout Hall.** Follow the track up past Lee House to reach Lee Lane, heading down the cobbles to the corner, where a path leads right above Ousel Hall. Cross a pair of stiles

3 At the end of the lane by **Lower Lime House,** continue straight on up the rough track. Turn left at the top and follow Bare Head Lane through the trees, keeping right to climb steadily out of the valley. Where a path leads right through the judd walls at **Bare Head Tunnel,** turn left along the fence. It is slightly overgrown in places, but leads pleasingly along the slope above **Hazelhurst Clough.** Beyond Upper Woodland Farm, stay along the top of the trees and head left of a holly bush to reach a gap in the wall beyond. Turn left to reach a bridge over the stream.

4 Climbing out of **Hazelhurst Clough,** turn left at a waymark post and follow a path back down the other side of the valley. Just before the remains of a second rough stile, look for a faint path zigzagging down through the trees. At the bottom you emerge on a path leading down to the fords at the heart of **Henacre Wood.** Cross the right-hand of the two streams and then keep right where the path forks to emerge from the wood. By a prominent ash tree, look for a path leading steeply up the slope to the right.

walls, where quarry waste has been piled up behind high retaining walls. Often the over-burden was removed from stone mines sunk for Elland flags from the late 19th century. The finest is the one the **Bare Head Tunnel** is built through. The large judd lumps had to be positioned by crane and carefully wedged in place.

A distinctive feature of the Shibden Valley are the **judd**

snowdrops

before reaching a broken-down wall, where the path climbs up the far side of the very overgrown Hag Lane. Fork left soon after, staying below **Howcans Wood** on a faint path that weaves for some distance down the rough ground to reach a stile. Skirt the bottom of the beech wood beyond and emerge at a stile leading onto the track below. Turn right then immediately fork left by a small stoop, skirting below **Spa House** and crossing the fields below. Head straight on to join a track by Long Side Farm and, where this bends through Shibden Fold, go straight on again to emerge on the A58 near **Stump Cross**.

2 Across the road below **Salterlee School**, follow a sign down some steps and turn right along the flagged path below. Continue across the fields to the road just above **Shibden Mill Inn**. Head straight down, then turn left down the lane at the end of The Dicken. Keep right, following Simm Carr Lane along the side of **Shibden Brook**. After half a mile, a possible shortcut turns left through a gate and crosses the stream to emerge near Scout Hall, but the main route stays on the lane.

1 From the A6036 in **Northowram** cut up a cobble path just up the hill from Chelsea Mansions, reaching the parking area by the tennis courts. Head straight across the road and follow Windmill Drive to its end, where a path leads on from its left corner. Follow the right fork to emerge above the trees of **Staups Common**. Turn right and, after about 100m, fork left steeply down the slope to a gate and follow a path that angles down across the heath below **Shroggs Wood**. Turn right at the bottom and, shortly before a scruffy gate at the far end, bear left down to a stile and continue through a gate below to emerge by the school.

8 Reaching a track, turn left over the bridge and climb up towards **Brian Scholes**. After the track bends right, turn sharp left through a gap and follow a fenced path up the hill into **Only House Wood**. Climb through the beech trees to join a track heading left down towards Only House. A path follows the wall to the right and leads straight on across the field beyond to a gap in the edge of **Jagger Wood**. At the far end is the A6036 on the edge of **Northowram**.

7 Cross the busy road and follow some steps opposite down to the old road, where you head straight on down Red Beck Road. Just before crossing the stream into the park **Shibden Park**, bear left on a track that leads along the edge of the woods. Continue past the miniature railway and fork left up to the road again. 100m to the right, turn left over a stile. The path crosses the fields of the **Chelsea Valley** via a series of narrow squeezes, eventually passing Belvidere (formerly Chelsea House) and leading to the stream edge. Cross a shallow ford over Jum Hole Beck into the beech trees on the edge of **Common Wood**.

The suffix '-owram' means 'on the slopes' and relates to two ridges of land running north-west from the Calder – on which stand **Northowram** and **Southowram**.

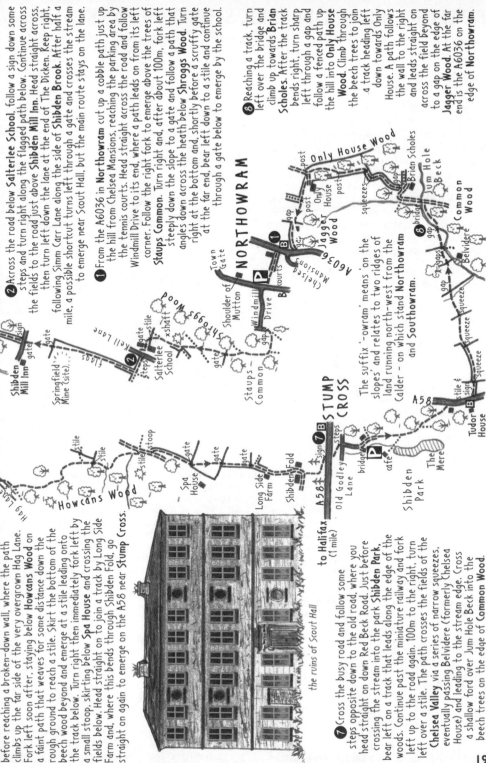

the ruins of Scout Hall

to Halifax (1 mile)

19

ROUTE 3: BEACON HILL, SHIBDEN PARK, SUNNY

Distance: 7 miles (11km)

Ascent: 450m

Parking: Numerous pay car parks in the centre of Halifax, as well as at Shibden Hall.

Public Transport: Halifax is on the main Caldervale railway line.

Character: A superbly varied walk that is full of interest throughout. Initially climbing out of the industrial heart of Halifax to its finest vantage point on Beacon Hill, the route then drops into the rich woods of Shibden Park, Chelsea Valley and Sunny Vale. Despite areas of abandoned industry, this is a surprisingly quiet and beautiful valley. This walk can also easily be started from Hipperholme or Southowram.

The whole of **Southowram Bank** was covered in trees in the Middle Ages and they are gradually returning.

The route follows the medieval **Wakefield Gate** (or Alta Via) onto Beacon Hill. This was the main packhorse route into Halifax until the turn-pike was built in the late 18th century. Little of its original surface remains, its much-repaired setts having been laid in the 1720s. The steep section up past the **Devil's Elbow** hairpin was known as Whiskam Dandy. There have been proposals for alternative ways up the hill – a rack-and-pinion railway in 1898 and cable car in 2005 – but none has ever come to fruition.

2 Retrace your steps along **Beacon Hill**, following the main path down to a busy junction. Head straight on through a pair of gates and follow the gravel path round past the ornamental ventilation shaft of **Walker Pit**. Nearing the road, turn right through a gate into **Cunnery Wood**, a former rabbit warren and kitchen garden. The gravel path winds down to a tunnel by the lower pond that leads beneath the road and emerges near **Shibden Hall**. Dogs are not allowed in Cunnery Wood, but an alternative crosses the road and follows the main tarmac track down to Shibden Hall.

1 From **Halifax railway station**, turn right along South Parade and follow the walkway towards the Ring of Bells. After looping around **Halifax Minster**, turn right down some steps and go straight on up Bank Bottom. At the bottom of Southowram Bank, head straight on up the setts of **Old Bank**. Turn right near the top and cross straight over Beacon Hall Road. At the sharp bend, carry straight on and pull steeply up through thinning trees to the path along the top of **Beacon Hill**, turning right to reach the beacon pan.

7 Turn right on the track at the top of **Sunny Bank Clough**, then bear left up Whitley Lane to the edge of **Southowram**. Turn right along the road at the top as far as the next bend, where you cut diagonally across the field to the left. Turn right on the next lane, then left through a heavy double gate beyond Pit Farm. The path leads to the trees at the corner of the field, then cuts diagonally down to a rough stile in the wall below. Head straight down the wall to join a track by **Snydal Farm**, bending right down into trees below.

Lilly Bridge stood alongside Lilly Mill, taking its name from one of its tenants, Edward Lilley. It was on the main route between Halifax and Southowram.

8 At the next bend, bear right into **High Grove Lane**, a walled path along the top of the wood. After 100m, cut through a rough gap in the wall to the left to some large graves at the corner of the old graveyard. Here, by an intriguing face carved into a tree, turn right down some rough steps covered in leaves and follow the slightly overgrown line of an old path down into **Stoney Royd Cemetery**. Keep right around the top of the graves until a cobbled path leads left down to the main cemetery road. From the entrance, turn left down the road, then right into Waterside. Bear left at the far end and duck under the railway line, before crossing a high footbridge by Eureka. Rejoin South Parade at the far end turning right to reach **Halifax railway station**.

20

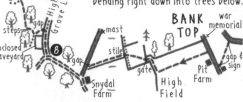

Pit Farm relates to **High Field Coal Pit** which was sunk in the field opposite, one of a series along this ridge of coal-rich high land east of Halifax.

VALE & CHELSEA VALLEY FROM HALIFAX

④ Reaching a vehicle track, double back right then left, climbing towards **Throstle Nest**. Head straight on up the slope here, skirting around the fence to a stile, from where a path leads up the wooded slope. Turn right at the top and keep right, following a path along the top of **Common Wood**. At the far end, bear right then left to follow a narrow path along the right side of a wall. Drop down through Sammy Wood and bear left at the bottom onto Upper Royd on the edge of **Hipperholme**.

Common earthballs litter the ground of our woods and look tempting until you split them open to reveal a black mass of earth-like spores in the middle.

earthballs

③ Turn right down some steps above a small pond near **Shibden Hall** and then bear right on one of a series of smaller paths through the beech trees of **North Wood**. These soon descend to join the main track. At the bottom, cut through or skirt around the play area (no dogs again) and join a path alongside the left side of the railway embankment which climbs up to the A58. Head straight across, following a path across the fields via a series of narrow squeezes to reach **Jum Hole Beck**. Cross this, not at a bridge, but a shallow ford just beyond, entering a beautiful beech grove.

Walker Pit ventilation shaft

⑤ At Lane Ends Green, turn right and cross the A58, descending Watergate to the **Travellers Inn**. Head straight on into Station Road; across the railway, bear left by a quarry face, following a path along the edge of **Sutcliffe Wood**. This climbs to reach a firepit, from where a tentative path bears left then immediately right down a gully to pick up a clearer route below. Follow this left for 100m, before turning sharp right along the top of a spoil heap. A path weaves on through the quarry spoil along the top of the slope, before joining another route to climb back to the top of Sutcliffe Wood near a noisy dog pen.

The **Who Could a' Thowt It** was a pub at the top of Sunny Bank Clough serving the many local delvers. It is said to have had a handy tunnel from its cellar into the adjacent Clough Head Cottage. It closed in 1933 and was demolished soon after, its stone said to have been used in the rebuilding of Coventry after the War.

SOUTHOWRAM

⑥ Stay along the top of **Sutcliffe Wood** until the path drops down to the lane. Duck through a gap alongside the aerial flight support (*a giant stone cube - see sketch on p14*) opposite and follow a path down to **Red Beck**, which meanders delightfully along this quiet section of the valley. Turn right and cross the fields, carrying straight on by Pinnell Bridge to pass below what was **Sunny Vale Pleasure Gardens** (see p17 for more information). Across the next bridge, follow the fence up to **Hipperholme Brickworks** and head straight on up the steps between the ruined buildings. Turn left at the top and head straight on into the wood at the foot of **Sunny Bank Clough**. A path climbs steadily up the left bank from a gap in the fence.

21

Map labels:
N
Chelsea Valley
Throstle Nest
stile
gap & ford
gaps
gates
squeeze
Belvidere
④
squeeze
Tudor House
squeezes
B
gate
stile
railway
Jum Hole Beck
Common Wood
spoil wall
steps
Underwood Cottage
gate
Sammy Wood
Kirk Lane
⑤
A58
HIPPERHOLME
railway
B
Travellers Inn
Badger Lane
sign
steps
fire
Sunny Mount
judd wall
Sutcliffe
spoil heaps
judd wall
dog pen
factory
⑥
Sutcliffe Wood
pylon
Alexandra Lake
steps
bridge
Sunny Vale Gardens (site)
Clough
shaft
Hipperholme Brickworks
Red Beck
sign
sign & stiles
Pinnell Bridge
Who Could a' Thowt It (site)
Sunny Bank Clough
gaps
Sunny Bank Wood
hearth
⑦
Ingfield Farm
Whitley Lane
sign
post
stables
gap
Beck
stile
aerial flight support
steps
stile
Law Lane
B
0 200 400 600
METRES

THE ASH

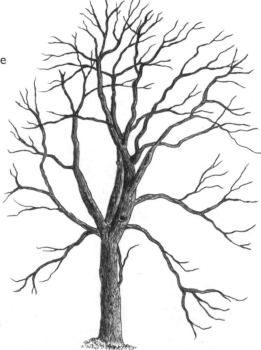

The mature ash is possibly the most graceful tree we have, a powerful yet benign presence in our woods and fields. In the winter, the ash's outline is the grandest and most shapely, its stout trunk contrasting with the fine curve of its branches and the lazy droop of the still-hanging keys. It is easy to see why in Norse mythology the universe sprang from an ash tree, Igradil (or the Tree of Life). In Britain, the ash was seen as a healing tree and burnt to ward off evil spirits.

The common ash is identifiable by its grey-green bark when young, but becomes deeply furrowed as an elder statesman. It has bowed drooping branches (always pointing up at the ends) and distinctive black buds that sprout long sprigs of odd-numbered leaflets. These drop while still green, but the tree's winged keys remain throughout the winter and can be blown up to 100m, at which time the long-dormant seed may germinate. The knotted nature of mature ash is partly due to frost damage, which tends to lead to unwanted forks and restricts its value as timber, but ash trees can still grow for over four hundred years. Because the ash is so susceptible to frost, it is the last tree to burst forth with life in the spring, to the point where you may be wondering if all the ash trees have died a mysterious death in the winter, when suddenly in late May they burst to life.

There are estimated to be eighty million ash trees in Britain, though they grow best on lime-rich, moist yet well-drained soils. As a result they don't develop particularly well on the sort of acid soils that dominate the Upper Calder Valley, except around stream-sides and springs, where the water is more calcareous due to the underlying limestone. Thick layers of soot further lowered the pH of the soil during the industrial era, and ash was among the trees that suffered most. Mature ash trees are far more commonly found in the east of the borough, a number of which stand out along the hedgerows of the Shibden Valley, where they would largely have been planted as ornamental landscape features. Ash saplings are now found more widely along the valley, though, as they grow well without much light and can develop for about fifteen years under the canopy of a wood in a way that oak cannot. However, these saplings may well die subsequently due to a lack of light, or even ash dieback, a fungus that blackens the leaves of mature ash and kills younger trees. This disease arrived in Britain in 2012, likely having been blown over the Channel, and has now spread across the whole country, thriving in damp climates like ours.

Ash is a very hard yet flexible timber and was known as the 'husbandman's tree'. It was widely coppiced and pollarded, though less commonly in this area. It was used before the advent of steel in things like ploughs, carts, wagons, wheel rims and dairy tools. It was used locally to make the spell for games of knur and spell, as well as tranditional tool handles and sporting bats (such as hurling sticks, for which ash are specially harvested). It is also a prized furniture wood, as its alternative name 'green ebony' suggests, and is said to 'make a fire fit for a queen'.

22

CHAPTER 3 - BRIGHOUSE & ELLAND

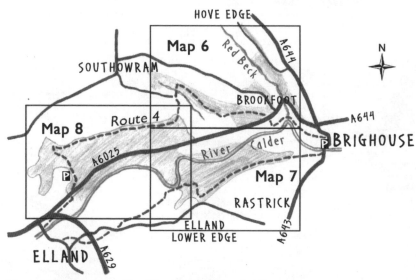

Map Sheet: Explorer 288 (Bradford & Huddersfield)

Public Transport: Brighouse is on the Caldervale and Huddersfield train lines and is well served by buses, including the 548/549 from Halifax. Regular 501/503 buses run from Halifax/Huddersfield to Elland.

Parking: Pay car parks in Brighouse and Elland. Free car park at Elland Crematorium.

This part of the Calder Valley was home to the great osier beds that provided willow for Halifax and Elland's wicker basket-weaving industry, as well as the stone quarries that Brighouse (the 'town of stone') was founded on. The durable Elland flags (the famous Yorkshire stone) have been quarried here for over 100 years, creating vast stone amphitheatres, with some now abandoned to nature once again. After decades of industry, the gravel pits of Cromwell Bottom are rewilding as a nature reserve full of the willows that were once cultivated on these marshes.

Elland, the second town in the borough to be granted a market charter after Halifax, was described in the early 19th century by T. D. Whitaker as 'beneath the union of two valleys, whose sides are hung with native oak'. Part of this would have been the parkland and hunting estate of the ancient Elland Hall, but there were once considerable oak woods all around Elland. Ainley Wood was substantial during the Middle Ages, but now only young scrub grows on the slopes below the motorway.

What does remain are Elland Park and Cromwell Woods, some of the finest woodlands in the valley, their dense oak canopies shrouding the hearths, trial holes, mines and fireclay works of years of industrial toil. In spring, the woods above the A6025 are a riot of colour and the carpet of bluebells is unsurpassed in the Calder Valley.

contour-like patterns on sycamore bark in Cromwell Wood

MAP 6: CROMWELL WOOD & BROOKFOOT

Cromwell and **Freeman's Woods** cloak the steep hillside above the A6025, providing a vibrant flank of bluebells in the spring, while **Sutcliffe, Slead Sike** and **Brighouse Woods** fringe the edge below the A644. The flat hilltops have been all been quarried away for the stone that built Brighouse's reputation as the 'town of stone', but the charming slopes below have been left well alone, including the secluded valley once known as Fairy Glen. It is an area easily accessed from both Brighouse and Southowram.

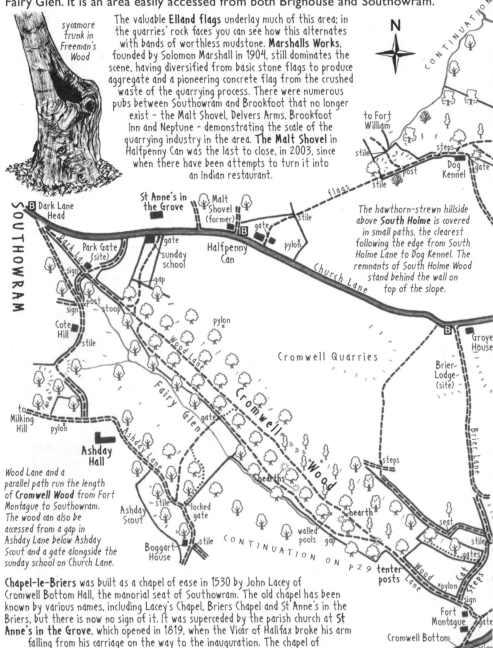

sycamore trunk in Freeman's Wood

The valuable **Elland flags** underlay much of this area; in the quarries' rock faces you can see how this alternates with bands of worthless mudstone. **Marshalls Works**, founded by Solomon Marshall in 1904, still dominates the scene, having diversified from basic stone flags to produce aggregate and a pioneering concrete flag from the crushed waste of the quarrying process. There were numerous pubs between Southowram and Brookfoot that no longer exist – the Malt Shovel, Delvers Arms, Brookfoot Inn and Neptune – demonstrating the scale of the quarrying industry in the area. **The Malt Shovel** in Halfpenny Can was the last to close, in 2003, since when there have been attempts to turn it into an Indian restaurant.

The hawthorn-strewn hillside above **South Holme** is covered in small paths, the clearest following the edge from South Holme Lane to Dog Kennel. The remnants of South Holme Wood stand behind the wall on top of the slope.

*Wood Lane and a parallel path run the length of **Cromwell Wood** from Fort Montague to Southowram. The wood can also be accessed from a gap in Ashday Lane below Ashday Scout and a gate alongside the sunday school on Church Lane.*

Chapel-le-Briers was built as a chapel of ease in 1530 by John Lacey of Cromwell Bottom Hall, the manorial seat of Southowram. The old chapel has been known by various names, including Lacey's Chapel, Briers Chapel and St Anne's in the Briers, but there is now no sign of it. It was superceded by the parish church at **St Anne's in the Grove**, which opened in 1819, when the Vicar of Halifax broke his arm falling from his carriage on the way to the inauguration. The chapel of Gimmerden Sough in *Wuthering Heights* is said to be based on the church.

24

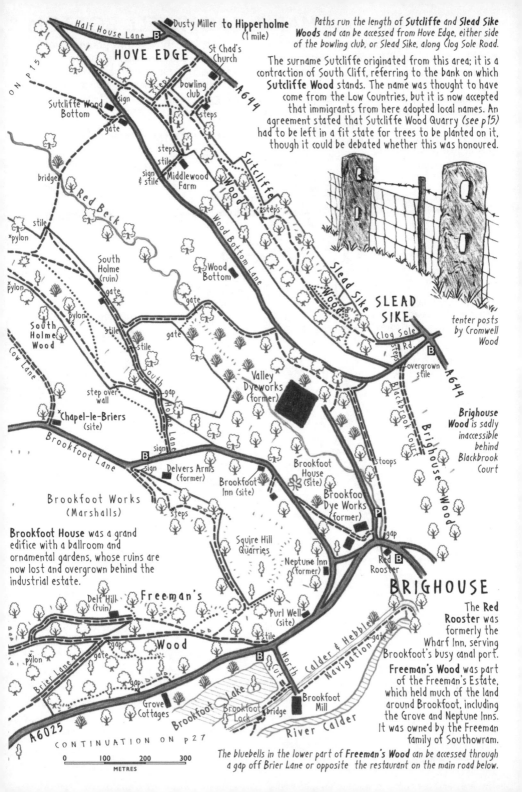

Paths run the length of **Sutcliffe** and **Slead Sike Woods** and can be accessed from Hove Edge, either side of the bowling club, or Slead Sike, along Clog Sole Road.

The surname Sutcliffe originated from this area; it is a contraction of South Cliff, referring to the bank on which **Sutcliffe Wood** stands. The name was thought to have come from the Low Countries, but it is now accepted that immigrants from here adopted local names. An agreement stated that Sutcliffe Wood Quarry (see p15) had to be left in a fit state for trees to be planted on it, though it could be debated whether this was honoured.

tenter posts by Cromwell Wood

Brighouse Wood is sadly inaccessible behind Blackbrook Court

Brookfoot House was a grand edifice with a ballroom and ornamental gardens, whose ruins are now lost and overgrown behind the industrial estate.

The **Red Rooster** was formerly the Wharf Inn, serving Brookfoot's busy canal port.

Freeman's Wood was part of the Freeman's Estate, which held much of the land around Brookfoot, including the Grove and Neptune Inns. It was owned by the Freeman family of Southowram.

The bluebells in the lower part of **Freeman's Wood** can be accessed through a gap off Brier Lane or opposite the restaurant on the main road below.

CONTINUATION ON p27

0   100   200   300
METRES

This is an area dominated by the local fireclay industry, both past and present, yet it remains full of wildlife and interesting trees. **Cromwell Bottom** was home to a series of gravel pits and refuse tips, but has been reinvented as a nature reserve with graceful lagoons and busy boating and fishing lakes. Its historic osier beds, used in the basket-making industry, remain and here you'll find the biggest willows in the district.
Strangstry Wood is less than half the size it once was, steadily eaten into by the workings of a vast shale quarry, but the oak woods that remain here and in Reins Wood are still delightful.

CONTINUATION ON P29

CONTINUATION ON P29

stoops

B

to Brighouse
(1 mile)

to Elland
(1 mile)

A6025

Cromwell House

Cromwell Bottom

waterskiing

Cromwell Lock

Crowther Bridge

P

milestone

gate

Freeman's Bridge

lagoon

pylon

Works

bird feeding

sign

bridge

pylon

The River Calder here was originally crossed by two sets of stepping stones. They were destroyed in an attempt to close the path, only to be relaid by quarrymen from Rastrick to get to work in Southowram.

sign

bridge

gate

River Calder

meadow

newt pond

pylon

Tag Lock (site)

wharf

Cromwell Bottom Nature Reserve is criss-crossed by easy paths around the meadow in the west and the lagoons in the east. A smaller path follows the edge of the old canal of **Tag Cut**, while the lagoon side can be reached from a tiny path over the berm at the riverside opposite the pylon.

Stony Fields

gate

Strangstry Bridge

Tag Cut Mill (site of)

stile

crossing

barrier

Tag Cut

post

Strangstry Wood

Harry Castle Hill

railway

stile

Calder Coal Mine & Fireclay Works (site)

discarded bricks

gap

slate wall

Strangstry Quarry

steps

Booth Royd Lane

Once far larger, **Strangstry Wood** is a maze of paths now squeezed in by the fence of the giant shale quarry. The quarry is private, but the former workings and vast floors of discarded bricks can be glimpsed via a gap in the fence alongside the railway.

Shaw Laithe (site)

gap

Shaw Lane

gate

shale quarry

pool

26

to Elland
B
(1/2 mile)

pylon

Lower Edge Road

B

Royal Oak

ELLAND LOWER EDGE

Strangstry Wood is first recorded as Strang-stigh Wood in 1394, its name thought to refer to an 'arduous path' in Old English or 'stairs' in local dialect. There is another recorded in Rawtonstall.

0   100   200   300
METRES

N

STRANGSTRY WOOD

CONTINUATION ON p25

Brookfoot Lake was formed in 1965, when the river flooded a gravel pit, before being split in two to be used by waterskiing and angling clubs.

The Lillands comes from *linlands*, which referred to flax-lands, and a Linland Royd Wood was recorded in 1709.

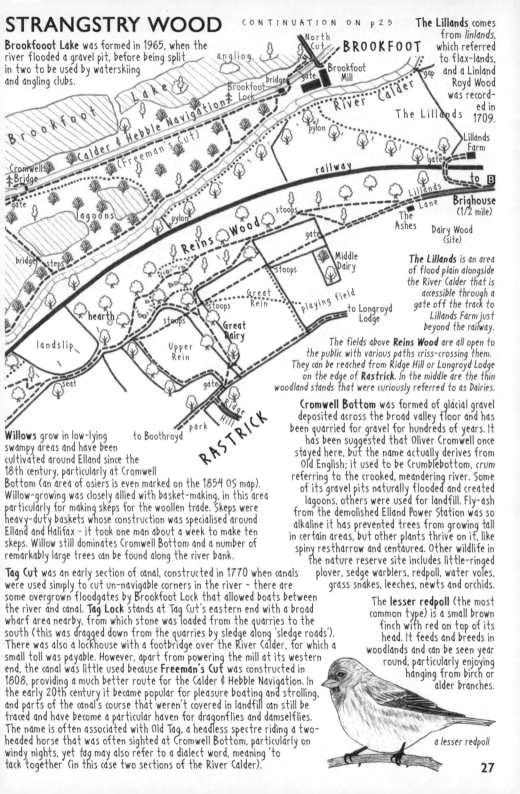

The Lillands is an area of flood plain alongside the River Calder that is accessible through a gate off the track to Lillands Farm just beyond the railway.

The fields above **Reins Wood** are all open to the public with various paths criss-crossing them. They can be reached from Ridge Hill or Longroyd Lodge on the edge of **Rastrick**. In the middle are the thin woodland stands that were curiously referred to as Dairies.

Cromwell Bottom was formed of glacial gravel deposited across the broad valley floor and has been quarried for gravel for hundreds of years. It has been suggested that Oliver Cromwell once stayed here, but the name actually derives from Old English; it used to be Crumblebottom, *crum* referring to the crooked, meandering river. Some of its gravel pits naturally flooded and created lagoons, others were used for landfill. Fly-ash from the demolished Elland Power Station was so alkaline it has prevented trees from growing tall in certain areas, but other plants thrive on it, like spiny restharrow and centaurea. Other wildlife on the nature reserve site includes little-ringed plover, sedge warblers, redpoll, water voles, grass snakes, leeches, newts and orchids.

Willows grow in low-lying swampy areas and have been cultivated around Elland since the 18th century, particularly at Cromwell Bottom (an area of osiers is even marked on the 1854 OS map). Willow-growing was closely allied with basket-making, in this area particularly for making skeps for the woollen trade. Skeps were heavy-duty baskets whose construction was specialised around Elland and Halifax – it took one man about a week to make ten skeps. Willow still dominates Cromwell Bottom and a number of remarkably large trees can be found along the river bank.

Tag Cut was an early section of canal, constructed in 1770 when canals were used simply to cut un-navigable corners in the river – there are some overgrown floodgates by Brookfoot Lock that allowed boats between the river and canal. **Tag Lock** stands at Tag Cut's eastern end with a broad wharf area nearby, from which stone was loaded from the quarries to the south (this was dragged down from the quarries by sledge along 'sledge roads'). There was also a lockhouse with a footbridge over the River Calder, for which a small toll was payable. However, apart from powering the mill at its western end, the canal was little used because **Freeman's Cut** was constructed in 1808, providing a much better route for the Calder & Hebble Navigation. In the early 20th century it became popular for pleasure boating and strolling, and parts of the canal's course that weren't covered in landfill can still be traced and have become a particular haven for dragonflies and damselflies. The name is often associated with Old Tag, a headless spectre riding a two-headed horse that was often sighted at Cromwell Bottom, particularly on windy nights, yet *tag* may also refer to a dialect word, meaning 'to tack together' (in this case two sections of the River Calder).

The **lesser redpoll** (the most common type) is a small brown finch with red on top of its head. It feeds and breeds in woodlands and can be seen year round, particularly enjoying hanging from birch or alder branches.

a lesser redpoll

27

MAP 8: ELLAND PARK WOOD & BINNS WOOD

Elland Park Wood is one of Calderdale's most treasured woods, a dense oak stand riddled with paths and possessing a rich history. Though the fires of the fireclay and brick industry raged within it, the shafts and quarries are long abandoned and the wood is a haven for wildlife in a busy industrial valley. **Binns Wood**'s sycamores are less well frequented, but comes alive in the spring when they are carpeted with bluebells.

*The brick track of **Plains Lane** is the main track up the western side of Elland Park Wood, but becomes abruptly private at the top of the wood. In fact, there is no public access through **Wood Nook**, with paths leading either up to Park Nook or over the tiny stream and across the fields towards Park Gate.*

Park Nook was known as a wartime beauty spot. The whole area has since suffered subsidence caused by the coal and fireclay mine that was located at Wood Nook and the cottages here were due to be torn down in the 1970s until the residents took the matter to the Historic Buildings Bureau.

The woolly boletus is recorded at **Robin Hood's Scar** at the top of Elland Park Wood in 1784. We now know this as the suede or yellow cracked bolete, an edible if unremarkable mushroom found infrequently under broadleaves. The scar itself was formed by a landslip.

*The heart of **Elland Park Wood** is a charming maze of paths, with most weaving across the slope past a series of shafts and trial holes. The only difficulties are encountered around **Ash Grove Fireclay Works**. The bottom path stops abruptly at its perimeter fence, but a couple of paths lead up the slope before the quarried section, allowing you to continue above the works. From the other direction, this well-used path is marked as 'Private' at a barrier that is easily by-passed.*

This corner of the wood is ancient semi-natural woodland and more likely a former coppice than the pure oak area above Plains Lane, which may have been a plantation.

The De Laci family granted the **Manor of Elland** to the Elands* in the 11th century along with permission to hunt across Elland Park Wood. There is a reference to it as Pudding Park Wood in 1855, when it was owned by Hugh Francis Ingram. The crematorium was built in 1956 by Marshalls.

*Interestingly Sir John de Eland was one of few to accept a knighthood; most, like the Listers and Clays, paid a fine instead as it was cheaper.

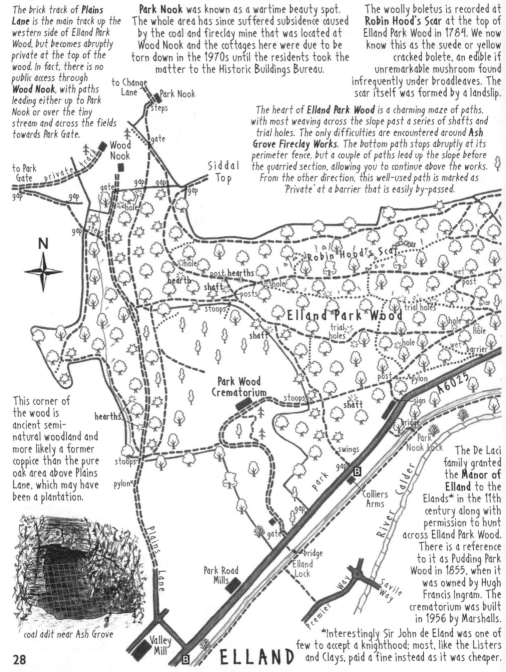

coal adit near Ash Grove

the suede bolete

The area above the woods was the **Binns Estate**, which had fine areas of trees that were ravaged by the quarrying of fireclay and shale. In the wood are some of the estate's distinctive walls with tall coping stones along the top.

Boggart House was erected in the 1830s as a gatehouse for the ancient residence at nearby Ashday Hall; at around the same time an observatory was built above Ashday Scout. It acquired the name after a series of supernatural occurences, such as lights going off and on and 'a little man with a ginger beard' appearing in a cupboard. Boggarts were household spirits, known to help with chores if rewarded satisfactorily with milk, but also to cause mischief around the house.

The bridleway of **Ashday Lane** is largely blocked by an inexplicable 3ft wall below Boggart House; still, it is easily by-passed on foot.

0   100   200   300
METRES

A clear path runs all the way along the top of Elland Park Wood, while that along the top of **Binns Wood** is slightly fainter. It sets off by scrambling up the bank from the bend near the top of Binns Top Lane, but then becomes obvious until the slope above the site of Far Binns - stay high here to avoid the wet ground.

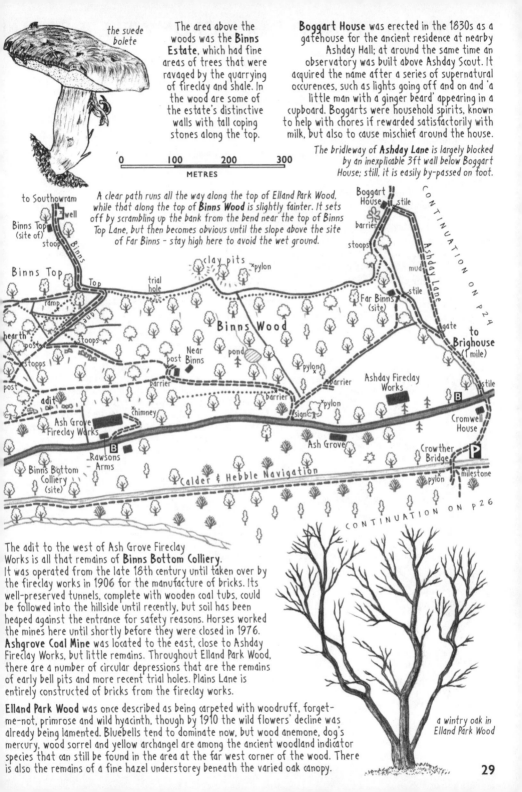

to Southowram

well

Binns Top (site of)

stoop

Binns Top Lane

Binns Top

Top

ramp

hearth

post

stoops

stoops

post

adit

Ash Grove Fireclay Works

B

Rawsons Arms

Binns Bottom Colliery (site)

clay pits

pylon

trial hole

Binns Wood

Near Binns

post

pond

barrier

chimney

barrier

barrier

sign

pylon

Ash Grove

Calder & Hebble Navigation

Boggart House

stile

barrier

stoops

mud

Far Binns (site)

stile

Ashday Lane

CONTINUATION ON P24

gate

to Brighouse (1 mile)

stile

Ashday Fireclay Works

pylon

B

Cromwell House

Crowther Bridge

P

milestone

pylon

CONTINUATION ON P26

The adit to the west of Ash Grove Fireclay Works is all that remains of **Binns Bottom Colliery**. It was operated from the late 18th century until taken over by the fireclay works in 1906 for the manufacture of bricks. Its well-preserved tunnels, complete with wooden coal tubs, could be followed into the hillside until recently, but soil has been heaped against the entrance for safety reasons. Horses worked the mines here until shortly before they were closed in 1976. **Ashgrove Coal Mine** was located to the east, close to Ashday Fireclay Works, but little remains. Throughout Elland Park Wood, there are a number of circular depressions that are the remains of early bell pits and more recent trial holes. Plains Lane is entirely constructed of bricks from the fireclay works.

Elland Park Wood was once described as being carpeted with woodruff, forget-me-not, primrose and wild hyacinth, though by 1910 the wild flowers' decline was already being lamented. Bluebells tend to dominate now, but wood anemone, dog's mercury, wood sorrel and yellow archangel are among the ancient woodland indicator species that can still be found in the area at the far west corner of the wood. There is also the remains of a fine hazel understorey beneath the varied oak canopy.

a wintry oak in Elland Park Wood

29

ROUTE 4: ELLAND PARK, CROMWELL & STRAN

Distance: 7.5 miles (12km)

Ascent: 250m

Parking: Pay car parks at Daisy Street or Owler Bank off the A643 in the centre of Brighouse. Street parking on Lillands Lane in Brighouse and Elland Lane in Elland.

Public Transport: Brighouse is on both the Huddersfield and Caldervale train routes. Elland is on the 501/503 bus routes between Halifax & Huddesfield, and the 278 route between Halifax & Wakefield.

Character: A surprisingly verdant walk linking these two neighbours in an apparently industrial section of the Calder Valley. Elland Park Wood and Cromwell Wood are delightful ancient oak groves divided by the Fairy Glen, and on the south side of the valley the land along the railway is cloaked in oak trees. Though the route doesn't include the charms of Cromwell Bottom Nature Reserve, a short loop through this area can easily be added.

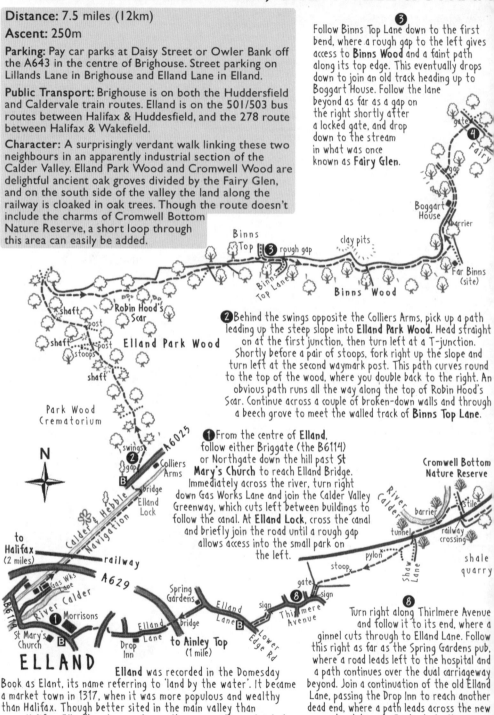

❸ Follow Binns Top Lane down to the first bend, where a rough gap to the left gives access to **Binns Wood** and a faint path along its top edge. This eventually drops down to join an old track heading up to Boggart House. Follow the lane beyond as far as a gap on the right shortly after a locked gate, and drop down to the stream in what was once known as **Fairy Glen.**

❷ Behind the swings opposite the Colliers Arms, pick up a path leading up the steep slope into **Elland Park Wood**. Head straight on at the first junction, then turn left at a T-junction. Shortly before a pair of stoops, fork right up the slope and turn left at the second waymark post. This path curves round to the top of the wood, where you double back to the right. An obvious path runs all the way along the top of Robin Hood's Scar. Continue across a couple of broken-down walls and through a beech grove to meet the walled track of **Binns Top Lane.**

❶ From the centre of **Elland,** follow either Briggate (the B6114) or Northgate down the hill past St Mary's Church to reach Elland Bridge. Immediately across the river, turn right down Gas Works Lane and join the Calder Valley Greenway, which cuts left between buildings to follow the canal. At **Elland Lock**, cross the canal and briefly join the road until a rough gap allows access into the small park on the left.

❽ Turn right along Thirlmere Avenue and follow it to its end, where a ginnel cuts through to Elland Lane. Follow this right as far as the Spring Gardens pub, where a road leads left to the hospital and a path continues over the dual carriageway beyond. Join a continuation of the old Elland Lane, passing the Drop Inn to reach another dead end, where a path leads across the new road and down to Eastgate by Morrisons. This leads back up into the centre of Elland.

ELLAND was recorded in the Domesday Book as Elant, its name referring to 'land by the water'. It became a market town in 1317, when it was more populous and wealthy than Halifax. Though better sited in the main valley than Halifax, Elland's subsequent growth was greatly restricted by the manorial system, which persisted far longer here.

4 Cross the stream to reach a gate and turn right on a lovely path along the foot of **Cromwell Wood** that emerges above Fort Montague. Drop down past the farm and, on a sharp bend, head straight on through a gate. Ascend steadily up a walled track into Freeman's Wood, then keep right along the wall to drop back down to the main road.

Bluebells uniquely brighten the spring scene in our woodlands and some of the finest locally are found along this stretch of the valley. In fact, the UK has almost half of the world's bluebells and it has been important plant since the Bronze Age. Bluebell sap has been used for attaching feathers to arrows and binding book pages

bluebells

5 Head straight across the A6025 into North Cut, turning left at its end to rejoin the Calder Valley Greenway. The canal provides a lovely walk into the heart of **Brighouse**. The station can be found by turning right up the second road the canal crosses, but the onward route turns right at the first (Anchor Bridge) by the Bridge Inn.

Cromwell Wood

Glen

Freeman's
Wood

sign
gate
Fort
Montague
gate

stile
A6025
B 5
Calder & Hebble
Navigation

Brookfoot
Mill

gate

The
Lillands

Ganny
Lock

bridge

BRIGHOUSE

The
Bridge

P

A643 B
Briggate

Atlas Mill

P

6

to
station

| 0 | 200 | 400 | 600 |

METRES

railway

Reins Wood

stoops

delfs

Two
Ashes

Lillands Lane

B

May Day temperance meetings were traditionally held on **Harry Castle Hill** in the late 19th and early 20th centuries.

landslip

seat

Strangstry
Wood

steps

Harry
Castle
Hill

7

to Rastrick
(1/2 mile)

6 Follow the A643 (Briggate) past the large Daisy Street car park near the centre of **Brighouse** and over the River Calder. Immediately beyond the railway arch, turn right along Scotty Bank and follow the footway alongside the railway until it joins Lillands Lane. Just beyond the point at which this turns into an unsurfaced road, bear right onto a path into **Reins Wood**. Follow the main path, passing a series of delfs and a fenced area where a landslip damaged the railway in 2008. Here you enter **Strangstry Wood**, staying along the top until the path forks by another delf; go right, climbing slightly onto the open crest of **Harry Castle Hill**, with great views over Cromwell Bottom and Elland.

The coal-powered **Elland Power Station** that once dominated Cromwell Bottom's landscape operated from 1959 to 1991 and was surrounded by ash settling ponds. It was cleared to make way for the Lowfields Industrial Estate.

Rastrick (whose name is likely to predate the Danes) was the older, more substantial settlement until the late 18th century, when the small village of **Brighouse** developed around the canal, turnpike and railway on land sold by the Kirklees Hall estate.

7 Just beyond the top of **Harry Castle Hill**, turn right down a slight gully and follow the path left down through the trees. Double back along the fence above the giant shale quarry, keeping left down the steps and following the fence round to the railway crossing by **Cromwell Bottom Nature Reserve**. If you have time, this lovely area can be explored further (see p26 for details), but the route turns left along the river bank. Beyond the railway, turn right and follow a path across the middle of the meadow towards houses on the outskirts of Elland, reached through a high metal gate.

flag walls in Strangstry Wood, possibly part of a sledge road used to transport quarried stone down to the river

THE WILLOW

The willow is an elegant if slightly melancholic tree of the riverbank, canalside and wet floodplain. It is known by many names, though these all have specific meanings; osier, sallow (as in the names Salford and Saltonstall), salice and withen. There are some 18 native willows and a great number of hybrid species in between; the most common in the Calder Valley is the 'lowly goat willow', also known as the pussy willow for the large fluffy catkins that emerge before its leaves in the spring. It has glossy oval leaves and branches that are more brittle than most willows. The goat willow's male catkins and the branches that carry them are known as palms because they were traditionally gathered on Palm Sunday, the last before Easter. Goat willow is a good coloniser of former industrial sites and, in some cases, was planted intentionally to improve the ground as it copes well with many industrial pollutants, heavy metals and poor soils.

Other willows tend to have more slender leaves and include the crack willow, white willow, grey willow, weeping willow (an ornamental hybrid), and the common osier. The latter was particularly cultivated in the low-lying swampy areas around Elland and Cromwell Bottom due to its use in basket-making. Willow grows rapidly in this sort of coppice and can be cut every three or four years, producing highly flexible withies that could be woven like strings. The trees were cut with a willow knife, before being soaked in tanks and peeled to be suitable for making into traps, carriages or skeps (the latter a heavy-duty basket used in the woollen industry and particularly common in this area). Eventually the high demand for skeps meant that willows had to be imported from elsewhere and the osier beds were abandoned, leaving a number of graceful older willows here. They can live to a very great age, their mature bark becoming steadily more rugged and fissured.

The willow is famously used for cricket bats as it absorbs impact well. The cricket bat willow, a hybrid of crack willow and white willow, is carefully grown to produce evenly grained trees for the purpose. Spade handles, thatching spars, artificial limbs and small boats were also traditionally made from willow, and its bark and leaves were used as a remedy for fevers and pains since the ancient Greeks, as it contains salicyclic acid, from which aspirin is made. Willow has more recently been coppiced for producing green biomass energy.

a coppiced osier

CHAPTER 4 - HALIFAX & COPLEY

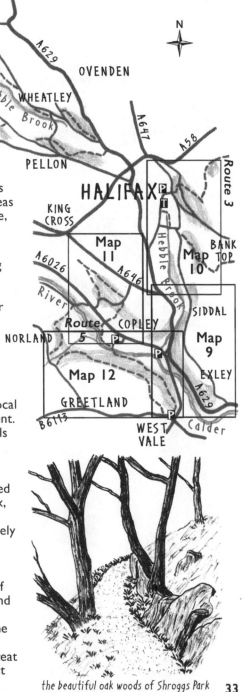

Map Sheet: Explorer 288 (Bradford & Huddersfield) and OL21 (South Pennines)

Public Transport: Halifax is on the main Caldervale railway line and the hub of most of the borough's public transport network. There are regular buses out to Copley, West Vale and Mixenden.

Parking: Various pay and display car parks in Halifax and West Vale. Free parking areas by the canal in Copley and at Salterhebble, as well as various street parking.

This chapter covers the urban heart of Calderdale, the town of Halifax sheltering a few sylvan treasures beneath its metropolitan cloak. Ancient woods have survived at North Dean Woods and Scarr Wood, while new swards of trees are growing across Beacon Hill and along Hebble Brook.

Halifax developed in the Middle Ages around the point at which the ancient Wakefield Gate crossed the Hebble (or Halifax) Brook, which later became the focal point for the town's industrial development. It is a curious town because the steep hills mean there are some very rural areas within and between its sprawling estates, while the town centre itself looks out on the green flank of Beacon Hill. The mapped areas are focussed to the south of Halifax, but I have included a route north along Hebble Brook. It is an area walked relatively little but, like all of our former industrial valleys, has some lovely pockets of varied woodland, particularly around the much-maligned Mixenden. Ogden, at the head of this valley, is a contraction of Oakdean, and along with Ovenden Wood indicates the earlier wooded nature of the valley. To the south, Copley is surrounded by the remnants of ancient woodland and is a great place from which to explore this rich part of the Calder Valley.

the beautiful oak woods of Shroggs Park   **33**

34

MAP 9: ELLAND WOOD & HEBBLE BROOK SOUTH

The Hebble Brook meets the Calder at Brooksmouth near Salterhebble Wharf amid a maze of railway tracks, canals and roads. The valley is fringed by a narrow band of fine woods, particularly between Elland and Exley and below Skircoat Green. It is most easily explored from the car park by Salterhebble Wharf.

The **Jew's ear** (or jelly ear) is a very distinctive rubbery fungus that often looks truly ear-like. The name is thought to derive from Judas ear, referring to the fact that they are often found on elder trees, the tree from which Judas hung himself. They are frost resistant and therefore found year round. Though rather chewy, they are perfectly edible and often added to Japanese soups, either in thin strips or powdered.

Bank House Wood is a nice oak stand, despite being small, steep and divided by the railway line. It can be reached easily from Skircoat Green either beside Back Dudwell Terrace or through All Saints churchyard. All paths lead down to the tracks of Bank House Lane or Cow Lane, though it is pretty impossible to reach the site of **Dud Well**, which gave the road above its name.

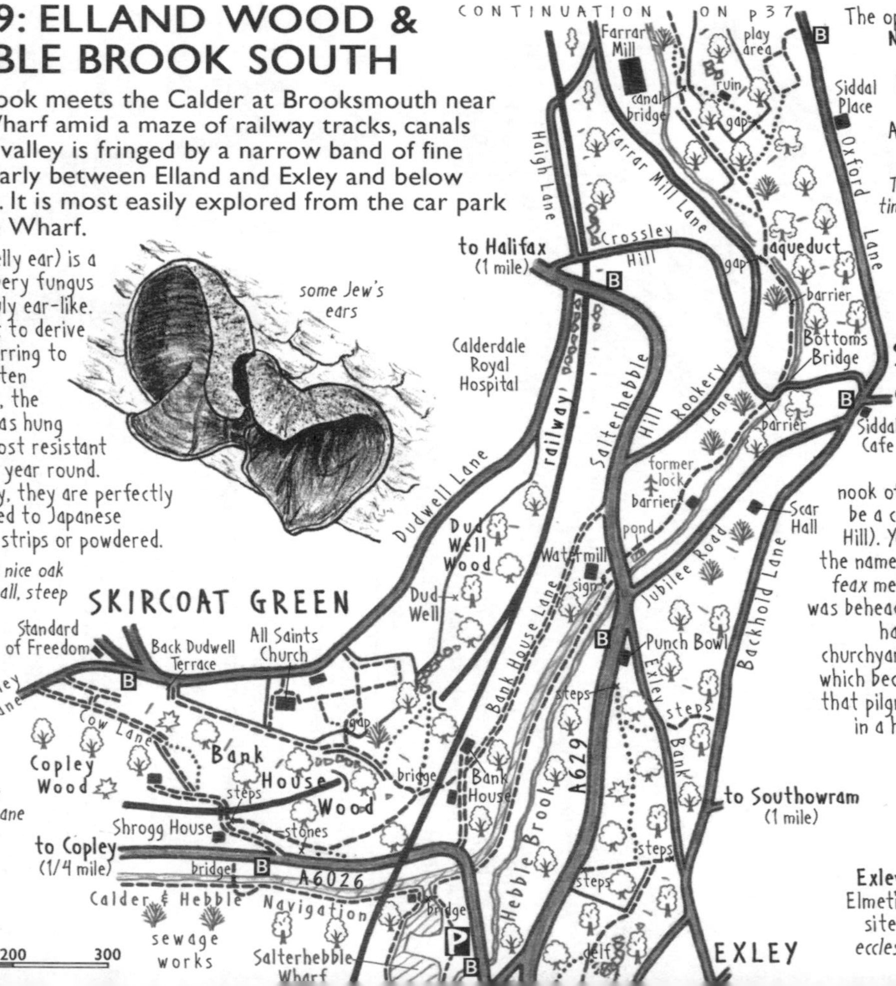

The opening of the Halifax branch of the **Calder & Hebble Navigation** in 1828 transformed this valley from an upmarket residential area into Halifax's industrial heart. Its course, followed by the Hebble Trail cycleway, had 14 locks on the way up to the basin by Albion Mills. It was abandoned in 1942 and soon filled in as it was unnecessary for drainage in the area.

The **Hebble Trail** follows the Hebble Brook throughout, at times picking up the obvious line of the old canal - a former lock is evident by Myrtle Cottage and a bridge opposite Farrar Mill. The only other path into the valley descends the steep bank from a play area off Oxford Lane.

The name **Hebble Brook** is thought to come from Salterhebble (*hebble* referring to a narrow bridge), having been Halifax Brook prior to the construction of the Calder & Hebble Canal, which originally was to end at Salterhebble. **Halifax** itself was first referred to around 1100 and the origin of its name is still debated. It may refer to *halh* (a nook of land) and *gefeaxe* (an area of coarse grassland), or be a corruption of Haley (which survives in the name Haley Hill). Yet in the Middle Ages, a myth developed, associating the name with 'holy hair': *halig* was Old English for 'holy' and *feax* meant 'hair'. This related to the story of a virgin who was beheaded after spurning the advances of a clergyman. Her hair caught in the fork of a yew tree in the Minster's churchyard and was for centuries said to survive in the tree, which became a site of pilgrimage. It has also been suggested that pilgrims believed the head of John the Baptist was held in a hermitage that was originally on the site of Halifax.

The woods of **Exley Bank** can be accessed via steps down from Exley or up from the A629, either behind the Punch Bowl or the traffic lights by the site of the old Calder & Hebble Inn. The focal point is a cavernous delf beneath the houses of Chevinedge Crescent.

Exley (formerly Eckisley) was the site of a 6th-century Elmetian church standing on a bluff above the valley. The site was likely that of Exley Hall, its name coming from eccles, an Old English word meaning church. It is said that all the Exleys in the world emanate from here.

some Jew's ears

CONTINUATION ON p.37

SIDDAL

Siddal Place
Oxford Lane
Siddal Hill
Siddal Cafe
Cinder Hill
Scar Hall

play area
Farrar Mill
Farrar Mill Lane
Canal bridge
Crossley Hill
Haigh Lane
aqueduct
Bottoms Bridge
barrier
gap
gap
Rookery Lane
former lock
barrier
pond
Salterhebble Hill
Backhold Lane
to Southowram (1 mile)

to Halifax (1 mile)

Calderdale Royal Hospital

railway

Watermill signs

EXLEY
Punch Bowl
Exley steps
Jubilee Road
Bank
A629
Hebble Brook
steps
Cliff
steps

Dudwell Lane
Dud Well Wood
Dud Well
Bank House Lane
Bank House
Wood
stones

SKIRCOAT GREEN
All Saints Church
Back Dudwell Terrace
Standard of Freedom
Copley Lane
Copley Wood
Cow Lane
Shrogg House
steps
bridge
Calder & Hebble Navigation
A6026
Salterhebble Wharf
sewage works
bridge

to Copley (1/4 mile)

0 100 200 300
METRES

There were originally staircase locks (like those in Bingley) at **Salterhebble Basin**, though these were replaced by conventional locks by 1780. Until the Halifax branch was constructed, barges had to unload at the basin here. Most of the craft on the canal were broad horse-drawn barges full of coal, grain or ready-milled flour from Halifax Flour Society.

Calder Bridge was originally Toll Bar Bridge, built on the Rochdale to Halifax and Elland Turnpike in 1824.

Elland Hall was an ancient seat inhabited by generations of the Eland Family, but it was tragically pulled down to build the by-pass in 1978. The 17th-century **Exley Hall** remains behind Exley Hall Farm, but the estate dates back further. Though just half a mile separates the two halls, they were bitterly divided during the notorious **Elland Feud** in the 14th century. Sir John de Eland's half-nephew was killed by an Exley during a siege of Conisborough Castle in 1317 and, despite being given land in compensation, he sought revenge. His attempt to kill Exley and those who sheltered him resulted in so much bloodshed across the county that by 1353 there were no male de Elands left and the hall passed to the Saviles. All in all it was a rather short-sighted affair.

The line of quarries above the east side of Hebble Brook (though not including those in Elland Wood) are dug into the **Elland flags**, a band of very durable stone found between the millstone grit to the west and the coal beds to the east. Sometimes referred to as the true 'Yorkshire stone', it was most used for paving slabs, as well as repairs to the Tower of London and London Bridge, and in many of Hamburg's buildings. Its quarrying was first recorded in 1314, when it would largely have been used for roofing thackstones, but much of the best surface stone was worked out by 1860 and many stone mines were subsequently sunk across the area.

Exley Hall was originally given to the Knights Hospitallers of St John of Jerusalem. **Annesley House** is recorded as Abulay Grange and was owned by monks of Fountains Abbey until the Dissolution in the 1550s. It is later recorded as Aneley House and its name probably has the some root as Ainley the other side of Elland.

Chevinedge Mansion was built in 1876 by James William Davis, taking its name from the rocky escarpment overlooking the Calder Valley. It acted as a private museum for Davis' renowned collection of fossils and geological specimens. In May 1909, Halifax Zoo & Amusement Park opened at Chevinedge, attracting 41,000 visitors over its first weekend. It had species from all around the world; lions, bears, wolves, monkeys, camels, rainforest birds, an elephant and an ornamental lake with exotic species like pelicans. Occasionally animals were known to escape, with a bear once chased by keepers down Exley Bank. Alongside were an Electric Theatre (early cinema), hall of mirrors, miniature railway and skating rink. It went out of fashion during the war and closed in 1917, with the lodge and tea rooms remained, the latter used by Siddal ARLFC as changing rooms for years.

Hall Wood is inaccessible above the A629, but a good path runs the length of Elland Wood. It can be picked up at the bottom of Elland Cemetery or up a bank beside Exley Lane just beyond Annesley House. At first it follows the top of the rocky crags before skirting around their foot all the way to Exley.

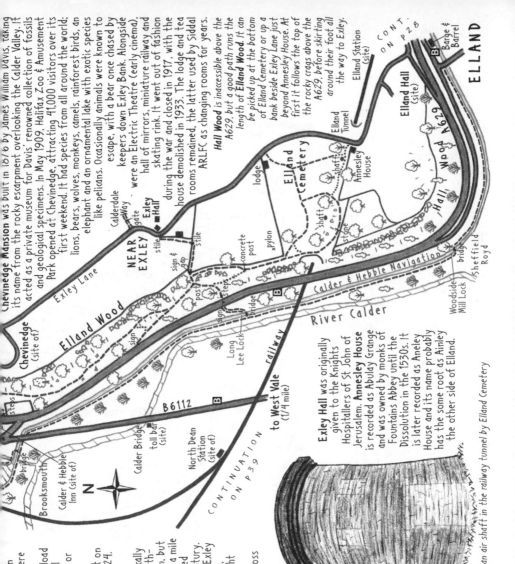

an air shaft in the railway tunnel by Elland Cemetery

CONT. ON P. 28

CONTINUATION ON P. 39

MAP 10: BEACON HILL & HEBBLE BROOK NORTH

The Hebble Brook provides a narrow green corridor right into the centre of Halifax, its woods largely composed of recent settlers (sycamore, birch and willow) on old industrial sites. On the hill above is the landscaped former estate of Stoney Royd Cemetery and the dense pines, birch and rhododendron of Beacon Hill Wood. Beacon Hill and the cemetery are the most obvious points of interest, but the mills along the brook are also interesting to explore.

There is a medieval grave from the mid-12th century in the graveyard of **Halifax Minster** that is carved with an elongated cavalry cross and pair of early shears.

The **cantilever walkway** above Hebble Brook was constructed to allow the expansion of the adjacent **canal basin**, which stood at the head of the Calder & Hebble Navigation.

The hounds for Halifax Hunt were kept at **Folly Hall** until the late 19th century. At that time it was a grand building on a completely bare hillside.

Prior to the construction of **Albion Mills** in the 1850s, the area alongside the Hebble Brook was the site of an extravagant bath house and ornamental garden, built in 1793 by Thomas Rawlinson and used by Halifax's elite. It was fed by natural springs and thought the most extensive suite of baths in Yorkshire, even rivalling those of Bath, but the springs were disturbed in the construction of the railway and it closed in 1853. Albion Mill itself was later used for making **Mackintosh's Toffee**, which began life as a pastry shop in 1890 and whose worldwide fame (with brands including Rolo and Quality Street) led to Halifax being known as Toffee Town in some quarters.

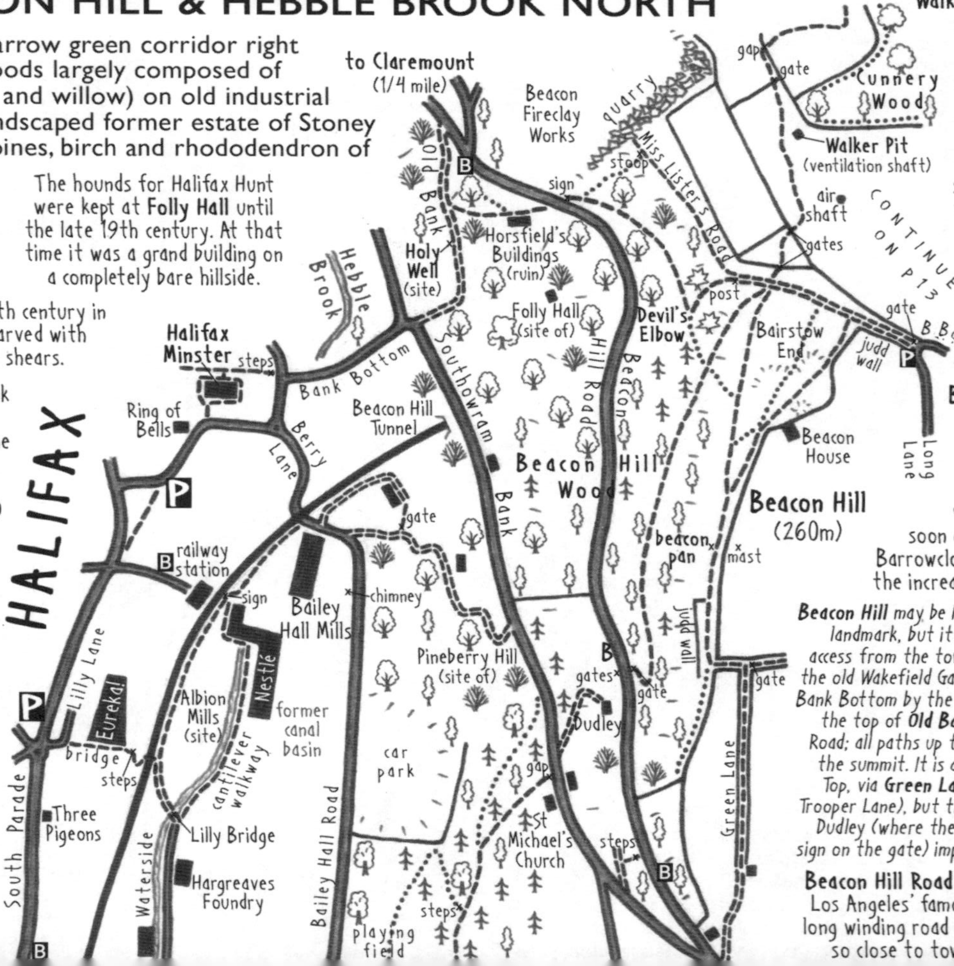

Walker Pit was a coal mine sunk in 1834 for Anne Lister of Shibden Hall with money aquired from her recent union with partner Ann Walker. The adorned folly-like ventilation shaft stands alongside the pit entrance, while the other shaft nearby is above the Beacon Hill Railway Tunnel.

Beacon House offered refreshments and a twopenny train ride to Victorian visitors. **Miss Lister's Road** was built in the 1830s soon after she had widened Barrowclough Lane to allow for the increased transport of coal.

Beacon Hill may be Halifax's most prominent landmark, but it isn't straightforward to access from the town. The main route up is the old Wakefield Gate, which climbs up from Bank Bottom by the Minster. Turn right near the top of **Old Bank** and cross Beacon Hill Road; all paths up to the right then lead to the summit. It is also accessible from Bank Top, via **Green Lane** (opposite the top of Trooper Lane), but the obstructed path past Dudley (where there is a very unwelcoming sign on the gate) impedes routes in between.

Beacon Hill Road is Halifax's version of Los Angeles' famous Mulholland Drive, a long winding road through hills that are so close to town yet feel so remote.

36

CONTINUED ON P13

HALIFAX

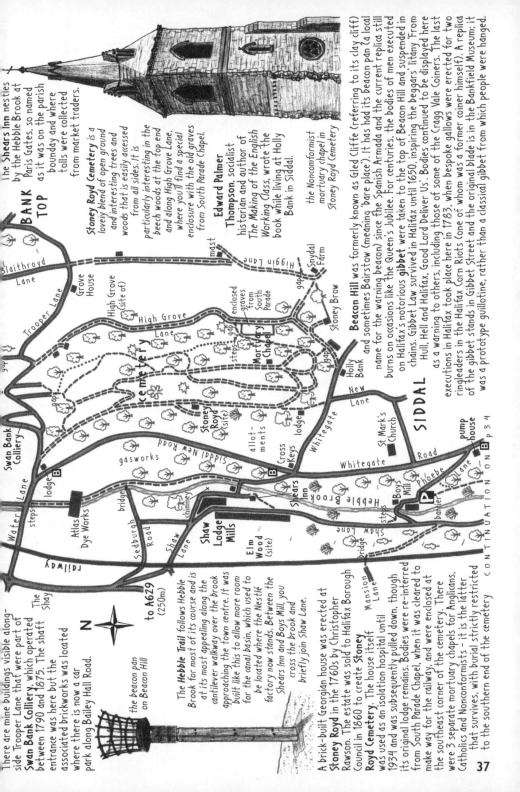

The Shears Inn nestles by the Hebble Brook at Paris Gates, so named as it was on the parish boundary and where tolls were collected from market traders.

Stoney Royd Cemetery is a lovely blend of open ground and interesting trees and woods that is easily accessed from all sides. It is particularly interesting in the beech woods at the top end and along High Grove Lane, where you'll find a special enclosure with the old graves from South Parade Chapel.

Edward Palmer Thompson, socialist historian and author of The Making of the English Working Class, wrote the book while living at Holly Bank in Siddal.

the Noncomformist mortuary chapel in Stoney Royd Cemetery

Beacon Hill was formerly known as Gled Cliffe (referring to its clay cliff) and sometimes Bairstow (meaning 'bare place'). It has had its beacon pan (a local name for the warning beacon) since the Spanish Armada and the current replica still burns on occasions like the Queen's Jubilee. For centuries, the bodies of men executed on Halifax's notorious gibbet were taken to the top of Beacon Hill and suspended in chains. Gibbet Law survived in Halifax until 1650, inspiring the beggars' litany 'From Hull, Hell and Halifax, Good Lord Deliver Us'. Bodies continued to be displayed here as a warning to others, including those of some of the Cragg Vale Coiners. The last executions in Halifax took place here in 1783, when bespoke gallows were erected for two ringleaders from the Halifax Corn Riots (one of whom was a former coiner himself). A replica of the gibbet stands in Gibbet Street and the original blade is in the Bankfield Museum; it was a prototype guillotine, rather than a classical gibbet from which people were hanged.

There are mine buildings visible alongside Trooper Lane that were part of Swan Bank Colliery, which operated between 1790 and 1875. The shaft entrance was here but the associated brickworks was located where there is now a car park along Bailey Hall Road.

the beacon pan on Beacon Hill

The Hebble Trail follows Hebble Brook for most of its course and is at its most appealing along the cantilever walkway over the brook approaching the town centre. It was built like this to allow more room for the canal basin, which used to be located where the Nestlé factory now stands. Between the Shears Inn and Boys Mill, you cross the brook and briefly join Shaw Lane.

A brick-built Georgian house was erected at Stoney Royd in the 1760s by Christopher Rawson. The estate was sold to Halifax Borough Council in 1860 to create Stoney Royd Cemetery. The house itself was used as an isolation hospital until 1934 and was subsequently pulled down, though its original lodge remains. Bodies were re-interred from South Parade Chapel, when it was cleared to make way for the railway, and were enclosed at the southeast corner of the cemetery. There were 3 separate mortuary chapels for Anglicans, Catholics and Nonconformists - it is the latter that survives, with burial strictly restricted to the southern end of the cemetery CONTINUATION ON B p 34

37

MAP 11: SKIRCOAT WOODS & DELPH HILL

The steep slope overlooking the Calder Valley on the south side of Halifax is very urban and yet fringed by beautiful oak woods. The ground here was considered so rough it was never much use for anything but trees. Scarr Wood and Long Wood are pure oak coppices, the former's low canopy of remarkably contorted trees having been stunted by years of pollution. Wainhouse Tower stands proudly at one end, while lost in its midst and rarely seen from afar, Wood House Scar forms an arresting series of crags. Further down the hill, scrub woodland has taken over around the Halifax Building Society's former head-quarters and along the canal and river, above which towers the magnificent structure of Copley Viaduct.

Robin Hood's Hotel

Wood House Scar is often simply referred to as the Rocks and forms a fine series of crenellations along the top of Scarr Wood. Albert Promenade was built along the top and provides one of Halifax's best viewpoints. Near the northern end of the crags, one of a number of holes in the face is engraved with 'Robin Hood's Hotel 1843'. A hoard of over 1000 Constantine Roman coins was discovered in another of these holes at the other end of the rocks by schoolchildren in 1915.

38

King Cross is named after an ancient wayside cross (also known as Mile Cross) that stood at the junction here until the 18th century. Although it is said to have acquired its name after an unknown king turned back from the hills at this spot on the road into Lancashire, it most likely took its name from a local family, the Kings. It was also the site of a Royalist Civil War garrison.

Skircoat Common, now Savile Park, was acquired for the town of Halifax from the Savile family in 1872 with a guarantee that it would remain unenclosed, as it does to this day. Horse races took place on the common as part of the annual June Fair between 1738 and 1740. Before moving to Thrum Hall, early football (always meaning rugby football) and cricket matches were also played here, as well as competitive running races, known as 'pedestrianism'. 20,000 Chartists gathered for a rally here on Good Friday 1848.

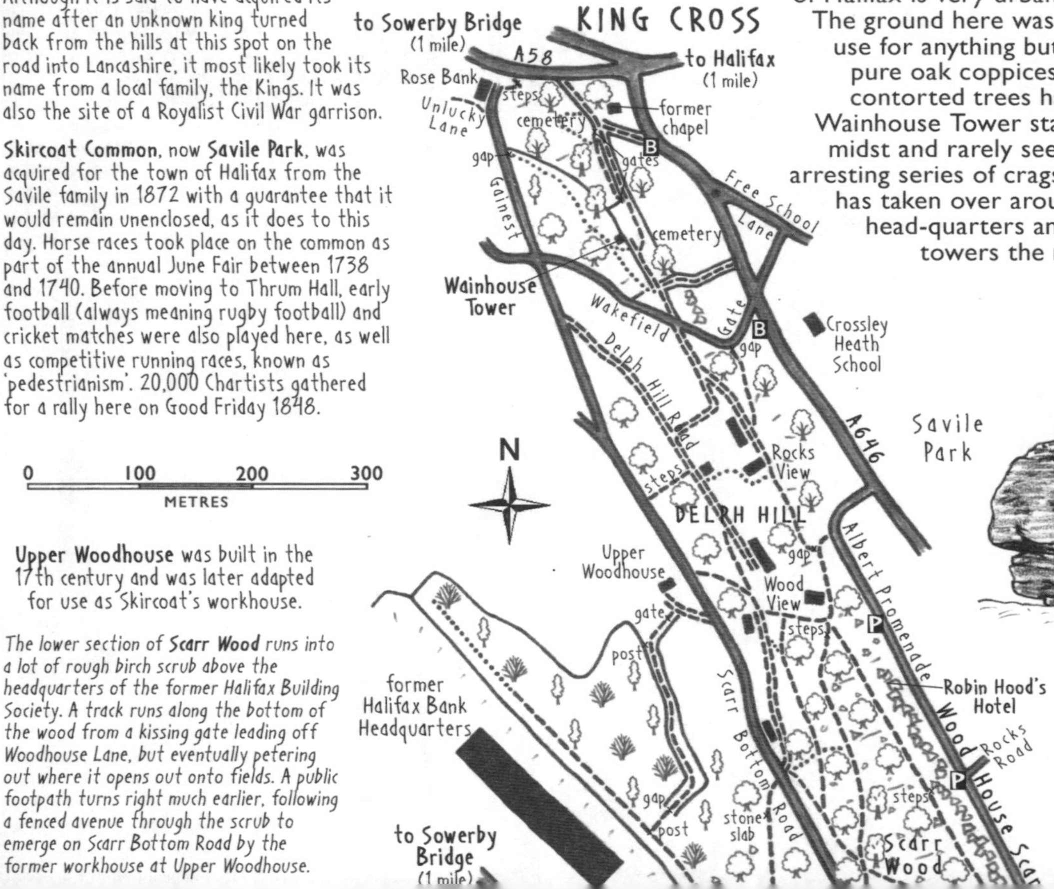

Upper Woodhouse was built in the 17th century and was later adapted for use as Skircoat's workhouse.

The lower section of **Scarr Wood** runs into a lot of rough birch scrub above the headquarters of the former Halifax Building Society. A track runs along the bottom of the wood from a kissing gate leading off Woodhouse Lane, but eventually petering out where it opens out onto fields. A public footpath turns right much earlier, following a fenced avenue through the scrub to emerge on Scarr Bottom Road by the former workhouse at Upper Woodhouse.

to Sowerby Bridge (1 mile)   **to Halifax** (1 mile)

KING CROSS

A58

Rose Bank

former chapel

Free School Lane

Crossley Heath School

A646

Savile Park

cemetery

Wakefield Gate

Delph Hill Road

Wainhouse Tower

Gainest

Unlucky Lane

DELPH HILL

Rocks View

Wood View

Albert Promenade

Robin Hood's Hotel

Wood Rocks Road

Wood House Scar

Scarr Wood

Scarr Bottom Road

Upper Woodhouse

stone slab

former Halifax Bank Headquarters

to Sowerby Bridge (1 mile)

N

0   100   200   300
METRES

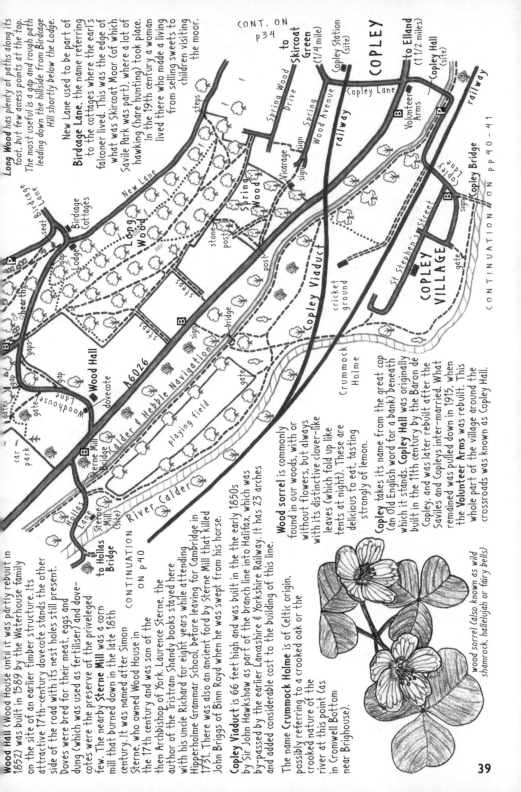

Long Wood has plenty of paths along its foot, but few access points at the top. The most useful is a gap and rough path leading down the hillside from Birdcage Hill directly below the Lodge.

New Lane used to be part of **Birdcage Lane**, the name referring to the cottages where the earl's falconer lived. This was the edge of what was Skircoat Moor (of which Savile Park was part), where a lot of hawking (hare hunting) took place. In the 19th century a woman lived there who made a living from selling sweets to children visiting the moor.

to **Skircoat Green** (1/4 mile)

COPLEY

to **Elland** (1 1/2 miles)

Copley Hall (site)

Copley Station (site)

Copley Lane

Spring Wood Drive

Volunteer Arms

Spring Wood

Copley Viaduct

Copley Bridge

Copley Lane

railway

CONTINUATION ON PP40–41

COPLEY VILLAGE

St Stephen's Street

cricket ground

Crummock Holme

playing field

River Calder

Calder & Hebble Navigation

A6026

♦ **Wood Hall**

dovecote

Woodhouse Lane

Sterne Mill Bridge

Hollas Lane

to **Hollas Bridge**

Sterne Mill (site)

CONTINUATION ON P40

Long Wood

New Lane

Birdcage Cottages

Lodge

Closet Birdcage Lane

hearths

car park

Vicarage

Wood Avenue

Wood Hall (Wood House until it was partly rebuilt in 1852) was built in 1589 by the Waterhouse family on the site of an earlier timber structure. Its attractive 17th-century dovecote stands the other side of the road with its nest holes still present. Doves were bred for their meat, eggs and dung (which was used as fertiliser) and dove-cotes were the preserve of the privileged few. The nearby **Sterne Mill** was a corn mill that burned down in the late 18th century. It was named after Simon Sterne, who owned Wood House in the 17th century and was son of the then Archbishop of York. Laurence Sterne, the author of the Tristram Shandy books stayed here with his uncle Richard for eight years while attending Hipperholme Grammar School, before leaving for Cambridge in 1731. There was also an ancient ford by Sterne Mill that killed John Briggs of Binn Royd when he was swept from his horse.

Copley Viaduct is 66 feet high and was built in the the early 1850s by Sir John Hawkshaw as part of the branch line into Halifax, which was by-passed by the earlier Lancashire & Yorkshire Railway. It has 23 arches and added considerable cost to the building of this line.

The name **Crummock Holme** is of Celtic origin, possibly referring to a crooked oak or the crooked nature of the river at this point (as in Cromwell Bottom near Brighouse).

Wood sorrel is commonly found in our woods, with or without flowers, but always with its distinctive clover-like leaves (which fold up like tents at night). These are delicious to eat, tasting strongly of lemon.

Copley takes its name from the great cop (an old English word for a bank) beneath which it stands. **Copley Hall** was originally built in the 11th century by the Baron de Copley, and was later rebuilt after the Saviles and Copleys inter-married. What remained was pulled down in 1915, when the **Volunteer Arms** was rebuilt. This whole part of the village around the crossroads was known as Copley Hall.

wood sorrel (also known as wild shamrock, hallelujah or fairy bells)

MAP 12: NORTH DEAN WOOD

North Dean Wood is one of the finest woodlands in the lower Calder Valley. It stretches some three miles from West Vale to Norland, though the eastern end may previously have been known separately as Kings Dean Wood. It is probably most easily accessed from Copley, above which its shaded slopes and long line of crags stand darkly. The whole wood is easy to explore, being Open Access land and full of interesting paths through the varied oak, beech and birch trees. Pickwood Scar is a wooded outlier to the west, the two separated by beautiful Maple Dean Clough.

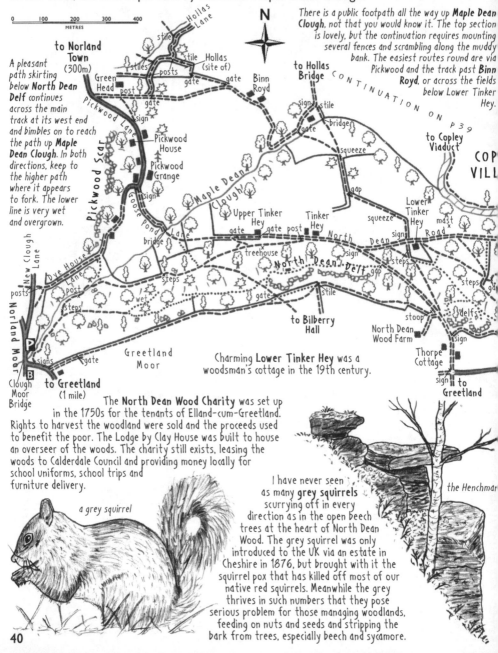

There is a public footpath all the way up **Maple Dean Clough**, not that you would know it. The top section is lovely, but the continuation requires mounting several fences and scrambling along the muddy bank. The easiest routes round are via Pickwood and the track past **Binn Royd**, or across the fields below Lower Tinker Hey.

A pleasant path skirting below **North Dean Delf** continues across the main track at its west end and bimbles on to reach the path up **Maple Dean Clough**. In both directions, keep to the higher path where it appears to fork. The lower line is very wet and overgrown.

Charming **Lower Tinker Hey** was a woodsman's cottage in the 19th century.

The **North Dean Wood Charity** was set up in the 1750s for the tenants of Elland-cum-Greetland. Rights to harvest the woodland were sold and the proceeds used to benefit the poor. The Lodge by Clay House was built to house an overseer of the woods. The charity still exists, leasing the woods to Calderdale Council and providing money locally for school uniforms, school trips and furniture delivery.

a grey squirrel

the Henchman

I have never seen as many **grey squirrels** scurrying off in every direction as in the open beech trees at the heart of North Dean Wood. The grey squirrel was only introduced to the UK via an estate in Cheshire in 1876, but brought with it the squirrel pox that has killed off most of our native red squirrels. Meanwhile the grey thrives in such numbers that they pose serious problem for those managing woodlands, feeding on nuts and seeds and stripping the bark from trees, especially beech and sycamore.

& PICKWOOD SCAR

The **Roman altar** found at Bank Top (see below) has had an interesting journey since its discovery in 1597. It has spent time at Bradley Hall (near Stainland), in a private collection, abandoned in a Cambridgeshire churchyard, then Trinity College's library, before its current home in the Museum of Archaeology and Anthropology at Cambridge University. It dates from around 205AD and is dedicated to Brigantia, the mother goddess of the Brigantes tribe that covered large parts of northern England.

Binn Royd is an elegant mansion that was built in the 16th century on the site of an earlier timber house on land owned by the Binns family. *Binn* was an Old English word for an animal's stall. Nearby **Hollas** was originally Hall House and so its name has nothing to do with holly, despite its proliferation along Hollas Lane.

the Bank Top Roman altar, of which there is a cast in Clay House

St Stephen's Church is an impressive neo-Gothic building built in the 1860s by subscription, but largely funded by Edward Akroyd. It was built in Greetland parish on the opposite bank of the river from the village because of the refusal of the vicar of All Saints Church in Halifax to have another church built in his parish. It is no longer used as a church, but preserved by the Churches Conservation Trust and open to the public as a museum, particularly for its stained glass windows.

Copley Village was constructed in 1847 at the same time as a new mill for Edward Akroyd, because there was little accommodation in the area. The lines of neat millworkers' cottages were built in English Old style and Akroyd paid particular attention to social conditions. There were plenty of allotments, a library, cricket team, evening classes, and rewards of excursions and book prizes. Akroyd subsequently built the Gothic model village of Akroydon on the other side of Halifax, originally planned to be a considerably larger settlement.

It is hard to follow paths through the open beech woods below **Shots Scar** at the heart of North Dean Wood, but then it is easy to wander anywhere over the thick leaf carpet. The main paths run from a couple of gaps in the wall near **St Stephen's Church**; the lower one peters out near a dry gulch but can be picked up again heading up the slope above a small pond to the right; the higher path climbs sooner to cut across the slope at the foot of Shots Scarr. Both then continue through the oak and birch woods of **Kings Dean**. An alternative to both of these is to pick up a faint path along the river bank then head up the slope beyond the dry gulch and follow a path that meanders alongside the railway all the way past Kings Dean.

Bank Top was formerly known as Thick Hollins, suggesting the existence of an earlier holly plantation. In 1597, a **Roman altar** to the goddess Victoria Brigantia was unearthed in its garden, and it was later suggested by John Horsley that this was the site of Cambodunum, an unidentified Roman fort on the York–Chester road. Although this is more commonly ascribed to a site at Slack near Outlane, that was thought abandoned by 125AD and the debate over its whereabouts continues.

The name **West Vale** was only created in 1851 for a new settlement in an area anciently known as Brook Brigge (the earlier form of Brow Bridge, which was built in 1770).

The area on the south side of the river by the railway bridge held rifle butts used by local volunteers until the late 19th century.

*North Dean Wood starts immediately outside **Lindwell** and **West Vale** and can be reached either through Clay House Park, along Clay House Lane or down Dean End (a track reached above the Star Inn). There is no path along the crags at the top of the woods here, though a nice path cuts through **Dean Top Delf** to join the main path.*

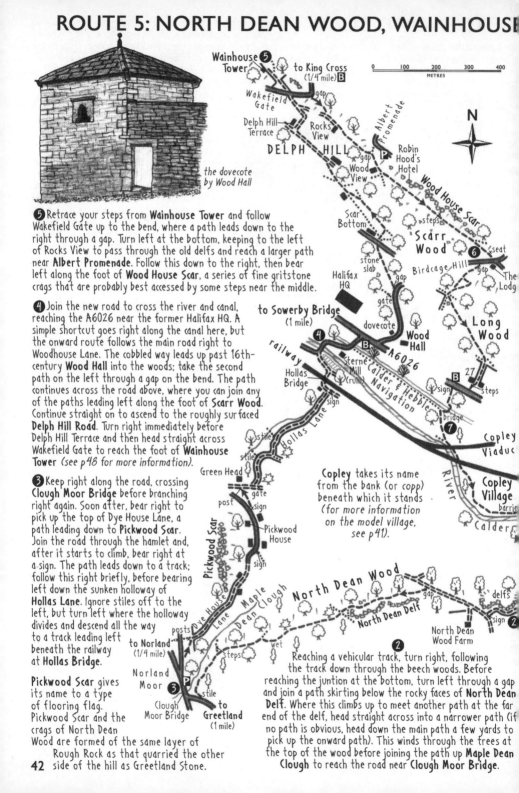

the dovecote by Wood Hall

5 Retrace your steps from **Wainhouse Tower** and follow Wakefield Gate up to the bend, where a path leads down to the right through a gap. Turn left at the bottom, keeping to the left of Rocks View to pass through the old delfs and reach a larger path near **Albert Promenade**. Follow this down to the right, then bear left along the foot of **Wood House Scar**, a series of fine gritstone crags that are probably best accessed by some steps near the middle.

4 Join the new road to cross the river and canal, reaching the A6026 near the former Halifax HQ. A simple shortcut goes right along the canal here, but the onward route follows the main road right to Woodhouse Lane. The cobbled way leads up past 16th-century **Wood Hall** into the woods; take the second path on the left through a gap on the bend. The path continues across the road above, where you can join any of the paths leading left along the foot of **Scarr Wood**. Continue straight on to ascend to the roughly surfaced **Delph Hill Road**. Turn right immediately before Delph Hill Terrace and then head straight across Wakefield Gate to reach the foot of **Wainhouse Tower** (see p48 for more information).

3 Keep right along the road, crossing **Clough Moor Bridge** before branching right again. Soon after, bear right to pick up the top of Dye House Lane, a path leading down to **Pickwood Scar**. Join the road through the hamlet and, after it starts to climb, bear right at a sign. The path leads down to a track; follow this right briefly, before bearing left down the sunken holloway of **Hollas Lane**. Ignore stiles off to the left, but turn left where the holloway divides and descend all the way to a track leading left beneath the railway at **Hollas Bridge**.

Pickwood Scar gives its name to a type of flooring flag. Pickwood Scar and the crags of North Dean Wood are formed of the same layer of Rough Rock as that quarried the other side of the hill as Greetland Stone.

Copley takes its name from the bank (or copp) beneath which it stands (for more information on the model village, see p41).

2 Reaching a vehicular track, turn right, following the track down through the beech woods. Before reaching the junction at the bottom, turn left through a gap and join a path skirting below the rocky faces of **North Dean Delf**. Where this climbs up to meet another path at the far end of the delf, head straight across into a narrower path (if no path is obvious, head down the main path a few yards to pick up the onward path). This winds through the trees at the top of the wood before joining the path up **Maple Dean Clough** to reach the road near **Clough Moor Bridge**.

TOWER & WOOD HOUSE SCAR FROM WEST VALE OR COPLEY

Distance: 7 miles (11km)
Ascent: 350m

Parking: Pay and display car park in West Vale by Brow Bridge. Free parking areas by the canal in Copley, on Albert Promenade near Savile Park, and by Clough Moor Bridge near Norland.

Public Transport: The 501/503 buses run regularly through West Vale between Halifax and Huddersfield. Copley is on the hourly 561/562/563 services from Halifax.

Character: An intricate round of the fine woods either side of the Calder Valley above Copley. Though backing right onto Halifax, the area is home to the ancient oak and beech woodland of North Dean Wood and Scarr Wood, and a number of dramatic crags. The route also takes in the local historical features of Wainhouse Tower, Wood Hall and Clay House. The easiest place to start is West Vale, but the route can also be undertaken from Copley or Norland. It can be shortened by a couple of miles by missing out the loop of Scarr Wood up to Wainhouse Tower.

❻ Reaching **Birdcage Hill**, turn right as far as the first gap on the left. A couple of paths weave down through **Long Wood** towards the corner of a wall. Here, take the middle of three paths down the hill, descending gently to the bottom edge of the wood. Look for a narrow gap in the wall, from which a ginnel leads down between houses to reach the main road again. 100m to the right, a path continues down to the left to a metal bridge over the canal.

❼ Over the bridge, head left away from the canal and join a path alongside the **River Calder** as it passes beneath the twin arms of the railway. The river can be followed right round **Copley model village** to Copley Bridge (where there is parking up the lane to the left).

Copley Bridge Bar is an early 19th-century toll house that has recently been renovated as a private house. It stands on North Dean Road and the original toll board is on the wall outside.

Clay House fountain

❽ Cross **Copley Bridge** and turn left opposite the old Bar House to pass through the churchyard of **St Stephen's Church**. Beyond a gap in the wall at the far end, keep left and follow a narrow path along the river bank. Ignore some steps up to the right, but at a hollow soon after, head straight up the short bank ahead. A path winds through the scrub beyond to pass a small pond and run parallel to the railway line. Reaching the line of an old wall, the path continues up the side of this to the main track through **North Dean Wood**. Keep left, following the newly surfaced Calderdale Way down to a lower track. After passing the path down to the car park on the B6112, keep left and head down through a gap in the wall to curve round to the front of **Clay House**.

Clay House is a Jacobean-style mid-17th century yeoman clothier's house built for John Clay on the site of a 13th-century timbered structure. It was inherited by John Wheelwright (the founder of Rishworth School) in 1713 and subsequently preserved by the Wheelwright Trust. It was then purchased by Greetland Urban District Council in 1923 and its grounds opened as a park shortly after. Jane Clay is said to haunt the house, weeping in a white dress.

❶ From the gates of **Clay House**, follow the B6113 briefly up out of West Vale, before turning right up some steps. At the top, turn left, then first right to reach another short flight of steps. Follow the track left, then bear right up the steps to the road above. Turn right, then double back to the left by **Bank Top**; this leads on to Collin Moor Lane, a green lane across the fields. Reaching the top of **North Dean Wood**, turn left and follow the fine path along the top of a series of crags.

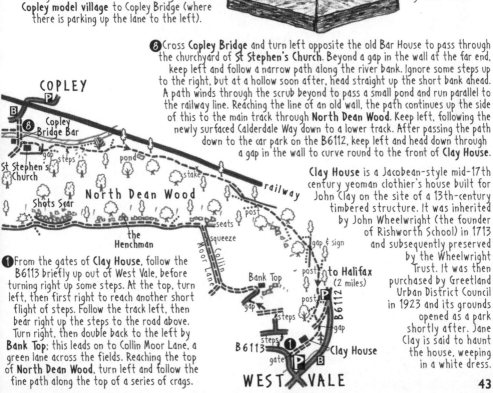

43

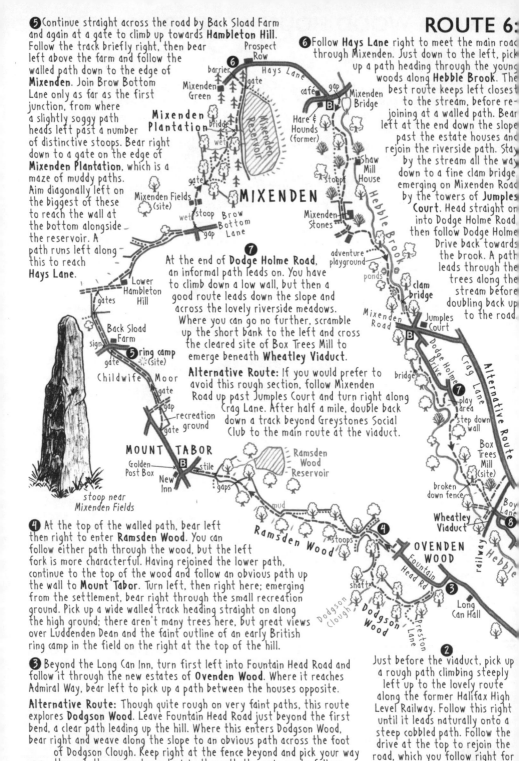

5 Continue straight across the road by Back Sload Farm and again at a gate to climb up towards **Hambleton Hill**. Follow the track briefly right, then bear left above the farm and follow the walled path down to the edge of **Mixenden**. Join Brow Bottom Lane only as far as the first junction, from where a slightly soggy path heads left past a number of distinctive stoops. Bear right down to a gate on the edge of **Mixenden Plantation**, which is a maze of muddy paths. Aim diagonally left on the biggest of these to reach the wall at the bottom alongside the reservoir. A path runs left along this to reach **Hays Lane**.

6 Follow **Hays Lane** right to meet the main road through Mixenden. Just down to the left, pick up a path heading through the young woods along **Hebble Brook**. The best route keeps left closest to the stream, before re-joining at a walled path. Bear left at the end down the slope past the estate houses and rejoin the riverside path. Stay by the stream all the way down to a fine clam bridge emerging on Mixenden Road by the towers of **Jumples Court**. Head straight on into Dodge Holme Road, then follow Dodge Holme Drive back towards the brook. A path leads through the trees along the stream before doubling back up to the road.

7 At the end of **Dodge Holme Road**, an informal path leads on. You have to climb down a low wall, but then a good route leads down the slope and across the lovely riverside meadows. Where you can go no further, scramble up the short bank to the left and cross the cleared site of Box Trees Mill to emerge beneath **Wheatley Viaduct**.

Alternative Route: If you would prefer to avoid this rough section, follow Mixenden Road up past Jumples Court and turn right along Crag Lane. After half a mile, double back down a track beyond Greystones Social Club to the main route at the viaduct.

4 At the top of the walled path, bear left then right to enter **Ramsden Wood**. You can follow either path through the wood, but the left fork is more characterful. Having rejoined the lower path, continue to the top of the wood and follow an obvious path up the wall to **Mount Tabor**. Turn left, then right here; emerging from the settlement, bear right through the small recreation ground. Pick up a wide walled track heading straight on along the high ground; there aren't many trees here, but great views over Luddenden Dean and the faint outline of an early British ring camp in the field on the right at the top of the hill.

3 Beyond the Long Can Inn, turn first left into Fountain Head Road and follow it through the new estates of **Ovenden Wood**. Where it reaches Admiral Way, bear left to pick up a path between the houses opposite.

Alternative Route: Though quite rough on very faint paths, this route explores **Dodgson Wood**. Leave Fountain Head Road just beyond the first bend, a clear path leading up the hill. Where this enters Dodgson Wood, bear right and weave along the slope to an obvious path across the foot of Dodgson Clough. Keep right at the fence beyond and pick your way through the young trees to join the path the main route follows.

Just before the viaduct, pick up a rough path climbing steeply left up to the lovely route along the former Halifax High Level Railway. Follow this right until it leads naturally onto a steep cobbled path. Follow the drive at the top to rejoin the road, which you follow right for half a mile to **Ovenden Wood**.

WHEATLEY VALLEY & MIXENDEN FROM HALIFAX

Distance: 10 miles (16km)
Ascent: 370m

Parking: Various pay car parks in Halifax, the best for this route being at North Bridge or Dean Clough Mills (which is free at the weekend). Various street parking along the route.

Public Transport: Halifax is easily accessible by bus and train. Buses also run regularly from Halifax to Mixenden and Wheatley, which enables the route to be shortened.

Character: A long but interesting exploration of an often overlooked corner of Calderdale. Though industry, landfill and housing developments have blighted the valley, it retains beautiful areas, like the charming oak woods of Shroggs and Ramsden Wood, and areas along the Hebble Brook where nature has re-established itself. This is not the simplest route though, largely due to quirks (and brazen obstructions) of the footpath network; hence there are a few sections with alternatives, but ultimately I hope it is a good guide to a difficult area to explore.

The route can be shortened to 8.5 miles (13km) by omitting the section between Halifax and Dean Clough Inn, starting the route in Wheatley, Ovenden Wood or Mixenden.

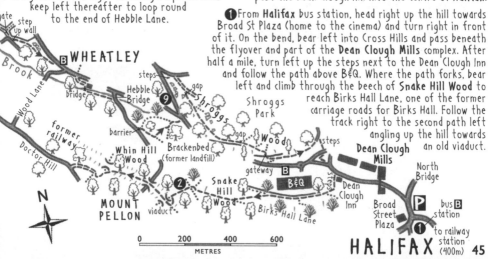

the clam bridge on the Hebble Brook at Mixenden

The name **Ovenden Wood** implies that this was once a far more wooded valley. The name Ovenden itself refers to the upper part of the valley, while **Mixenden** refers to a valley of dung-hills. The housing devlopment here is on the site of the former Webster's Brewery, which dominated the valley until its closure in 1996

Wheatley Viaduct and the railway that is followed through Whin Hill Wood is part of Halifax High Level Railway, built in the 1880s. The line ran from the Halifax-Queensbury line to St Paul's Station (near Queens Road), but the passenger service lasted just 26 years. In the 1890s a vast road bridge was also proposed across the valley near Shroggs Park.

8 Beyond the **viaduct**, turn right along Hops Lane and, near the end, cut through a path to Larch Close. At the road, immediately bear left up the wall - there is a bit of a step up the new gabions, but the path winds nicely through **Larch Close Wood** to Long Lane. Head down past Wood Lane, then take the next track on the right to pick up a path along the brook. At the end, turn right up Brackenbed Lane to an entrance to the former landfill site on the left. This was previously the more salubrious site of Birks Hall. There is a narrow path off to the left, but it can be overgrown so the right fork may be preferable; keep left thereafter to loop round to the end of Hebble Lane.

9 Head left up **Shroggs Road** to some steps leading up to the right and enter Shroggs Park. Bear right off the main track at a former gate and follow a delightful path through the oak trees and crags of **Shroggs Wood**. Keep right to descend through a formal gateway, but don't join the road; instead pick up a path along the bottom of the hillside. Where this reaches a road, turn right down the steps and cross Shroggs Road. A path leads down to Lee Bridge, which can be followed back past the Dean Clough Inn into the centre of **Halifax**.

1 From **Halifax** bus station, head right up the hill towards Broad St Plaza (home to the cinema) and turn right in front of it. On the bend, bear left into Cross Hills and pass beneath the flyover and part of the **Dean Clough Mills** complex. After half a mile, turn left up the steps next to the Dean Clough Inn and follow the path above B&Q. Where the path forks, bear left and climb through the beech of **Snake Hill Wood** to reach Birks Hall Lane, one of the former carriage roads for Birks Hall. Follow the track right to the second path left angling up the hill towards an old viaduct.

WAINHOUSE TOWER

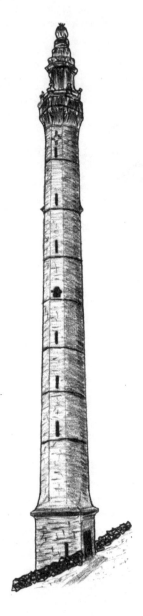

Wainhouse Tower is one of Halifax's most familiar
landmarks, standing sentinel over this part of the
Calder Valley and emitting an eerie green light by
night that has seen it compared to the Eye of Sauron
in *Lord of the Rings*. The octagonal tower was begun
in 1871 by John Wainhouse to release smoke from
his nearby Washer Lane Dye Works. This was
shortly after the Smoke Abatement Act of 1870, and
Wainhouse believed in improving the air of the town
by releasing the smoke as high has possible. However,
by the time it was completed in 1875, Wainhouse
had sold the works and the new owner wasn't
interested in the costly chimney. It was therefore
embellished with a gothic cupola and gallery and
used only as an observatory tower, although it was
said that the stonework was so ornate that there
was no room for any scientific equipment in the end.

It is sometimes referred to as the Tower of Spite
as it was thought Wainhouse built it to spy on his
neighbour, Sir Henry Edwards. The two had fought
over water rights and Edwards declared proudly that
no-one in the valley could see into his grounds. He
also profoundly disliked chimney towers, so he was
incredibly angered by Wainhouse's new viewing
gallery, claiming that Wainhouse was using it to spy
on his wife rather than the stars.

Wainhouse Tower was illuminated to celebrate the
Queen's Jubilee in 1977 and remains lit to this day. It
is the world's tallest folly and its 403 steps are now
open to the public on bank holidays.

CHAPTER 5 - BLACKBURN & HOLYWELL VALLEYS

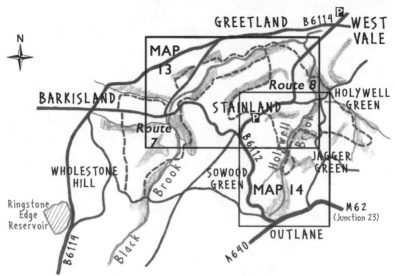

Map Sheet: OL21 (South Pennines)

Public Transport: Stainland, Holywell Green and West Vale are on the 536/537 bus routes between Halifax and Huddersfield, and the 539 from Halifax. Barkisland is on the following bus routes: 559 from Halifax, E7/E8 from Brighouse and 901 between Huddersfield and Hebden Bridge (the latter also goes through Sowood Green).

Parking: Free car parks in Stainland and West Vale, and layby near Barkisland Mill.

This quiet corner at the southern edge of Calderdale is too often overlooked. Though there is little substantial woodland in the area, the number of different groves and dingles give these valleys a verdant feel during the summer, and much of the surrounding area feels like the sort of grand parkland through which hunts would have taken place. This area was all part of the chapelry of Elland, which was made up of a number of parishes whose name all end in '-land', each defined by a separate ridge of land. Stainland and Greetland are thought to refer to stony or gravelly ground, while Soyland relates to swampy ground and Norland is self-evident. Barkisland is more complicated, deriving from Barsland (like nearby Barsey Clough) and referring possibly to an area of either wolves or birches. Both suggest a wild wooded area, and certainly the Blackburn Valley was far more wooded in the past, though it hasn't maintained its woodland as other tributaries of the Calder have.

The Black Brook (or Blackburn) flows from Scammonden and Deanhead Reservoirs, beneath the M62 and down through West Vale to join the River Calder. It is a largely quiet valley with little settlement on its course, yet is dominated by a line of substantial mills, particularly lower down where the bulk of the woodlands are concentrated. Access is particularly good here, whether from Stainland, Barkisland, Greetland or West Vale.

Holywell Brook joins it on the edge of West Vale, the amalgamation of a number of narrow wooded streams flowing down from Outlane and Old Lindley Moor. Access is more difficult along the Holywell Brook due to industry, private estates and a frustrating footpath network, but it is charming countryside with a patchwork of interesting small copses.

47

MAP 13: BLACKBURN VALLEY

The Black Brook flows through a valley that is still very industrial and has lost large chunks of its older woodland, but the lower end of the valley between West Vale, Stainland and Barkisland retains a distinct wooded charm. Beestones Wood is the finest ancient wood here, but Fall Spring Wood, Stubbing Wood, Zachariah Wood and North Wood are also rewarding. Bradley Hall golf course is squeezed in by the woods, but paths abound and the whole area is particularly accessible from Stainland.

The strangled body of Margaret Simpson was found in **Zachariah Wood** in 1964 and, despite stories linking it to the Yorkshire Ripper, no-one has ever been accused of her murder.

lion carving in Fall Spring Wood

0   100   200   300
METRES

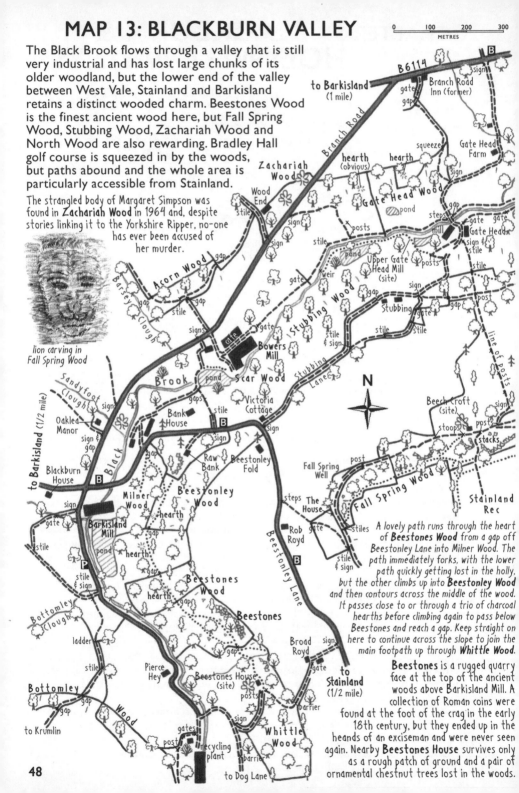

A lovely path runs through the heart of **Beestones Wood** from a gap of Beestonley Lane into Milner Wood. The path immediately forks, with the lower path quickly getting lost in the holly, but the other climbs up into **Beestonley Wood** and then contours across the middle of the wood. It passes close to or through a trio of charcoal hearths before climbing again to pass below Beestones and reach a gap. Keep straight on here to continue across the slope to join the main footpath up through **Whittle Wood**.

Beestones is a rugged quarry face at the top of the ancient woods above Barkisland Mill. A collection of Roman coins were found at the foot of the crag in the early 18th century, but they ended up in the heands of an exciseman and were never seen again. Nearby **Beestones House** survives only as a rough patch of ground and a pair of ornamental chestnut trees lost in the woods.

48

Barkisland Mill was built in the early 1900s on the site of an old burnt out mill, but it quickly closed down when the owner died soon after. It has now been converted into apartments. The last of **Ellistones Mill** was torn down very recently, leaving only modern factories along the valley and dim memories of the vast Greetland Dye Works. It was previously known as Outram's Mill after Benjamin Outram, who was the first to use alpaca wool in England, and had a large dam above that was a popular local beauty spot. This part of the valley is featured on novelty postcards in the early 20th century promoting **Outram's Valley**. Outram's Dam has since been lost beneath the factories, but there are is a pleasant pond just upstream where one can imagine promenading Edwardians.

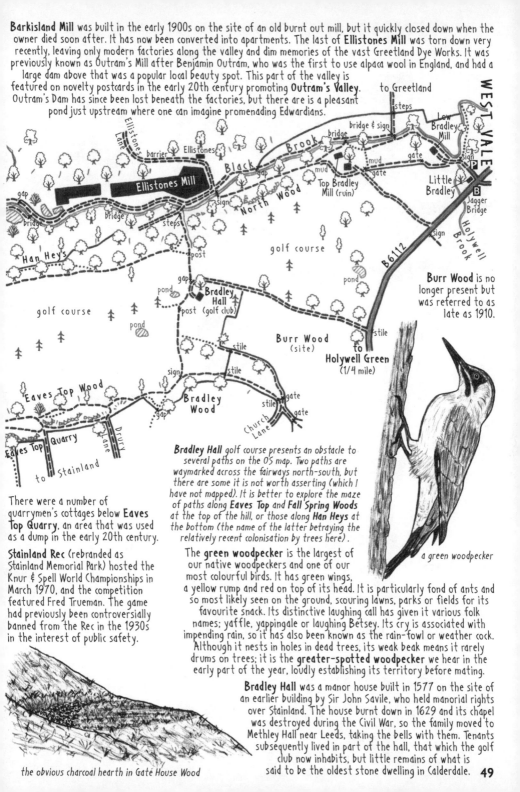

WEST VALE

to Greetland

steps

bridge & sign

Low Bradley Mill

bridge

gate

Little Bradley

Jagger Bridge

mud

gate

Top Bradley Mill (ruin)

Ellistones Lane

barrier

Ellistones

Black Brook

North Wood

sign

bridge

steps

sign

gap

Ellistones Mill

Han Heys

bridge

post

golf course

pond

B6112

Holywell Brook

sign

Burr Wood is no longer present but was referred to as late as 1910.

gap

pond

Bradley Hall (golf club)

post

pond

golf course

pond

stile

stile

Burr Wood (site)

to Holywell Green (1/4 mile)

stile

sign

stile

Eaves Top Wood

gap

Bradley Wood

stile

gate

gate

Church Lane

Drury Lane

Eaves Top Quarry

to Stainland

Bradley Hall golf course presents an obstacle to several paths on the OS map. Two paths are waymarked across the fairways north-south, but there are some it is not worth asserting (which I have not mapped). It is better to explore the maze of paths along **Eaves Top** and **Fall Spring Woods** at the top of the hill, or those along **Han Heys** at the bottom (the name of the latter betraying the relatively recent colonisation by trees here).

There were a number of quarrymen's cottages below **Eaves Top Quarry**, an area that was used as a dump in the early 20th century.

Stainland Rec (rebranded as Stainland Memorial Park) hosted the Knur & Spell World Championships in March 1970, and the competition featured Fred Trueman. The game had previously been controversially banned from the Rec in the 1930s in the interest of public safety.

The **green woodpecker** is the largest of our native woodpeckers and one of our most colourful birds. It has green wings, a yellow rump and red on top of its head. It is particularly fond of ants and so most likely seen on the ground, scouring lawns, parks or fields for its favourite snack. Its distinctive laughing call has given it various folk names; yaffle, yappingale or laughing Betsey. Its cry is associated with impending rain, so it has also been known as the rain-fowl or weather cock. Although it nests in holes in dead trees, its weak beak means it rarely drums on trees; it is the **greater-spotted woodpecker** we hear in the early part of the year, loudly establishing its territory before mating.

a green woodpecker

Bradley Hall was a manor house built in 1577 on the site of an earlier building by Sir John Savile, who held manorial rights over Stainland. The house burnt down in 1629 and its chapel was destroyed during the Civil War, so the family moved to Methley Hall near Leeds, taking the bells with them. Tenants subsequently lived in part of the hall, that which the golf club now inhabits, but little remains of what is said to be the oldest stone dwelling in Calderdale.

the obvious charcoal hearth in Gate House Wood

49

MAP 14: HOLYWELL BROOK & GOSPORT CLOUGH

Holywell Brook is a charming wooded enclave that is crossed by no roads between Stainland, Holywell Brook, Outlane and Sowood. Stumbling across the area for the first time, with its grand estates and ornamental trees, it doesn't feel like part of Calderdale. The only frustration is that the limited footpath network makes it difficult to come up with a decent round walk. Yet it is an area well worth exploring, if only to see the Thunnerley red deer.

The houses of Brooklands Avenue are built on the site of Brooklands House with some of the same stone. It was built in 1865 by Samuel Shaw, who owned Brookroyd Mills and was a great bird lover. The steps leading up to the house remain at the top of Shaw Park, which was originally its grounds. As well as the ornamental lake and arches, the remains of a number of castellated follies can be seen, the finest being the two aviaries in the north-west corner.

There are two routes south out of *Stainland*. One follows the well-defined Carr Hall Lane from Stainland Cross. The other goes down Cliffe Lane and across a garden, before following a wall across a series of fields to reach Stanley Lane.

The tracks up Holywell Brook, Carr Hall and Castle Farm are all private, but a lovely path follows the top of *Thunnerley Wood* to the east of the stream and joins Carr Hall Lane above Castle Farm.

Carr Hall Castle (originally Redman's Farm) was built in the 19th century by the Shaws of Brooklands House as a folly to improve their view, but also served as quarters for those looking after their shire horses. It was recently restored and won the TV show / Own *Britain's Best Home*.

Thunnerley is a corruption of Thornilees. The beautiful red deer in the park below Thunnerley Wood are want to make extra-ordinary noises. It starts out as a baa and ends sounding like a whale.

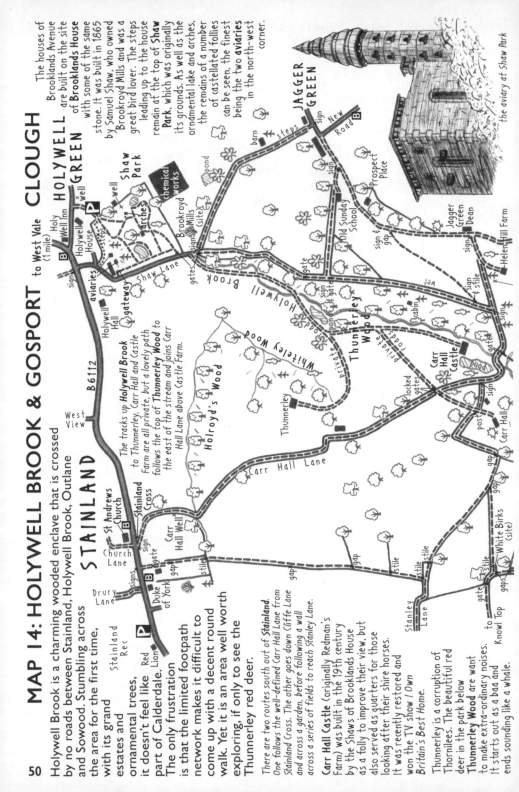

the aviary at Shaw Park

to West Vale (1 mile)

STAINLAND
B6112
West View
HOLYWELL GREEN
JAGGER GREEN
Shaw Park
Holywell Hall
Shaw Lane
Holywell Brook
Whiteley Wood
Holroyd's Wood
Thunnerley Wood
Carr Hall Lane
Carr Hall Castle
Carr Hall
Carr Hall Well
St Andrews Church
Stainland Cross
Church Lane
Drury Lane
Duke of York
Red Lion
Stainland Rec
Holywell House
Holy Well Inn
Brookroyd Mills (site)
chemical works
Old Sunday School
Prospect Place
Jagger Green Dean
Helen Hill Farm
New Road
Stanley Lane
White Birks (site)
to Knowl Top
Thunnerley

The **Holy Well Inn** in Holywell Green was renamed in 1980 when a 60ft well was discovered beneath an outhouse there. Previously it was the Waggon and Horses, then the Station Hotel after the Stainland and Holywell Green terminus of the branch line in the valley below. Yet neither this, nor the other nearby wells – a stone trough by the road declaring 'Holy Well Improved 1843' and the rebuilt **Stainland Well in Shaw Park** – are thought to be the holy well after which the village is named. In fact, it is likely that **St Helen's Well** (alongside Helen Hill Farm near Jagger Green) was a pre-Christian well later dedicated to St Helen, like many in Yorkshire. The mother of Constantine the Great is often held to be a Brigantine princess and so was venerated across the north of England. The well was a popular site of pilgrimage in the Middle Ages and had a medieval chantry chapel alongside. The well still has water flowing through three basins built in the 18th century, but is on private land. With the Victorian fashion for reviving old springs, a spring in the village was restored as a makeshift holy well in 1843, though it is little more than a flowerbed today.

A tramp known as Treacle (after he tried to buy a yard of treacle) lived in the stables at **Carr Hall** and sold curative herbs around the area.

The most appealing and accessible section of **Holywell Brook** lies between Carr Hall Lane and Gosport Clough. There are plenty of paths here between groves of both beech and oak. Beyond Gosport Clough, Holywell Brook can be followed all the way up to a track on the edge of **Sowood**, though the trees quickly thin out. **Gosport Clough** is a more appealing dingle but can only be reached by the path between Far Sowood and Mulehouse Lane.

Sowood would seem to be an obvious contraction of south wood, but may also refer to a medieval pig farm, which the manors often established in areas of woodland.

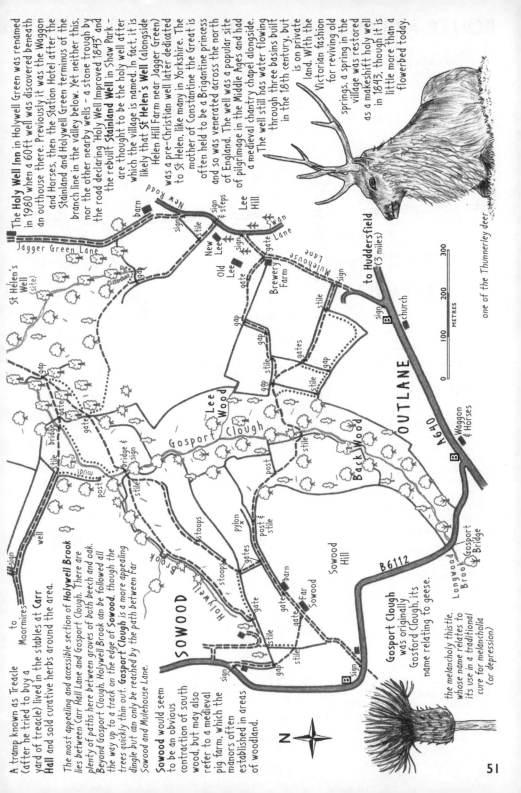

Gosport Clough was originally Gosford Clough, its name relating to geese.

the melancholy thistle, whose name relates to its use in a traditional cure for melancholia (or depression)

one of the Thurnerley deer

to Moormires

Jagger Green Lane — New Road — St Helen's Well (site) — New Lee — Old Lee — Lee Lane — Lee Hill — Brewery Farm — Mulehouse Lane — to Huddersfield (3 miles) — church — OUTLANE — A640 — Waggon & Horses — Back Wood — Lee Wood — Gosport Clough — Sowood Hill — Far Sowood — SOWOOD — Holywell Brook — Longwood Brook — Gosport Bridge — B6112

METRES 0 100 200 300

N

ROUTE 7: BLACKBURN VALLEY FROM BARKISLAND

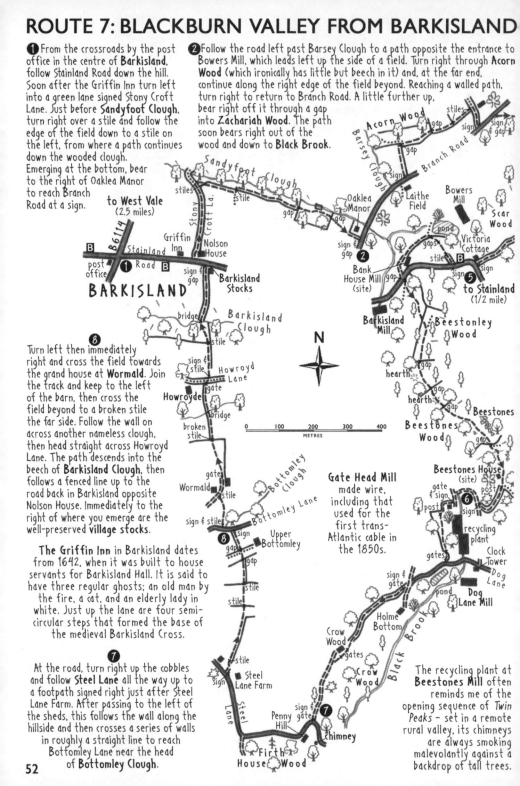

1 From the crossroads by the post office in the centre of **Barkisland**, follow Stainland Road down the hill. Soon after the Griffin Inn turn left into a green lane signed Stony Croft Lane. Just before **Sandyfoot Clough**, turn right over a stile and follow the edge of the field down to a stile on the left, from where a path continues down the wooded clough. Emerging at the bottom, bear to the right of Oaklea Manor to reach Branch Road at a sign.

2 Follow the road left past Barsey Clough to a path opposite the entrance to Bowers Mill, which leads left up the side of a field. Turn right through **Acorn Wood** (which ironically has little but beech in it) and, at the far end, continue along the right edge of the field beyond. Reaching a walled path, turn right to return to Branch Road. A little further up, bear right off it through a gap into **Zachariah Wood**. The path soon bears right out of the wood and down to **Black Brook**.

8 Turn left then immediately right and cross the field towards the grand house at **Wormald**. Join the track and keep to the left of the barn, then cross the field beyond to a broken stile the far side. Follow the wall on across another nameless clough, then head straight across Howroyd Lane. The path descends into the beech of **Barkisland Clough**, then follows a fenced line up to the road back in Barkisland opposite Nolson House. Immediately to the right of where you emerge are the well-preserved **village stocks**.

The **Griffin Inn** in Barkisland dates from 1642, when it was built to house servants for Barkisland Hall. It is said to have three regular ghosts; an old man by the fire, a cat, and an elderly lady in white. Just up the lane are four semi-circular steps that formed the base of the medieval Barkisland Cross.

7 At the road, turn right up the cobbles and follow **Steel Lane** all the way up to a footpath signed right just after Steel Lane Farm. After passing on the left of the sheds, this follows the wall along the hillside and then crosses a series of walls in roughly a straight line to reach Bottomley Lane near the head of Bottomley Clough.

Gate Head Mill made wire, including that used for the first trans-Atlantic cable in the 1850s.

The recycling plant at **Beestones Mill** often reminds me of the opening sequence of *Twin Peaks* – set in a remote rural valley, its chimneys are always smoking malevolantly against a backdrop of tall trees.

to West Vale (2.5 miles)

to Stainland (1/2 mile)

3 Follow the path left along the side of Black Brook to a track by the ruins of **Gate Head Mill**. Cross the bridge and turn left through a kissing gate to follow the other side of the river to an attractive pond. Soon after, cross the river again and continue along it join the road alongside the large factory on the site of the old **Ellistones Mill**.

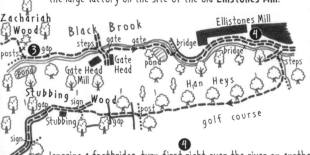

Barkisland Stocks

Howroyde Hall was built in 1642 on the site of an earlier hall by the prominent Horton family, after whom Great and Little Horton in Bradford are named (interestingly these were originally christened Horton Magna and Horton Parva). In the 1940s, Ivor Novello wrote We'll Gather Green Lilacs in the Spring Again while visiting Howroyde. Nearby **Barkisland Hall** was built four years earlier by John Gledhill, whose brother Richard died in the Civil War and is said to haunt the area. There is no doubt the area around Barkisland retains the air of an open estate; Howroyde was surrounded by a deer park and much of the area was used by the hunt from Barkisland Hall's kennels.

4 Ignoring a footbridge, turn first right over the river on another factory road, then immediately go left up some steps. Follow the stream until a muddy path forks right up the bank; this becomes a clear path along the edge of the golf course above, following the top of the woods all the way. Reaching a waymark post, continue straight on along the top of the older trees of **Stubbing Wood**. Go straight on along the track at the far end, passing in front of Stubbing to join the walled bridleway along the top of the wood. Follow the beautifully oak- and ash-lined **Stubbing Lane** all the way to Beestonley Lane.

5 Turn right down the hill, which it is is possible to stay on, but to avoid the narrow kerbs, turn right at a sign part way down. The path descends steeply to the stream, where you turn left through the site of Bank House Mill. Follow the track round to the road and then duck through a gap opposite into **Milner Wood**. Fork left immediately and ascend to a path through the birch trees of Beestonley Wood. Continue across a trio of broken down walls in **Beestones Wood** and bear left up towards the quarried face of **Beestones**. At a gap beyond, carry straight on across the slope to reach a clear path near the site of **Beestones House**. Bear right to descend to the road.

The **wood anemone** (also known as windflower or smell fox) is one of the best indicator species for ancient woodland, as it spreads only through its roots and is said to travel at just six feet every hundred years. Its name relates to the Greek wind god Anemos, who arrived in the spring and, at this time of year, it carpets woodlands like Beestones Wood with a galaxy of star-like white flowers. Cow wheat, lesser stitchwort and wood speedwell are also found in this beautiful woodland. Though the wood anemone is poisonous to both man and beast, the hoverfly remains particularly keen on pollinating it.

wood anemone

Distance: 6 miles (9.5km)

Ascent: 290m

Parking: Street parking in Barkisland along Stainland Road near the post office.

Public Transport: Barkisland is on the following bus routes: 559 from Halifax, E7/E8 from Brighouse and 901 between Huddersfield and Hebden Bridge.

Character: A choice exploration of the middle of the Blackburn Valley, taking in the charms of Sandyfoot Clough, Zachariah Wood, Stubbing Wood and Beestones Wood, before heading up the less wooded upper valley and returning via the former parkland on the slopes above. All the walking is straightforward on fairly obvious paths.

6 Turn right along the road round the large recycling plant. Turn left beyond the stream, and then go right through a gate just before a bungalow. A path winds through the trees above to emerge on **Dog Lane**, which you follow right up the hill. At the top, head straight on through a gate into a green lane that leads up to **Crow Wood**. Keep left of the farm through a series of gates before rejoining the track on through the replanted woodland.

ROUTE 8: HOLYWELL BROOK FROM STAINLAND

Distance: 6 miles (9.5km)

Ascent: 280m

Parking: Free car park on B6112 by Stainland Memorial Park.

Public Transport: Stainland is on the 536/537 bus routes between Halifax and Huddersfield, and the 539 from Halifax.

Character: A relatively simple circuit of the woods around Stainland and Holywell Green, taking in a number of tree-lined valleys, as well as the quarries of Eaves Top. The frustrating path network means a short optional loop leads from the main route up to Gosport Clough, but this is one of the most charming corners in the area.

There are medieval walls in **Fall Spring Wood** that were originally thought to date from the Iron Age. There are also a number of interesting carvings on stones in the wood, thought to be the work of Victorian quarrymen – look out for a lion (see p48), a face and a house, the latter very close to the route.

①

From the car park in the middle of **Stainland**, go through the arch into Stainland Memorial Park (known as Stainland Rec) and keep left along the wall. At the far end, turn right down a vehicle track and follow it round to the left until it opens out into a field. Keep left along the wall, following it round to a stile, almost immediately after which you turn right over another stile. Follow a narrow path along the top of **Fall Spring Wood** and, beyond a large quarry, fork left down a rough path. Rejoin the main path by a stoop at the foot of another quarry.

②

Head straight across the open area of **Eaves Top Quarry**, then bear left shortly before some railings to stay below the rocks. Fork left again before the path doubles back. Continue along the slope to a sign, where you bear left across the golf course. Head down the slope to the left of a grove of trees and the track by **Bradley Hall**, dropping into a wooded hollow. Pick up a path alongside the stream here that emerges by the site of **Ellistones Mill**.

③

Back on the main route, continue down the walled path of Carr Hall Lane to cross Holywell Brook by the restored house at **Carr Hall Castle**. Stay on the track for half a mile all the way back into the village. Emerging by **Stainland Cross**, turn left to return to the car park.

Though its shaft is thought to be Saxon, **Stainland Cross** is of uncertain origin, and may have served as a medieval wayside cross. It was moved into its current position when cottages on the site were taken down and the road realigned. Its head is carved on each side with St Andrew's Cross (the saltire), but may have been added when **St Andrew's Church** was built in 1839. Previously the chapel here was independent, serving all denominations (Wesleyans, Methodists and Anglicans) as it was the only place of worship in the area.

Stainland Cross

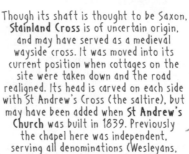

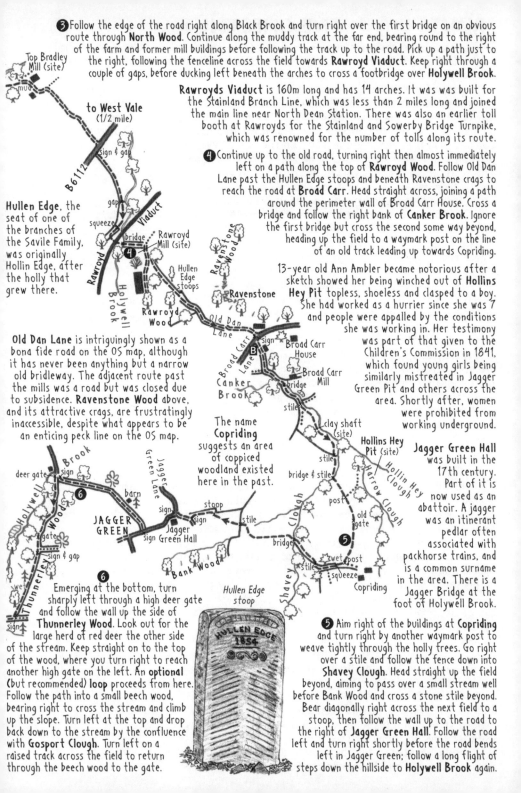

3 Follow the edge of the road right along Black Brook and turn right over the first bridge on an obvious route through **North Wood**. Continue along the muddy track at the far end, bearing round to the right of the farm and former mill buildings before following the track up to the road. Pick up a path just to the right, following the fenceline across the field towards **Rawroyd Viaduct**. Keep right through a couple of gaps, before ducking left beneath the arches to cross a footbridge over **Holywell Brook**.

Rawroyds Viaduct is 160m long and has 14 arches. It was was built for the Stainland Branch Line, which was less than 2 miles long and joined the main line near North Dean Station. There was also an earlier toll booth at Rawroyds for the Stainland and Sowerby Bridge Turnpike, which was renowned for the number of tolls along its route.

4 Continue up to the old road, turning right then almost immediately left on a path along the top of **Rawroyd Wood**. Follow Old Dan Lane past the Hullen Edge stoops and beneath Ravenstone crags to reach the road at **Broad Carr**. Head straight across, joining a path around the perimeter wall of Broad Carr House. Cross a bridge and follow the right bank of **Canker Brook**. Ignore the first bridge but cross the second some way beyond, heading up the field to a waymark post on the line of an old track leading up towards Copriding.

13-year old Ann Ambler became notorious after a sketch showed her being winched out of **Hollins Hey Pit** topless, shoeless and clasped to a boy. She had worked as a hurrier since she was 7 and people were appalled by the conditions she was working in. Her testimony was part of that given to the Children's Commission in 1841, which found young girls being similarly mistreated in Jagger Green Pit and others across the area. Shortly after, women were prohibited from working underground.

Jagger Green Hall was built in the 17th century. Part of it is now used as an abattoir. A jagger was an itinerant pedlar often associated with packhorse trains, and is a common surname in the area. There is a Jagger Bridge at the foot of Holywell Brook.

Hullen Edge, the seat of one of the branches of the Savile Family, was originally Hollin Edge, after the holly that grew there.

Old Dan Lane is intriguingly shown as a bona fide road on the OS map, although it has never been anything but a narrow old bridleway. The adjacent route past the mills was a road but was closed due to subsidence. **Ravenstone Wood** above, and its attractive crags, are frustratingly inaccessible, despite what appears to be an enticing peck line on the OS map.

The name **Copriding** suggests an area of coppiced woodland existed here in the past.

6 Emerging at the bottom, turn sharply left through a high deer gate and follow the wall up the side of **Thunnerley Wood**. Look out for the large herd of red deer the other side of the stream. Keep straight on to the top of the wood, where you turn right to reach another high gate on the left. An **optional** (but recommended) loop proceeds from here. Follow the path into a small beech wood, bearing right to cross the stream and climb up the slope. Turn left at the top and drop back down to the stream by the confluence with **Gosport Clough**. Turn left on a raised track across the field to return through the beech wood to the gate.

Hullen Edge stoop

HULLEN EDGE 1854

5 Aim right of the buildings at **Copriding** and turn right by another waymark post to weave tightly through the holly trees. Go right over a stile and follow the fence down into **Shavey Clough**. Head straight up the field beyond, aiming to pass over a small stream well before Bank Wood and cross a stone stile beyond. Bear diagonally right across the next field to a stoop, then follow the wall up to the road to the right of **Jagger Green Hall**. Follow the road left and turn right shortly before the road bends left in Jagger Green; follow a long flight of steps down the hillside to **Holywell Brook** again.

Map labels: Top Bradley Mill (site), mud, to West Vale (1/2 mile), B6112, sign & gap, gap, squeeze, Viaduct, bridge, Rawroyd Mill (site), Rawroyd, Holywell Brook, Rawroyd Wood, Hullen Edge stoops, Ravenstone Wood, Ravenstone, Old Dan Lane, sign, Broad Carr House, Broad Carr Lane, Broad Carr Mill, bridge, Canker Brook, stile, clay shaft (site), stile, bridge & stile, Hollins Hey Pit (site), Hollin Hey Clough, Harrow Clough, post, old gate, Clough, Shavey, squeeze, wet post, stile, Copriding, Holywell Brook, deer gate, sign, barn, Jagger Green Lane, sign, stoop, stile, JAGGER GREEN, sign, Jagger Green Hall, bridge, Bank Wood, gate, sign & gap, Thunnerley Wood, wet, sign

THE CHESTNUT

The name chestnut comes from the Latin *castanea* and relates to a whole family of trees native to the Mediterranean and North America. Interestingly the horse chestnut is not one of these; it is actually an unrelated tree native only to a small part of the Balkans. It was not introduced until the late 16th century, but quickly became popular as an ornamental tree because of its remarkable candelabra-like flowers. It is striking in all seasons, whether for its thick pendulous limbs or its huge palmate leaves. We of course know it best for its inedible seeds. Though the game of conkers was first recorded in 1848 on the Isle of Wight, it is thought to have been played earlier with shells, the name a derivation of 'conch'.

The wood itself is of very little use other than general turnery, so the tree has remained almost entirely ornamental. In recent years, horse chestnuts have been attacked by disease and many of our local trees are identifiable by their mottled brown leaves and the bleeding canker oozing out of their cracked bark.

The sweet chestnut is a fine tree with toothed leaves and a spiralling growth that can be seen in the patterns in its bark. It is generally thought to have been introduced by the Romans, though some chestnut charcoal hearths have now been identified in ancient campsites. It is now naturalised, but occurs as pure woodland only on the sandstone ridges of the Weald in south-east England, where it was widely coppiced for use as hop-poles. There are very few in the Calder Valley, though, as it does not produce viable seed at this latitude. Its edible seeds are known as marrons and, though growing smaller than in the Mediterranean, can still make a great nut loaf.

horse chestnut flowers

THE LIME

The lime is a romantic tree, beautifully formed with heart-shaped leaves and distinctive drooping branches. It tends to have a lot of growth around its base and is able to self-sucker when these branches reach the ground, so much so that it is very hard to kill a lime tree. They can also be identified by the sticky black mess beneath them; known as honeydew, this is the waste from aphids feeding on the sap and helps generate nitrogen-fixing bacteria in the soil. Both the small-leafed lime (also known as pry) and large-leafed lime are native to Britain, but are now far less common than the hybrid common lime. The small-leaved lime once covered most of lowland England, but its presence steadily dwindled and it is now rarely found as pure woodland.

At this latitude, however, lime does not seed naturally, so it can be assumed that all lime trees in the area were planted; although there is a Pry Farm in Rawtonstall, *pry* may also be dialect for some types of coarse grass. Lime trees were planted, often in avenues, in urban parks and places like Linden House in Hebden Bridge (*linden* originally referred to something made from lime) as they were pollution resistant, much like London planes. Lime is fine grained and doesn't warp, so it was prized for carving, as well as making shields and piano keys. Its inner bark (or bast) was used for making ropes, mats and other fibres, while the medicinal scent of its blossom resulted in it being planted along roads and being renowned as a cure for epilepsy.

lime leaf

CHAPTER 6 - RYBURN VALLEY

Map Sheet: OL21 (South Pennines)

Public Transport: Sowerby Bridge is on the main Caldervale train line. Ripponden and Sowerby Bridge are on the regular 560/561/562 bus routes, the former continuing to Rishworth. The 901 runs more infrequently through Ripponden between Huddersfield and Hebden Bridge.

Parking: Free car parks in Ripponden, Sowerby Bridge and by Ryburn Reservoir.

The **Ryburn Valley** is one of the major tributaries of the Calder Valley – so much so that I mistook it for the main valley on my first visit to the area. Joining the Calder at Sowerby Bridge, the River Ryburn cascades attractively off the moors via a series of reservoirs, before powering the mills of Rishworth, Ripponden, Kebroyd and Triangle. The name *ryburn* has been said to refer to either a fierce or reedy stream, or possibly a roebuck. The northern end of the valley has also been known as Sowerby Dean.

Writing in 1816, T. D. Whitaker described the Ryburn Valley as 'hanging oak woods... the most pleasing of the dependencies of the Calder'. Even now, driving up the A58, one is struck by the wall of woods lining the steep eastern side of the valley, even if they are now composed as much of beech and sycamore as oak. Many of these trees were planted by John Rawson, a landowner responsible for planting 100,000 trees in the late 19th century. Further up the valley, Ryburn Reservoir is idyllically shrouded in trees and Turner Wood (in Booth Dean Clough) is one of the area's most surprising corners of woodland. The valley is best explored from the beautiful conservation village of Ripponden.

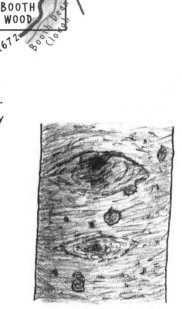

beech eyes in Rough Hey Wood

MAP 15: LOWER RYBURN VALLEY

The Lower Ryburn Valley, between Kebroyd and Sowerby Bridge, was dominated by mills and industry, but retains a dense swathe of trees until Watson Mills on the edge of Sowerby Bridge. The closure of the old Rishworth Branch Line in 1958 means there is now a fine bridleway through the heart of the woods, with various paths leading off from the numerous bridges. Rough Hey, Butterworth End and Highlee Woods climb steeply up the eastern side of the valley and offer plenty of fine walking among the mixed woodland. The whole area is easily accessed various places along the A58.

The Ryburn Valley is renowned for its rush-**bearing festival** in early September. As across much of the north-west, several townships in Calderdale (Lumbutts, Cragg Vale, Midgley, Brighouse and Illingworth) used to have a similar festival in the week leading up to the Thump Sunday. This celebrated the start of the new church year, when fresh rushes were cut and laid on the church floor for the winter. With folk dancing at pubs along the way, these events had a tendency to dissolve into drunken occasions, with brawls between rival rushcarts. Some were banned and many simply fell out of fashion. Sowerby Bridge revived a centuries-old tradition in 1977 to celebrate the Queen's Silver Jubilee. A lavish rushcart (designed to replicate that seen in images from 1906) is pulled along a nine-mile route between Warley and Ripponden over two days by sixty men in clogs and Panama hats, and there is still much drinking and dancing.

The **Triangle** area was known as Stansfield Pond before the construction of the Halifax and Blackstone Edge Turnpike in 1635, which created a triangle at the bottom of Mill Bank road. This was one of the country's first turnpike trusts and its line is followed by the A58. The Triangle was built as a coaching inn on this area in 1767, giving its name to the village. The adjacent **Stile** area was formerly Chapel Stile.

There are a number of paths through the open beech trees of **Dodge Royd Wood**. The old railway line is muddy and often best left to horses and bikes, but a clear path follows its northern embankment while another cuts down past the former **Millhouse Dyeworks**.

The house name **Bullace Trees** refers to a bolace, a wild plum tree.

Stansfield Mill Bridge is cast iron and assumed to have been built shortly after the great Ripponden flood of 1722, replacing an earlier stone structure.

The long straight section of Rochdale Road leading out of Sowerby Bridge is known as **Long Chimney** after the 50ft high octagonal mill chimney near the bottom of Lower Brook Well Lane. It served Millhouse Mill, but has been shortened in the last few years and is no longer deserving of its nickname.

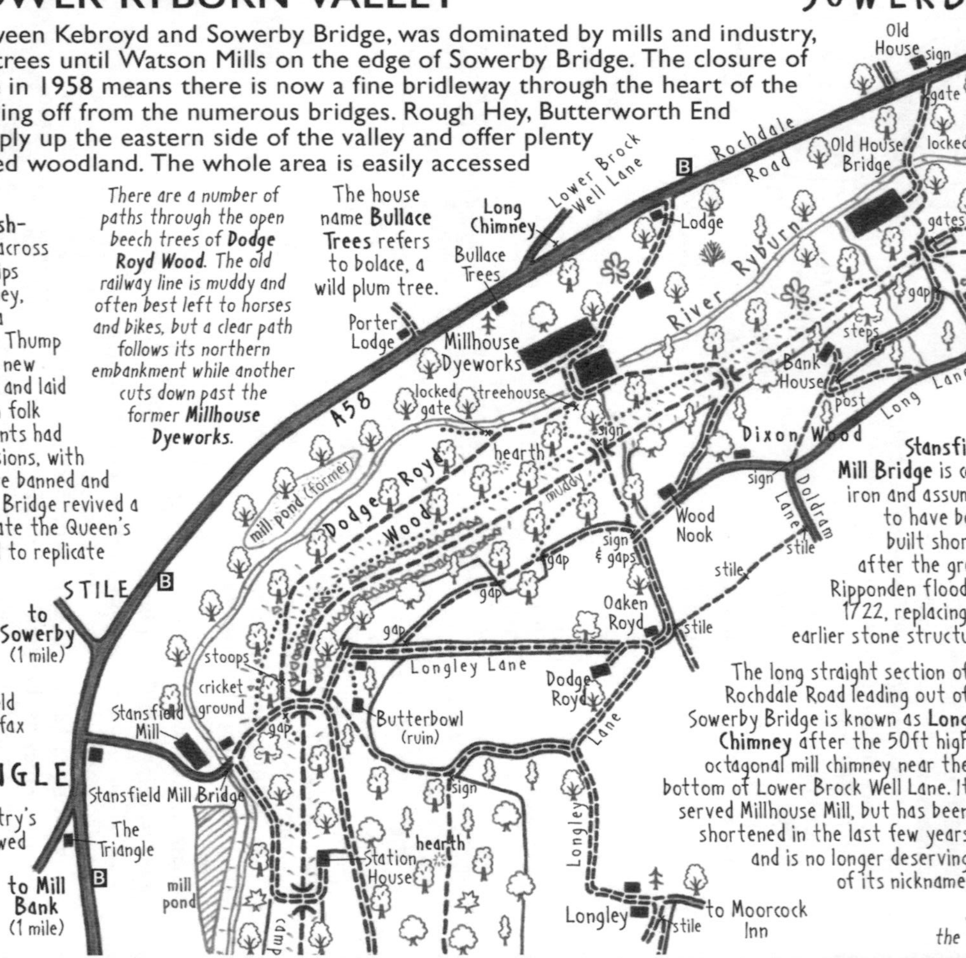

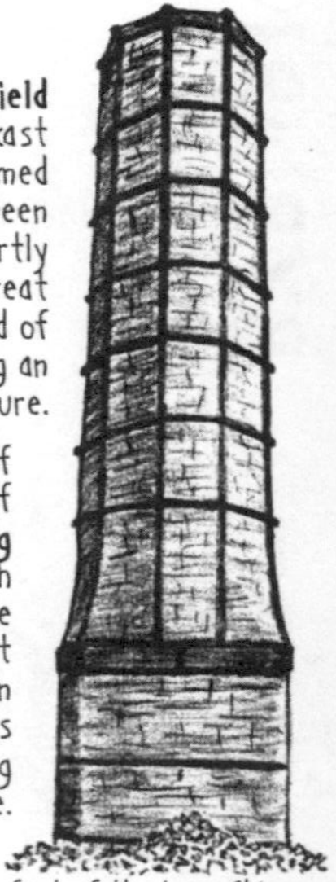

the foot of the Long Chimney

The mills of the Ryburn Valley were renowned for producing **kersey**, a coarse and thick cloth produced from inferior wool. It was a narrow cloth that could be produced by a family in one week, and Daniel Defoe describes descending the valley in 1774 and finding tenters outside every house with kersey drying on each one. Its blue cloth was said to have clothed the entire British navy. Yet by the early 19th century, nearly every mill in the valley had been adapted almost overnight for the spinning of cotton as a result of the labour-saving machinery developed in the cotton industry.

Rough Hey Wood is largely owned by Calderdale Council and is Open Access other than around Rough Hey itself. The areas of beech plantation have recently been thinned to allow birch and oak regeneration, and brash barriers laid to stop soil erosion. Rough Hey itself is now a pet cemetery.

Little Haven (originally Little Heaven) was the site of an Edwardian tea garden with camping grounds, and was reached by the former stepping stones at Alexandra Bridge.

The path across *Highlee Clough* from Little Haven can be hard to trace, especially near the clough where it is marked only by yellow splodges of paint on the trees. It emerges by a waymarker at a junction of paths; the path leading uncertainly left down the hill becomes a lovely way along the top of **Rough Hey Wood.**

N

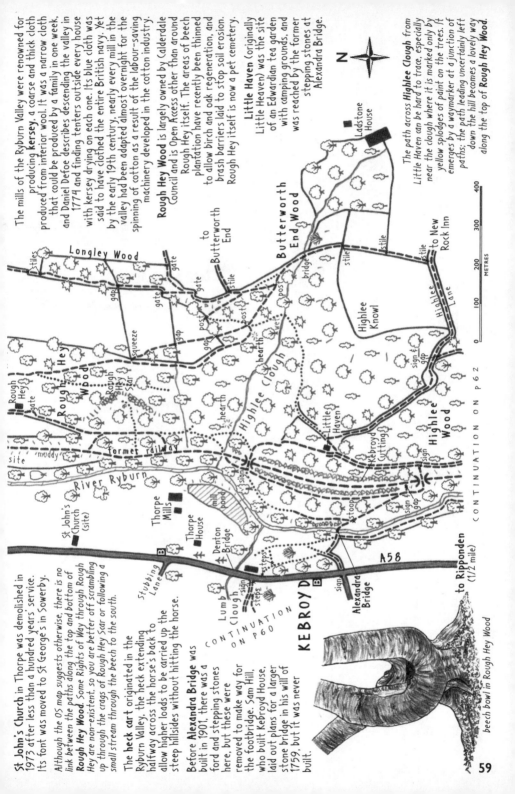

Ladstone House

to Butterworth End

Longley Wood

Butterworth End Wood

to New Rock Inn

Highlee Lane

Highlee Knowl

Rough Hey Wood

Rough Hey

Rough Hey Star

squeeze

Highlee Clough

hearth

hearth

hearth

Little Haven

Highlee Wood

Kebroyd Cutting

stile

post

post

gate

gate

gate

gate

stile

bridge

stile

gap

gap

gap

gap

gap

gap

gap

post

well

sign & gap

sign

sign & gap

sign

Rough Hey

gate

gate

site

muddy

former railway

River Ryburn

St John's Church (site)

Thorpe Mills

Thorpe House

mill pond

Denton Bridge

sign

sign

stoop

stile

stile

KEBROYD

Stubbing Lane

Lumb Clough

steps

sign

stile

steps

sign

sign

Alexandra Bridge

A58

to Ripponden (1/2 mile)

0 100 200 300 400
METRES

CONTINUATION ON P62

CONTINUATION ON P60

St John's Church in Thorpe was demolished in 1973 after less than a hundred years' service. Its font was moved to St George's in Sowerby.

Although the OS map suggests otherwise, there is no link between the paths along the top and bottom of *Rough Hey Wood.* Some Rights of Way through Rough Hey are non-existent, so you are better off scrambling up through the crags of Rough Hey Star or following a small stream through the beech to the south.

The **heck cart** originated in the Ryburn Valley, the heck extending halfway across the horse's back to allow higher loads to be carried up the steep hillsides without hitting the horse.

Before **Alexandra Bridge** was built in 1901, there was a ford and stepping stones here, but these were removed to make way for the footbridge. Sam Hill, who built Kebroyd House, laid out plans for a larger stone bridge in his will of 1759, but it was never built.

beech bowl in Rough Hey Wood

59

MAP 16: LUMB & SEVERHILLS CLOUGHS

These wooded cloughs form an attractive siding off the main Ryburn Valley that is largely dominated by beech plantations. Fiddle (or Kebroyd) Wood is open and easily accessed from Kebroyd or Mill Bank, but access is more difficult beyond the junction of Lumb and Severhills Cloughs. The upper part of Lumb Clough is entirely inaccessible, while there are limited paths in Severhills Clough. The latter once housed a number of mills, including Soyland Mill, now an evocative ruin.

The name **lumb** is given to the valley by the ancient settlement upstream from Mill Bank. In Yorkshire it either refers to a wooded section of a clough or a small pool, and remains a local Sowerby surname to this day.

Severhills Clough (also known as Shaw Edge or Blackshaw Clough) is a beautiful valley but hard to access beyond the path across the valley between Shaw Edge and Clay House, which is overgrown on the north side of the valley but otherwise fairly clear. Where the Calderdale Way heads off up Gough Lane, there is supposed to be another public footpath from Wood End to Severhills Mill but the only traceable path follows the top of Gough Wood and eventually links up with the other path.

Rather than referring to elves, **Aufhole** appears to be a corruption of Haughole.

There were mills at the **Kebroyd Mills** site from the 17th century. The largest, used for silk spinning, was destroyed by fire in 1904, when only a blackened Bible was salvaged from the ruins.

This bible was subsequently displayed in a glass case when the mill was rebuilt. In 2006 fire raged again, this time suspected arson, and now little remains of the site on Lumb Clough.

As well as the main paths through **Fiddle Wood**, a good path follows the stream and then a line of mill ponds down **Lumb Clough**. It re-emerges by the site of **Kebroyd Mills** at the downstream end.

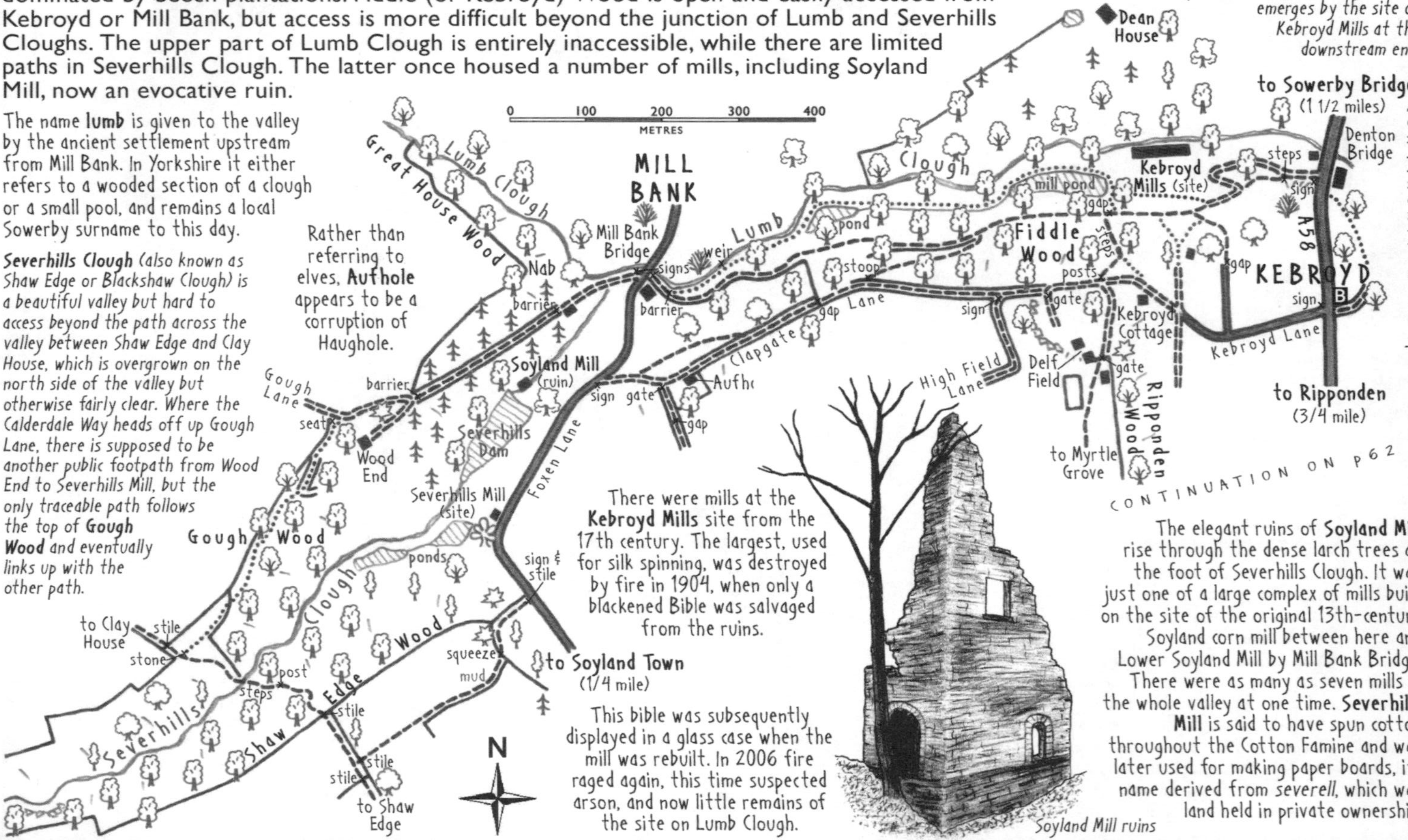

The elegant ruins of **Soyland Mill** rise through the dense larch trees at the foot of Severhills Clough. It was just one of a large complex of mills built on the site of the original 13th-century Soyland corn mill between here and **Lower Soyland Mill** by Mill Bank Bridge. There were as many as seven mills in the whole valley at one time. **Severhills Mill** is said to have spun cotton throughout the Cotton Famine and was later used for making paper boards, its name derived from severell, which was land held in private ownership.

Soyland Mill ruins

CONTINUATION ON p59

CONTINUATION ON p62

to Sowerby Bridge (1½ miles)

to Ripponden (¾ mile)

Denton Bridge

KEBROYD

A58

Dean House

Kebroyd Mills (site)

Kebroyd Cottage

Kebroyd Lane

Ripponden Wood

to Myrtle Grove

Fiddle Wood

Del Field

High Field Lane

mill pond

Clough

Lumb

Clough

Stoop

Pond

Capgate

Aufh.

weir

signs

barrier

MILL BANK

Mill Bank Bridge

Soyland Mill (ruin)

Mab

barrier

Severhills Dam

Severhills Mill (site)

ponds

Lumb Clough

Great House Wood

Gough Lane

Wood End

barrier

Gough Wood

Foxen Lane

sign gate

sign

to Soyland Town (¼ mile)

stile

squeeze

mud

Severhills

Clough

to Shaw Edge

stile

post

steps

stone

stile

to Clay House

N

METRES
0   100   200   300   400

THE SYCAMORE

The sycamore has attracted a bad reputation for its tendency to colonise large areas and reduce biodiversity, and as a non-native outsider is the victim of a certain nationalist mentality. John Evelyn wrote scathingly in *Sylva* in 1664, 'the honey-dew leaves… turn to mucilage and noxious insects, and putrefy with the first moisture of the season, so as they contaminate and mar our walks'. Sure enough, the sycamore's extensive shading does inhibit the growth of younger native trees, while its heavy leaf-fall results in a dull mushy woodland floor with little of interest (a particular disappointment as a member of the maple family that produce such flourishes of colour in so many other species). However, in spring the sycamore is in its element. Its leaves emerge among the first of the broadleaves, brightening up the woods as early as March, and are often accompanied by vast swathes of bluebells which thrive beneath better drained areas of sycamore. Its pale green flowers hang from its branches like bunches of grapes and the bark of its older trees becomes a patchwork of craggy plates, often leaving underneath a contour-like map of lines that is among its most appealing features. The latter is why it was known as the plane tree in Scotland and has the proper name *Acer pseudoplatanus* (literally 'like a plane tree').

The sycamore is an unrivalled success story. Introduced sometime in the late Medieval period, having originated in the Balkans, it was rare until the 1600s, but began to spread widely with the aid of its winged 'helicopter' seeds, exploiting disturbed ground and capable of establishing on most soils. It became more common in the north-west as it withstands pollution particularly well, because it sheds its bark to get rid of toxins, and was widely planted for making the shuttles that drove the weaving industry. The soot also killed the tar spot fungus which so quickly disfigures many sycamore leaves. As it withstands exposure, it was also planted to shelter farms and other outbuildings, as well as to shade dairies before the advent of fridges. Hence it is still found around buildings and otherwise lonely ruins today. Sycamore is rarely dominant in any woodland, but often forms the edges of beech woods.

The sycamore's bark is smooth until the tree is about sixty years old, when it starts to break up and the tree develops its vast shading crown, 'the spreading sycamore'. In winter it is identifiable by its single green buds and the broccoli-like branching of its crown. It is very fast growing and produces good even-grained timber that is favoured by wood turners. It doesn't warp in water or taint food, and is easily worked while green, so became particularly popular by the 19th century. It also satisfied the mills' demand for cylindrical rollers, shuttles and perfectly smooth bobbins, and was used more than beech for making clog soles. Elsewhere it is used in violin-making, including by the great Stradivari family.

sycamore leaves and flowers

61

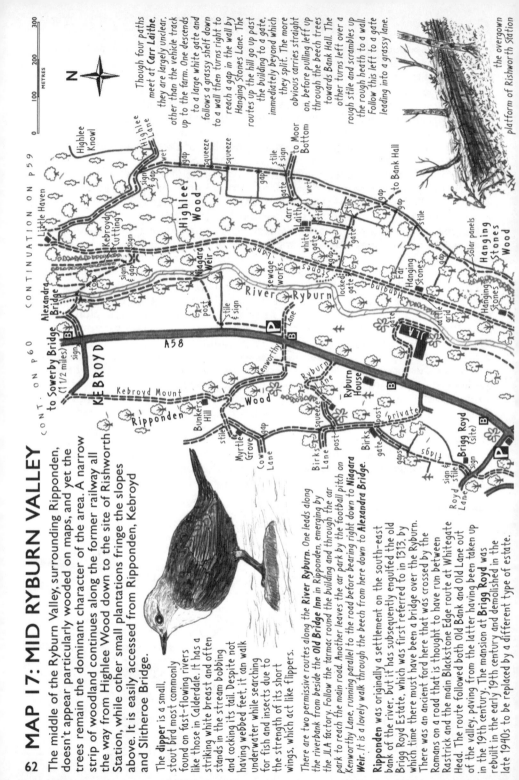

The middle of the Ryburn Valley, surrounding Ripponden, doesn't appear particularly wooded on maps, and yet the trees remain the dominant character of the area. A narrow strip of woodland continues along the former railway all the way from Highlee Wood down to the site of Rishworth Station, while other small plantations fringe the slopes above. It is easily accessed from Ripponden, Kebroyd and Slitheroe Bridge.

The **dipper** is a small, stout bird most commonly found on fast-flowing rivers like those in Calderdale. It has a striking white breast and often stands in the stream bobbing and cocking its tail. Despite not having webbed feet, it can walk underwater while searching for fish and insects due to the strength of its short wings, which act like flippers.

There are two permissive routes along the **River Ryburn**. One leads along the riverbank from beside the **Old Bridge Inn** in Ripponden, emerging by the JLA factory. Follow the tarmac round the building and through the car park to reach the main road. Another leaves the car park by the football pitch on Kenworthy Lane, running parallel to the road before bearing right down to **Niagara Weir**. It is a lovely walk through the beech from here down to **Alexandra Bridge**.

Ripponden was originally a settlement on the south-east bank of the river, but it has subsequently engulfed the old Brigg Royd Estate, which was first referred to in 1313, by which time there must have been a bridge over the Ryburn. There was an ancient ford here that was crossed by the Romans on a road that is thought to have run between Rastrick and the main Blackstone Edge route at Whitegate Head. The route followed both Old Bank and Old Lane out of the valley, paving from the latter having been taken up in the 19th century. The mansion at **Brigg Royd** was rebuilt in the early 19th century and demolished in the late 1940s to be replaced by a different type of estate.

Though four paths meet at **Carr Laithe**, they are largely unclear, other than the vehicle track up to the farm. One descends to a large white gate and follows a grassy shelf down to a wall then turns right to reach a gap in the wall by Hanging Stones Lane. The routes up the hill go up past the building to a gate, immediately beyond which they split. The more obvious route carries straight on, before pulling left up through the beech trees towards **Bank Hall**. The other turns left over a rough stile and scrambles up the rough heath to a wall. Follow this left to a gate leading into a grassy lane.

the overgrown platform of Rishworth Station

CONTINUATION ON P 59
CONT. ON P 60
to Sowerby Bridge (1 1/2 miles)

Map labels:

N

0 100 200 300
METRES

Little Haven
Highlee Knowl
Highlee Lane
Highlee Wood
Kebroyd Cutting
Niagara Weir
Alexandra Bridge
A58
KEBROYD
Kebroyd Mount
Ripponden
Bunkers Hill
Kebroyd Wood
Myrtle Grove
Cow Lane
Birks Lane
Birks
Squeeze Lane
Ryburn Lane
Ryburn House
River Ryburn
Stones Lane
sewage works
Carr Laithe
To Moor Bottom
white gate
Hanging Stones
Hanging Stones Wood
solar panels
to Bank Hall
Brigg Royd (site)
Royd Lane
Birchcliffe
private
squeeze
stiles
stile & sign
post
gap
squeeze
wet
stile
cattle grid
cattle grid

RIPPONDEN

There is some debate over the claim on the **Old Bridge Inn**'s blue plaque that it is probably the oldest hostelry in Yorkshire. Although an inn is recorded in the vicinity in 1307, the current building dates from the 16th century and the first reference to the pub is in 1754. It was renamed the Old Waterloo Inn for a time after Wellington's victory, as was the bridge itself.

It is generally held that the first co-operative shop was set up in Rochdale in 1844, yet **Ripponden Co-operative Society** was founded in 1832 with a shop in a cottage, and there may be even earlier examples elsewhere. Involving members from Ripponden, the Rochdale Pioneers learnt from their predecessors and set out a model that was subsequently widely copied.

Hollins Lane is followed by the path that leads down to Pretoria Bridge. **Hollins Mill** was located at the bottom and known locally as Tread Mill, as it had been an early walk mill.

Slitheroe Mills were built around 1640 on a site originally called Lower Oakes. There were both fulling and corn mills on the site, before being used for making paper. They were unusual in the area for never being converted to cotton mills. Its name may well refer to the steep approach down Dyson Lane to the old bridge here (originally Brow Bridge). The bulk of the mill was demolished but what remains is the Robins Mill Business Complex.

St Bartholomew's Church was constructed in 1868, the fourth to be built on the site. The church was originally said to be of Royal foundation, after Richard I granted a licence for it because the tenants in the farthest corners of Sowerbyshire were deemed too far from a church. The second church was destroyed by a flood in 1722 which washed away the font and exhumed various graves, not helped by the fact that Cob Clough runs beneath the church. The yew trees were planted in 1751 and were considered one of the finest yew hedges in the country. The fine Old Bridge survived the flood, as did the adjacent pub, which was owned by the church until 1697.

Though ultimately an unsuccessful venture, the **Ryburn Valley Branch Line** opened on 5th August 1878 to great local fanfare. In Ripponden, a cannon was fired and workers were given the day off to travel on the line. **Rishworth Station** was opened in 1881, and originally an extension west beneath Blackstone Edge was planned, but landslides meant this was quickly abandoned. Motor trains known as Rishworth Pigs were used after 1907 and the line closed in 1958, though it had been closed to passengers since 1929. The platform is still visible amid the undergrowth at Rishworth Station, while the station entrance is marked by a plaque on Slitheroe Bridge, from which a high trestle bridge led across the clough to the platform.

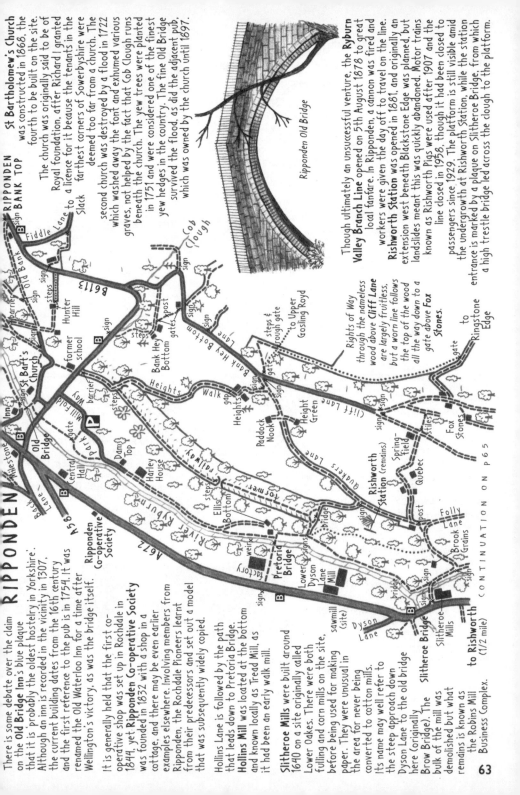

Ripponden Old Bridge

RIPPONDEN BANK TOP

Fiddle Lane — to Slack

Rights of Way through the nameless wood above **Cliff Lane** are largely fruitless, but a worn line follows the top of the wood all the way down to a gate above *Fox Stones*.

CONTINUATION ON P 65

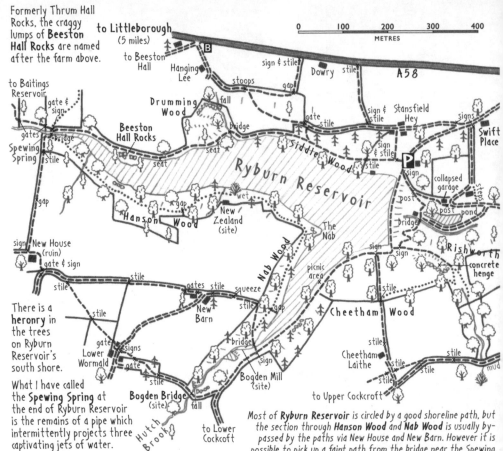

Formerly Thrum Hall Rocks, the craggy lumps of **Beeston Hall Rocks** are named after the farm above.

to Littleborough (5 miles)

to Beeston Hall

B

Hanging Lee

stoops

sign & stile

Dowry stile

A58

to Baitings Reservoir

gate & sign

fall

Drumming Wood

bridge

sign & stile

Stansfield Hey

signs

Swift Place

gates

bridge

Beeston Hall Rocks

seat

sign & stile

gate stile

Siddle Wood

sign & stile

collapsed garage

Spewing Spring

stile

seat

Ryburn Reservoir

stile

P

sign

steps

post

pond

gap

Hanson Wood

gap

wet

New Zealand (site)

The Nab

Nab Wood

post

bridge

Rishworth

concrete henge

sign

New House (ruin)

gate & sign

picnic area

sign

There is a **heronry** in the trees on Ryburn Reservoir's south shore.

stile

stile

gates stile

squeeze

New Barn

stile

gap

stile

Cheetham Wood

stile

gate signs

Lower Wormald

gate

bridge

sign

Cheetham Laithe

stile

stile

stile

stile

mud

What I have called the **Spewing Spring** at the end of Ryburn Reservoir is the remains of a pipe which intermittently projects three captivating jets of water.

stile

Bogden Bridge (site)

fall

Bogden Mill (site)

Hutch Brook

to Lower Cockcroft

to Upper Cockcroft

Bogden Bridge was a packhorse bridge known locally as Roman Bridge. Bogden Mill was built just downstream in 1792 as a cotton carding mill. In its few years of service it confusingly also went by the names Hazel Grove Mill, Hutch Royd Mill and Cockcroft Mill. However, it burnt down in 1882 and was abandoned as ruins, which helped Bogden Clough become a fashionable Edwardian beauty spot. When the valley was flooded in the 1920s, 'Farewell to Bogden' postcards were printed. Even though the reservoir was initially called Bogden Clough Reservoir, the name has subsequently disappeared, as has every other reference to Bogden, a name now consigned to history.

Ryburn Reservoir was the first built in the valley and has a particularly impressive gravity dam wall, its shape modelled on that of Hoover Dam. Construction began in 1925 by the Wakefield Corporation, which subsequently planted many of the spruce and larch trees around the reservoir. However, the valley was already very wooded, as the old wood names attest. Hanging Lee Mill was used as a hostel during construction. Nowadays Ryburn is used only as a compensation reservoir for

64 maintaining levels in the river downstream.

Most of **Ryburn Reservoir** is circled by a good shoreline path, but the section through **Hanson Wood** and **Nab Wood** is usually by-passed by the paths via New House and New Barn. However it is possible to pick up a faint path from the bridge near the Spewing Spring. Beyond the gap in the wall in Hanson Wood, descend through the beech trees to the shore near New Zealand. There is a short wet section, but if you pick your way through the willows you'll be rewarded with a better path continuing around **The Nab** - a charming spot - to rejoin the main path near the bridge over **Bogden Clough**.

the stores on Snow Hill

The undefined stone stores below **Snow Hill** are an intriguing feature. Marked on OS maps as a cave, they appear to be some kind of store that would have been larger and covered with earth. I have been told they were used for keeping pheasant and partridge chicks by the Wheelwrights' gamekeeper at the turn of the century, but whether this was their original purpose is unclear. A hut can be traced in the rhododendron nearby, known by locals at the Magic Hut.

MAP 18: UPPER RYBURN VALLEY

The Ryburn Valley continues up from Slitheroe Bridge to Ryburn Reservoir, which is surrounded by attractive beech and larch plantations. It is joined by Booth Dean Clough, a beautiful remote stream flowing north from Booth Wood through the ancient Turner Wood. Ryburn Reservoir is a particularly popular spot, but the whole area is reasonably accessible via paths from Rishworth or the two main roads.

Little remains of the mills of the Upper Ryburn Valley other than a number of mill ponds, which have become features of the luxury properties that have recently been built here. **Ryburndale Paper Mill** (previously Soyland Paper Mill and Upper Swift Place Mill) was the last to operate, eventually closing in 1990.

Booth Dean Clough is said to be home to a unique hybrid of bilberry and cowberry.

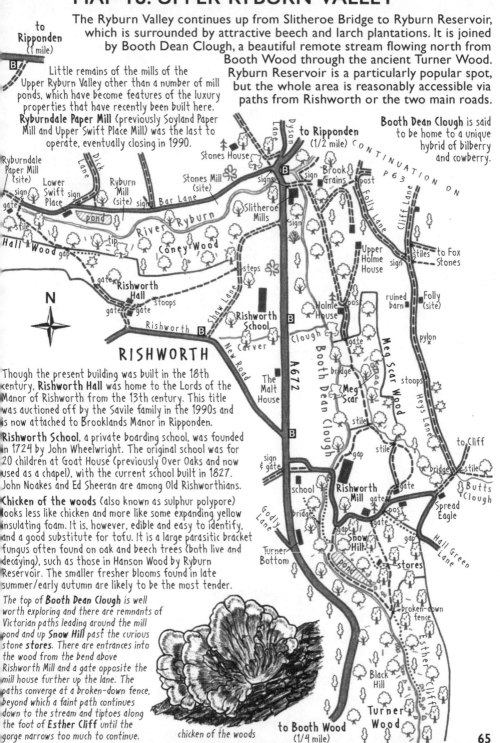

to Ripponden (1 mile)

to Ripponden (1/2 mile)

CONTINUATION ON P 63

Ryburndale Paper Mill (site)

Lower Swift Place

Ryburn Mill (site)

Dick Lane

Bar Lane

Dyson Lane

Stones House

Stones Mill (site)

signs

sign

Brook Grains

post

Folly Lane

Cliff Lane

Slitheroe Mills

River Ryburn

pond

stile

gate

tip

Coney Wood

gap

Hall Wood

gate

Rishworth Hall

stoops

gate   gate

Rishworth

steps

Shaw Lane

Rishworth School

Carver

New Road

Upper Holme House

sign

stiles to Fox Stones

ruined barn

Folly (site)

pylon x

Holme House

post

gate

Booth Dean Clough

Meg Scar Wood

stoops

Heys Lane

RISHWORTH

Though the present building was built in the 18th century, **Rishworth Hall** was home to the Lords of the Manor of Rishworth from the 13th century. This title was auctioned off by the Savile family in the 1990s and is now attached to Brooklands Manor in Ripponden.

Rishworth School, a private boarding school, was founded in 1724 by John Wheelwright. The original school was for 20 children at Goat House (previously Over Oaks and now used as a chapel), with the current school built in 1827. John Noakes and Ed Sheeran are among Old Rishworthians.

Chicken of the woods (also known as sulphur polypore) looks less like chicken and more like some expanding yellow insulating foam. It is, however, edible and easy to identify, and a good substitute for tofu. It is a large parasitic bracket fungus often found on oak and beech trees (both live and decaying), such as those in Hanson Wood by Ryburn Reservoir. The smaller fresher blooms found in late summer/early autumn are likely to be the most tender.

The top of **Booth Dean Clough** is well worth exploring and there are remnants of Victorian paths leading around the mill pond and up **Snow Hill** past the curious stone **stores**. There are entrances into the wood from the bend above Rishworth Mill and a gate opposite the mill house further up the lane. The paths converge at a broken-down fence, beyond which a faint path continues down to the stream and tiptoes along the foot of **Esther Cliff** until the gorge narrows too much to continue.

The Malt House

A 672

Meg Scar

bridge

stile

gap

stile

to Cliff

bridge   stile

Butts Clough

Spread Eagle

Hall Green Lane

sign & gate

Godly Lane

school

bridge

Rishworth Mill

gate

post

gate

gap

gap

Snow Hill

stores

Turner Bottom

pond

broken-down fence

Black Hill

Esther Cliff

Turner Wood

chicken of the woods

to Booth Wood (1/4 mile)

65

ROUTE 9: LOWER RYBURN VALLEY FROM SOWERBY BRIDGE

SOWERBY BRIDGE

Distance: 8 miles (12.5km)

Ascent: 450m

Parking: Free parking at Sowerby Bridge station and behind the Conservative Club in Ripponden. Plentiful street parking along Sowerby Street.

Public Transport: Sowerby Bridge is on the main Caldervale train and bus routes.

Character: A beautiful route that reveals the Ryburn Valley for the rich tapestry that it is. The woods here are so narrow that the outward route follows the open ground to the west, but this makes it a walk of great variety. The return is via the varied woodlands that cloak the east side of the valley, leading all the way back into the industrial heart of Sowerby Bridge. The going is generally good, though there are some muddy stretches and a couple of paths need care with navigation. The route can also be started from Ripponden.

The name **Sowerby** is of Scandinavian origin and refers to a farmstead on sour ground.

① From the centre of **Sowerby Bridge**, follow the A58 over the river and under the railway, then bear right up Sowerby Street past Tesco. On the bend, carry straight on up the hill past the Royal Oak and do the same at the next bend, following Haugh End Lane past the former St George's Church. After 300m, fork right up Brockwell Gate, a beech-lined avenue leading up to **Brockwell House**. Follow the track through the buildings and round to the left, before bearing right onto a path into the trees. This follows a wall to reach some steps climbing up towards **Ryburn Valley High School**.

② Skirt round to the left of the school grounds and keep left around the playing field to reach a gap in the wall. Just before the road beyond, turn left onto a path across the field and down steps by **The Breck**. Turn right on the track and left upon reaching the lane. On the bend, bear right at the second footpath sign, skirting around Sowerby Parsonage before dropping down to the squelchy ground around **Nether End Beck**. Bear right then left up through the small beech wood to reach a gap in the far wall. Follow the left-hand edge of the field beyond to another gap and, ignoring a rough stile to the right, follow the fence on across the slope.

③

John Rawson lived at **Brockwell House** and was responsible for planting over 100,000 trees in the Ryburn Valley in the late 19th century, including Rawson Wood (now a housing estate on the edge of Sowerby village). A woollen mill and dye house stood alongside the house.

⑧ Follow the only clear path down through **Rough Hey Wood** to reach Stansfield Mill Lane, following the setts down to the bridge over the old railway. Turn right beyond the bridge and fork left away from the railway to skirt along the bottom of **Dodge Royd Wood**. Head straight on by the former dyeworks to pick up a path climbing back up to the railway, following its left side until the path drops down into the cutting itself. Turn right under the footbridge beyond, then immediately left to follow the setts out of the wood. Reaching **Long Lane**, turn left along the road.

⑨ Follow **Long Lane** to its end and bear right, only to fork left soon after and descend Scar Head Road. Across **Stirk Bridge**, turn right along the river, then left at the end to emerge on the A58 by the Long Chimney pub. Turn right to return to the centre of **Sowerby Bridge**.

A stirk was a young heifer and the route over **Stirk Bridge** would have been used by farmers coming to market when it was just a ford. A ducking stool was erected alongside in the 17th century

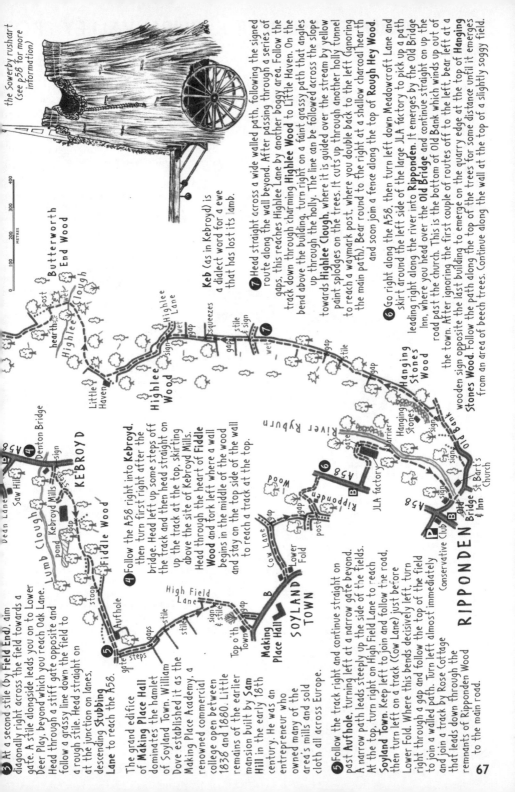

the Sowerby rushcart (see p58 for more information)

Butterworth End Wood

Keb (as in Kebroyd) is a dialect word for a ewe that has lost its lamb.

7 Head straight across a wide walled path, following the signed route along the wall beyond. After passing through a series of gaps, this reaches Highlee Lane by another boggy area. Follow the track down through charming **Highlee Wood** to Little Haven. On the bend above the building, turn right on a faint grassy path that angles up through the holly. The line can be followed across the slope towards **Highlee Clough**, where it is guided over the stream by yellow paint splodges on the trees. It cuts up through another holly funnel to reach a waymark post, where you double back to the left (ignoring the main path). Bear round to the right at a shallow charcoal hearth and soon join a fence along the top of **Rough Hey Wood**.

6 Go right along the A58, then turn left down Meadowcroft Lane and skirt around the left side of the large JLA factory to pick up a path leading right along the river into **Ripponden**. It emerges by the Old Bridge Inn, where you head over the **Old Bridge** and continue straight on up the road past the church. This is the bottom of Old Bank which winds up out of the town. After ignoring the first couple of routes off to the left, bear left at a wooden sign opposite the last building to emerge on the quarry edge at the top of **Hanging Stones Wood**. Follow the path along the top of the trees for some distance until it emerges from an area of beech trees. Continue along the wall at the top of a slightly soggy field.

3 At a second stile (by **Field End**), aim diagonally right across the field towards a gate. A stile alongside leads you on to Lower Deer Play, beyond which you reach Oak Lane. Head through a stiff gate opposite and follow a grassy line down the field to a rough stile. Head straight on at the junction on lanes, descending **Stubbing Lane** to reach the A58.

The grand edifice of **Making Place Hall** dominates the hamlet of Soyland Town. William Dove established it as the Making Place Academy, a renowned commercial college open between 1838 and 1880. Little remains of the earlier mansion built by **Sam Hill** in the early 18th century. He was an entrepreneur who owned many of the area's mills and sold cloth all across Europe.

4 Follow the A58 right into **Kebroyd**, then turn first right after the bridge. Head left up some steps off the track and then head straight on up the track at the top, skirting above the site of Kebroyd Mills. Head through the heart of **Fiddle Wood** and fork left where a wall begins in the middle of the wood and stay on the top side of the wall to reach a track at the top.

5 Follow the track right and continue straight on past **Aufhole**, turning left at a narrow gate beyond. A narrow path leads steeply up the side of the fields. At the top, turn right on High Field Lane to reach **Soyland Town**. Keep left to join and follow the road, then turn left on a track (Cow Lane) just before Lower Fold. Where this bends decisively left, turn right through a gap and follow the top of the field to join a walled path. Turn left almost immediately and join a track by Rose Cottage that leads down through the remnants of Ripponden Wood to the main road.

KEBROYD

Denton Bridge
Saw Hill
Dean Lane
Kebroyd Mills
pond
Lumb Clough
Fiddle Wood
stoop
Aufhole
gate
steps
gaps
stile
stiles
High Field Lane
sign & stile
Top o'th' Town
Making Place Hall
SOYLAND TOWN
Lower Fold
Cow Lane
Conservative Club

Highlee Lane
sign
wet
squeezes
stile & sign
Highlee Wood
Little Haven
Highlee Clough
hearth
wet post

RIPPONDEN
River Ryburn
Hanging Stones Wood
Hanging Stones
JLA factory
Ripponden Wood
Old Bank
Bridge
Inn
St Bart's Church
sign
gate
barrier
post

Hanging Stones Wood

METRES 0 100 200 300 400

ROUTE 10: UPPER RYBURN VALLEY FROM

Distance: 7.5 miles (12km)

Ascent: 290m

Parking: Free car parks on Mill Fold Way in Ripponden, or by both Ryburn and Baitings Reservoirs.

Public Transport: Ripponden is on the regular X58 and 560/561/562 bus routes from Halifax and Sowerby Bridge, as well as the 901 service from Hebden Bridge and Huddersfield.

Character: A varied walk combining the reservoirs at the head of the Ryburn Valley with the beautiful woods in Booth Dean Clough. Though many of the woods here are small, there is great variety among Baitings' larch plantations, Ryburn's beech stands and the ancient oaks of Turner Wood, as well as plenty of open hillsides in between. The walking is on good paths throughout and fairly straightforward to follow.

Baitings Reservoir (originally New Top Reservoir) was constructed in the 1950s to supply Wakefield (like Ryburn Reservoir). At the time it was the highest dam in England at 255ft and the IRA threatened to blow it up an hour before its opening on 3rd May 1957. It was surrounded by larch and spruce plantations, but storms in 2004 damaged the plantation on the north shore, which was subsequently replanted with oak, birch, hazel, and rowan. When the reservoir is low, the old road and **Baitings Bridge** are visible just upstream of the recently rebuilt Baitings Viaduct.

❸ Reaching the bridge at the end of the reservo... (and the impressive **Spewing Spring** alongside... stay on the right bank of the river through... series of gates. A fenced path then leads on u... to the car park by **Baitings Reservoir**. Joi... the road briefly here, before bearing left at... sign beyond the former New Inn to pick up... good path along the north shore. At the en... cross **Baitings Viaduct** and then turn lef... into the conifer woods tha... fringe the southern shore...

❹ At the end of **Baitings Reservoir**, turn right up the fenced track to Upper Schole Carr. Turn left in front of the farm through a gate leading across the fields towards Higher Wormald. Bear left around the building there, picking up a walled path through another gate beyond. At the ruins of **New House**, turn right up the slope to a narrow gate and head left along the path. Carry on along the edge of the fields and drop down a narrow path behind the buildings of New Barn. Head straight on to another stile and drop down the left edge of the field to the top of **Nab Wood**.

The name **Wormald** is found only locally, and is probably derived from the Anglo-Saxon word *wyrm* for a reptile or serpent.

❺ Drop down through the trees to cross **Bogden Clough** and head left along the south shore of **Ryburn Reservoir**. Just before the dam wall, turn right up through **Cheetham Wood**. Follow the path past Cheetham Laithe, turning left by the old gateposts into a narrow walled path that can be muddy in places. It emerges by the playing field on the edge of **Rishworth** and follows the track down to the road. If you don't have a dog, you can head straight on across the playing field opposite. Otherwise follow the road left for 100m, then turn right up some steps and follow the edge of the playing fields. Ignore the first path off to the left, and at the next junction turn left through a stone arch to descend to **Godly Lane**.

The huge building at **Rishworth Mill** (now flats going b... the name of Rishworth Palace) was built in the 1860s b... the Wheelwright family, largely as a means to keep th... workers occupied during the Cotton Famine. There wer... several older mills on the site, including a corn mi... mentioned in 1601. It was driven by a 57ft waterwhee... and produced cotton textiles until the early 1990s

Beeston Hall Rocks

New Inn (former) sign

B P gate & sign

Lower Beestonhirst

A58

Bridge

to Littleborough (4 miles)

Baitings Reservoir

N

sign

Baitings Viaduct

Baitings Bridge (remains)

sign

Baitings Gate Road

gate

❹ gate

gate

gates

Upper Schole Carr gates

stoops

Higher Wormald

New House (ruin) sign & gate

sign

Drumming Wood

gate ❸ gates Beeston Hall Rocks bridge

Spewing Spring bridge seat

seat

Hanson Wood

stile gates stile stile

❺ New Barn bridge

Bogden Mill (site)

RIPPONDEN

The boletus edulis is known by many names; the French **cep**, the English **penny bun**, the Italian porcini, or indeed the German steinpilz (stone mushroom). It can be identified by its brown, slightly slimy cap and chunky cream-coloured stem, and is highly prized for cooking. However, like all boletes, it quickly turns mushy and maggoty, so must be found fresh, usually in late summer.

① From the centre of **Ripponden**, follow the B6113 (Elland Road) over the river. Shortly after Mill Fold Way (and the main car park), turn right up a walled path. Before the bridge, bear right along the side of the **former railway**. The path soon drops into the cutting. At the next bridge, turn right down the slope towards the River Ryburn. Follow the path left along the river bank, turning right at the end to reach the main road. Go right over **Slitheroe Bridge** then immediately left along Bar Lane.

a cep or penny bun

② Follow **Bar Lane** all the way up the valley, its industry replaced by new housing estates. Continue straight on until the track bends sharply right, where you head straight on past an old garage and climb up to the car park by **Ryburn Reservoir**. Turn left opposite the car park, crossing a field before entering **Siddle Wood** near the boathouse. The obvious path continues along the reservoir's lovely wooded shore.

⑦ Follow the road up to a sharp bend by the former Spread Eagle and head straight on down the track. This continues beyond Butts Clough all the way up the hill and joins the tarmac of Cliff Lane. Near the end of a nameless beech wood, turn left at a signed farm track, then immediately right down through the buildings of Heights. Bear right to follow Heights Walk back down over the old railway into Ripponden.

St John's Church was built in 1927 rather appropriately in the Godly area of Rishworth, though the name was actually Anglo-Saxon for 'good clearing'. The church is shaded by a line of fine lime trees.

⑥ Follow Godly Lane right past **St John's Church** then turn left down a tarmac path. Head straight across the main road, joining Rishworth Mill Lane. Over the bridge by Rishworth Mill, it is possible to step over the wall to the right and follow the river (unless you have a dog with you). This soon joins the larger path leading right from the next bend, which skirts the charming mill pond and heads up **Booth Dean Clough**. Just before a broken-down fence, double back to the left and ascend through the beech trees. A little off to the left are the intriguing stone **stores** (see p64 for more information) and the attractive lump of Snow Hill. The path continues to a narrow gate back onto the lane.

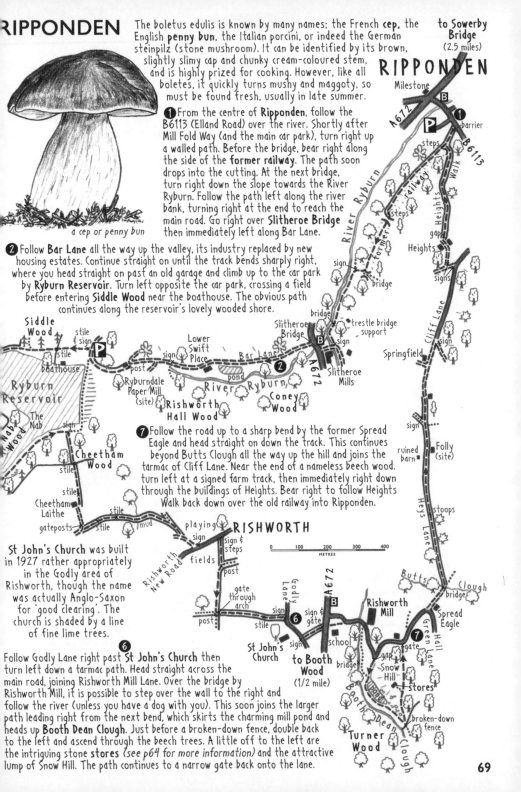

to Sowerby Bridge (2.5 miles)

RIPPONDEN

Milestone

River Ryburn

former railway

Heights Walk

Heights

Cliff Lane

Springfield

sign

Folly (site)

ruined barn

Heys Lane

stoops

Slitheroe Bridge

trestle bridge support

bridge

Slitheroe Mills

A672

Bar Lane

Lower Swift Place

pond

River Ryburn

Coney Wood

Rishworth Hall Wood

Ryburndale Paper Mill (site)

Siddle Wood

boathouse

Ryburn Reservoir

The Nab

Nab Wood

Cheetham Wood

Cheetham Laithe

gateposts

mud

playing fields

RISHWORTH

Rishworth New Road

0 100 200 300 400
METRES

St John's Church

to Booth Wood (1/2 mile)

Godly Lane

A672

school

Rishworth Mill

bridge

Snow Hill

stores

Butts Clough

bridge

Spread Eagle

Hall Green Lane

gate

gap

Booth Dean Clough

Turner Wood

broken-down fence

69

THE CONIFERS

The conifers are much misunderstood and easily viewed as a single monolithic entity because of their association with large-scale plantation. The use of the terms conifer, fir, evergreen and pine are often conflated – indeed the term fir was originally used to refer to conifers as a whole, with the name fir-apple used for their cones (which were gathered as fuel). However, fir, pine, spruce and larch are very different trees and not all are evergreen (unlike holly or holm oak), so conifer is the only satisfactory catch-all. Explore the forests of northern Europe or even Scotland and you leave with a far greater appreciation of the varied beauty of these trees. Though we have none of the majesterial Douglas or Grand firs (or vast swathes of pine wood) that grace the forests of the north, there are still enough introduced conifers in the valley to provide plenty of interest.

The Scots pine is Britain's only native pine, but survives in its natural state in parts of Scotland alone. Though the vast Caledonian pinewoods were reduced by nearly 99% by the 20th century, it has been re-established in many areas and remains our second most common tree. In the South Pennines it is always planted, largely as an ornamental species, to give variety to estates like Hardcastle Crags. Perhaps the most appealing local pine plantation, though, is that by Mixenden Reservoir near Halifax. Scots pine grows tall and straight and provides a great habitat for wildlife like red squirrels, capercaillie and pine marten. It was valued for ships' masts, telegraph poles, pit props and furniture, and its resin tapped for preservatives, inks and waxes. It can be identified by its reddish scaly bark that flakes rather like the sycamore.

The larch is probably the most appealing conifer, largely because it is not evergreen. It has a graceful outline, and once the needles turn a charming orange or yellow in the autumn they form a beautiful carpet through the forest. The European larch was probably introduced to Britain in the 17th century, with most trees now planted being fast-growing hybrids of this and the later arrival, the Japanese larch. Its female flowers (often a vibrant pink) are known as larch roses and ripen into the small brown cones that line a larch trees branches, where they can stay for many years. They are found locally in plantations in Severhills Clough and around reservoirs like Ogden Water and Baitings.

Spruce, particularly the blue-tinged Sitka, gets the worst reputation of all the conifers. It forms the dense cloaks of the most impenetrable forestry plantations, like those above Portsmouth and in Sunderland Plantation (near Stoodley Pike), yet where there are paths beneath the canopy these are invariably darkly atmospheric. Spruce is a survivor and the world's oldest tree is thought to be a 9,550-year-old stunted spruce in Sweden. Valued for its strength, rapid growth and lightness, it was widely planted in the 20th century and is now Britain's commonest tree. It was used in making the earliest aeroplanes, high-quality paper production, fencing and building frames.

Scots pine needles and cone

CHAPTER 7 - LUDDENDEN DEAN

Map Sheet: OL21 (South Pennines)

Public Transport: Luddendenfoot is on the main Caldervale bus routes. Bus 574 runs hourly from Halifax to Luddenden.

Parking: Free car parks on Luddenden Lane and at Jerusalem Farm, Booth.

Luddenden Dean is a beautiful patchwork of fields and woodland, seemingly a world away from the bustling Calder Valley. At the head of the valley is the impenetrable Castle Carr estate, a warren of intriguing plantations. Further down, there are appealing woods around Jerusalem Farm, and it is on these two areas I have focused, though Route 11 gives a full tour of the valley from the comely village of Luddenden.

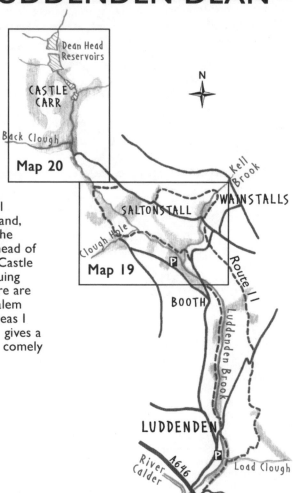

tree carving in Wade Wood

Luddenden was originally Luddingdene (which would probably have been easier to say) and referred to a clearing in the valley of the loud river (from the Old English word *hlud*). These days we know the stream that flows through the valley as the Luddenden Brook, but it could equally be the River Ludd. It is first mentioned in 1284, soon after which the corn mill for the Graveship of Warley was moved down to Luddenden Brook, the first of many mills to take advantage of the fast-flowing stream. Ironstone was also quarried and worked near Booth, the adjacent woods providing fuel for these industries.

These days Luddenden Dean is as quiet as anywhere in the borough and a place whose charms are enchanting on a warm summer day.

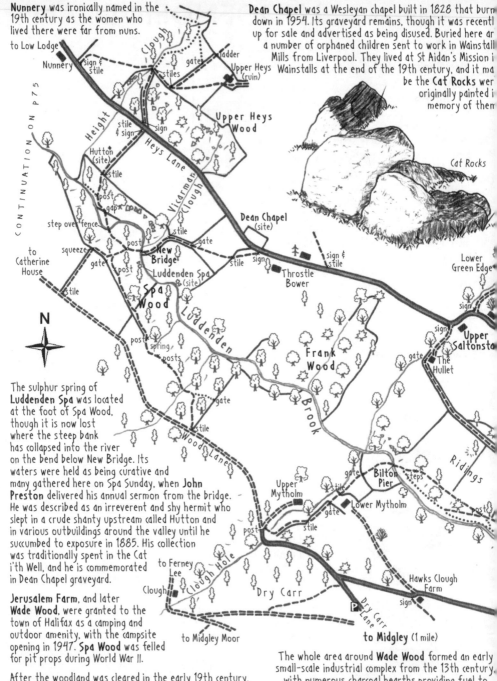

Nunnery was ironically named in the 19th century as the women who lived there were far from nuns.

to Low Lodge

Nunnery · sign & stile

Dean Chapel was a Wesleyan chapel built in 1828 that burn down in 1954. Its graveyard remains, though it was recentl up for sale and advertised as being disused. Buried here ar a number of orphaned children sent to work in Wainstall Mills from Liverpool. They lived at St Aidan's Mission i Wainstalls at the end of the 19th century, and it ma be the **Cat Rocks** wer originally painted i memory of them

Clough

gate

ladder

stiles

Upper Heys (ruin)

Upper Heys Wood

Cat Rocks

CONTINUATION ON P75

Height

stile & sign

sign

Heys Lane

Hutton (site)

stile

Vicarman Clough

post

gap

step over fence

Dean Chapel (site)

squeeze

stile

gate

New Bridge

stile

sign

Throstle Bower

sign & stile

Lower Green Edge

to Catherine House

gate

post

Luddenden Spa (site)

Spa Wood

sign

stile

sign

Upper Saltonsta

The Hullet

N

post

spring

posts

Luddenden

Frank Wood

gate

gate

The sulphur spring of
Luddenden Spa was located
at the foot of Spa Wood,
though it is now lost
where the steep bank
has collapsed into the river
on the bend below New Bridge. Its
waters were held as being curative and
many gathered here on Spa Sunday, when **John
Preston** delivered his annual sermon from the bridge.
He was described as an irreverent and shy hermit who
slept in a crude shanty upstream called Hutton and
in various outbuildings around the valley until he
succumbed to exposure in 1885. His collection
was traditionally spent in the Cat
i'th Well, and he is commemorated
in Dean Chapel graveyard.

gate

stile

Wood Lane

Brook

Ridings

Upper Mytholm

gate

stile

Bilton Pier

steps

Lower Mytholm

post

gate

stile

post

Jerusalem Farm, and later
Wade Wood, were granted to the
town of Halifax as a camping and
outdoor amenity, with the campsite
opening in 1947. **Spa Wood** was felled
for pit props during World War II.

to Ferney Lee

Clough

Clough Hole

Dry Carr

Hawks Clough Farm

sign

P

Dry Carr Lane

to Midgley Moor

to Midgley (1 mile)

After the woodland was cleared in the early 19th century,
there was a beehive enclosure that can still be traced on the
Ridings (the name, like royd, referring to a clearing). Bees
were kept from the 17th century, at a time when honey was
the only sweetener available. It is thought that more honey
was produced locally before the Industrial Revolution,
whose smoke damaged both the bees and the fruit.

The whole area around **Wade Wood** formed an early
small-scale industrial complex from the 13th century,
with numerous charcoal hearths providing fuel to
smelt iron at bloomeries by Bilton Pier and
Jerusalem Farm. Ironstone was quarried and mined in
a seam all along the north bank of the river, but the
large coal-fired blast furnace at Holme House Bridge
Ironworks quickly replaced the whole industry in the
19th century and functioned until 1936.

MAP 19: LUDDENDEN DEAN SOUTH

Luddenden Dean is at its most wooded around Jerusalem Farm, and the car park here is the best place from which to explore. The sylvan delights of Wade Wood lead to paths along the winding Luddenden Brook and up Wainstalls Clough to Cat i'th Well and Cat Rocks. Further upstream, the birch of Spa Wood is great for autumn mushrooms and Upper Heys Wood is full of birdboxes and their visitors.

Caty Well, a 17th-century stone cistern alongside the road, is thought to be a corruption of St Catherine's Well, named after St Catherine of Alexandria. The painted rocks on the hill above are known as **Cat Rocks** and, from the right angle, they appear rather cat-like. Though it is said Robin Hood began the custom of painting the rocks when he hid out in a priest hole in the pub, on Spaw Sunday in 1890 it was reported that people were surprised to see the rocks freshly painted and no-one knew by whose hand. The tradition continues every year, though superstition has it the landlord of the **Cat i'th Well** does it to ensure good business for the pub.

Cat Rocks stand just out of the trees on the hillside above **Cat i'th Well**, but the path straight up to them from the gate opposite the pub is unclear and very wet. A more pleasant route follows the path immediately over the brook up the stream to **New Mill** at Wainstalls. Keep left here and contour across the slope to eventually emerge above the white rocks.

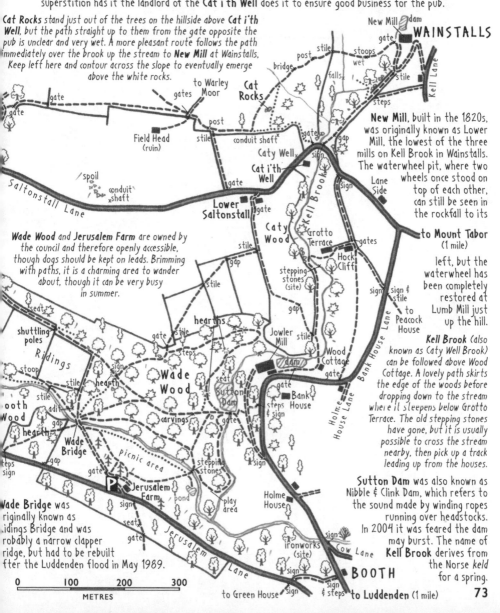

Wade Wood and **Jerusalem Farm** are owned by the council and therefore openly accessible, though dogs should be kept on leads. Brimming with paths, it is a charming area to wander about, though it can be very busy in summer.

Wade Bridge was originally known as Ridings Bridge and was probably a narrow clapper bridge, but had to be rebuilt after the Luddenden flood in May 1989.

New Mill, built in the 1820s, was originally known as Lower Mill, the lowest of the three mills on Kell Brook in Wainstalls. The waterwheel pit, where two wheels once stood on top of each other, can still be seen in the rockfall to its

to Mount Tabor (1 mile)

left, but the waterwheel has been completely restored at Lumb Mill just up the hill.

Kell Brook (also known as Caty Well Brook) can be followed above Wood Cottage. A lovely path skirts the edge of the woods before dropping down to the stream where it steepens below Grotto Terrace. The old stepping stones have gone, but it is usually possible to cross the stream nearby, then pick up a track leading up from the houses.

Sutton Dam was also known as Nibble & Clink Dam, which refers to the sound made by winding ropes running over headstocks. In 2004 it was feared the dam may burst. The name of **Kell Brook** derives from the Norse *keld* for a spring.

0   100   200   300
METRES

73

MAP 20: LUDDENDEN DEAN NORTH
(Castle Carr Estate)

The head of Luddenden Dean is almost entirely taken up by the beautiful but unreachable Castle Carr Estate. Other than the surrounding moorland, it is private land, open only on occasions like the annual walk to the fountain in July. I have mapped it more for its historical interest than for practical exploration. The estate was assembled in the mid-19th century as an attempt to recreate a Scottish shooting estate in West Yorkshire, Joseph Priestley Edwards buying up many of the farms in the valley which now stand as ruins.

In 1868, Joseph Priestley Edwards closed to the public all roads and paths through the estate, paying only a small compensation and granting a Right of Way across Warley Moor to the east. As well as the obvious routes that remain, the 1854 map shows footpaths between Castle Carr and a farm at Dean Head (now submerged), and across some stepping stones to the farm at Deep Clough. Another went from Head House Bridge up Shore End to join Limers Gate. A local man, Sam Murgatroyd, was caught on one of these in 1896; when he took it to the High Court, he was ordered to pay costs equivalent to half a million today. The judge decreed that the compensation Priestley paid was a just price, and those paths have been shut off to this day.

When negotiations for the Castle Carr and Dean Head Reservoirs began between the Halifax Corporation and Joseph Priestley Edwards, there was going to be just one large reservoir on the estate, beneath the house. Construction began in 1859, but it was soon deemed unsafe and they re-negotiated the existing system of smaller dams. Edwards was paid £4000 and provided with the fountain and cascades on the lower reservoir. An existing dam built by mill-owners (cont. below...)

For most of the year, the closest you can get to the Castle Carr Estate is via the track from Warley Moor Reservoir or the faint (and often very wet) path down the side of Horse Pasture Clough from the moor above. Reaching the rhododendrons around the reservoirs, the latter path skirts the boundary fence around the Upper Reservoir then climbs up towards the head of Luddenden Brook, though a fell-runners' trod branches straight up the slope above Bare Clough to reach the conduit on the moor above.

In 1842, Joseph Savile Scott wrote about and sketched a group of likely Bronze Age barrows in the Castle Carr Estate. There is no other reference to these features and it is generally thought these were lost in the construction of the reservoirs. Yet from the lithographs, at least one of the barrows appears to stand above the reservoirs' level, possibly on the south side of Broadfield Clough. It has also suggested that there is a possible cairn circle on the southern flank of Dean Head Upper Reservoir.

Most of the paths in the Castle Carr estate are around the smaller ornamental reservoirs, as this is the area that is open to the public on occasions when the fountains are on display. A path can be followed through the rhododendrons and great yew trees alongside Luddenden Brook to Stony Spot Plantation, but it soon peters out, as does another in Fulshaw Clough.

74

Map labels:
line of old track
Sheep(cote Brinks)
to Warley Moor Reservoir
Warley Moor
Oxenhope Moor
Upper Dean Head Reservoir
Lower Dean Head Reservoir
Bare Clough
bridge
Bob Hill
gate
gate
gate
gate
stoops
Dean Head (site)
stoops
Broadfield Clough
Durham (ruin)
Fulshaw Clough
Fulshaw (ruin)
wooden tower
stoops
Castle Carr Reservoir
Castle Carr (ruin)
gate
feeding area
very wet
feeding area
barrier
Horse Pasture Clough
Horse Pasture
Castle Scout Plantation
Wadsworth Moor
stoops
N
0 100 200 300
METRES

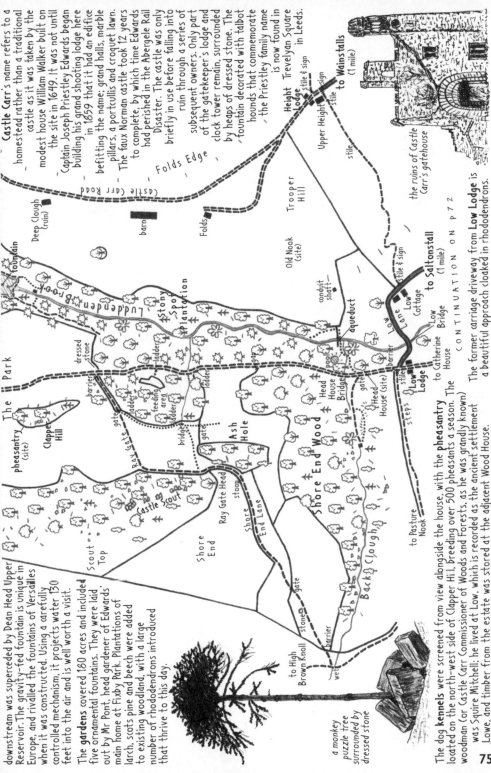

Castle Carr's name refers to a homestead rather than a traditional castle as it was taken by the modest house William Walker built on the site in 1649. It was not until Captain Joseph Priestley Edwards began building his grand shooting lodge here in 1859 that it had an edifice befitting the name; grand halls, marble pillars, a portcullis and croquet lawn. The faux Norman castle took 12 years to complete, by which time Edwards had perished in the Abergele Rail Disaster. The castle was only briefly in use before falling into ruin through a series of subsequent owners. Only part of the gatekeeper's lodge and clock tower remain, surrounded by heaps of dressed stone. The fountain decorated with talbot hounds that commemorate the Priestley family name is now found in Trevelyan Square in Leeds.

downstream was superceded by Dean Head Upper Reservoir. The gravity-fed fountain is unique in Europe, and rivalled the fountains of Versailles when it was constructed. Using a carefully controlled mechanism, it projects water 130 feet into the air and is well worth a visit.

The **gardens** covered 180 acres and included five ornamental fountains. They were laid out by Mr Pont, head gardener of Edwards' main home at Fixby Park. Plantations of larch, scots pine and beech were added to existing woodland, with a large number of rhododendrons introduced that thrive to this day.

The dog **kennels** were screened from view alongside the house, with the **pheasantry** located on the north-west side of Clapper Hill, breeding over 500 pheasants a season. The woodman (or Castle Carr Commissioner of Woods and Forests, as he was grandly known) was Squire Mitchell; he lived at Low, which is recorded as the ancient settlement Lowe, and timber from the estate was stored at the adjacent Wood House.

The former carriage driveway from **Low Lodge** is a beautiful approach cloaked in rhododendrons.

CONTINUATION ON P72

75

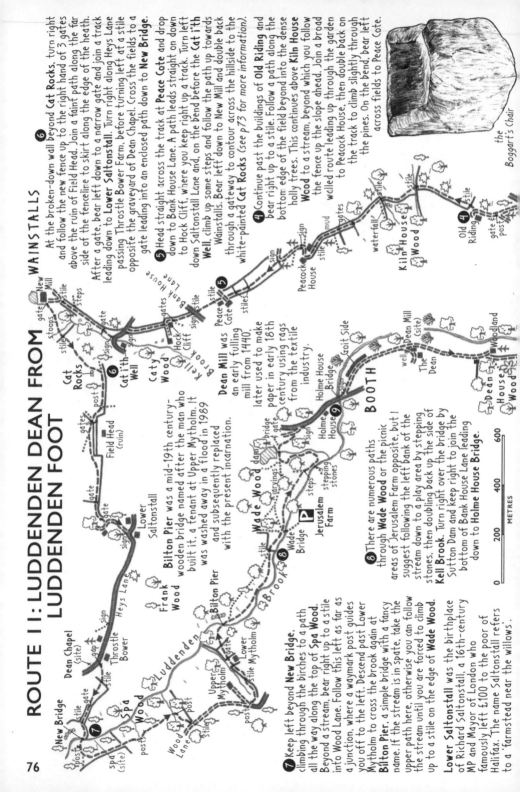

ROUTE 11: LUDDENDEN DEAN FROM LUDDENDEN FOOT

WAINSTALLS

6 At the broken-down wall beyond **Cat Rocks**, turn right and follow the new fence up to the right hand of 3 gates above the ruin of Field Head. Join a faint path along the far side of the fenceline to skirt along the edge of the heath. After a gate, bear left down to a narrow gate and join a track leading down to **Lower Saltonstall**. Turn right along Heys Lane passing Throstle Bower Farm, before turning left at a stile opposite the graveyard of Dean Chapel. Cross the fields to a gate leading into an enclosed path down to **New Bridge**.

5 Head straight across the track at **Peace Cote** and drop down to Bank House Lane. A path leads straight on down to Hock Cliff, where you keep right up a track. Turn left down Saltonstall Lane and, on the bend before the **Cat i'th Well**, climb up some steps and follow the path up towards Wainstalls. Bear left down to New Mill and double back through a gateway to contour across the hillside to the white-painted **Cat Rocks** (see p73 for more information).

4 Continue past the buildings of **Old Riding** and bear right up to a stile. Follow a path along the bottom edge of the field beyond into the dense holly trees. This continues above **Kiln House Wood** to a stream, beyond which you follow the fence up the slope ahead. Join a broad walled route leading up through the garden to Peacock House, then double back on the track to climb slightly through the pines. On the bend, bear left across fields to Peace Cote.

Dean Mill was an early fulling mill from 1440, later used to make paper in early 18th century using rags from the textile industry.

Bilton Pier was a mid-19th-century wooden bridge named after the man who built it, a tenant at Upper Mytholm. It was washed away in a flood in 1989 and subsequently replaced with the present incarnation.

7 Keep left beyond **New Bridge**, climbing through the birches to a path all the way along the top of **Spa Wood**. Beyond a stream, bear right up to a stile into Wood Lane. Follow this left as far as a junction, where a waymark post guides you off to the left. Descend past Lower Mytholm to cross the brook again at **Bilton Pier**, a simple bridge with a fancy name. If the stream is in spate, take the upper path here, otherwise you can follow the stream until you are forced to climb up to a stile on the edge of **Wade Wood**.

Lower Saltonstall was the birthplace of Richard Saltonstall, a 16th-century MP and Mayor of London who famously left £100 to the poor of Halifax. The name Saltonstall refers to a farmstead near the willows.

8 There are numerous paths through **Wade Wood** or the picnic areas of Jerusalem Farm opposite, but I suggest following the left bank of the stream down to a play area by stepping stones, then doubling back up the side of **Kell Brook**. Turn right over the bridge by Sutton Dam and keep right to join the bottom of Bank House Lane leading down to **Holme House Bridge**.

BOOTH

the Boggart's chair

76

Distance: 7.5 miles (12km)

Ascent: 350m

Parking: Free car parks on Luddenden Lane and at Jerusalem Farm. Limited street parking in Luddenden Foot.

Public Transport: Luddenden Foot is on the 590/592 bus routes between Halifax and Rochdale/Burnley. Bus 574 from Halifax runs up Luddenden Lane.

Character: Luddenden Dean is a tranquil retreat from the busy Calder Valley and, though not covered with trees, it is littered with various small woodlands. The lower section from Luddenden Foot to Booth is not covered elsewhere in the book, as there is little access, but this route provides the best way of linking up all the different areas. It meanders across the charming hillsides above Luddenden and Booth to Wainstalls, before following the busy brook all the way back to Luddenden Foot.

The **Lord Nelson** was built in 1634 as a private dwelling, then served as the Black Swan until the Battle of Trafalgar. It is notable for its association with Branwell Brontë, who drank here while working in Luddenden Foot.

The **Boggart's Chair** stands in the far corner of St Mary's Church. It is actually the oldest of four fonts, but was removed to the garden of Ellen Royd House when the church was attacked during the Civil War. It was only recognised in 1902, by which time it had acquired its new name; it was said to have become worn by a boggart sitting in it. (Coincidentally, an almost identical tale exists about a large boulder on the lawn of another Ellen Royd in Elland.

Until 2004, **Luddenden Foot Mill** and its mill pond stood on the site of the housing estate below Roebucks Wood. The pond, which had become a local nature reserve, was controversially filled in before planning permission was granted.

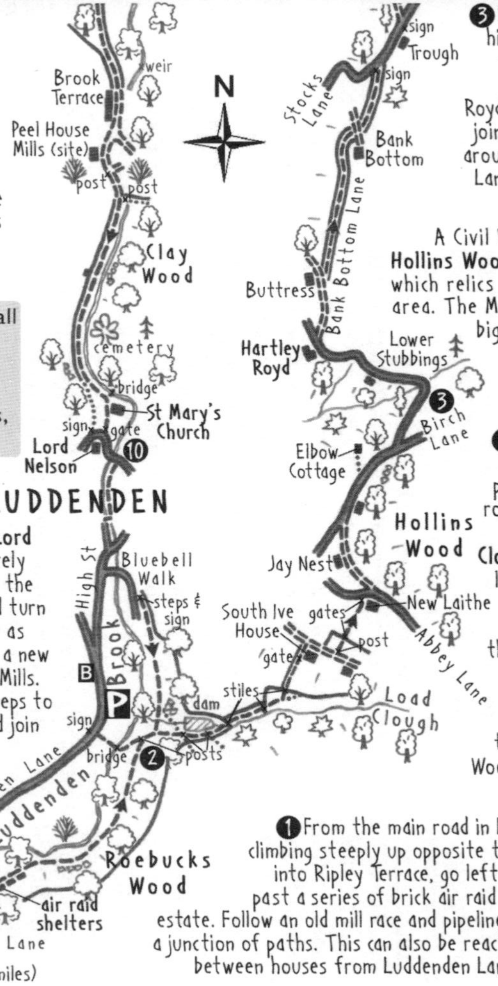

1 From the main road in **Luddenden Foot**, join Danny Lane climbing steeply up from opposite the Post Office. Where this forks into Ripley Terrace, go left down some steps and join a path past a series of brick air raid shelters above the new housing estate. Follow an old mill race and pipeline on through **Roebucks Wood** to a junction of paths. This can also be reached by a narrow path down steps between houses from Luddenden Lane 100m along from the car park.

2 Turn right up to the site of an old dam, then ignore a couple of paths off to the right to reach a rough stile at its far end. A muddy path leads up the side of **Load Clough**. After a stile, keep high and look for steps leading up the wall to the left of South Ive House. Follow the track briefly right, then climb steeply up through the next garden to reach a gate by New Laithe. Turn right on the road, then immediately left on a track along the bottom of Hollins Wood past Jay Nest. Join Birch Lane for 300m before forking left.

3 Follow the lane round the hillside high above Luddenden village, then fork right up a track just beyond the grand residence of Hartley Royd. At the next houses, keep right, joining an old green lane as if skirts around Bank Bottom to reach Stocks Lane. Follow this uphill briefly, then drop down Old Riding Lane.

A Civil War skirmish was fought just above **Hollins Wood** on 23rd October 1643, from which relics are regularly unearthed in the area. The Murgatroyds of the Hollins were big Royalist supporters and their arms store here was raided by a sizeable Parliamentarian force and quickly seized.

9 Turn left immediately over **Holme House Bridge** and follow the rough road along the side of Luddenden Brook to Woodland, where a path continues along the bottom of **Dean House Wood**. Join another track at Brook Terrace and keep right through the scrub around the site of Peel House Mills. The path continues all the way along the stream until it emerges through the churchyard of **St Mary's** in the middle of Luddenden village.

10 Follow the road down past the **Lord Nelson** and turn right immediately beyond Luddenden Bridge. Follow the brook through to Spring Bank and turn right on High Street only as far as Bluebell Walk, which leads through a new estate on the site of Luddenden Mills. Near the end, bear left up some steps to dip back into **Roebucks Wood** and join the outward route at the foot of Load Clough.

Map labels: N — weir — Brook Terrace — Post — Clay Wood — Peel House Mills (site) — cemetery — bridge — gate — sign — St Mary's Church — Lord Nelson — High St — BROOK — Bluebell Walk — steps & sign — sign — LUDDENDEN — Trough — sign — Bank Bottom — Stocks Lane — Bank Bottom Lane — Buttress — Hartley Royd — Lower Stubbings — Birch Lane — Elbow Cottage — Hollins Wood — Jay Nest — New Laithe — Abbey Lane — South Ive House — Load Clough — gates — gate — post — stiles — posts — dam — Roebucks Wood — air raid shelters — steps — Danny Lane — LUDDENDEN FOOT — Old Brandy Wine — to Halifax (4 miles) — to Mytholmroyd (2 miles) — Luddenden Lane estate — to Halifax

77

THE YEW

You might not come across many yews in the Pennines, but where you do they stand out as truly remarkable trees. Their potential for living to an incredible age (possibly over 10,000 years) meant the druids venerated them as much as the oak and performed rituals in yew groves. Its thick fluted trunk and matted canopy mean it is also the best tree to shelter under when it is raining – it is still possible to draw maps beneath them without returning home with a soggy mush of pulp.

The European yew is one of only three conifers native to Britain, but it is found naturally only on thin dry soils like chalk or limestone. It tends to dominate areas of woodland with its dense shading – dog's mercury is one of the few flowers than can survive beneath it. Elsewhere it has been widely planted as an ornamental tree and does well anywhere but on waterlogged soils; unlike most conifers it is tolerant of pollution. Branches that reach the ground can produce roots and new growth that often outlives the original trunk, which ends up rotten at its core and thus difficult to date. The oldest trees in Britain, the Fortingall Yew and the Llangernyw Yew, are cases in point; they are both estimated to be over 4000 years old.

The yew is not naturally suited to this area and there are relatively few in the Calder Valley except around churches and great houses, the woods of the Castle Carr Estate being the only place I know where they are part of the fabric of a woodland. They are easier to find in graveyards, where it is said they were planted because their evergreen nature and long lifespan symbolised the immortality of those buried there. However, churches were often built on important pagan sites, where yews may already have been present, or it may be simply that they were planted to keep cattle out.

Yew is not planted commercially, as it is so slow growing and short, and instead often forms an understorey in beech woods. However, its dense, hard wood is highly valuable; medieval longbows were formed of yew as the wood was tough and the sap could be used as poison on the arrows. Ironically some of the bows used to defeat the French in the Middle Ages were made of trees imported from France. The yew is often associated with death and funerary customs as it is totally poisonous except for its fruit. Though the seeds inside them are poisonous, these red berry-like fruits (known as arils) that the yew produces in late autumn are particularly favoured by the blackbird.

a gnarled Yew trunk

CHAPTER 8 - MYTHOLMROYD & CRAGG VALE

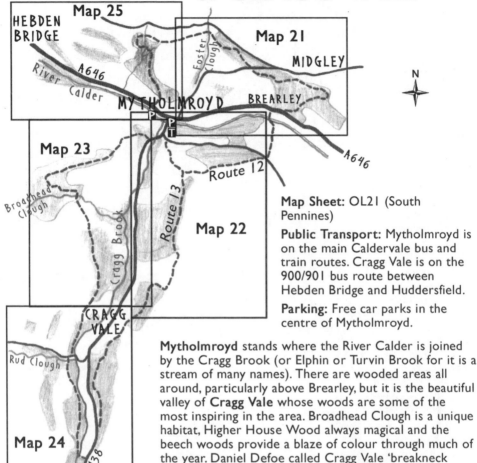

Map Sheet: OL21 (South Pennines)

Public Transport: Mytholmroyd is on the main Caldervale bus and train routes. Cragg Vale is on the 900/901 bus route between Hebden Bridge and Huddersfield.

Parking: Free car parks in the centre of Mytholmroyd.

Mytholmroyd stands where the River Calder is joined by the Cragg Brook (or Elphin or Turvin Brook for it is a stream of many names). There are wooded areas all around, particularly above Brearley, but it is the beautiful valley of **Cragg Vale** whose woods are some of the most inspiring in the area. Broadhead Clough is a unique habitat, Higher House Wood always magical and the beech woods provide a blaze of colour through much of the year. Daniel Defoe called Cragg Vale 'breakneck country' and the trees do cascade impressively down the precipitous walls of this enchanting valley.

Though it remains a largely wooded enclave, Cragg Vale's trees have been particularly threatened during the last hundred years. The Twelve Apostles (near Twist Clough) and the whole of Sutcliffe and Holderness Woods (which have been subsequently replanted) were felled during the World Wars, and much of the woodland at the head of the valley was scheduled to be clear-felled by the Wakefield Corporation and replaced with conifer plantations in the 1950s. The work was begun in Tenter Wood, Hove Yard Wood and Round Hill, but practical difficulties (poor accessibility and bad weather) and local opposition meant much of the plan was shelved and a number of fine ancient woodlands were fortunately preserved. Walking up the top of the valley, where lichen-covered oaks line the stream, it is hard to imagine this landscape populated by dark spruce trees.

old stoop in Knowl Wood

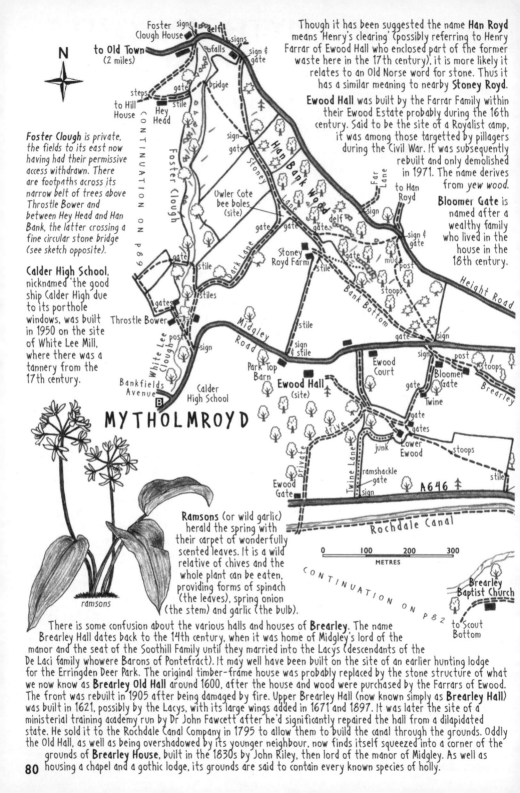

N

to Old Town
(2 miles)

Foster
Clough House — sign · delf
signs
falls
sign & gate

Though it has been suggested the name **Han Royd** means 'Henry's clearing' (possibly referring to Henry Farrar of Ewood Hall who enclosed part of the former waste here in the 17th century), it is more likely it has a similar meaning to nearby **Stoney Royd**.

Ewood Hall was built by the Farrar Family within their Ewood Estate probably during the 16th century. Said to be the site of a Royalist camp, it was among those targetted by pillagers during the Civil War. It was subsequently rebuilt and only demolished in 1971. The name derives from yew wood.

Bloomer Gate is named after a wealthy family who lived in the house in the 18th century.

steps
to Hill House
gate
bridge
stile
Hey Head
sign · gate

Foster Clough is private, the fields to its east now having had their permissive access withdrawn. There are footpaths across its narrow belt of trees above Throstle Bower and between Hey Head and Han Bank, the latter crossing a fine circular stone bridge (see sketch opposite).

Calder High School, nicknamed 'the good ship Calder High' due to its porthole windows, was built in 1950 on the site of White Lee Mill, where there was a tannery from the 17th century.

CONTINUATION ON P.89

Foster Clough
Han Bank Wood
Stoney Lane
Far Lane
to Han Royd
sign
Owler Cote bee boles (site)
Dark Lane
gate · gate · gate
delf
sign & gate
gate · stile
Stoney Royd Farm
stile
mud · post
Bank Bottom
stoops
Height Road

gate
stile
gates
stiles
Throstle Bower
post
sign
White Lee Clough
Bankfields Avenue
B
Calder High School

MYTHOLMROYD

Midgley Road
sign & stile
stile
gate
sign
post
stoops
Park Top Barn
Ewood Hall (site)
Ewood Court
gate
Bloomer Gate
Twine
gate
gates
Brearley
junk
Lower Ewood
stoops
drive
Twine Lane
ramshackle gate
Ewood Gate
sign
A646
stile

Ramsons (or wild garlic) herald the spring with their carpet of wonderfully scented leaves. It is a wild relative of chives and the whole plant can be eaten, providing forms of spinach (the leaves), spring onion (the stem) and garlic (the bulb).

ramsons

Rochdale Canal

0   100   200   300
METRES

CONTINUATION ON P.82

Brearley Baptist Church
to Scout Bottom

There is some confusion about the various halls and houses of **Brearley**. The name Brearley Hall dates back to the 14th century, when it was home of Midgley's lord of the manor and the seat of the Soothill Family until they married into the Lacys (descendants of the De Laci family who were Barons of Pontefract). It may well have been built on the site of an earlier hunting lodge for the Erringden Deer Park. The original timber-frame house was probably replaced by the stone structure of what we now know as **Brearley Old Hall** around 1600, after the house and wood were purchased by the Farrars of Ewood. The front was rebuilt in 1905 after being damaged by fire. Upper Brearley Hall (now known simply as **Brearley Hall**) was built in 1621, possibly by the Lacys, with its large wings added in 1671 and 1897. It was later the site of a ministerial training academy run by Dr John Fawcett after he'd significantly repaired the hall from a dilapidated state. He sold it to the Rochdale Canal Company in 1795 to allow them to build the canal through the grounds. Oddly the Old Hall, as well as being overshadowed by its younger neighbour, now finds itself squeezed into a corner of the grounds of **Brearley House**, built in the 1830s by John Riley, then lord of the manor of Midgley. As well as housing a chapel and a gothic lodge, its grounds are said to contain every known species of holly.

MAP 21: BREARLEY & HAN BANK WOODS

Brearley Wood and **Han Bank Wood** form a near continuous strip of woodland the northern side of the Calder Valley between Luddenden and Mytholmroyd. The 'umbrageous greenery' of Brearley Wood is a broad area of predominantly oak woodland around the twin mansions of Brearley Hall and Brearley House, though it has many different aspects. Beech covers the narrower strip of Han Bank Wood, while Foster Clough provides a slender wooded passage into Mytholmroyd.

*The public footpaths below **Black Scout** are hard to follow, despite a number of signs. This is particularly true coming from Brearley Gate, where the path peters out near an old timber cycle ramp across a couple of fallen trees. In the open area beyond, the most interesting route continues straight ahead towards the rocks at the foot of Black Scout. It picks its way between them to join a narrow path along the steep rocky slope that emerges at the top of the wood below Midgley village. The other route drops down the slope to the right and crosses an open area behind Brearley House.*

A 30ft passage was dug into the rocks of **Black Scout** (also known as Scout Head Rocks) in an attempt to find coal in the 1760s, but the seam was ultimately only three inches deep. Similarly unfruitful searches occurred all across the side of the moor above Midgley. The name Scout Head relates to the building that housed the old Lord Nelson and Black Rock Inns on the edge of Midgley.

bridge in Foster Clough

*A delightful narrow path winds its way along the top of **Brearley Wood**, branching off the main path by a pair of stone stoops. The far eastern end of the wood is somewhat cut off by Brearley Hall, but contains some old carriageways and a lovely area of larch, planted in the 1950s after part of the wood was clear-felled.*

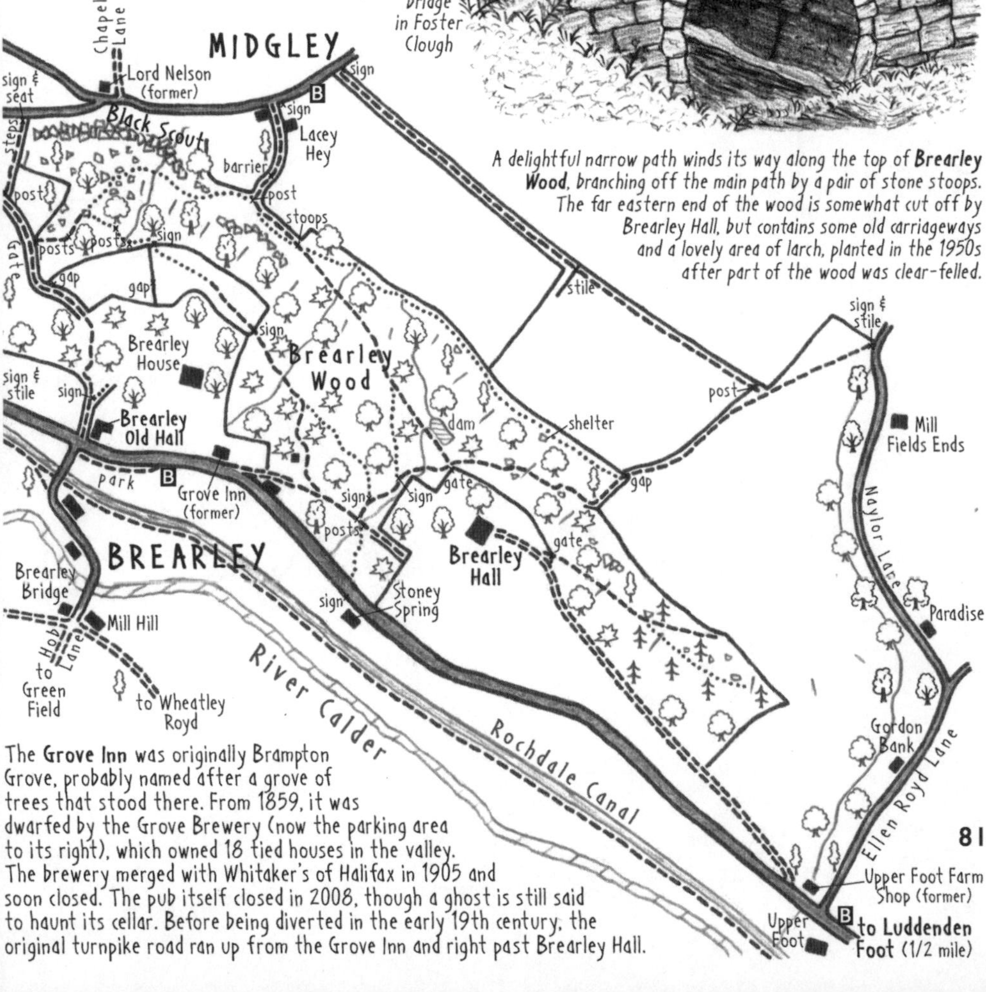

The **Grove Inn** was originally Brampton Grove, probably named after a grove of trees that stood there. From 1859, it was dwarfed by the Grove Brewery (now the parking area to its right), which owned 18 tied houses in the valley. The brewery merged with Whitaker's of Halifax in 1905 and soon closed. The pub itself closed in 2008, though a ghost is still said to haunt its cellar. Before being diverted in the early 19th century, the original turnpike road ran up from the Grove Inn and right past Brearley Hall.

81

MAP 22: HATHERSHELF SCOUT & HOLLIN HEY WOOD

South of Mytholmroyd rises the dark wooded face of Hathershelf Scout. The trees continue, with the holly of Hollin Hey Bank leading into those above the bottom of Cragg Road – the fine beech and birch of Hollin Hey, Holderness and Sutcliffe Woods, crested by Robin Hood Rocks among others.

Top Land Business Park is built on the site of Thornber's poultry farm, established in 1907 during a weavers' strike. Some of its timber buildings were incorporated into the hatchery-style design of the business park.

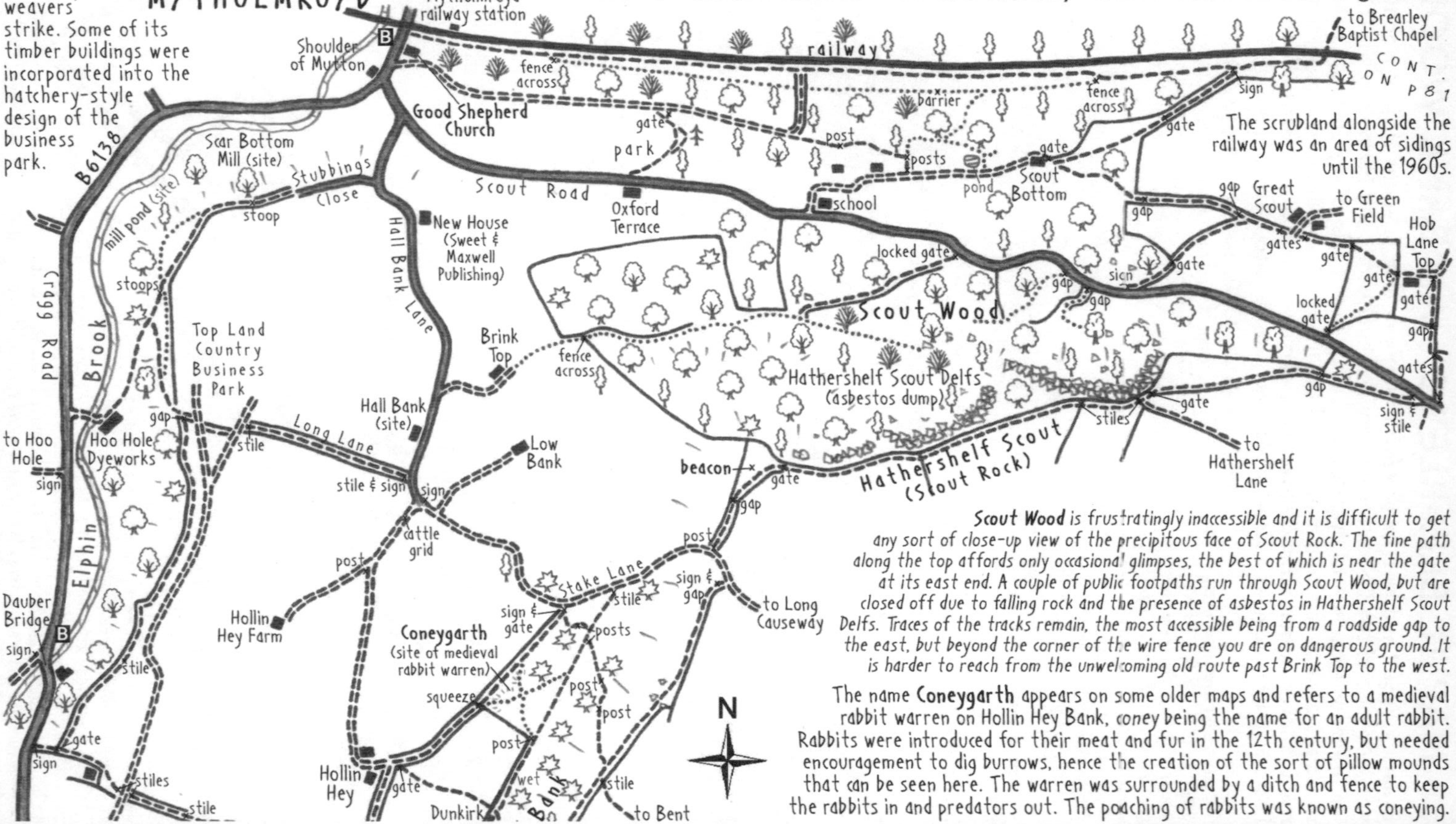

Scout Wood is frustratingly inaccessible and it is difficult to get any sort of close-up view of the precipitous face of Scout Rock. The fine path along the top affords only occasional glimpses, the best of which is near the gate at its east end. A couple of public footpaths run through Scout Wood, but are closed off due to falling rock and the presence of asbestos in Hathershelf Scout Delfs. Traces of the tracks remain, the most accessible being from a roadside gap to the east, but beyond the corner of the wire fence you are on dangerous ground. It is harder to reach from the unwelcoming old route past Brink Top to the west.

The name **Coneygarth** appears on some older maps and refers to a medieval rabbit warren on Hollin Hey Bank, coney being the name for an adult rabbit. Rabbits were introduced for their meat and fur in the 12th century, but needed encouragement to dig burrows, hence the creation of the sort of pillow mounds that can be seen here. The warren was surrounded by a ditch and fence to keep the rabbits in and predators out. The poaching of rabbits was known as coneying.

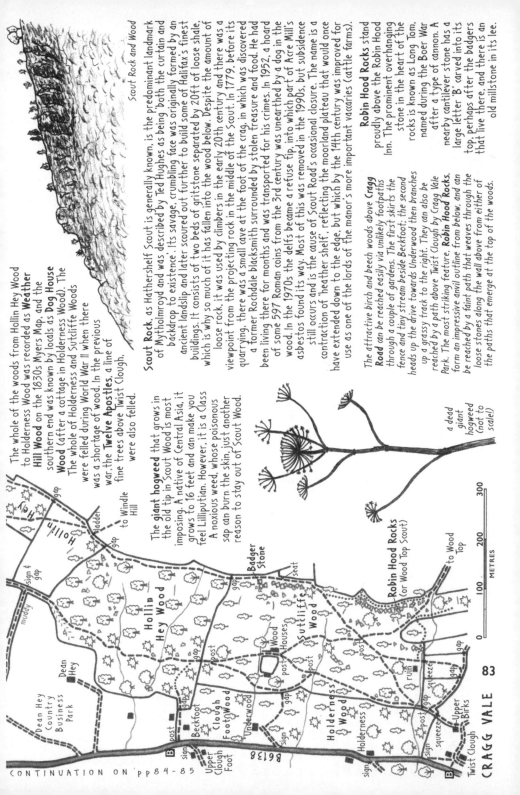

Scout Rock and Wood

The whole of the woods from Hollin Hey Wood to Holderness Wood was recorded as **Wether Hill Wood** on the 1830s Myers Map, and the southern end was known by locals as **Dog House Wood** (after a cottage in Holderness Wood). The whole of Holderness and Sutcliffe Woods were felled during World War II when there was a shortage of wood. In the previous war, the **Twelve Apostles**, a line of fine trees above Twist Clough, were also felled.

Scout Rock, as Hathershelf Scout is generally known, is the predominant landmark of Mytholmroyd and was described by Ted Hughes as being 'both the curtain and backdrop to existence'. Its savage, crumbling face was originally formed by an ancient landslip and later scoured out further to build some of Halifax's finest buildings. It consists of two beds of gritstone separated by 20ft of loose shale, which is why so much of it has fallen into the wood below. Despite the amount of loose rock, it was used by climbers in the early 20th century and there was a viewpoint from the projecting rock in the middle of the Scout. In 1779, before its quarrying, there was a small cave at the foot of the crag, in which was discovered a former Rochdale blacksmith surrounded by stolen treasure and food. He had been living there for months and was transported for his crimes. In 1952, a hoard of some 597 Roman coins from the 3rd century was unearthed by a dog in the wood. In the 1970s the delfs became a refuse tip, into which part of Acre Mill's asbestos found its way. Most of this was removed in the 1990s, but subsidence still occurs and is the cause of Scout Road's occasional closure. The name is a contraction of 'heather shelf', reflecting the moorland plateau that would once have extended down to the edge, but which by the 14th century was improved for use as one of the lords of the manor's more important vaccaries (cattle farms).

The **giant hogweed** that grows in the old tip in Scout Wood is most imposing. A native of Central Asia, it grows to 16 feet and can make you feel Lilliputian. However, it is a Class A noxious weed, whose poisonous sap can burn the skin, just another reason to stay out of Scout Wood.

The attractive birch and beech woods above **Cragg Road** can be reached easily via unlikely footpaths through a couple of gardens. The first skirts the fence and tiny stream beside Beckfoot; the second heads up the drive towards Underwood then branches up a grassy track to the right. They can also be reached by a path above Twist Clough by Cragg Vale Park. The most striking feature, **Robin Hood Rocks**, form an impressive anvil outline from below, and can be reached by a faint path that weaves through the loose stones along the wall above from either of the paths that emerge at the top of the woods.

Robin Hood Rocks stand proudly above the Robin Hood Inn. The prominent overhanging stone in the heart of the rocks is known as Long Tom, named during the Boer War after a type of cannon. A nearby cantilever stone has a large letter 'B' carved into its top, perhaps after the badgers that live there, and there is an old millstone in its lee.

a dead giant hogweed (not to scale!)

to Windle Hill

Holliп H

ladder

Dean Hey Country Business Park

Dean Hey

Holliп Hey Wood

Badger Stone

Wood Houses

Sutcliffe Wood

Robin Hood Rocks (or Wood Top Scout)

to Wood Top

Beckfoot

Upper Clough Foot

Clough Foot Wood

Underwood

Holderness Wood

Holderness

Upper Birks

Twist Clough

ruin

squeeze

squeeze

post

seat

muddy

sign

sign

sign

post

post

post

post

post

post

94p

94p

94p

94p

94p

94p

94p

94p

94p

94p

94p

0   100   200   300
METRES

B6138

83

CRAGG VALE

CONTINUATION ON pp84-85

MAP 23: CRAGG VALE NORTH

This part of Cragg Vale centres around the long arm of Parrock/ Broadhead Clough, an ancient oak woodland that is now a Local Nature Reserve because of its rare woodland bog habitat. Elsewhere the steep faces of Lord, Whams, and Paper Mill Woods rise above the attractive Cragg Brook, and Martin Wood is a pleasant Open Access area on the fringe of Mytholmroyd. Other than the boggy heart of Broadhead Clough, the area is all fairly easily explored from the B6138.

From the mid 13th century, the whole of Erringden Moor and surrounding areas were enclosed as **Erringden Deer Park**, which stocked deer to supply parkland across the Manor of Wakefield. It was enclosed by a boundary ditch and wooden palisade fence, and the remains of the original boundary can be seen clearly in the open ground on both north and south sides of Broadhead Clough. The park was subsequently expanded all the way down to Cragg Brook. The names of Bell House (which may have had a bell to call the deer in for winter feeding), Tower Hill (where it is thought there was a lookout tower), and Park Fold (below Hey Edge) are all thought to date from this period.

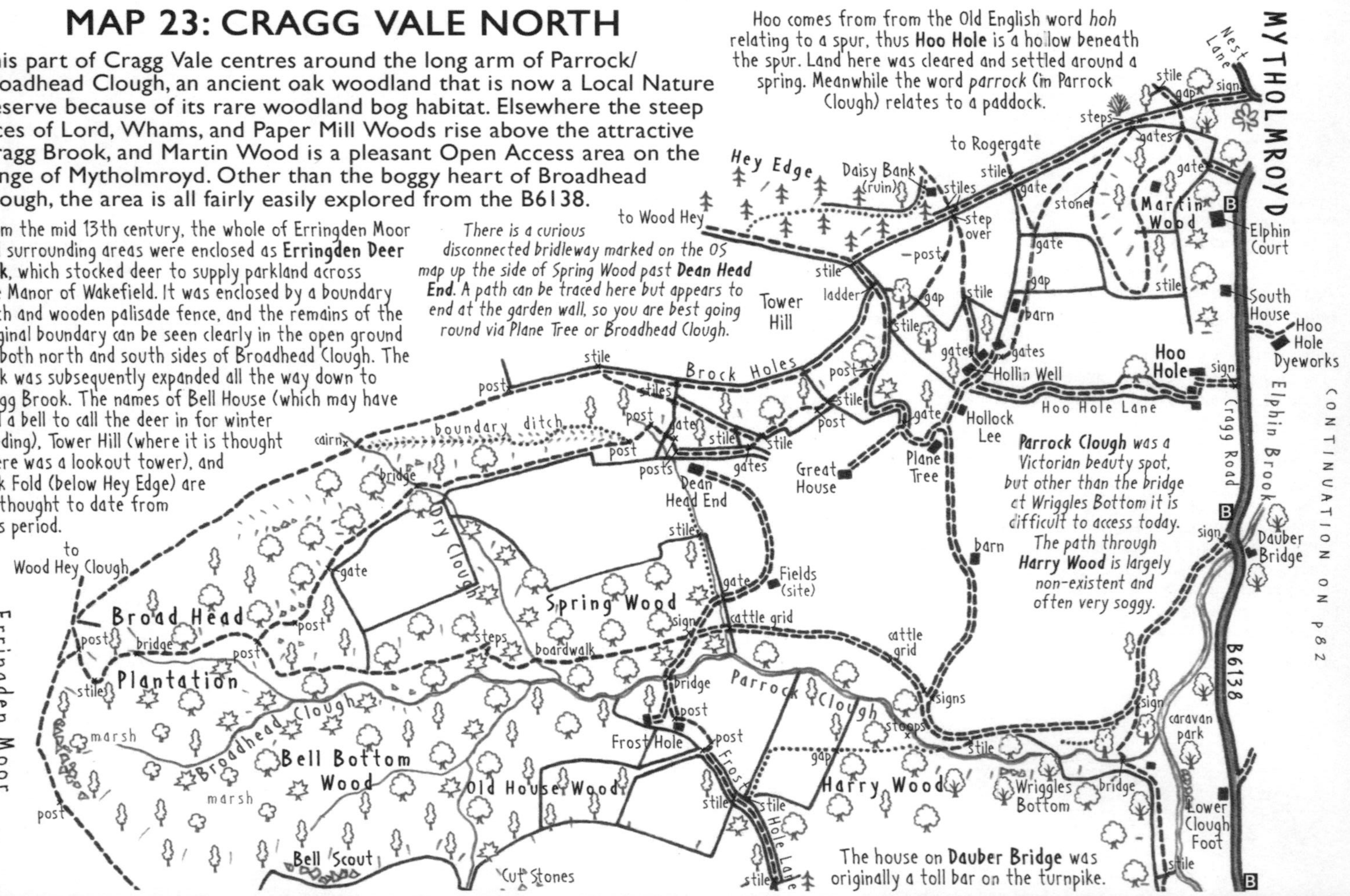

Hoo comes from from the Old English word *hoh* relating to a spur, thus **Hoo Hole** is a hollow beneath the spur. Land here was cleared and settled around a spring. Meanwhile the word *parrock* (in Parrock Clough) relates to a paddock.
*There is a curious disconnected bridleway marked on the OS map up the side of Spring Wood past **Dean Head End**. A path can be traced here but appears to end at the garden wall, so you are best going round via Plane Tree or Broadhead Clough.*
Parrock Clough was a Victorian beauty spot, but other than the bridge at Wriggles Bottom it is difficult to access today.
The path through **Harry Wood** is largely non-existent and often very soggy.
The house on **Dauber Bridge** was originally a toll bar on the turnpike.
MYTHOLMROYD
Nest Lane
Hey Edge
Daisy Bank (ruin)
to Rogergate
to Wood Hey
Martin Wood
Elphin Court
South House
Hoo Hole Dyeworks
Hoo Hole
Hoo Hole Lane
Hollin Well
Hollock Lee
Plane Tree
Great House
Tower Hill
Brock Holes
boundary ditch
Dean Head End
Fields (site)
Spring Wood
Dry Clough
Broad Head
Plantation
Broadhead Clough
Bell Bottom Wood
Old House Wood
Bell Scout
Cut Stones
Frost Hole
Frost Hole Lane
Parrock Clough
Harry Wood
Wriggles Bottom
Lower Clough Foot
caravan park
Dauber Bridge
Cragg Road
Elphin Brook
B6138
to Wood Hey Clough
Erringden Moor
marsh
cairn
boardwalk
cattle grid
stoops
barn
stile
gate
gates
post
steps
stone
sign
bridge
ladder
step over

CONTINUATION ON p82

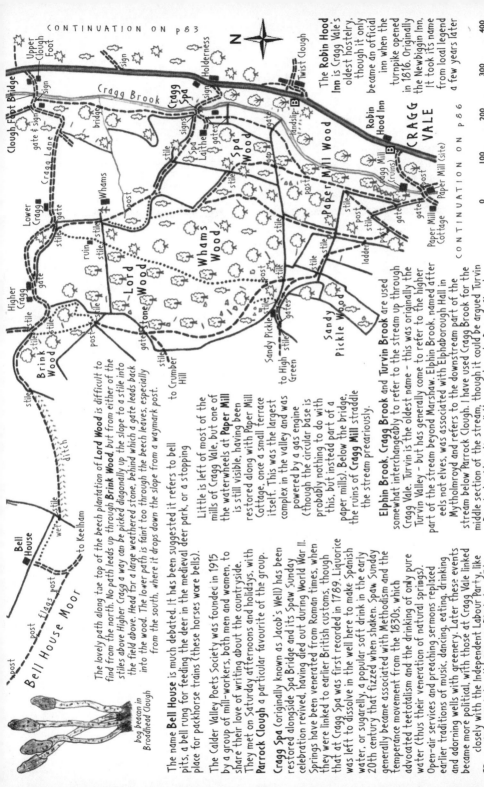

CONTINUATION ON p83

N

Upper Clough Foot
Clough Foot Bridge
sign
sign
Cragg Brook
Cragg Lane
bridge
Lower Cragg
gate & sign
gate
stile
stile
gate
stile
post
ruin
stile
stile
Higher Cragg
stile
stile
Brink Wood
post
stile
stile
gate
Stone Wood
Lord Wood
Whams Wood
Whams
sign
Spa Laithe
Cragg Spa
Holderness
Twist Clough
sign
Spa Wood
gates
gap
stile
stile
stile
stile
stile
stile
stile
post
gates
Sandy Pickle
stile
Sandy Pickle Wood
to High Green
to Crumber Hill
handslip B
Paper Mill Wood
Robin Hood Inn
B
Cragg Mill (ruins)
post
stile
ladder
Paper Mill (site)
gate
post
gate
Paper Mill Cottage

The **Robin Hood Inn** is Cragg Vale's oldest hostelry, though it only became an official inn when the turnpike opened in 1816. Originally the Newbiggin Inn, it took its name from local legend a few years later.

CRAGG VALE

CONTINUATION ON p86

0 100 200 300 400
METRES

Bell House
Bell House Moor
post
flags
post
wet
stile
ditch
to Keelham

bog beacon in Broadhead Clough

The lovely path along the top of the beech plantation of **Lord Wood** is difficult to find from the north. No path leads up through **Brink Wood**, but from either of the stiles above Higher Cragg a way can be picked diagonally up the slope to a stile into the field above. Head for a large weathered stone, behind which a gate leads back into the wood. The lower path is faint too through the beech leaves, especially from the south, where it drops down the slope from a waymark post.

The name **Bell House** is much debated. It has been suggested it refers to bell pits, a bell rung for feeding the deer in the medieval deer park, or a stopping place for packhorse trains (these horses wore bells).

The Calder Valley Poets Society was founded in 1915 by a group of mill-workers, both men and women, to share their love of writing about the countryside. They met on Saturday afternoons and holidays, with **Parrock Clough** a particular favourite of the group.

Cragg Spa (originally known as Jacob's Well) has been restored alongside Spa Bridge and its Spaw Sunday celebration revived, having died out during World War II. Springs have been venerated from Roman times, when they were linked to earlier British customs, though that at Cragg Spa was first recorded in 1789. Liquorice was left to dissolve in the well here to make Spanish water, or sugarelly, a popular soft drink in the early 20th century that fizzed when shaken. Spaw Sunday generally became associated with Methodism and the temperance movement from the 1830s, which advocated teetotalism and the drinking of only pure water (thus their veneration of natural springs). Open-air services and preaching sermons replaced earlier traditions of music, dancing, eating, drinking and adorning wells with greenery. Later these events became more political, with those at Cragg Vale linked closely with the Independent Labour Party, like earlier socialist gatherings on Blackstone² Edge.

Little is left of most of the mills of Cragg Vale, but one of the waterwheels at **Paper Mill** is still visible, having been restored along with Paper Mill Cottage, once a small terrace itself. This was the largest complex in the valley and was powered by a gas engine (though the circular base is probably nothing to do with this, but instead part of a paper mill). Below the bridge, the ruins of **Cragg Mill** straddle the stream precariously.

Elphin Brook, Cragg Brook and **Turvin Brook** are used somewhat interchangeably to refer to the stream up through Cragg Vale. Turvin is the oldest name – this was originally the Turvin Valley – but has generally come to refer to the higher part of the stream beyond Marshaw. Elphin Brook, named after eels not elves, was associated with Elphaborough Hall in Mytholmroyd and refers to the downstream part of the stream below Parrock Clough. I have used Cragg Brook for the middle section of the stream, though it could be argued Turvin Brook should continue all the way down to Parrock Clough.

85

MAP 24: CRAGG VALE SOUTH

The wooded part of Turvin Brook is among Calderdale's most charming landscapes. Squeezed in tightly by the moorland, it is like a little corner of the Lake District. Elsewhere, the hillsides above Cragg Vale are home to numerous smaller woods, linked by a maze of paths, and the valley floor is strewn with the detritus of its dozen or so mills. Like those on all sides, this idyllic rural valley once thrummed to the sound of manufacturing.

Deacon Hill Wood is a mix of open beech and dense tangles of rhododendron. The only satisfactory path through it runs up from Springfield Terrace. Theoretically there is also one up beside Fair View, though this leaves you scrambling through the bushes. In contrast, **Bank Top Wood** is riddled with paths and crested by the **Bull Fall Stone**, a fine vantage point. Adjacent Bank Top is a contender for the scruffiest farm in Calderdale and its maze of metal and mud is best avoided by following the path along the top of the wood.

Both Hove Yard Wood and the woods up Rud Clough are private, though the moorland edge above the walls is designated as Open Access. An old track (now fenced off) runs up through **Tenter Wood** and then zigzags up to Turley Holes Edge, while another can be traced from the remains of New Mill's dam up the side of Rud Clough. **Hove Yard Wood** is a lovely mixed plantation surrounded by an impressively constructed but precarious looking dry stone wall (thought to have been built by Irish labourers in their native style).

CONTINUATION ON p 85

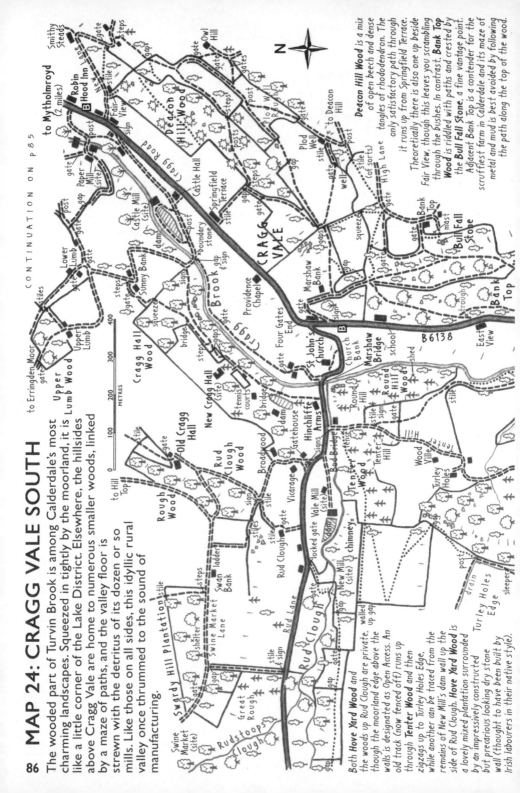

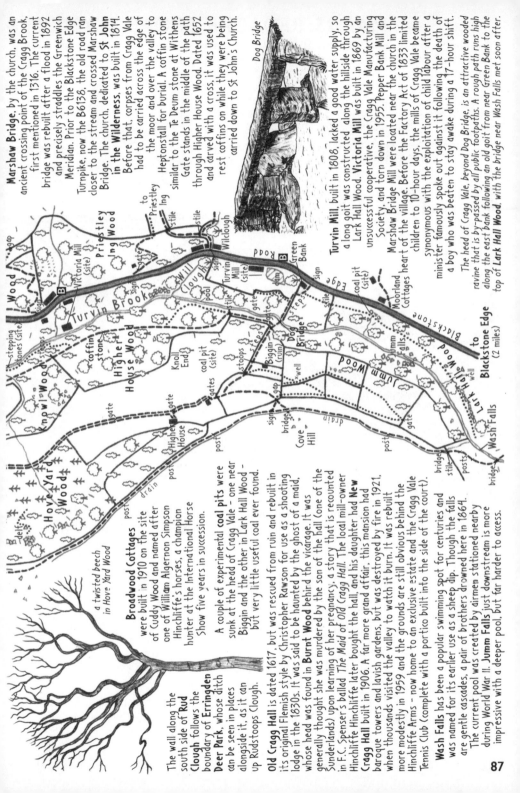

Marshaw Bridge, by the church, straddles the Cragg Brook, first mentioned in 1316. The current bridge was rebuilt after a flood in 1892 and precisely straddles the Greenwich Meridian. Prior to the Blackstone Edge Turnpike, now the B6138, the old road ran closer to the stream and crossed Marshaw Bridge. The church, dedicated to **St John in the Wilderness**, was built in 1814. Before that, corpses from Cragg Vale had to be carried across the edge of the moor and over the valley to Heptonstall for burial. A coffin stone similar to the Te Deum stone at Withens Gate stands in the middle of the path through Higher House Wood. Dated 1652 and carved with a cross, it was used to rest coffins on while they were being carried down to St John's Church.

Dog Bridge

Turvin Mill, built in 1808, lacked a good water supply, so a long goit was constructed along the hillside through **Lark Hall Wood**. **Victoria Mill** was built in 1869 by an unsuccessful cooperative, the Cragg Vale Manufacturing Society, and torn down in 1955. Pepper Bank Mill and Marshaw Bridge Mill were located near the church in the heart of the village. Before the Factory Act of 1833 limited children to 10-hour days, the mills of Cragg Vale became synonymous with the exploitation of child labour after a minister famously spoke out against it following the death of a boy who was beaten to stay awake during a 17-hour shift.

The head of Cragg Vale, beyond Dog Bridge, is an attractive wooded ravine that is by-passed by all public footpaths. A rough path runs high along the east bank following an old goit from near Green Bank to the top of **Lark Hall Wood**, with the bridge near Wash Falls met soon after.

The wall along the south side of **Rud Clough** follows the boundary of **Erringden Deer Park**, whose ditch can be seen in places alongside it, as it can up Rudstoops Clough.

a twisted beech in Hove Yard Wood

Broadwood Cottages were built in 1910 on the site of Cuddy Wood and named after one of William Algernon Simpson Hinchliffe's horses, a champion hunter at the International Horse Show five years in succession.

A couple of experimental **coal pits** were sunk at the head of Cragg Vale – one near Biggin and the other in Lark Hall Wood – but very little useful coal ever found.

Old Cragg Hall is dated 1617, but was rescued from ruin and rebuilt in its original Flemish style by Christopher Rawson for use as a shooting lodge in the 1830s. It was said to be haunted by the ghost of a maid, whose head was found in **Burnt Wood** behind the vicarage. It was generally thought she was murdered by the son of the hall (one of the Sunderlands) upon learning of her pregnancy, a story that is recounted in F.C. Spenser's ballad *The Maid of Old Cragg Hall*. The local mill-owner Hinchliffe Hinchliffe later bought the hall, and his daughter had **New Cragg Hall** built in 1906. A far more grand affair, this mansion had baroque towers and lavish gardens, but was destroyed by fire in 1921, when thousands visited the valley to watch it burn. It was rebuilt more modestly in 1959 and the grounds are still obvious behind the Cragg Vale Tennis Club (complete with a portico built into the side of the court).

Wash Falls has been a popular swimming spot for centuries and was named for its earlier use as a sheep dip. Though the falls are gentle cascades, a pair of brothers drowned here in 1864. The current pool was created by airmen stationed nearby during World War II. **Jumm Falls** just downstream is more impressive with a deeper pool, but far harder to access.

87

MAP 25: REDACRE, BROAD BOTTOM &

The northern side of the Calder Valley between Mytholmroyd and Hebden Bridge consists of a series of narrow strips of woodland that combine to give a good impression of a richly clad slope. Most of the woods here are beech, planted in the 19th century, though the oak of Redacre Wood are an exception. There are few features here other than the bright beech leaves themselves and the large houses they shroud at May Rod, Falling Royd and Broad Bottom.

Common Bank Wood was once known as Hollins, like the house on the road below, suggesting it may have been a holly plantation for providing winter feed.

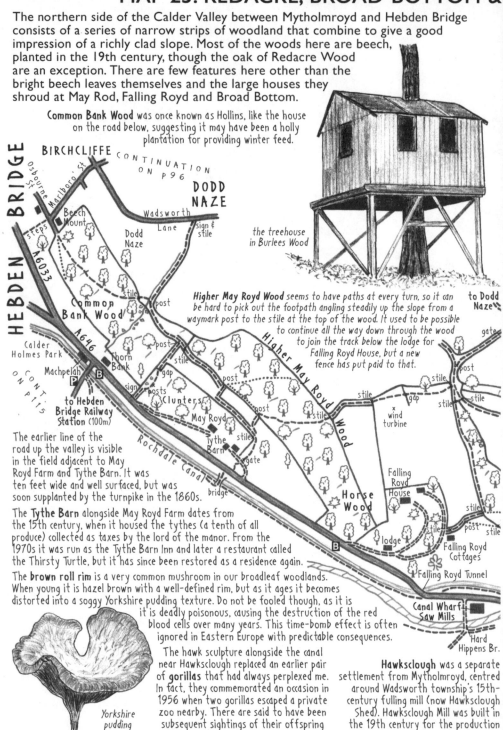

the treehouse in Burlees Wood

CONTINUATION ON P.96

Higher May Royd Wood seems to have paths at every turn, so it can be hard to pick out the footpath angling steadily up the slope from a waymark post to the stile at the top of the wood. It used to be possible to continue all the way down through the wood to join the track below the lodge for Falling Royd House, but a new fence has put paid to that.

to Dodd Naze

The earlier line of the road up the valley is visible in the field adjacent to May Royd Farm and Tythe Barn. It was ten feet wide and well surfaced, but was soon supplanted by the turnpike in the 1860s.

The Tythe Barn alongside May Royd Farm dates from the 15th century, when it housed the tythes (a tenth of all produce) collected as taxes by the lord of the manor. From the 1970s it was run as the Tythe Barn Inn and later a restaurant called the Thirsty Turtle, but it has since been restored as a residence again.

The brown roll rim is a very common mushroom in our broadleaf woodlands. When young it is hazel brown with a well-defined rim, but as it ages it becomes distorted into a soggy Yorkshire pudding texture. Do not be fooled though, as it is it is deadly poisonous, causing the destruction of the red blood cells over many years. This time-bomb effect is often ignored in Eastern Europe with predictable consequences.

Yorkshire pudding fungus

The hawk sculpture alongside the canal near Hawksclough replaced an earlier pair of gorillas that had always perplexed me. In fact, they commemorated an occasion in 1956 when two gorillas escaped a private zoo nearby. There are said to have been subsequent sightings of their offspring living in the woods along the valley.

Hawksclough was a separate settlement from Mytholmroyd, centred around Wadsworth township's 15th-century fulling mill (now Hawksclough Shed). Hawksclough Mill was built in the 19th century for the production of fustian and later aerated water.

MAY ROYD WOODS

There was a dam at the top of **Hill House Clough** that was built for the fulling mill at Broad Bottom and supplied Hill House Farm until recently.

The large houses scattered along the south-facing side of the valley – **Falling Royd, Burlees, May Royd, Redacre** and **Broad Bottom** – are legacies of the yeoman clothiers who prospered from the early textile industry in the 17th century. Yeoman was a term used for someone socially immediately below a gentleman, normally a farmer done good. The clothier usually had a workshop for both shearing and weaving. Between these processes, the wool was spun and carded in nearby cottages. After weaving, the cloth (usually kersey or later worsted) was fulled, dried and finished before the clothier shipped it for sale at the local cloth hall. With the income from this trade they were able to build these grand houses, often on the site of older properties, and they came to dominate local society, religion and politics. **Falling Royd House** was built by the Drapers of Broad Bottom in 1604. **May Royd Hall**, built where Thornhollin once stood, was home to the Sutcliffe and Cockcroft families at different times. William Thomas of **Broad Bottom** (or Broad Bottom Old Hall as it was) was one of the largest clothiers, possessing a fulling mill and as many as five looms. The hall retained some medieval carving within its timber frame (part of a minstrels' gallery), as well as a private 14th-century chapel. It is also said to have a tunnel linking it with one of the adjacent woods, though it is unclear why. Lavena Saltonstall, the suffragette after whom a room has been named at Hebden Bridge Town Hall, described conjuring up haunted spirits at Broad Bottom.

Ted Hughes wrote of playing in **Redacre Wood**, where there was an animal-shaped rock said to be the grave of the ancient Briton. It is now thought to have been buried beneath a landslip. Redacre was first recorded in the 13th century and its name may derive from 'reedy-carr'.

Redacre Delf can be explored by a couple of gaps in the fence to Redacre Wood. There is little to see but it forms a pleasant glade on the fringe of the Wadsworth Bank Fields estate.

The path through **Broad Bottom Wood** becomes suddenly vague amid the fallen beech trees, but continues roughly on a level through the heart of the wood to reach the higher of two stiles at the far side.

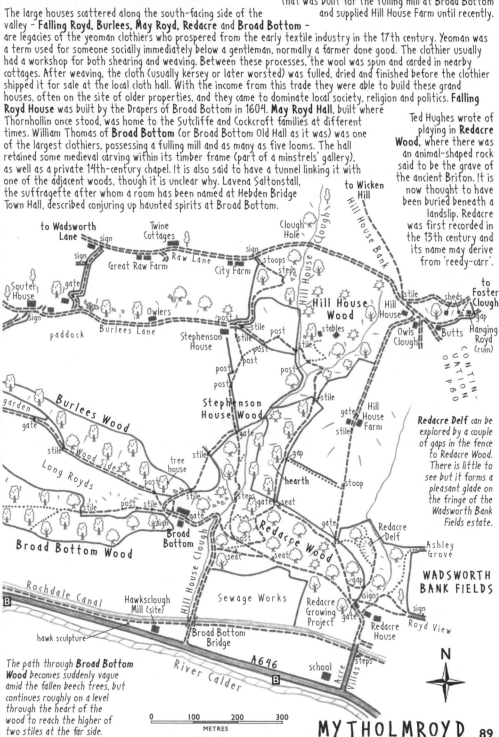

2 Follow the track right to join a tarmac track heading down past **Hill House**. Keep to the left of the houses, following a path above Butts up the hill to a ruined farm (Hanging Royd). Through a gap to its right, follow a grassy trod across the hillside to **Old Castle**. Carry straight on past the farm to reach Hey Head, following the drive down past the house to a path leading straight on through the garden and down to a bridge in **Foster Clough**. Continue across the hillside to join a walled path below **Han Bank Wood**. Keep left above Stoney Royd Farm, entering the beech woods at a gate and climbing past a quarry delf. Turn right before the gate at the top and angle steeply back down through the dense holly to emerge on **Midgley Road**.

Mytholmroyd refers to the clearing (*royd*) of a meadow at a junction of rivers (*mytholm*). It was the site of an early ford across the River Calder, and the first stone packhorse bridge built here in 1634 replaced an earlier timber structure. However, there was little development other than scattered farms like Redacre, Mytholmroyd Farm and Elphaborough Hall until the Industrial Revolution. The County Bridge was constructed for the Blackstone Edge Turnpike in 1824 with the remains of the old packhorse bridge left beneath it. The railway and parish church were built in the 1840s, and a largely Victorian town developed around them.

3 Head straight across Midgley Road and keep left to follow a waymarked path above Bloomer Gate. Skirt the edge of **Brearley Wood** and bear left through a gap on the bend. Fork left at the next post to scramble over a fallen tree. Continue to the far end of the flat area and try pick up a faint path heading straight on up through the fallen rocks at the foot of the crags of **Black Scout**. This bears round to the right, clinging to the steep slope as it climbs to the top of the wood.

Alternative Route: If you want to avoid this precarious path it is simple to continue down Brearley Gate along the edge of the wood to reach the main road at **Brearley Lane Top**.

1 Follow the A646 west out of the centre of **Mytholmroyd** towards Hebden Bridge and turn right at Acre Villas just before the school. Follow the road over the canal and bear left at the end into **Redacre Wood**. Fork right immediately and ascend to follow a path left along the top of this lovely wood. Keep right until the path eventually descends to cross the two streams of Hill House Clough. Climb across the field beyond towards **Stephenson House**, where you double back to the right and keep climbing through **Hill House Wood** to reach a track running across the hillside.

6 At the end of **Hathershelf Scout**, the path continues along the edge past the beacon to reach the top of **Stake Lane**. Follow the old track all the way down to the top of Hall Bank Lane. Soon after joining the tarmac, turn left at the second sign and follow a fenced path down to Top Land Business Park. Skirt round the business park and enter the woods above **Elphin Brook**, keeping right throughout to emerge at the end of Stubbings Close. At the T-junction, turn left down to the Shoulder of Mutton and follow the road right back under the railway into the middle of **Mytholmroyd**.

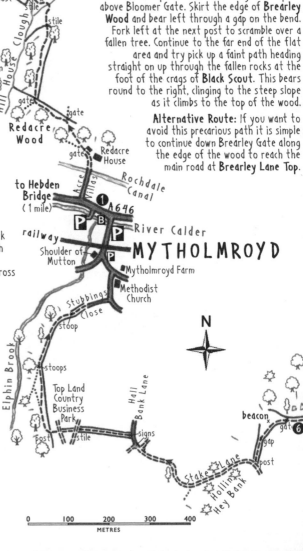

WOOD & SCOUT ROCK FROM MYTHOLMROYD

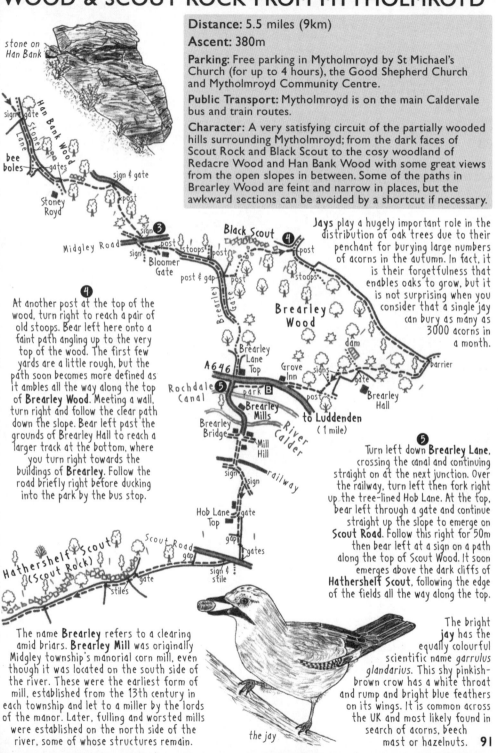

stone on Han Bank

Distance: 5.5 miles (9km)

Ascent: 380m

Parking: Free parking in Mytholmroyd by St Michael's Church (for up to 4 hours), the Good Shepherd Church and Mytholmroyd Community Centre.

Public Transport: Mytholmroyd is on the main Caldervale bus and train routes.

Character: A very satisfying circuit of the partially wooded hills surrounding Mytholmroyd; from the dark faces of Scout Rock and Black Scout to the cosy woodland of Redacre Wood and Han Bank Wood with some great views from the open slopes in between. Some of the paths in Brearley Wood are feint and narrow in places, but the awkward sections can be avoided by a shortcut if necessary.

(map labels: sign & gate, Han Bank Wood, Stoney Lane, bee boles, gates, sign & gate, Stoney Royd, post, sign, Midgley Road, Bloomer Gate, post & gap, post, stoops, post, Black Scout ❹, post, stoops, Brearley Gate, Brearley Wood, dam, barrier, Brearley Lane Top, A646, Grove Inn, signs, gate, Brearley Hall, Rochdale Canal, park B, Brearley Mills, post, to Luddenden (1 mile), River Calder, Brearley Bridge, Mill Hill, sign, sign, railway, Hob Lane Top, gap, gates, Scout Road, gap, sign & stile, Hathershelf Scout (Scout Rock), gate, stiles)

Jays play a hugely important role in the distribution of oak trees due to their penchant for burying large numbers of acorns in the autumn. In fact, it is their forgetfulness that enables oaks to grow, but it is not surprising when you consider that a single jay can bury as many as 3000 acorns in a month.

❹ At another post at the top of the wood, turn right to reach a pair of old stoops. Bear left here onto a faint path angling up to the very top of the wood. The first few yards are a little rough, but the path soon becomes more defined as it ambles all the way along the top of **Brearley Wood**. Meeting a wall, turn right and follow the clear path down the slope. Bear left past the grounds of Brearley Hall to reach a larger track at the bottom, where you turn right towards the buildings of **Brearley**. Follow the road briefly right before ducking into the park by the bus stop.

❺ Turn left down **Brearley Lane**, crossing the canal and continuing straight on at the next junction. Over the railway, turn left then fork right up the tree-lined Hob Lane. At the top, bear left through a gate and continue straight up the slope to emerge on **Scout Road**. Follow this right for 50m then bear left at a sign on a path along the top of Scout Wood. It soon emerges above the dark cliffs of **Hathershelf Scout**, following the edge of the fields all the way along the top.

The name **Brearley** refers to a clearing amid briars. **Brearley Mill** was originally Midgley township's manorial corn mill, even though it was located on the south side of the river. These were the earliest form of mill, established from the 13th century in each township and let to a miller by the lords of the manor. Later, fulling and worsted mills were established on the north side of the river, some of whose structures remain.

The bright **jay** has the equally colourful scientific name *garrulus glandarius*. This shy pinkish-brown crow has a white throat and rump and bright blue feathers on its wings. It is common across the UK and most likely found in search of acorns, beech mast or hazelnuts.

the jay

ROUTE 13: CRAGG VALE FROM MYTHOLMROYD

1 From the centre of **Mytholmroyd**, follow the B6138 out past the Shoulder of Mutton and turn right up Stocks Lane by the old fire station. Go left into Nest Lane, then turn left up a signed track (towards Daisy Bank) which leads up through the edge of **Martin Wood**. Follow the fenced path straight on up the shoulder to a stile below the plantation on Hey Edge. Immediately beyond, step over the low fence to the left and pick up a path leading diagonally up the slope.

2 Beyond a small beech wood, turn left at a stile and then fork right by a waymark post to wind through the trees by **Brock Holes**. Emerging at a stile above Dean Head End, fork left to join a fenced path above the farm. Follow the well waymarked route along the foot of the slope beyond; in summer it can be awkward to push through the dense bracken here. Continue into **Broad Head Plantation** and its beautiful nature reserve, then turn left at the first obvious junction. This leads down into **Broadhead Clough**.

3 Reaching the track at the foot of **Broadhead Clough**, turn right (signed Bell House Moor). Skirt round to the left of the buildings at Frost Hole and join a path above the wall by a tall stoop. This leads up past Harry Wood to a fenced track, which you head straight across, climbing diagonally left up through **Brink Wood** from the stile. There is little more than sheeptracks, but you should reach the top of the wood and a stile shortly before a wall comes in from the left. Cross the field to find a gate by a distinctive weathered stone and continue through the open beech at the top of **Lord Wood**.

8 Where the track bends sharply right, bear left into a walled path, then continue along the field edge to Weather Hill. Pass in front of the farm and turn left on the track beyond. Just before Wood Top, turn left down a walled path to reach the top of **Sutcliffe Wood**. Where the main path descends, keep right along the wall to clamber up onto the impressive cantilever viewpoint of **Robin Hood Rocks**. A faint path continues along the wall before dropping down to join a larger path. Follow this right past further rocky outcrops, including the B-arved Badger Stone, and on along the top of **Hollin Hey Wood**.

9 As you emerge from Hollin Hey Wood, bear left down to the foot of **Hollin Hey Bank**. By the barn at Dunkirk, carry straight on along the wall and follow a broad grassy avenue through the holly as far as a waymark post (possibly lying on the ground). Head left steeply down the bank here to a gate into **Stake Lane**, which leads down to the top of Hall Bank Lane. Follow the road all the way down into Mytholmroyd, turning left at the bottom to rejoin the B6138.

Broadhead Clough was a plantation in the mid-19th century, but the natural wet woodland has been allowed to redevelop. Its flatter marshy areas, riddled with smaller streams, are formed of thick peat and continually fed by numerous rotting trees. They are important habitats for mosses and sedges, as well as woodpeckers, curlews, redstart, flycatchers, cuckoos, twite and woodcocks, the last two being particularly rare. It is carefully managed as a Nature Reserve by Yorkshire Wildlife Trust and people are asked to keep dogs on leads and stay on the paths.

Map: MYTHOLMROYD

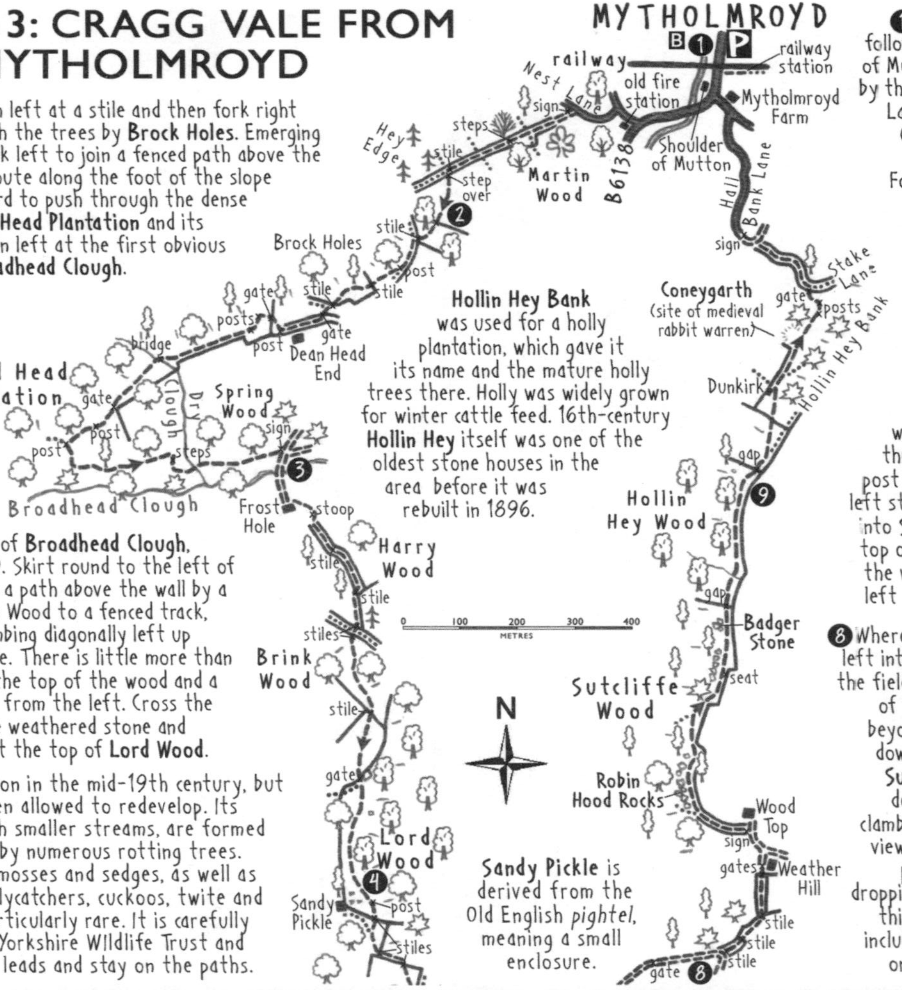

Hollin Hey Bank was used for a holly plantation, which gave it its name and the mature holly trees there. Holly was widely grown for winter cattle feed. 16th-century **Hollin Hey** itself was one of the oldest stone houses in the area before it was rebuilt in 1896.

Sandy Pickle is derived from the Old English *pightel*, meaning a small enclosure.

Map labels: railway, railway station, P, old fire station, Nest Lane, B6138, Martin Wood, Hey Edge, steps, step over, stile, post, Brock Holes, gated stile, post, gate, Dean Head End, posts, sign, Spring Wood, Dry Clough, steps, bridge, gate, post, Broad Head Plantation, Broadhead Clough, weathered stone above Lord Wood, Frost Hole, stoop, Harry Wood, Brink Wood, stiles, Lord Wood, Sandy Pickle, gate, Coneygarth (site of medieval rabbit warren), Dunkirk, gap, Hollin Hey Wood, Hall Bank Lane, Stake Lane, gate posts, Hollin Hey Bank, Mytholmroyd Farm, Shoulder of Mutton, Sutcliffe Wood, Robin Hood Rocks, Badger Stone, seat, Wood Top, Weather Hill, sign, gates, stile, gate

N

METRES 100 200 300 400

7) Climb to some rough steps at the top of **Deacon Hill Wood** and follow the wall along until it drops down a little. Here, continue along the slope to join a clearer path heading down to the track by Lower Brig Hey. Follow the track left down to Smithy Steads, where you head straight on at the bend. A path above the farm leads to another track, which you follow back up the hillside.

porcelain fungus

The **porcelain fungus** (also known as the poached egg fungus) is an eerily translucent mushroom that grows exclusively on dead beech trees. Its glassy white caps are covered in slime, but are delicious once this is removed.

Cragg Vale had its own rushbearing festival known as **Cragg Fair**, held on the second Tuesday in August. It originated around Sam's Race, a naked race from the Robin Hood Inn organised by its landlord Sam Hinchliffe, that ended in the 1870s.

6) Turn left down the B6138 and follow it to the second cluster of buildings on the right, Victoria Buildings, shortly after which a path leads up into **Bank Top Wood**. Bear left at the first bend and stay along the bottom of the wood, soon joining another path to climb up through the oaks to a major junction. The faint path leading straight on offers a possible shortcut, bending round to the left beyond an old wall, but the more obvious way heads left down the clear path. Turn right above Marshaw Bank and climb back up the slope to rejoin the shortcut. Beyond a gap, an obvious path continues straight on, but duck through another gap to the left and pick up a path on the opposite side of the wall. This soon leads down below the wood. Turn right at the bottom, climbing steps into **Deacon Hill Wood** to pick your way through the intricate mass of rhododendron.

Distance: 7 miles (11km)
Ascent: 540m

Parking: Free car parks in the centre of Mytholmroyd at St Michael's Church, by Russell Dean and at Community Centre.

Public Transport: Mytholmroyd is on the main Caldervale train & bus routes.

Character: One of the finest woodland walks anywhere and a real personal favourite. The route takes in many of Cragg Vale's varied oak, beech, holly and rhododendron woods, as well as Broad Head Clough nature reserve, Robin Hood Rocks and the beautiful Turvin Brook. There are plenty of ups and downs, but the paths are largely good and easy to follow.

4) At the far side of **Lord Wood**, a stile leads onto a path heading down from Sandy Pickle. Turn right over a stile halfway down and descend diagonally to a path along the top of the trees below. Keep right along the wall to reach a gate near the chalet at Lower Lumb Lodge. Follow the track and keep left; just before Sunny Bank, turn right up some steep steps to skirt around the top side of the property. A squeeze leads into **Cragg Hall Wood** and the path leads obviously on past the site of New Cragg Hall and its gardens, to emerge by the **Hinchliffe Arms**.

The **Hinchliffe Arms** was originally the Cragg Vale Inn, first built in the early 18th century. The current building dates from 1879 and was rechristened around 1912 after the Hinchliffe family. There was also a Sportsman's Inn on the main road at the northern end of Four Gates End until 1959.

5) Turn right on the road by the **Hinchliffe Arms**, then first left over Bod Bridge. Where the track bends, head straight on along a signed path that soon emerges alongside **Turvin Brook**. Keep left along the stream until the path climbs up to rejoin the main route through **Higher House Wood**. This eventually returns to the stream to reach **Dog Bridge**, a beautiful clapper bridge that you cross before climbing steeply to emerge on the road to the right of Green Bank.

Long Tom on Robin Hood Rocks

THE HOLLY

It is easy to think of the holly as a bush not a tree, but it is a native hardwood timber that has long been highly valued as firewood and its foliage as winter feed. It is the most shade-tolerant tree in the UK and grows well under a canopy of oak or beech because it retains its evergreen leaves for up to four years. It suckers well from its roots and thus often forms dense clusters, where the smooth grey bark of its boughs are all but hidden under the foliage. Though slow growing, it can reach anything up to 300 years old, growing pretty much anywhere except on waterlogged soil, and is largely unaffected by pollution.

Holly has separate male and female trees in about equal numbers, though confusingly the Silver Queen is male while the Golden King and Silver Milkboy varieties are female. Only female trees over the age of about twenty produce flowers and berries, and even then not where there is dense shade or in repeatedly clipped hedgerows. Good holly berry years are thought to coincide with good beech mast years. Holly was brought home during the winter for centuries to ward off evil spirits and witches, though it traditionally could not be brought into the home until Christmas Eve. Later its leaves came to represent Jesus' crown of thorns and the berries his blood. The berries are guarded robustly by the mistle thrush to stop other birds getting to them.

Holly was widely grown in the Calder Valley as winter feed for livestock, which is reflected in the number of places called Hollins that can be found. The leaves are actually very palatable to animals and only those on the bottom two metres of the tree tend to be spiky to prevent them being grazed. These leaves were probably crushed and combined with the smooth upper leaves to produce a feed known as husset. When Erringden was a deer park, it was the practice to coppice the holly where it was getting too thick, old and prickly to provide new shoots for grazing. However, its palatability does mean holly is particularly susceptible to browsing by deer, especially younger trees, and consequently the average holly tree only lives a few years.

During the Industrial Revolution holly was imported from as far afield as Ireland to be used for making bobbins, such was the local demand. It was said that 186,000 holly trees in the Needwood Forest were cut down in one year in 1802 to send to Lancashire for bobbin-making. The density of its timber meant it was also used for walking sticks, handles, bowls, musical instruments and whips. The holly-oak is the holm oak, an evergreen introduced to Britain that has glossy and spiny leaves like holly, and many similar uses.

CHAPTER 9 - HEBDEN DALE

Map Sheet: OL21 (South Pennines)

Public Transport: Hebden Bridge is on the main Caldervale train and bus routes. Bus 906 runs from Hebden Bridge to Midgehole on weekends between April and September.

Parking: Pay car parks for the National Trust's Hardcastle Crags estate at Midgehole and Clough Hole, near Slack. Free car parks in Heptonstall and pay car parks in Hebden Bridge.

Hebden Dale is generally thought to be the jewel in the crown of the Calder Valley's woodlands. Certainly it is the most well visited, with the busy Hardcastle Crags estate comprising a large part of the valley. Known by the Victorians as Little Switzerland, it was visited by as many as 20,000 in a single Whit weekend.

Before the area was an estate, it was described as 'a terrible gorge choked with great fallen boulders and trees whose roots sneaked like snakes between the gaps in the rocks', and was renowned as the hiding place for the outlaw Tom Bell (whose cave can still be found). The whole of the valley was working woodland, renowned for the quality of its timber, and there are hundreds of charcoal hearths and some early iron smelting sites to be found here.

The beautiful, mixed woods we see today were planted by the Saviles in the 1870s to improve the views on the approach to their Walshaw estate and to hide the industrial scars in the landscape while staying there. This explains the prominence of beech and the existence of various ornamental species in small pockets along the valley, including hornbeam, lime, ash and horse chestnut. Scots pine and sycamore were also planted, probably with a view to providing more commercial timber. Parts of the Saviles' woodland estate were given to the National Trust in 1950, as was land owned by Henry Mitchell Ingham and Abraham Gibson, but it was managed by the local council until 1984. Further planting took place, including that beneath Black Scout, where larch and Swedish whitebeam were planted.

It might have been very different. Plans were submitted in 1934 to make part of Hardcastle Crags near Over Wood into a reservoir, and were resubmitted in 1948 and 1967, until finally being rejected after opposition from the Hardcastle Crags Preservation Society and Calder Civic Trust, which was initially founded to fight this cause. Large pylons across the valley were also threatened, but what is retained is a beautifully embowered dean that manages to swallow all of its visitors and still hold something back.

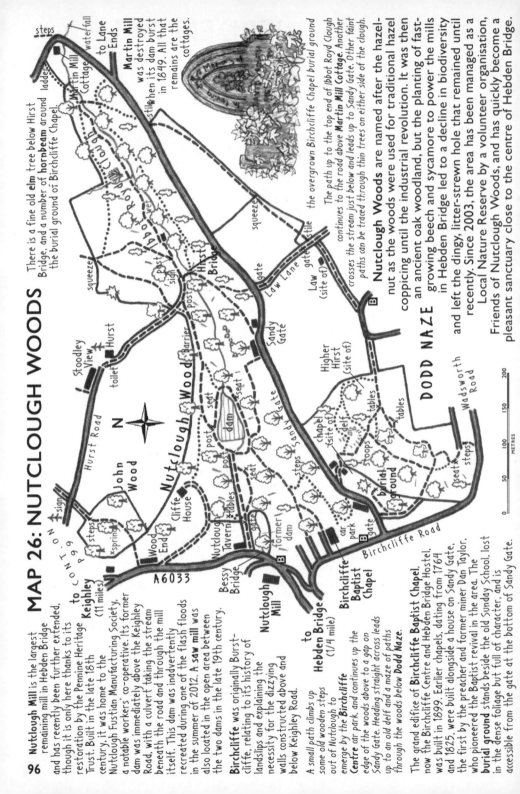

Nutclough Mill is the largest remaining mill in Hebden Bridge and has recently been further extended, though it is only here thanks to its restoration by the Pennine Heritage Trust. Built in the late 18th century, it was home to the Nutclough Fustian Manufacturing Society, a notable workers' co-operative. Its former dam was immediately above the Keighley Road, with a culvert taking the stream beneath the road and through the mill itself. This dam was inadvertently recreated during one of the flash floods in the summer of 2012. A **saw mill** was also located in the open area between the two dams in the late 19th century.

Birchcliffe was originally Burstcliffe, relating to its history of landslips and explaining the necessity for the dizzying walls constructed above and below Keighley Road.

A small path climbs up some old wooden steps out of Nutclough to emerge by the **Birchcliffe Centre** car park, and continues up the edge of the woods above to a gap on Sandy Gate. Heading straight across leads up to an old delf and a maze of paths through the woods below **Dodd Naze**.

The grand edifice of **Birchcliffe Baptist Chapel**, now the Birchcliffe Centre and Hebden Bridge Hostel, was built in 1899. Earlier chapels, dating from 1764 and 1825, were built alongside a house on Sandy Gate, the first by the preacher and former miner Dan Taylor, who pioneered the Baptist revival in the area. The **burial ground** stands beside the old Sunday School, lost in the dense foliage but full of character, and is accessible from the gate at the bottom of Sandy Gate.

There is a fine old **elm** tree below Hirst Bridge, and a number of **hornbeam** around the burial ground of Birchcliffe Chapel.

The path up to the top end of Ibbot Royd Clough continues to the road above **Martin Mill Cottage.** Another crosses the stream just below and leads up to Sandy Gate. Other faint paths can be traced through thin trees on either side of the clough.

Nutclough Woods are named after the hazel-nut as the woods were used for traditional hazel coppicing until the industrial revolution. It was then an ancient oak woodland, but the planting of fast-growing beech and sycamore to power the mills in Hebden Bridge led to a decline in biodiversity and left the dingy, litter-strewn hole that remained until recently. Since 2003, the area has been managed as a Local Nature Reserve by a volunteer organisation, Friends of Nutclough Woods, and has quickly become a pleasant sanctuary close to the centre of Hebden Bridge.

Martin Mill was destroyed when its dam burst in 1849. All that remains are the cottages.

to Lane Ends

steps
waterfall
ladder
Martin Mill Cottage
Clough
Hirst
Stoodley View
Hurst
toilet
Hurst Road
squeeze
squeeze
Post
sign
Hirst Bridge
Post
sign
stile
stile
Law Lane
gate
Sandy Gate
Law gate
(site of)
B
John Wood
steps
spring
Wood End
Cliffe House
Nutclough Wood
barrier
seat
post
post
dam
seat
post
seat
tables
Nutclough Tavern
tables
gate
formerly dam
car park
B
gate
Bessy Bridge
Nutclough Mill
A6033
Birchcliffe Centre
Birchcliffe Baptist Chapel
Birchcliffe Road
B
Sandy Gate
steps
chapel (site of)
delf
stoops
burial ground
tables
tables
Higher Hirst (site of)
B
Wadsworth Road
DODD NAZE
seat
steps

CONTOUR 199

N

to Keighley (11 miles)

to Hebden Bridge (¼ mile)

0   50   100   150   200
METRES

TREES WITH MAGICAL PROPERTIES

THE HAZEL

The hazel has a long history in this area, having dominated large parts of the northern uplands during its prehistory, before later providing a productive understorey in oak woodlands. As hazel naturally forms multiple stems, it is an easy tree to coppice and was widely used for this purpose until it fell out of fashion in the 19th century and was increasingly shaded out. Nutclough is named after the hazel it was once covered in, but like many places was planted with ornamental beech and sycamore by the Victorians. As a result, hazel is not seen in much ancient woodland in the South Pennines and is largely absent from the seed bank, despite appearing to thrive here.

hazelnuts

The tree of the poets, the hazel is also profoundly magical, used by water diviners and often found surrounding holy wells, where it held the offerings of pilgrims in its twisted branches. From it are gathered the nuts of knowledge, the cob or hedge nuts that were used in All Hallows Eve games. It also supports more wildlife species than any other tree. Yet, in Yorkshire slang, we have still managed to associate this wonderful tree with the term 'hazeling', which means flogging someone with a hazel bough.

THE ROWAN

Though commonly known as the mountain ash because of its pattern of leaves, this small tree is entirely unrelated to the ash. It was also known as kern or quickbeam, a name that became corrupted to witchen or wicken (as in Wicken Hill above Mytholmroyd or Wickenberry Clough near Todmorden) because of its long association with witches. Thought to protect against witchcraft, rowan was often grown near a dwelling to ward off evil spirits and, on Rowan Tree Day (May 2nd), rowan twigs were placed above every door. Witch posts were popular in West Yorkshire until the early 20th century; carved from rowan and covered in cross patterns, they framed the screen in front of the hearth, which was thought a possible entry point for a witch. There is one still at Stocks House in Barkisland.

THE HAWTHORN

Hawthorn is so ubiquitous as a hedgerow plant that it has acquired many names, including May tree, whitethorn, albespine, quickthorn and azzy-tree. The name hawthorn itself derives from an Anglo-Saxon word for hedge, and it was used to delineate many old tracks – anywhere known as The Haigh was enclosed by hawthorn hedges not walls. Its cheery blossom contrasts sharply with its thorny branches and marks the arrival of summer. At this time, boughs were traditionally brought into the house, but for the rest of the year it was thought a bad omen. As well as haws, its bitter berries have been known as eagleberries, peggles and thornapples.

THE ELDER

Elder is a robust little tree that will grow anywhere it has light. Also known as the ellen, scaw or buttery tree, it was said to bleed when cut, possibly as it was the wood from which the cross is supposed to have been made. It was thought unlucky to burn or cut down elder, or even have one close to the house, as it was possible for them to be possessed by witches – hence its alternative name, witchwood. Its main use has always been as food or drink.

MAP 27: HEBDEN DALE SOUTH (Hebden Bridge to Midgehole)

The lower portion of the Hebden Water, leading out of Hebden Bridge, is surrounded by various woods, all cut through by a number of roads that can make them hard to walk in. Lee Wood is the most accessible. Above Midgehole itself stand the beautiful beeches of Kitling Clough and Crimsworth Wood, crested by the Stoodley Pike-inspired war memorial on Smeekin Hill.

The **birch polypore** is a large spongy bracket fungus, common in the birchwoods of Hebden Dale. It doesn't have a pleasant taste, but has long been held to have medicinal properties and was found on the body of Ötzi, a 5300-year old mummy found in the Alps.

Pecket Well Clough only becomes so above Kitling Bridge. The more familiar ravine below is correctly known as **Kitling Clough** and has an impressive but hard-to-access waterfall (Great Fall) in its midst.

The name **Akroyd** refers to an oak clearing, dating from the 13th century when the site was first occupied.

Crimsworth Dyeworks were built on the site of an earlier spinning mill in the 1860s by a Salford firm to take advantage of the local water for the dyeing and finishing of **fustian**. This dense hard-wearing cotton fabric, used in corduroy, moleskin and whipcord clothing, was originally made in Manchester, but Hebden Bridge soon became the centre for its production as well as finishing, a shift that has been suggested as having started at this very mill. Its chimney was only demolished in recent years and the Hebden Dyeing and Finishing Company used the premises until 2009.

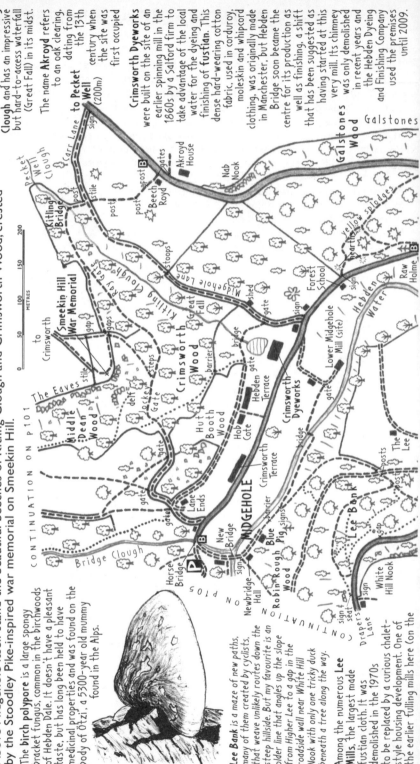

Map labels:
to Pecket Well (200m)
Pecket Well Clough
Carr Lane
sign
Kitling Bridge
post
stile
post
post B
gates
Beech Royd
Akroyd House
Nab Nook
Galstones Wood
Galstones
yellow splodges
hearths
B
Smeekin Hill War Memorial
stoops
Midgehole Lane
to Crimsworth
Kay gate
Kitling Clough
gap
gaps
Great Fall
shed
gate
sign
Forest School
Hebden Water
Raw Holme
B
The Eaves
stile
steps
Locke Gate
delf
Crimsworth Wood
barrier
bridge
gate
Hebden Terrace
Crimsworth Dyeworks
Middle Dean Wood
gate
Hut Booth Wood
Hob Cote
Crimsworth Terrace
gate
Lane Ends
gate
barrier
MIDGEHOLE
gate
Lower Midgehole Mill (site)
gate
bridge
posts
The Lee
post
Lee Bank
gap
New Bridge
B
Blue Pig
sign
signs
Horse Bridge
P
Robin Rough Wood
sign
White Hill Nook
Bridge Clough
Newbridge Hall
Drapers Lane
sign & seat
sign

CONTINUATION ON P101

CONTINUATION ON P105

METRES
0 50 100 150 200

Lee Bank is a maze of new paths, many of them created by cyclists, that weave unlikely routes down the steep hillside. But my favourite is an older line that angles up the slope from Higher Lee to a gap in the roadside wall near White Hill Nook with only one tricky duck beneath a tree along the way.

Among the numerous **Lee Mills**, the largest made fustian cloth. It was demolished in the 1970s to be replaced by a curious chalet-style housing development. One of the earlier fulling mills here (on the

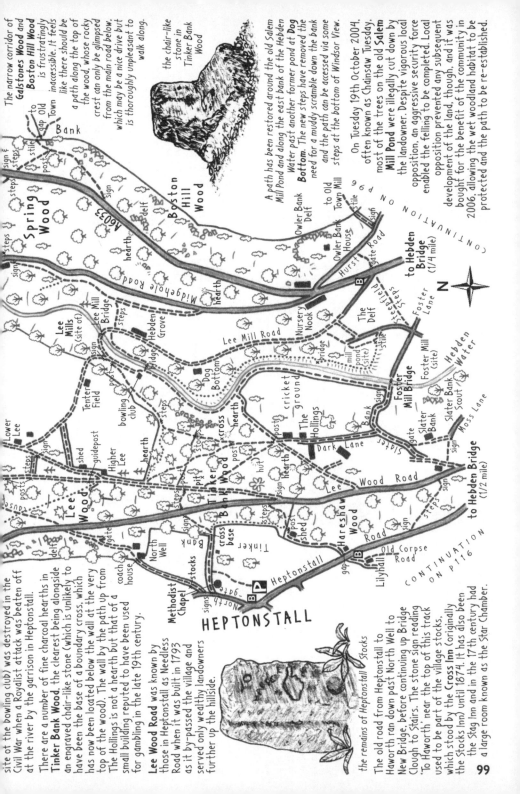

The narrow corridor of **Galstones Wood** and **Boston Hill Wood** is frustratingly inaccessible. It feels like there should be a path along the top of the wood, whose rocky crest can only be glimpsed from the main road below, which may be a nice drive but is thoroughly unpleasant to walk along.

the chair-like stone in Tinker Bank Wood

A path has been restored around the old Salem Mill Pond and along the east bank of the Hebden Water past another former pond at **Dog Bottom**. The new steps have removed the need for a muddy scramble down the bank and the path can be accessed via some steps at the bottom of Windsor View.

On Tuesday 19th October 2004, often known as Chainsaw Tuesday, most of the trees on the old **Salem Mill Pond** were illegally cut down by the landowner. Despite vigorous local opposition, an aggressive security force enabled the felling to be completed. Local opposition prevented any subsequent development of the land, though, and it was bought for the benefit of the community in 2006, allowing the wet woodland habitat to be protected and the path to be re-established.

site at the bowling club) was destroyed in the Civil War when a Royalist attack was beaten off at the river by the garrison in Heptonstall.

There are a number of fine charcoal hearths in **Tinker Bank Wood**, the clearest being alongside an engraved chair-like stone (which is unlikely to have been the base of a boundary cross, which has now been located below the wall at the very top of the wood). The wall by the path up from The Hollings is not a hearth but that of a small building reputed to have been used for gambling in the late 19th century.

Lee Wood Road was known by those in Heptonstall as Needless Road when it was built in 1793 as it bypassed the village and served only wealthy landowners further up the hillside.

The old road from Heptonstall to Haworth ran down past North Well to New Bridge, before continuing up Bridge Clough to Stairs. The stone sign reading 'To Haworth' near the top of this track used to be part of the village stocks, which stood by the **Cross Inn** (originally the Stocks Inn) until 1874. It has also been the Stag Inn and in the 17th century had a large room known as the Star Chamber.

the remains of Heptonstall Stocks

Spring Wood

Bank

to Old Town

gap

Old Bank

stile

signs

steps

post

sign

steps

steps

signs

A6033

Boston Hill Wood

delf

hearth

sign

hearth

Midgehole Road

Owler Bank Delf

to Old Town Mill

Owler Bank House

Hurst Road

stile

to Hebden Bridge (1/4 mile)

CONTINUATION ON P96

B

Steeplefield Road

steps

Foster Lane

N

hearth

Lee Mills (site of)

Lee Mill Bridge

steps

Bridge

Hebden Grove

Lee Mill Road

Nursery Nook

The Delf

stile

mill pond (site)

Hebden Water

Foster Mill Bridge

Foster Mill (site)

Dog Bottom

bridge

Lower Lee

sign

guidepost

shed

Higher Lee

bowling club

hearth

steps

Tenter Field

cricket ground

The Hollings

cross

stoops

post

hearth

Slater Bank

Slater Bank Scout

Moss Lane

Dark Lane

gate

sign

Lee Wood

delf

gate

sign

steps

pit

hut

sign

shed

Tinker Bank Wood

cross base

sign

Lee Wood Road

Hareshaw Wood

sign

steps

to Hebden Bridge (1/2 mile)

crust

posts

steps

North Well

stocks

Tinker

gap

Lilyhall

Old Corpse Road

B

CONTINUATION ON P116

Methodist Chapel

coach house

North gate

signs

P

Heptonstall

HEPTONSTALL

99

MAP 28: CRIMSWORTH DEAN

Crimsworth Dean stretches up from Midgehole to the bottom of Stairs, its lower wooded section forming part of the National Trust's Hardcastle Crags estate. The mixed beech, pine and oak woods are as attractive as the woods along the Hebden Water, but much more secluded and less trodden. The whole valley is a SSSI for its geological exposures of Kinderscoutian sandstone.

The name **Helliwell Wood** appears to relate to an early British holy well, but there is little record of its location. The West Yorkshire Archaeological Survey records it closer to Green Hirst, around which there were three wells, but there are springs all along the steep valley sides here that may once have been consecrated by our medieval forebears.

It was at **Great Mount Quarry** that Ted Hughes' family camped and hunted rabbits, calling the place happy valley. He only went there once, at the age of 7 with his much older brother Gerald in the late 1930s, but it was an experience that he said inspired him to become a poet: "It was in Crimsworth Dean... that I had the dream that turned later into all my writing. *The Deadfall* recounts this tale, in which he awakes in the tent at night to be led to a fox caught in a gamekeeper's trap by its spirit in the form of an old woman. Upon burying the unfortunate fox, he digs up a small ivory fox that he treasures thereafter. After the war, the quarry was used as a council dump.

The series of dams in **Bridge Clough** were built in the 1860s by the Worrall family to supply water to the Crimsworth Dye Works at the foot of Kitling Clough (see p.98). This was a valuable source of work during the Cotton Famine, as was the construction of Keppit Holme Dam for New Bridge Mill. The conduit ran down to the tank below the aqueduct bridge, along the river bank and then across the fields below Hebden Terrace, and is still largely traceable.

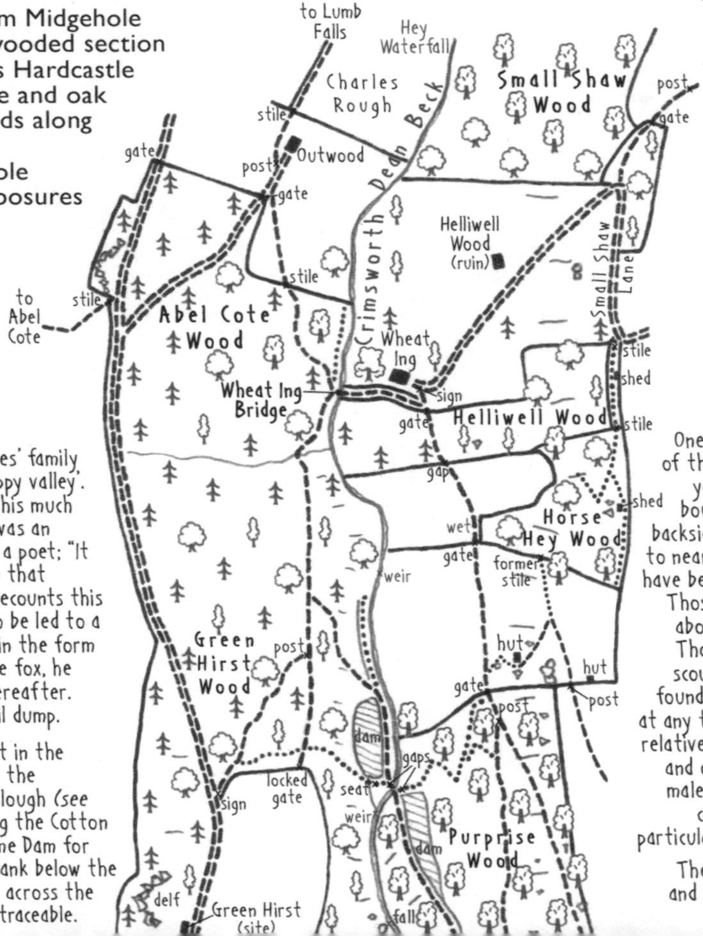

One of the great pleasures of wandering the woods of the Upper Calder Valley is the frequency with which you come face to face with roe deer, before they bounce off through the trees flashing their white backsides. Though native to Britain, they were hunted to near-extinction in England by the 18th century, but have been successfully reintroduced in many areas since. Those in Upper Calder were released onto the moors above Cragg Vale in the middle of the 20th century. Though they have proliferated and are considered a scourge by some, a recent survey in Hardcastle Crags found there were approximately twenty in the estate at any time, hardly an alarming population. Roe deer are relatively small and reddish-brown (darkening in winter) and only the females have the white rump, while the males have short antlers. They are generally solitary creatures other than during the winter, and feed particularly on the shoots and leaves of holly and beech.

The section of open ground between Purprise Wood and Horse Hey Wood was also once woodland, marked on 19th-century maps as **Brotherton Wood**.

a female roe deer

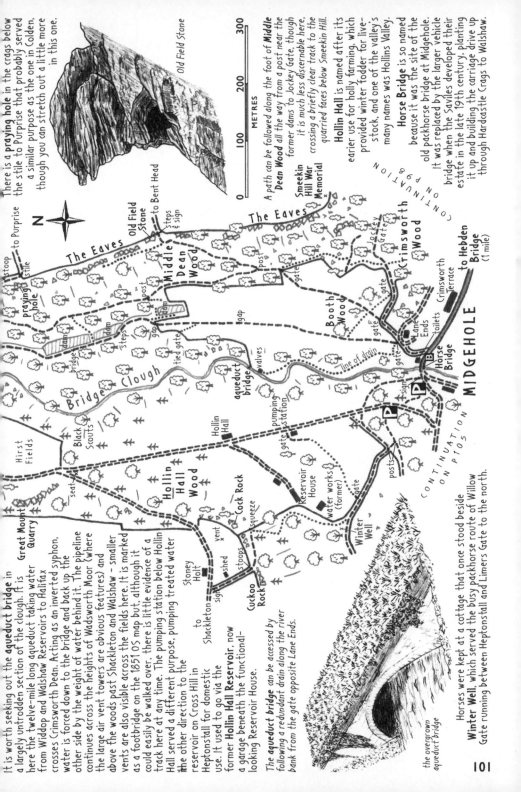

It is worth seeking out the **aqueduct bridge** in a largely untrodden section of the clough. It is here the twelve-mile long aqueduct taking water from Widdop and Walshaw Reservoirs to Halifax crosses Crimsworth Dean. Acting as an inverted syphon, water is forced down to the bridge and back up the other side by the weight of water behind it. The pipeline continues across the heights of Wadsworth Moor (where the large air vent towers are obvious features) and above the woods past Shackleton and Walshaw – smaller vents are also visible across the fields here. It is marked as a footbridge on the 1:25 105 map but, although it could easily be walked over, there is little evidence of a track here at any time. The pumping station below Hollin Hall served a different purpose, pumping treated water the other direction to the reservoir on Cross Hill in Heptonstall for domestic use. It used to go via the former **Hollin Hall Reservoir**, now a garage beneath the functional-looking Reservoir House.

The **aqueduct bridge** can be accessed by following a redundant drain along the river bank from the gate opposite Lane Ends.

Horses were kept at a cottage that once stood beside **Winter Well**, which served the busy packhorse route of Willow Gate running between Heptonstall and Limers Gate to the north.

the overgrown aqueduct bridge

There is a **praying hole** in the crags below the stile to Purprise that probably served a similar purpose as the one in Colden, though you can stretch out a little more in this one.

Old Field Stone

A path can be followed along the foot of **Middle Dean Wood** all the way from a post near the former dams to Jockey Gate, though it is much less discernable here, crossing a briefly clear track to the quarried faces below Smeekin Hill.

Hollin Hall is named after its earier use for holly farming, which provided winter fodder for live-stock, and one of the valley's many names was Hollins Valley.

Horse Bridge is so named because it was the site of the old packhorse bridge at Midgehole. It was replaced by the larger vehicle bridge when the Saviles developed their estate in the late 19th century, planting it up and building the carriage drive up through Hardcastle Crags to Walshaw.

CONTINUATION ON P98

CONTINUATION ON P105

Map labels: to Purprise · stoop · stile · N · praying hole · The Eaves · Old Field Stone · steps & sign · to Bent Head · The Eaves · Middle Dean Wood · post · dam · dam · bridge · steps · dam · gap · gap · tied gate · post · gap · Bridge Clough · Hirst Fields · Black Scouts · seat · Great Mount Quarry · to Shackleton · Stoney Holt · sign · shed · stoops · Cuckoo Rock · vent · Cock Rock · squeeze · Hollin Hall Wood · Hollin Hall · valves · aqueduct bridge · line of drain · pumping station · Reservoir House · water works (former) · gate · Winter Well · posts · gate · Booth Wood · gate · gate · Crimsworth Wood · Jockey Gate · gate · Lane Ends · Crimsworth Terrace · toilets · gate · Horse Bridge · sign · P · P · B · MIDGEHOLE · to Hebden Bridge (1 mile) · Smeekin Hill War Memorial

METRES · 0 · 100 · 200 · 300

101

ROUTE 14: CRIMSWORTH DEAN & LUMB FALLS FROM HEBDEN BRIDGE

Distance: 6 miles (11km)
Ascent: 370m

Parking: Various pay & display car parks and street parking in Hebden Bridge.

Public Transport: Hebden Bridge is on the main Caldervale train & bus routes.

Character: A thorough exploration of Crimsworth Dean that follows the open valley side from Smeekin Hill War Memorial up to Lumb Hole and returns via the varied woodlands of the valley. The route follows good paths throughout, passing through a mix of different landscapes, and taking in Kitling Clough, the aqueduct bridge and Tinker Bank Wood.

Lumb Bridge

③ At the top of the clough, turn left by a waymark post and cross **Kitling Bridge**. After 200m, scramble up off the track to pick up a path following the fenceline right up to **Smeekin Hill War Memorial**. The path continues round to the right, following a wall up to **Lower Crimsworth Farm**. Follow the track left in front of the farm and continue up the hill as far as a bridle gate on the left. This path follows the wall round to **Purprise**. Turn left at the track above the farm and squeeze through a couple of gates to emerge in the field to the right. Head diagonally down the slope slightly (aiming below the prominent ash tree) to reach a waymark post. A worn line then zigzags roughly down the open slope past a small ruined hut. Turn right along the obvious path at the bottom and follow this to **Wheat Ing**.

Purprise was marked on an early map as Poorprice, suggesting it was a cheap undesirable area of land, rather than from the French word *pourpris* for an enclosure or close.

④ At **Wheat Ing**, there is an obvious shortcut left across the bridge, but the route continues straight ahead, following the tarmac track up the hill. At the bend, bear left through the edge of **Small Shaw Wood**. Emerging in a field beyond, bear right to aim for a gap in the far corner. Follow the wall up to the corner and turn left over a stone stile, staying in the fields to pass past Upper Small Shaw. The well waymarked route continues past Barker Cote and Gib to join **Haworth Old Road**, which can be picked up earlier if in doubt. Turn left at the sign beyond and follow Lumb Lane down to **Lumb Hole**.

⑤ Cross **Horse Bridge** above the falls and climb as far as a post, leading left onto a path across **Charles Rough** high above Crimsworth Dean. Beyond Outwood, this drops down to a track. Bear left before the gate to descend to a stile on the edge of **Abel Cote Wood**. Continue past **Wheat Ing Bridge**, climbing back through the pines before bearing left at the first junction. If you reach a waymark post you've gone too far, but can still easily cut down to the other path.

Lumb Bridge stood on Limers Gate, a pack-horse route between Lancashire and Halifax, and used to be known as Horse Bridge (and the valley Horse–bridge Clough). It is said to be haunted by a White Lady, the ghost of a woman who committed suicide by jumping from the bridge into the falls. However, it is clearly impossible to reach the falls from the bridge, and you only have to watch the kids jumping into the pool from the rocks high above **Lumb Hole waterfall** to know that this is hardly a way to certain death.

102

6 Skirt around the dam and turn left through a metal gap to join a path along the side of another series of dams in **Middle Dean Wood**. Beyond a short set of steps, keep right before the last dam to squeeze through a gap into the field. A clear path leads steadily down to Lane Ends, but if you want to see the **aqueduct bridge** (see page 101), head right down the slope at the first gap. A faint path along the river can then be picked up by the concrete tank near the bridge and leads back up to the gate at **Lane Ends.**

2 Head straight across Lee Mill Road and turn left at the top of the steps, cutting through the woods to Raw Holme. Though you can follow Midgehole Road, it is more pleasant to climb the steps opposite and keep left along the bottom of **Spring Wood.** Rejoin the road briefly and turn right before Ivy House into a walled path that leads up the side of **Kitling Clough.**

1 From the centre of **Hebden Bridge,** follow pedestrianised Bridge Gate to its end and turn left by the Shoulder of Mutton. Over the bridge, turn immediately right, joining a footway along the river bank until you are forced back to the road. Follow Valley Road right, crossing the river again before turning second right up Windsor Road. Climb the hill and bear left before the houses, then look for some steps leading down to the site of the old mill pond. A lovely path leads around the pond and along the river all the way to **Lee Mill Road.**

Spring Wood

Midgehole Road

Lee Mill Rd

Smeekin Hill War Memorial

Great Fall

Clough

Clough

Ivy House

semi-circular hut

stoops

sign

sign & steps

Raw Holme

steps

steps

sign

MIDGEHOLE

gate 7

Lane Ends

barrier

signs

Blue Pig

gap

gap

aqueduct bridge

tank

toilets

P

B

Hebden Water

A boggart is said to reside beneath **Kitling Bridge,** whose name is thought to refer to a young animal, or specifically a kitten.

The White Lion, built in 1657, is the oldest building in Hebden Bridge and was known as King's Farm, after the family that owned it and served liquor to passing travellers. Another pub across the road, the White Horse, also began life as Bannister's Farm. Later the White Lion was the starting point for the renowned T'Brig Races; until 1820, men ran to Mayroyd and back naked (the women were allowed chemises) for prizes hung above the door.

METRES

0   100   200   300   400

N

Higher Lee

post

Lee Wood

Tinker Bank Wood

bowling post club

The Hollings

Hebden

bridge

Windsor Rd

steps

Slater Bank

P

Foster Mill Bridge

Hebden Water

Valley Rd

Town Hall

P

Shoulder of Mutton

to Keighley (11 miles)

to Mytholmroyd (1 mile)

A6033

A646

1

B

HEBDEN BRIDGE

to Todmorden (4 miles)

The **Smeekin Hill War Memorial** is dedicated to those from Wadsworth Parish who fell in both World Wars. It was built by public subscription and is a direct copy of the earlier monument on Stoodley Pike, commanding a fine view over the valleys on all sides.

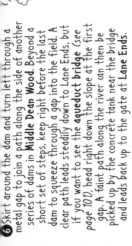

Smeekin Hill War Memorial

7 From Lane Ends, follow the path right down to Midgehole Road. Turn right then fork left to cross New Bridge and pass the **Blue Pig.** Carry on into the woods and fork right, climbing up to join a tarmac track along the foot of **Lee Wood.** Beyond Higher Lee, bear left where the wood opens out again, not down the wall but weaving diagonally through **Tinker Bank Wood.** Carry straight on at the end of the wood to pass between the shaded buildings of **The Hollings.** Turn sharp left at the junction with Slater Bank Lane and descend the cobbles to reach **Foster Bridge.** Carry straight on into Foster Lane to rejoin the outward route at Windsor Road, turning right to head back into **Hebden Bridge.**

Foster Mill Bridge was originally a private packhorse bridge built and owned by Thomas Foster in the 17th century to serve the adjacent fulling mill. **Foster Mill** (and the adjacent Hebden Vale Iron Works) filled much of the land at the end of Foster Lane now covered in housing developments and was operated by Redman Brothers until the 1990s. Its owners built the terraces of Windsor Road for their workers and provided the Delf opposite for allotments and green space.

The National Trust-owned woods of the **Hardcastle Crags** estate divide nicely in two at Gibson Mill. This section is the most trodden, busy with a warren of paths through the delightful mixed woodland on the north side of Hebden Water and crested by a series of interesting rocky outcrops. The south side is mostly private woodland and has fewer paths as it is not Open Access land. However, it is still full of sites of interest, particularly around Hebden Hey, where the outlaw Tom Bell is said to have lived and died in his cave.

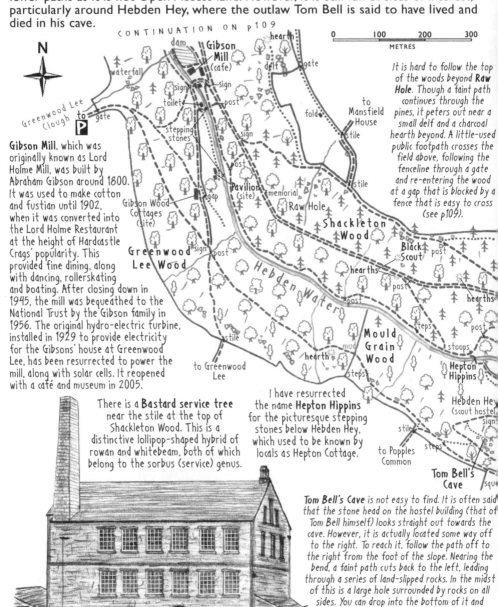

CONTINUATION ON p109

It is hard to follow the top of the woods beyond **Raw Hole**. Though a faint path continues through the pines, it peters out near a small delf and a charcoal hearth beyond. A little-used public footpath crosses the field above, following the fenceline through a gate and re-entering the wood at a gap that is blocked by a fence that is easy to cross (see p109).

Gibson Mill, which was originally known as Lord Holme Mill, was built by Abraham Gibson around 1800. It was used to make cotton and fustian until 1902, when it was converted into the Lord Holme Restaurant at the height of Hardcastle Crags' popularity. This provided fine dining, along with dancing, rollerskating and boating. After closing down in 1945, the mill was bequeathed to the National Trust by the Gibson family in 1956. The original hydro-electric turbine, installed in 1929 to provide electricity for the Gibsons' house at Greenwood Lee, has been resurrected to power the mill, along with solar cells. It reopened with a café and museum in 2005.

There is a **Bastard service tree** near the stile at the top of Shackleton Wood. This is a distinctive lollipop-shaped hybrid of rowan and whitebeam, both of which belong to the sorbus (service) genus.

I have resurrected the name **Hepton Hippins** for the picturesque stepping stones below Hebden Hey, which used to be known by locals as Hepton Cottage.

Tom Bell's Cave is not easy to find. It is often said that the stone head on the hostel building (that of Tom Bell himself) looks straight out towards the cave. However, it is actually located some way off to the right. To reach it, follow the path off to the right from the foot of the slope. Nearing the bend, a faint path cuts back to the left, leading through a series of land-slipped rocks. In the midst of this is a large hole surrounded by rocks on all sides. You can drop into the bottom of it and peer into the cave on its western side, but the actual entrance is up above, with a 5m drop down into a large chamber, from which it is hard to see how you could access the alleged tunnels under the hill (see p106 for more information).

Gibson Mill

Gibson Mill)

With as many as 500,000 people a year visiting the Hardcastle Crags estate at the turn of the century, many refreshment rooms were set up, including Wood & Sutcliffe's Refreshment Rooms and Dance Saloon at New Bridge Mill (later Lello's Tea Room), Thorntons Tea Room (later Cosy Corner Cafe) at Hebden Hey, the Lord Holme Restaurant at Gibson Mill, and further refreshment rooms at Hawden Hole. The Pavilion Tea Rooms was the very first in 1894, in a wooden chalet below Gibson Wood that was removed recently due to rot. These days only 150,000 visitors a year come, and yet it can still feel very busy.

It is possible to follow the top of the woods on the northern side of the valley all the way up to Raw Hole, from where a path drops down towards Gibson Mill. The only tricky section is around Rabbit Hole, but an easier path cuts through the wood below the delf, heading straight on where the red Mill Walk is signed down the steps to the left. This becomes fainter through the pines but soon joins a larger path heading up over Black Scout.

The grooves down **Slurring Rock** have been worn by the clog-irons of thousands of children sliding down the face of the rock.

In the 19th century, an eccentric geologist and botanist called William Pickles lived at the **Lodge** at the entrance to the Hardcastle Crags estate.

Rom Folly may refer (like Bracken's Folly on Midgley Moor) to the walled open area that was cleared of stones for grazing, or it may be that in doing so a remarkable heap of stones was created on the rock in the middle. It was used by the horses that worked in the woods, dragging timber out of steep inaccessible slopes, a practice known as **snigging**. This tradition has been resurrected because of its minimal intereference with the soil and other wildlife, and has recently been employed on the steep slopes of the Hardcastle Crags estate again.

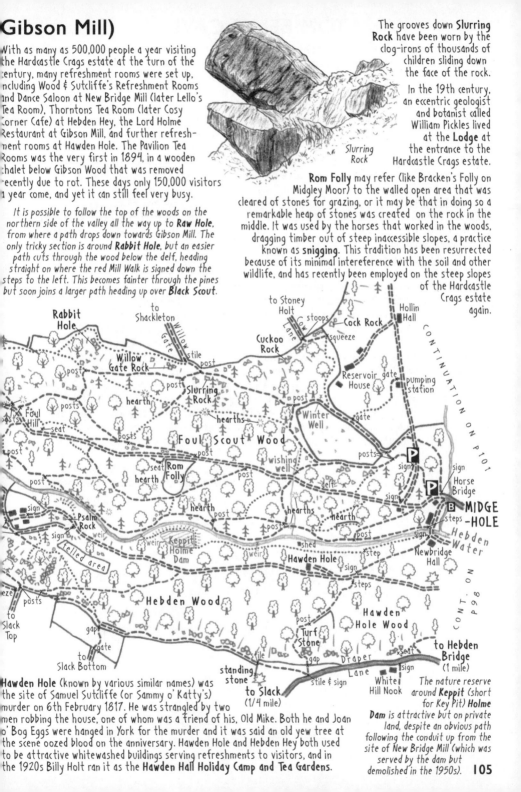

Hawden Hole (known by various similar names) was the site of Samuel Sutcliffe (or Sammy o' Katty's) murder on 6th February 1817. He was strangled by two men robbing the house, one of whom was a friend of his, Old Mike. Both he and Joan o' Bog Eggs were hanged in York for the murder and it was said an old yew tree at the scene oozed blood on the anniversary. Hawden Hole and Hebden Hey both used to be attractive whitewashed buildings serving refreshments to visitors, and in the 1920s Billy Holt ran it as the **Hawden Hall Holiday Camp and Tea Gardens**.

The nature reserve around **Keppit** (short for Key Pit) **Holme Dam** is attractive but on private land, despite an obvious path following the conduit up from the site of New Bridge Mill (which was served by the dam but demolished in the 1950s).

TOM BELL'S CAVE

In the land-slipped rocky outcrops above Hebden Hey lies the entrance to a rather impressive cave. If you pick your way through the boulders and drop into the dark with a torch and some rope, you can explore what may have been the hideaway of an outlaw called Tom Bell. He was said to be clothed in iron chains that clanked as he moved, yet emerged by night to steal food and valuables that he stored in his cave. There are supposed to have been further entrances to the cave at Eaves Bottom, which enabled him to evade capture, as did his habit of wearing special metal shoes that made it look like he was walking the other way. Legend has it that he eventually died through over-eating and was found illuminated by the green phosporescence of rotting tree roots by his only known companion, Willie the Woodsman.

In 1899 Herbert Cooper, the son-in-law of the then owner of Hebden Hey, claimed to have found a human skull in a crevice in the back of the cave, as well as a number of other bones, including a rhino skull. It was declared to be prehistoric by a Professor Dawkins and thought to be evidence of Neolithic man's practice of cave burial across the area (like those at Creswell Crags and Dowel Cave in Derbyshire). After a few public appearances, though, the skull disappeared, prompting speculation that it was merely a bit of marketing for tourism, rather like the mummified cat that had also suddenly appeared in the cave.

After this controversy, the legend of Tom Bell began to grow. The early 19th century poems of William Broadbent and William Dearden were further embellished by D.T. Wilcock in 1918 as a cautionary tale for children, in which two boys discover the outlaw's corpse. The legend may originally have been based on Joseph Bailey, a blacksmith from Rochdale who was found living in a cave in Hathershelf Scout near Mytholmroyd with a hoard of stolen treasure in 1779. It was said he had other hiding places, which may have included Tom Bell's Cave (indeed Bell may have been a corruption of Bailey). But the story also drew on other legends handed down by generations, from that of the wholesome Willie the Woodsman to outlaws like Robin Hood (likely a conflation of numerous local legends).

The cave now known as Tom Bell's Cave may not be the original one; it is thought the original was walled up after a child was lost there some years before 1879. The few tiny passages from the current cave have now been explored, reaching only 140 feet and thought never to have gone further. There is a stone head on the building at Hebden Hey hostel that is said to be Tom Bell looking out directly at his lair. However, this no longer looks towards the cave. Though the head was obviously moved when the old farmhouse was taken down in the 1970s, the new building is similarly aligned to the old farm and the cave is marked on numerous old maps as being some 100m to the east. Cavers have discovered several other small caves in the area, including the chamber of Hebden Valley Cave, but none continues far beneath the hillside. So, who knows, maybe the real Tom Bell's Cave is still out there among the tumbled rocks and moss of the crags?

the entrance to Tom Bell's Cave

THE BIRCH

The birch is known as the Lady of the Woods, or ribbon tree, for its elegant feminine beauty and frail limbs. Its pale bark is particularly striking in the thin winter sunshine, when it stands out from the drab greys of the rest of the trees. The birch is among the earliest trees to come into leaf in spring, though its tiny leaves do little to shade anything else. In late autumn its red buds stand out across the hillsides of the Calder Valley and demonstrate quite how much birch there is. Its suitability to the soils of the area and small size mean it is quite possibly the most numerous tree in the borough.

The birch tolerates poor soil and as a result is a very successful pioneer species that colonises derelict areas like old buildings and the sides of railways, as well as moorsides and ungrazed grassland. It grows quickly, but is short lived, rarely growing to be more 20m tall. It is not competitive, its thin leaves giving plenty of scope for other things to grow, and it often provides shelter for trees like oak. For the Celts the birch was a symbol of renewal, used to drive out the spirits of the old year. It improves the nutrients in the soil and produces a vast amount of pollen (meaning it is a common cause of hay fever). Since it tolerates some shade, it will also be found among larger trees – indeed it often makes up more than half of the trees in any oak woodland.

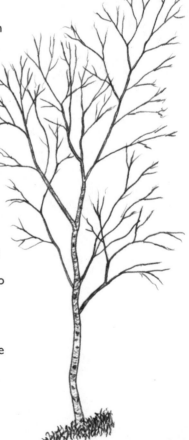

There are two native birches, silver and downy, and they are difficult to distinguish. Although a great deal of hybridisation between the two means it is often difficult to tell, the downy birch is far more common in this area than the silver birch. It is more likely to be found in the wetter parts of woods (like Broadhead Clough or Edge End Moss) and can grow on very peaty soil on the edges of the moor. Despite the names, the downy birch has similarly (if slightly less silvery) pale bark and is easier to discern by its leaves. The silver birch's leaves are triangular, hairless and double-toothed, while the downy birch's are more rounded, hairy and single-toothed.

Birch was used locally for making besoms, bundles of its fine twigs making a good brush and traditionally being made by a broom squire. It was once so widespread in the valley that it was used in clog soles and cotton bobbins when other wood was in short supply, as well as for firewood. In the absence of oak, its bark was also for tanning leather. In Canada, its waterproof bark was used for canoes and, in the Scottish Highlands, the birch was so proliferous that it was used for almost everything from houses to ropes. Birch sap wine was also traditionally made when the sap was rising in the early spring by drilling and tapping the trunk of the silver birch. Many mushrooms can be found in its lee; milk caps, russulas and chanterelles are good finds, while birch polypores are the huge rubbery bracket funghi that clasp to many birch trunks.

MAP 30: HEBDEN DALE NORTH
(Gibson Mill to Blake Dean)

The northern section of Hebden Dale beyond Gibson Mill is further from the car parks and therefore refreshingly quieter than the south end. It is also the most dramatic part of the valley, with Hebden Water carving its course steeply from the Pennine rocks. The Hardcastle Crags themselves stand sentinel over the upper part of the valley; often bypassed, they, like the Hell Holes upstream, are worthy of closer inspection. All of the woods are Open Access except Over Wood and Rowshaw Clough, which the National Trust does not own.

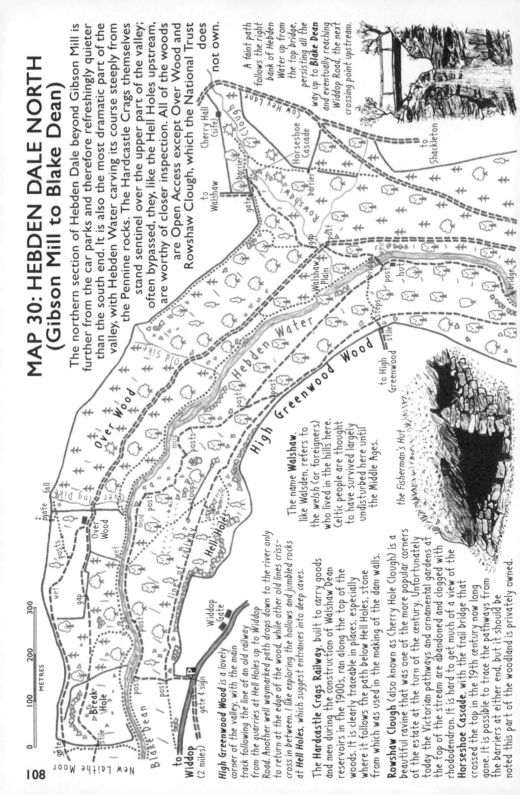

A faint path follows the right bank of Hebden Water up from the top bridge, persisting all the way up to **Blake Dean** and eventually reaching Widdop Road, the next crossing point upstream.

the Fisherman's Hut

The name **Walshaw**, like Walsden, refers to the **welsh** (or foreigners) who lived in the hills here. Celtic people are thought to have survived largely undisturbed here until the Middle Ages.

High Greenwood Wood is a lovely corner of the valley, with the main track following the line of an old railway from the quarries at Hell Holes up to Widdop Road. Another well waymarked path drops down to the river only to return at the edge of the wood, while other old lines criss-cross in between. I like exploring the hollows and jumbled rocks at **Hell Holes**, which suggest entrances into deep caves.

The **Hardcastle Crags Railway**, built to carry goods and men during the construction of Walshaw Dean reservoirs in the 1900s, ran along the top of the woods. It is clearly traceable in places, especially where it follows the path below Hell Holes, stone from which was used in the making of the dam walls.

Rowshaw Clough (also known as Cherry Hole Clough) is a beautiful ravine that was one of the more popular corners of the estate at the turn of the century. Unfortunately today the Victorian pathways and ornamental gardens at the top of the stream are abandoned and clogged with rhododendron. It is hard to get much of a view of the **Horseshoe Cascade**, with the frail bridge that crossed the top in the 19th century now long gone. It is possible to trace the pathways from the barriers at either end, but it should be noted this part of the woodland is privately owned.

Horseshoe Cascade when the old bridge was still present

Among the conifers planted in the Savile's woodland estate were Scots pine, Austrian pine, Corsican pine, Norway spruce and the European larch, to go with the broadleaf beech, sycamore, hornbeam, lime and chestnut. The variety is part of the estate's enduring appeal.

There was a school at **Lady Royd** for tenants of the Savile estate from 1874 to 1948. The open area below Hardcastle Hills was known as **Cricket Field**, and used by the children here.

The top of the woods is hard to follow above **Gibson Mill**. The only path up the west side follows the riverbank, while the faint paths along the east side peter out near a small delf above Gibson Mill. Soon after this, the line of an old but largely unused track can be picked up zigzagging down to the main track.

to Mansfield House

CONTINUATION ON P104

The **Fisherman's Hut** now refers to a tiny shelter tucked beneath a large rock on the river bank, though it was originally an Edwardian stone hut when this upper part of the river was well used by trout fishermen. The area of Rom Hole, a flatter area beneath the steep cliffs, was popular with the ladies of the Savile Estate for picnicking while the men were out shooting, and remained so when it was opened to the public. There is no sign of the stepping stones here any more, nor the precipitous path that ran up to the Hardcastle Hills above.

The **Hardcastle Hills**, like Foul Hill further down the valley, are formed from land that has slipped in the distant past from the higher slopes, and thus comprises of jumbled heaps of boulders thrust from the valley side. At one time it was thought that these represented the ruins of an ancient castle, but the name Hardcastle refers to a herdsman's village or hamlet 'which may have needed to be defended at times. The **Hardcastle Crags** crest the highest of these and form a narrow ridge overlooking the main track. On the top is a distinctive weathered rock and a fine vantage point over the valley.

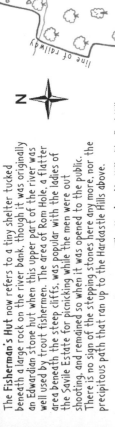

the rock perched on top of the highest of the Hardcastle Crags

Greenwood Lee stands on one of the most ancient settlements in Halifax parish and gave its name to the Greenwood family in the 12th century, from which it is thought all other Greenwoods are descended. In 1762 it was bought by an inebriated Abraham Gibson, who established a cotton spinning mill there before building Gibson Mill in the valley below.

Over 40 **charcoal burning hearths** have been identified in the woods of Hardcastle Crags. I have simply mapped the more obvious ones I have found. Look for small bits of charred wood in the soil on the downslope face of these flattened circular areas – it is particularly obvious where the track cuts through the middle of them. There were also related **iron bloomeries** in the area, and their slag heaps have been identified in Walshaw Wood near Rom Hole Stone.

109

Hardcastle Crags are reached either by scrambling straight up the crag from the track, or by following a more obvious path further south. This leads up to a slight hollow between crags, where you bear right towards a distinctive rock on the horizon. The path then leads on along the ridge, forking left to reach the summit.

to Heptonstall (1 mile)

Lady Royd Field · Lady Royd · stile to Lady Royd · rocking stone · Hardcastle Crags · Walshaw Wood · Bloomery slag · post · Rom Hole Stone · Ram Hole · bridge · post · Fisherman's Hut · seats · stepping stones (site) · viewing rock · Hardcastle Hills · Shackleton Wood · Cricket Field · step · fence across · hearth · delf · timber store · barn · bridge · weir · dam · Gibson Mill · stepping stones · Gibson Wood Bridge · steps · toilet · stile to Mansfield House · gate · Hebden Water · weir · dam · steps · stepping stones (site) · waterfall · stoop · Ingham Wood · Mould Grain Clough · Pisser Clough · line of railway · gate · post · Lee Clough · Greenwood Clough · gate · sign · P · sign · to Heptonstall

N

ROUTE 15: HARDCASTLE CRAGS & HEBDEN DALE FROM MIDGEHOLE

Distance: 4.5 miles (7km)

Ascent: 280m

Parking: National Trust car park at Midgehole (pay and display).

Public Transport: Midgehole is the terminus of the 906 bus service, which runs from Hebden Bridge six times a day on weekends and Bank Holidays from April to September.

Character: There are already many well-known routes through the Hardcastle Crags estate, some of which are signed by the National Trust's own coloured markers (i.e. the Red route follows the most popular routes up to Gibson Mill and back), so I have tried to find a route less trodden that nevertheless takes in many of the estate's most interesting features. While visiting Black Scout, Gibson Mill, Turf Stone, Tom Bell's Cave, Rom Hole, and of course the Hardcastle Crags themselves, this route includes a couple of slightly rougher sections of path and requires (at time of writing) climbing one easy fence. The route can be shortened in a number of places by returning along the main vehicle track to the car park.

The route can also be undertaken from Hebden Bridge, following either the road or part of Route 14 (see p103) to Midgehole. This extends the route to 7 miles (11km).

There are over 500 species of **mosses, liverworts** and **lichens** in Hardcastle Crags, particularly on the damp, dark southern flank. Many important mosses and liverworts were discovered here by the botanists John Nowell, Samuel Gibson and James Needham, including Atrichum Moss and Miss Hutchins' hollywort.

Black Scout

The **northern hairy wood ant** is distinguished by its hairy eyebrows, unfortunately visible only under a microscope. They have formed a number of large anthills in Hardcastle Crags, mainly in areas of pine trees. There are about half a million ants in each nest, which extend underground through a labyrinth of tunnels.

4 Reaching **Rowshaw Clough**, turn sharply left before the stream to cross Hebden Water at the highest bridge in the woods. The charming river can then be followed all the way back down to the café at **Gibson Mill. At Rom Hole**, the precipitous bank forces you briefly to the opposite bank, and soon after the **Fisherman's Hut** shelters beneath a rock on the river bank.

3 The track can be followed all the way up through **Walshaw Wood** but, to explore the **Hardcastle Crags** themselves, turn left off the track almost immediately. A path leads up between low outcrops. On the brow, bear right towards a distinctive rock on the crest above. A path continues along the ridge towards the highest of the crags, forking left to reach the weathered pillar on its crest. A couple of paths lead down to the left from the top, the most obvious descending a short rocky scramble to return to the main track. A narrower but less rocky path drops down further to the left. Continue along the track through the scattered pines of Walshaw Wood, forking left before the rather unremarkable **Rom Hole Stone.**

2 Beyond **Black Scout**, bear right over a stile out of the woods. Where the walled path opens out into a field, continue straight on along the fenceline to reach the corner of the wood again. Go through the gate to

Slag from a medieval iron **bloomery** was found below the track near the junction by Rom Hole Stone, but there is little to be seen at the site.

to Blake Dean

Rowshaw Clough

High Greenwood Wood

Walshaw Wood

Hardcastle Crags

Rom Hole

Rom Hole Stone

bloomery (site)

seats

Hardcastle Hills

distinctive rock

fence across gap

Fisherman's Hut

Hebden Water

Ingham Wood

dam

steps

110

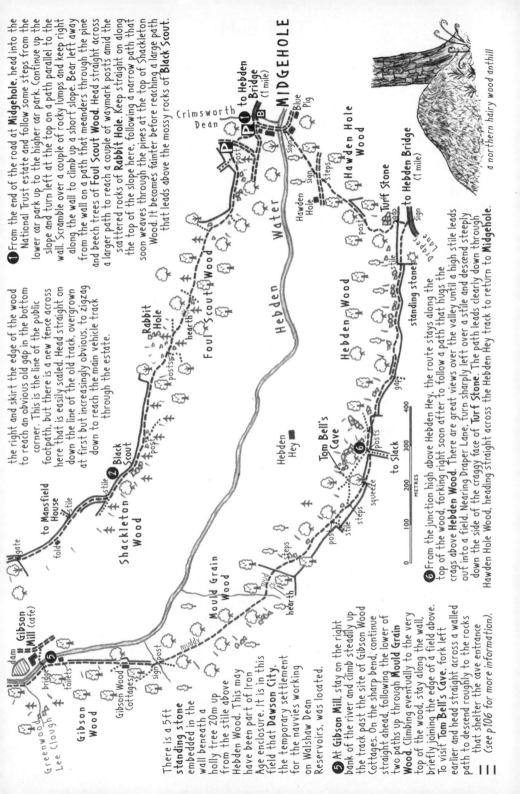

① From the end of the road at **Midgehole**, head into the National Trust estate and follow some steps from the lower car park up to the higher car park. Continue up the slope and turn left at the top on a path parallel to the wall. Scramble over a couple of rocky lumps and keep right along the wall to climb up a short slope. Bear left away from the wall on a path that meanders through the pine and beech trees of **Foul Scout Wood**. Head straight across a larger path to reach a couple of waymark posts amid the scattered rocks of **Rabbit Hole**. Keep straight on along the top of the slope here, following a narrow path that soon weaves through the pines at the top of **Shackleton Wood**. It becomes fainter before reaching a large path that leads above the mossy rocks of **Black Scout**.

the right and skirt the edge of the wood to reach an obvious old gap in the bottom corner. This is the line of the public footpath, but there is a new fence across here that is easily scaled. Head straight on down the line of the old track, overgrown at first but increasingly obvious, to zigzag down to reach the main vehicle track through the estate.

There is a 5ft **standing stone** embedded in the wall beneath a holly tree 20m up from the stile above Hebden Wood. This may have been part of Iron Age enclosure. It is in this field that **Dawson City**, the temporary settlement for the navvies working on Walshaw Dean Reservoirs, was located.

⑤ At Gibson Mill, stay on the right bank of the river and climb steadily up the track past the site of Gibson Wood Cottages. On the sharp bend, continue straight ahead, following the lower of two paths up through **Mould Grain Wood**. Climbing eventually to the very top of the wood, stay along the wall, briefly joining the edge of a field above. To visit **Tom Bell's Cave**, fork left earlier and head straight across a walled path to descend roughly to the rocks that shelter the cave entrance (see p106 for more information).

⑥ From the junction high above Hebden Hey, the route stays along the top of the wood, forking right soon after to follow a path that hugs the crags above **Hebden Wood**. There are great views over the valley until a high stile leads out into a field. Nearing Draper Lane, turn sharply left over a stile and descend steeply down the side of the craggy face of **Turf Stone**. The path leads clearly down through Hawden Hole Wood, heading straight across the Hebden Hey track to return to **Midgehole**.

a northern hairy wood anthill

THE ELM

For a long time it was assumed that the English elm was a native of Britain, but it is now thought more likely to have been was brought here by the Romans. Indeed the name comes from the Latin *ulmus*, and Italian grapes were long cultivated on the boughs of what we know as English elms. The smaller wych elm, on the other hand, is native; the word *wych* means supple or bendy in Anglo-Saxon. Wych elms have large and very rough leaves with virtually no stalk, and are found in woodland edges and hedgerows. Until fifty years ago English elms were common trees of the hedgerow, tending to grow in rich lowland soils, and were seen as suited to adapting to urban advances. Wild elm woods were rare, though, even before these trees were ravaged by disease in the 20th century.

Dutch elm disease didn't come from Holland, but was first identified there in 1921. It is caused by a fungus spread by the elm bark beetle. Though it arrived in the UK in the 1920s, it didn't develop an aggressive strain until the 1960s, when it quickly spread across the south-east. The first cases in Yorkshire were in 1975 and, despite great efforts to prevent its spread, the elm was largely wiped out. Widely planted as a genetically superior tree to the native wych elm, the English elm was particularly susceptible as it doesn't produce viable seed. The tree was introduced as a single genetic clone and, because it could only sucker to reproduce, its subsequent genetic variations were minimal. The disease probably has an even longer history, and may have been responsible for what was termed the Elm Decline that happened very suddenly about 4000BC.

Though elm timber was said to be 'good for nowt but gates and coffins', elm was useful in places where it would be constantly wet (i.e. buckets for mill waterwheels, ship keels, wharves, paddles, lock gates and traditional weather boarding). Elm's other strength is that it very rarely splits, so it was also good for chopping blocks, bakers' trays and the naves of wheels. It was also used for early water pipes, with the trunk hollowed out. When 17th-century elm pipes were unearthed in London in the 1930s, they were found to be still functional. Elm is said to have been used for the mains in Halifax around the same time. Elms were also known as 'widow makers' for their tendency to drop branches one by one as they die, rather than toppling over.

It is said that Calderdale was once full of elm trees, but there is little sign of this left. Wych elm is the most common species locally; as well as surviving the disease better, it is also best suited to this climate. Younger saplings can be found in places, such as along the Hebden Water near Salem Field, but there are only a few older elms scattered around the area that survived the disease. It is said that if you can hug an elm, it is almost certainly a survivor, and one of the finest is almost a hundred years old near Hirst Bridge in Nutclough – the ravages of the disease can still be seen in its contorted trunk.

wych elm leaves and seeds, which are known as samaras

CHAPTER 10 - HEBDEN BRIDGE TO TODMORDEN

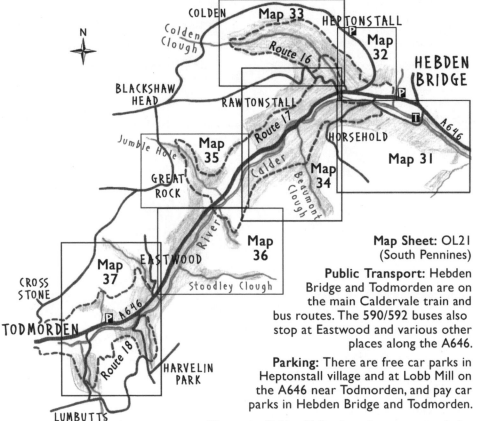

Map Sheet: OL21 (South Pennines)

Public Transport: Hebden Bridge and Todmorden are on the main Caldervale train and bus routes. The 590/592 buses also stop at Eastwood and various other places along the A646.

Parking: There are free car parks in Heptonstall village and at Lobb Mill on the A646 near Todmorden, and pay car parks in Hebden Bridge and Todmorden.

The main Calder Valley is at its most wooded along the beautiful stretch between Hebden Bridge and Todmorden. The steep valley sides are cloaked in trees throughout, with rocky crags like Horsehold Crag, Foster's Stone, and Lad Stones peering out from their crest. Numerous cloughs dive steeply down to join the Calder, including Colden Clough, Jumble Hole, Stoodley Clough and Lumbutts Clough, and these provide some of the most magical woodland hideaways in the area.

Climbing out of Hebden Bridge, one struggles to escape the clutch of the trees as networks of paths weave across these dense hillsides. As well as plantations of beech, there is an abundance of twisted oak here that makes every corner seem like a new world. You can spend hours in tiny Jumble Hole without retreading the same ground, and I discover new corners of Colden Clough every time I visit. It is this slightly fantastical nature of the landscape that is captured by the imagination of William Dearden (see p117 for more information on the Bard of Caldene).

The ancient woodland in this part of the valley possesses its finest charcoal hearths (in the aptly named Burnt Acres Wood) and sites of primitive iron smelting (in Beaumont Clough and Rawtonstall Wood), as well as industrial era mills, dams and tanneries, now romantically lost deep in the trees. There are few more rewarding landscapes in this area.

Crow Nest Wood and Hebble End Wood are dark caverns of beech that capture little sun and cloak the hillside above the Fairfield area of Hebden Bridge. It is an easy area to explore from the town and links straight into the woods of Horsehold and Cragg Vale, the latter via Wood Top and Wood Hey Clough.

Hebble End is the name of the area around the bridge over the Calder at the western end of Hebden Bridge. It was known as Litthouse Bridge in the 16th and 17th centuries, a litt-house being another name for a dyeworks, which stood alongside. The more prominent bridge that spans the canal is actually Neptune Bridge after the pub that once stood alongside.

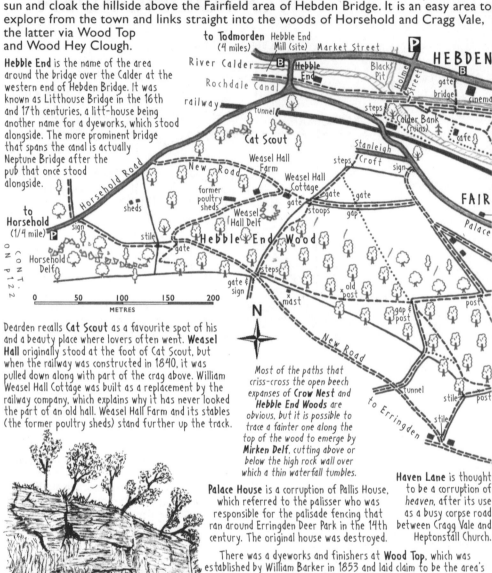

Dearden recalls **Cat Scout** as a favourite spot of his and a beauty place where lovers often went. **Weasel Hall** originally stood at the foot of Cat Scout, but when the railway was constructed in 1840, it was pulled down along with part of the crag above. William Weasel Hall Cottage was built as a replacement by the railway company, which explains why it has never looked the part of an old hall. Weasel Hall Farm and its stables (the former poultry sheds) stand further up the track.

Most of the paths that criss-cross the open beech expanses of Crow Nest and Hebble End Woods are obvious, but it is possible to trace a fainter one along the top of the wood to emerge by Mirken Delf, cutting above or below the high rock wall over which a thin waterfall tumbles.

Palace House is a corruption of Pallis House, which referred to the palisser who was responsible for the palisade fencing that ran around Erringden Deer Park in the 14th century. The original house was destroyed.

Haven Lane is thought to be a corruption of heaven, after its use as a busy corpse road between Cragg Vale and Heptonstall Church.

There was a dyeworks and finishers at **Wood Top**, which was established by William Barker in 1853 and laid claim to be the area's first wholesale clothier. It is one of the many dyeworks around Hebden Bridge because the area's water was so well suited to the process. Here cloth that had come off the looms was washed, cut, dyed, brushed, and often stiffened ready to be made into clothing. Each dyeworks tended to specialise in certain types of cloth, but nearly all were some type of fustian, the heavy-duty cotton fabric so closely associated with the town. Cloth was often brought in from elsewhere, but left the town as finished garments, whether corduroy trousers, moleskin jackets or whipcord overalls. Wood Top employed about 100 people, as cutters, machinists, tailors and finishers, some of these working at Old Chamber. It was just one of the twenty wholesale clothiers in Hebden Bridge by the early 20th century.

the waterfall at Wood Top Delf

END WOOD & WOOD HEY CLOUGH

Canal Wharf Saw Mills were built in 1851 and became renowned for clog manufacturing, first under **James Maude** and later **Walkley Clogs**, which took over the mill in 1978. Clogs were popular footwear in mills, where the floor was permanently wet, as the high wooden soles raised the feet enough to avoid this. Maude's also operated as a timber merchant to ensure a supply of wood, increasingly imported from Norway or Ireland as local woods dwindled. Traditionally clogs were made from alder or beech, but sycamore and birch were also used in this area. After World War II, when boots and shoes were rationed, clogs were cheap to produce and Maude's operated at their busiest, producing 120,000 pairs a year. More recently clogs became fashion accessories and Walkley Clogs operated as a minor tourist attraction until 1996, when it moved to Elland. It is still one of the UK's last manufacturers of clogs, now trading on Midgley Road, while the old mill sadly crumbles.

Machpelah was named in 1803 by Baptist minister, Dr Fawcett, after the biblical cave in Hebron where Abraham and his descendants were buried. He bought the plot of land for his own family's burial, but changed his mind when the area became built up. He is buried at Wainsgate and his grandson built Machpelah House on the site in 1842.

the Maude sole clog

BRIDGE
A646

Machpelah

Calder Holmes Park

sign

CONTINUATION ON p88

FIELD

May Royd Mill

Victoria Mill (site)

Palace House (site)

railway station

House Road

gasworks (site)

sign

bridge

Rochdale Canal

Falling Royd Tunnel was constructed upon the reopening of the Rochdale Canal in the 1960s after being blocked up for some years following the removal of the old Falling Royd Bridge.

A646

B

Falling Royd Tunnel

to Mytholm -royd
(1/2 mile)

post

Crow Nest

Crow Nest Wood

Wood Top Road

Mirken Wood

Mirken Delf

post

stile

waterfall

pond

sign

Wood Top

Thrush Hole Wood

dam

The Pines

gate

River Calder

Hard Hippens Bridge

Canal Wharf Saw Mills

sign

Carr Bridge

railway

Carr Lane

The name **Stubb** (like Stubbing) refers to a cleared area of woodland, the stubs being the stumps of felled trees. There is little woodland left here, other than along the stream.

Old Chamber

stile

stile

Spencer Lane

Wood Hey Lane

Fair View

sign & squeeze

Carr Green

bridge

Carr House

Stubb Clough

gate

pools

Shroggs

stile

stile

stile

Lane Side

to Nest Lane

Great Jumps

gates

Butts Bottom

Moorside Farm

The names **Shroggs** and Shroggs Wood Top (at Great Jumps) suggests an area of scrub woodland formerly existed on this slope. The name is also found in Shroggs Park in Halifax, Shroggs Wood in Northowram, and Birchcliffe Shroggs (an early name for Nutclough in Hebden Bridge).

Haven Wood

Wood Hey Clough

Haven Lane

sign

stile

to Erringden Moor

to Broad Head End

Amethyst deceivers are among the easiest mushrooms to spot and identify – an array of lilac caps emerging from the leaf litter of beech woodland from late summer. They make a pleasant addition to a stir fry and, though the colour fades (hence the deceiver part of the name), so too does the flavour.

115

MAP 32: GRANNY WOOD & WHINS

Granny Wood and the heath above known as **Whins** cover only a small area, but their accessibility from Hebden Bridge and Heptonstall mean they are rightly popular and full of paths. The quarries of Brock Holes Delf and Hell Hole form the most obvious features, but it is also worth seeking out the Victorian walkways in Eaves Wood and the chimney stump lost in Granny Wood. There are great views from Whins and Top o'the Eaves over Hebden Bridge and Mytholm, the former being my favourite in the area.

Granny Wood is marked on early 19th-century maps as Brock Holes Wood, named after badger setts.

Acres Lane in Heptonstall is a corruption of Thackers Lane, which refers to the medieval profession of thatchering.

the marker stone in Granny Wood on the line of the old corpse road

Hell Hole refers to the largest of the quarries on the hillside, a vast climbers' amphitheatre with the distinctive pinnacle of **Lad's Law** facing it (see p118). Stone from the quarry was used to rebuild St Thomas' Church in Heptonstall after the old church was damaged in a storm in 1847.

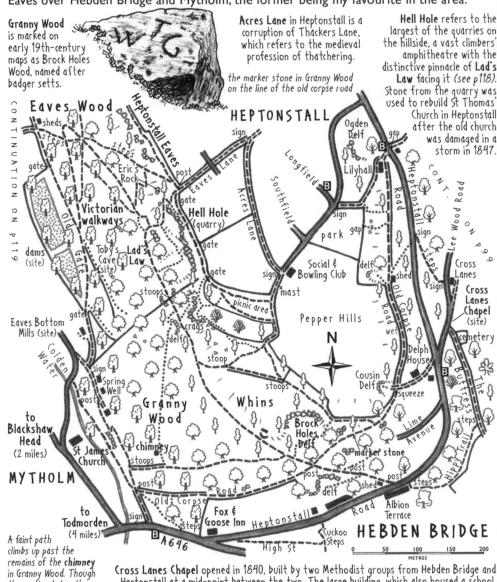

A faint path climbs up past the remains of the **chimney** in Granny Wood. Though the section below the chimney is overgrown, the path continues up an old level all the way to a small delf just below the main path.

116

Cross Lanes Chapel opened in 1840, built by two Methodist groups from Hebden Bridge and Heptonstall at a mid-point between the two. The large building, which also housed a school, closed in 1950 and was damaged by fire soon after. The graveyard remains, though, perched on the hillside a few yards down The Buttress. **The Buttress** carried the old packhorse route between Hebden Bridge and Heptonstall (the old track can still be seen in the centre), and it would have carried straight across what is now Lee Wood Road to reach Heptonstall Road. Another route to Heptonstall Church followed the **Old Corpse Road** from the foot of Granny Wood. The lower part of Heptonstall Road was not built until 1782, when it was known as New Road.

WILLIAM DEARDEN, THE BARD OF CALDENE

"The trees, that seem to stand like so many sentinels in green, to guard the mountain from the devastation which the hand of man is making among some of his ancient compeers. The dark waters of the Calder, once majestic and musical in their flow, before they were held in cassalage to commerce – now languid and feeble – fret impotently at his feet." (William Dearden, from *The Star-seer*)

William Dearden was an intriguing early 19th-century romantic poet, whose work reveals much about the woodlands of the Upper Calder Valley. He was born in Hebden Bridge in 1803 and as a boy lived at the original Weasel Hall, before the railway required its removal. He became a teacher of classics and later principal of Warley Grammar School, living at the Hollins in Warley, where he set up a boarding school. From 1839, he produced *Dearden's Miscellany*, a magazine of poetry, literature and science. A friend of Branwell Brontë, he famously challenged him to a poetry contest in 1842, held in the Cross Roads Inn near Haworth. It is thought Brontë had picked up the wrong manuscript and read from an early version of *Wuthering Heights*, leading Dearden to believe he was the true author of that work. He published numerous poems under the pseudonym William Oakendale and became known as the Bard of Caldene. He was President of the Huddersfield Philosophical Society and its Literary Institute. He died in 1889 and is buried at Heptonstall Church.

Though a man of science, Dearden was fascinated by astrology, trying to understand how it was possible to use the stars to tell the future. Ultimately he declared it fraudulent, but it didn't stop him romanticising about an astrologer he was told about in local lore. His most famous poem, *The Star-seer*, was published in 1837 and told the story of an astrologer, Harold, who resided at Oswald Tower, a castle said to have stood on Horsehold Scout in centuries past. It recounts his search for a woman whose destiny was tied up with his own via a unique comet; Editha herslf worshipped in the glades of Kirklees Priory.

He followed this up with *The Vale of Caldene* in 1844, another epic set in the Colden Valley and surrounding woods. There are recurrent landscapes within the works, most of it taking place within an enchanted woodland landscape on the west edge of Hebden Bridge, a landscape that in Dearden's life was rapidly diminished and taken over by the might of industry. It is a predictably romanticised view of the area from one who was acquainted with Wordsworth, Southey and Coleridge, but it reveals much about the early 19th-century folklore of these woods. Though in truth his sprawling five-part poems are hard to work through – dense nests of recurrent romantic imagery – the footnotes that accompany them are fascinating. Through these I have been able to locate the crags of Turret (distinct from the rocky eminence of Castle Hill to the west), confidently name both Lumb Waterfall and the distinctive rock of Lads Law below Hell Hole, as well as dig up local characters of his time. The 'wild man of the wood', Old Neddy, Willie the Woodsman and St Tobias. He also reveals more of himself through these notes; so we hear him mourning the 'sordid churl' who felled his beloved Whitebark, a mighty old oak near High Greenwood in Hebden Dale, the sort that he saw becoming increasingly rare in an industrial age; or cursing the railway for destroying his childhood home and the magical crag above at Cat Scout. Now, when I look at the woodlands that have re-cloaked so much of the Calder Valley since the industry has gone, I imagine how pleased Dearden would have been to see his beloved Caldene returning to what he saw as its rightful enchanted state.

MAP 33: COLDEN CLOUGH & EAVES WOOD

Colden Clough is one of the gems of the Upper Calder Valley, a sort of locals version of Hardcastle Crags. It has been suggested the name Colden is a contraction of Coaldene, a reference to the charcoal-making that was practiced here, though in picturesque railway images in the early 20th century it was marketed as Golden Valley. It remains picturesque ancient woodland, its birch and sessile oak mingling with beech and Scots pine plantations, all of it laced with beautiful pathways.

The **praying hole**, often referred to as a cave even though it is little more than two feet deep, was used by various dissenters in the 19th century. John Wesley is said to have preached here, and a Nonconformist service is still held here on Spa Sunday.

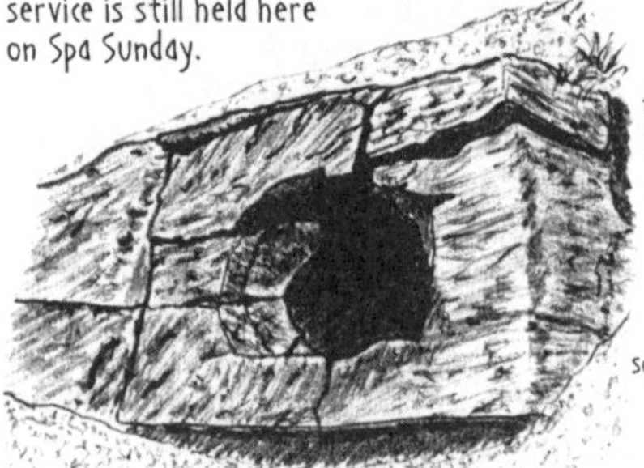

Dill Scout (also referred to as Dell Scout) is thought to be a contraction of *devil*, and is said to have a giant's face looking out at the valley. The woods beneath it were replanted with downy birch and Scots pine after a fire in the 1990s.

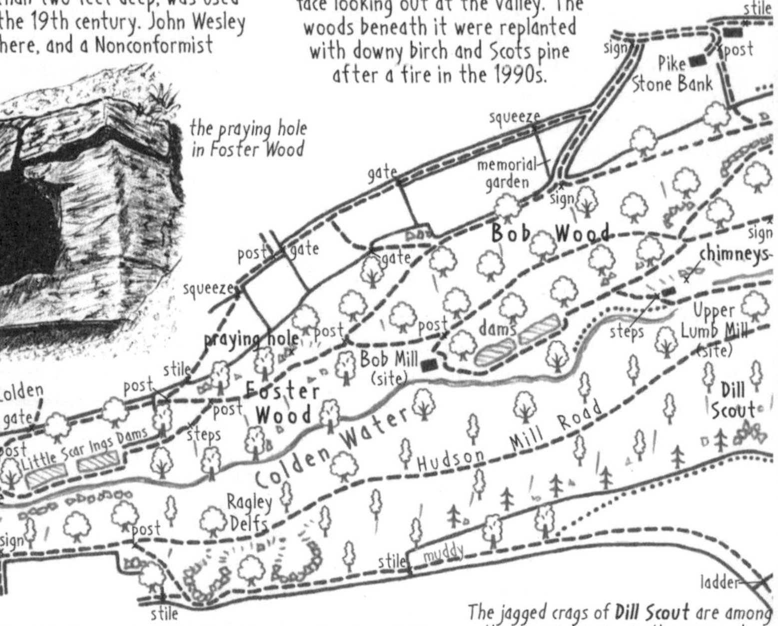

the praying hole in Foster Wood

(map labels) stile · sign · post · Pike Stone Bank · squeeze · memorial garden · sign · gate · gate · gate · post · gate · Bob Wood · sign · chimneys · squeeze · praying hole · post · post · dams · steps · Upper Lumb Mill (site) · stile · post · Bob Mill (site) · Dill Scout · to Colden · gate · post · steps · Foster Wood · Dill Scout · clapper bridge · steps · post · Little Scar Ings Dams · steps · Colden Water · Hudson Mill Road · post · Hebble Hole · Ragley Delfs · post · post · sign · post · stile · muddy · to Jack Bridge · stile · ladder

Hudson Mill, located a short distance above Hebble Hole, was the site of the earliest mill in Colden Clough, founded as Rawtonstall Corn Mill in the 13th century. It is named after Thomas Hudson, who served as the parish grave in 1570 and under whose ownership this served as Heptonstall's fulling mill. Only its former warehouse remains. Both Lumb Mills were built by Gamaliel Sutcliffe, as was Colden Road (then known as Gamaliel Road). **Upper Lumb Mill** was one of the largest in the valley. It had its own gas plant (which can still be seen) and a school for the 51 children it employed, and coal was shunted down the bank to it from Hudson Mill Road. But it was eventually considered to be too far from the railway and broken up for stone in the early 20th century. The ruins of **Bob Mill** had been a partly inhabited ruin since a fire in 1808, but its atmospheric walls were deliberately knocked down in 1967.

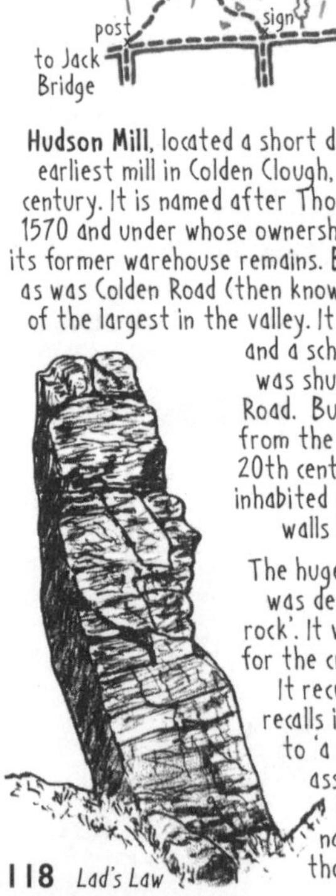

The huge boulder below Hell Hole quarry known as **Lad's Law** was described in the 1830s as 'a singular and magnificent rock'. It was never quarried because it was used as a backstay for the crane with which stone has hauled up out of the delf. It recurs regularly in the work of William Dearden, who recalls it previously having several companions. He likened it to 'a stony god' and suggests it was an altar for sacrifice associated with Druidic practices. There is another Lad Law on Boulsworth Hill, the 'hill of slaughter'. The name refers to a rock burial place, though *lad* itself is thought to date back no further than the Middle Ages.

The jagged crags of **Dill Scout** are among the more intriguing in the area and are relatively easily accessed by following the broken-down wall along the top of Dill Scout's Wood. The best viewpoint is from the lone crag at the northern end of the edge, overlooking Lumb Mills, but this can only be accessed by ducking through the fence along the pine-clad edge. A faint path follows this fence for some distance.

to Blackshaw (1 mile)

Badger

The **Long Causeway** followed the line of a primitive trackway across the Pennines that predates the 11th-century Manor of Wakefield. It followed Badger Lane and descended Rawtonstall Bank, the name *badger* (referring to an itinerant corn dealer) suggesting its antiquity. Only when the chapel was built in Heptonstall in the 12th century did that take over as the main trade route via Jack Bridge.

Lumb Waterfall drops impressively away by the chimney of **Lower Lumb Mill**, but is only clearly visible from below. Dearden describes its 'seed-toned roar' before the mills quietened it. The determined can follow the stream up from Milking Bridge, though the path gives up fairly soon and you may need to get your feet wet to reach the waterfall.

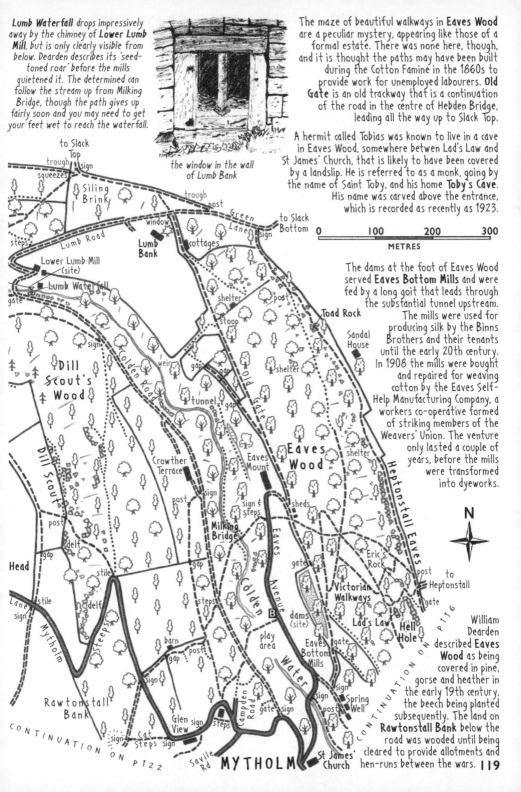

the window in the wall of Lumb Bank

The maze of beautiful walkways in **Eaves Wood** are a peculiar mystery, appearing like those of a formal estate. There was none here, though, and it is thought the paths may have been built during the Cotton Famine in the 1860s to provide work for unemployed labourers. **Old Gate** is an old trackway that is a continuation of the road in the centre of Hebden Bridge, leading all the way up to Slack Top.

A hermit called Tobias was known to live in a cave in Eaves Wood, somewhere between Lad's Law and St James' Church, that is likely to have been covered by a landslip. He is referred to as a monk, going by the name of Saint Toby, and his home **Toby's Cave**. His name was carved above the entrance, which is recorded as recently as 1923.

0   100   200   300
METRES

The dams at the foot of Eaves Wood served **Eaves Bottom Mills** and were fed by a long goit that leads through the substantial tunnel upstream. The mills were used for producing silk by the Binns Brothers and their tenants until the early 20th century. In 1908 the mills were bought and repaired for weaving cotton by the Eaves Self-Help Manufacturing Company, a workers co-operative formed of striking members of the Weavers' Union. The venture only lasted a couple of years, before the mills were transformed into dyeworks.

N

William Dearden described **Eaves Wood** as being covered in pine, gorse and heather in the early 19th century, the beech being planted subsequently. The land on **Rawtonstall Bank** below the road was wooded until being cleared to provide allotments and hen-runs between the wars. **119**

to Slack Top
trough
sign
squeezes
Siling Brink
trough
post
Green Lane
window
sign
to Slack Bottom
steps
Lumb Road
Lumb Bank
cottages
Lower Lumb Mill (site)
Lumb Waterfall
gate
shelter
post
stoop
Toad Rock
Sandal House
Dill Scout's Wood
Colden Road
weir
gap
gap
shelter
tunnel
gap
Old Gate
Eaves Wood
Dill Scout
Crowther Terrace
post
sign
Eaves Mount
shelter
Heptonstall Eaves
post
delf
gap
Head
stile
Milking Bridge
sign & steps
sheds
Eric's Rock
post
to Heptonstall
gate
Lane
stile
sign
delf
gap
steps
Eaves Avenue
gate
Victorian Walkways
Mytholm
Steps
barn
gap
post
play area
Colden
B
dams (site)
Lad's Law
Hell Hole
Rawtonstall Bank
sign
Eaves Bottom Mills
gate
sign
Water
CONTINUATION ON P116
Glen View
sign
steps
Campden Road
gate
sign
Spring Well
sign
post
CONTINUATION ON P122
sign
Cat Steps
sign
Savile Rd
MYTHOLM
St James' Church

ROUTE 16: COLDEN CLOUGH & EAVES

Distance: 4 miles (6.5km)   **Ascent:** 320m

Parking: Pay & display car parks and various street parking in Hebden Bridge.

Public Transport: Hebden Bridge is on the main Caldervale train & bus routes.

Character: Colden Clough is a small but dense area of woodland that reveals more on each visit. This straightforward route combines the imposing crags of both Heptonstall Eaves and Dill Scout with the charming ancient woods of the clough itself, and makes a great half day's outing from Hebden Bridge. There are some slightly rougher paths, but the route is largely easy to follow.

A **hebble** was a dialect word that could refer to a narrow wooden bridge or the handrail beside it. It seems likely the name predates the elegant 15th-century stone clapper bridge that still marks this popular picnic spot today. **Clapper bridges** are said to be named for the clattering sound of a packhorse train crossing them. They originally didn't have rails, so the wide packhorses could cross, but this one was intentionally narrowed in the 19th century.
The stone squeeze was built to prevent its use by packhorses and force them onto the newly built turnpike in the valley.

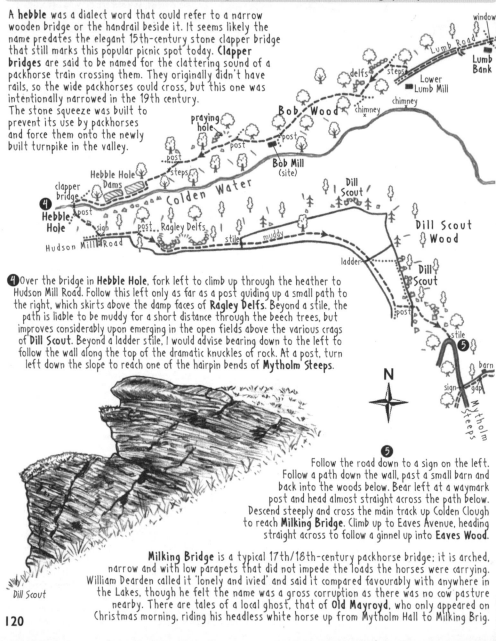

4 Over the bridge in **Hebble Hole**, fork left to climb up through the heather to Hudson Mill Road. Follow this left only as far as a post guiding up a small path to the right, which skirts above the damp faces of **Ragley Delfs**. Beyond a stile, the path is liable to be muddy for a short distance through the beech trees, but improves considerably upon emerging in the open fields above the various crags of **Dill Scout**. Beyond a ladder stile, I would advise bearing down to the left to follow the wall along the top of the dramatic knuckles of rock. At a post, turn left down the slope to reach one of the hairpin bends of **Mytholm Steeps**.

N

5 Follow the road down to a sign on the left. Follow a path down the wall, past a small barn and back into the woods below. Bear left at a waymark post and head almost straight across the path below. Descend steeply and cross the main track up Colden Clough to reach **Milking Bridge**. Climb up to Eaves Avenue, heading straight across to follow a ginnel up into **Eaves Wood**.

Milking Bridge is a typical 17th/18th-century packhorse bridge; it is arched, narrow and with low parapets that did not impede the loads the horses were carrying. William Dearden called it 'lonely and ivied' and said it compared favourably with anywhere in the Lakes, though he felt the name was a gross corruption as there was no cow pasture nearby. There are tales of a local ghost, that of **Old Mayroyd**, who only appeared on Christmas morning, riding his headless white horse up from Mytholm Hall to Milking Brig.

Dill Scout

WOOD FROM HEBDEN BRIDGE

❸ Follow the track down past **Lumb Bank**, hidden behind a high wall with an interesting mullioned window in it. Above the buildings of Lower Lumb Mill, turn right up some inconspicuous steps to reach a large path through the woods. Follow this down to the bottom and turn right, climbing again on a lovely path through the heart of **Bob Wood**. Dropping down once more, fork right above the ruins of Bob Mill and bear left at the next junction. As you pass through some beech woods, there is a tiny **praying hole** up to the right, where it is said John Wesley once preached. After climbing briefly, turn left at the next post and descend some steps to skirt around the **Hebble Hole Dams**. The delightful Colden Water is finally at hand and is soon crossed by the 15th-century **clapper bridge** in Hebble Hole.

❷ Keep right through the **Whins** heather to climb steadily towards Heptonstall. Just before the mast on the edge of the village, turn left and follow a clear path along the top of the quarried faces of **Hell Hole** and then the crags of **Heptonstall Eaves**. At Toad Rock, the path drops into the top of Eaves Wood, weaving through the rocks to reach **Lumb Road**.

Lumb Bank was built by the owner of Lower Lumb Mill in the 18th century. It was bought by Ted Hughes in 1969, though it was never really his home (he largely lived in Devon from the 1960s onwards) and was leased to the Arvon Foundation, who continue to use it as a place for writers' retreats.

The Buttress may take its name from a butt-tress (a place where archers rested their butts), though it may also be a local word for the steep mountain-like nature of the hillside (another is found on similar terrain in Warley).

Milking Bridge

❶ From Bridge Gate, cross the **packhorse bridge** in the centre of Hebden Bridge and head straight up the steep hill opposite, the cobbled track of The Buttress. Take the second path off to the left, doubling back up some steps and following a path round to Heptonstall Road beside Albion Terrace. Cross the road and follow a path opposite into **Granny Wood**. Shortly after the second waymark post, turn right on a small path into **Brock Holes Delf**. After this climbs steeply up the slope by the quarry, turn left to emerge on the cosy heath of **Whins**, my favourite vantage point over Hebden Bridge.

❻ There are various ways back through **Eaves Wood** that rejoin the outward route, but the easiest follows the path right along the foot of the wood. Descending to a tarmac track, turn left and, just before the gate of Spring Well, follow a path round to the right. After a short zigzag around a collapsed section, this descends steadily to the main road on the edge of Hebden Bridge handily near the **Fox & Goose Inn**. Follow the main road left back into centre of town.

HEBDEN BRIDGE

MAP 34: RAWTONSTALL, KNOTT, HORSEHOLD & CALLIS WOODS

This is one of the most beautiful wood-cloaked sections of the Calder Valley, with a series of imposing crags jutting out from the crests. Horsehold Scout and Foster's Stone are the best vantage points, but all the woods below are fascinating; Rawtonstall Wood is a particualr warren of twisted oak. It is a great area to explore from Hebden Bridge and Nazebottom.

The **Charlestown Curve**, between the Pen and Nazebottom, was a notorious section of the railway, even before the crash there on 21st June 1912. Originally a tunnel was planned, but the loose shale meant it was impossible to dig anything other than a deep cutting (which itself was liable to landslip). The curve had to be taken very slowly and was eventually straightened, with the old line still visible behind Nazebottom. This still didn't prevent the accident, which killed four people and was found to have been caused by a smaller carriage near the front of the train.

Castle Hill is an intriguing name on the map, thought to refer to a lump separated from the cliff face and the likely result of a landslip. It was cited by William Dearden as the site of a fortification since the Saxons that may have been used in feuds between the Roses. Thomas Whitaker described Rawtonstall Manor in the early 19th century as having existed within living memory, surrounded by a moat with a castle on the hill above. There is little evidence for either and it seems unlikely this would have been in the woods, given the unstable nature of the ground, so prone to landslips the railway company partially drained the whole hillside. The name may simply have sprung, like the nearby crags of **Turret**, from the castellated appearance of these rocks from the valley below.

Mytholm Mill was driven by springs diverted from Rawtonstall Wood to the small dam still present and a larger one alongside. It was founded by James King, after whom nearby King Street was named.

The crags of **Turret** at the top of Rawtonstall Wood are largely tree-clad and almost inaccessible.

A narrow path climbs up towards them from near Savile Bowling Club, bearing left below the stones to reach a gap in the wall by the composting toilet of the Knott Wood Coppicers. The top of the crag can be accessed from the path above, though it is rough and heathery.

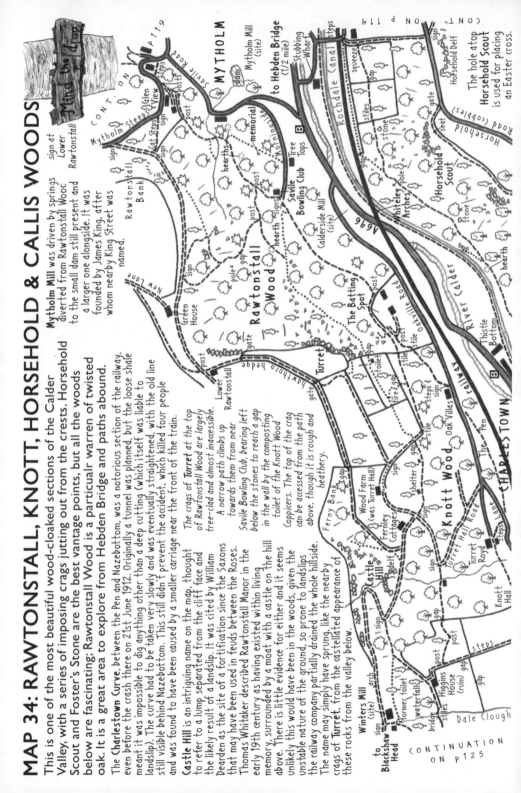

The hole atop Horsehold Scout is used for placing an Easter cross.

CONTINUATION ON p125

to Blackshaw Head

to Hebden Bridge (1/2 mile)

CONT ON p 114

CONT ON p 119

sign at Lower Rawtonstall

Mytholm Steep / Glen View

MYTHOLM

Mytholm Mill (site)

Stubbing Wharf

Rochdale Canal

Horsehold Road (cobbles)

Horsehold Delf

Horsehold Scout

Whiteley Arches

River Calder

Rawtonstall Bank

Rawtonstall Wood

Savile Bowling Club Tops

Calderside Mill (site)

The Batting Spot

Oakville Road

Thistle Bottom

New Lane

Green House

hawthorn hedge

Lower Rawtonstall

Turret

A646

CHARLESTOWN

Knott Wood

Oak Villas

The Pen

Ferny Bank

Wood Farm (was Turret Hall)

Fernley Cottages

Castle Hill

Turret Hall Road

Turret Royd

Knott Hall

Winters Mill (site)

Higgins House (ruin)

Dale Clough

Knott Delf

railway

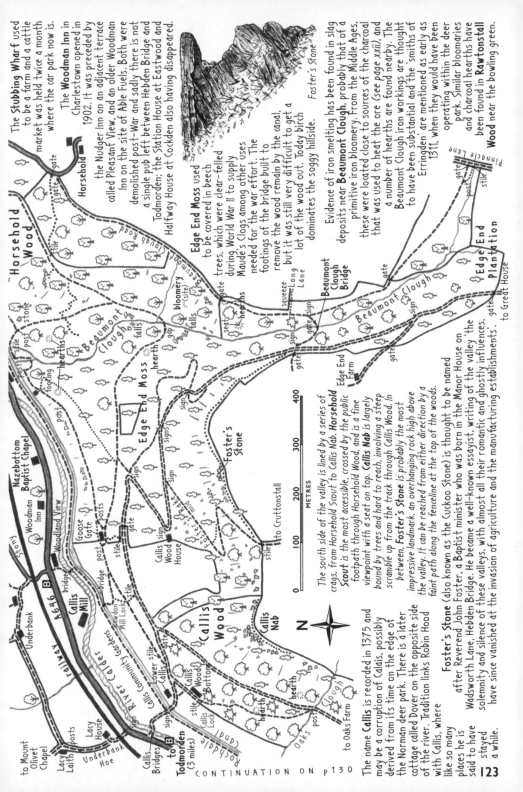

The **Stubbing Wharf** used to be a farm and a cattle market was held twice a month where the car park now is.

The **Woodman Inn** in Charlestown opened in 1902. It was preceded by the Nudger Inn on an adjacent terrace called Pleasant View, and an older Woodman Inn on the site of Able Fuels. Both were demolished post-War and sadly there is not a single pub left between Hebden Bridge and Todmorden; the Station House at Eastwood and Halfway House at Cockden also having disappeared.

Foster's Stone

Edge End Moss used to be covered in beech trees, which were clear-felled during World War II to supply Maude's Clogs among other uses needed for the war effort. The footings of the bridge built to remove the wood remain by the canal, but it was still very difficult to get a lot of the wood out. Today birch dominates the soggy hillside.

Evidence of iron smelting has been found in slag deposits near **Beaumont Clough**, probably that of a primitive iron bloomery. From the Middle Ages, these were located close to sources of the charcoal that was used to heat the ore (see page xxii), and a number of hearths are found nearby. The Beaumont Clough iron workings are thought to have been substantial and the 'smiths of Erringden' are mentioned as early as 1311, when they would have been operating within the deer park. Similar bloomeries and charcoal hearths have been found in **Rawtonstall Wood** near the bowling green.

The south side of the valley is lined by a series of crags, from Horsehold Scout to Callis Nab. **Horsehold Scout** is the most accessible, crossed by the public footpath through Horsehold Wood, and is a fine viewpoint with a seat on top. **Callis Nab** is largely bound by trees and hard to reach, involving a steep scramble up from the track through Callis Wood. In between, **Foster's Stone** is probably the most impressive landmark, an overhanging rock high above the valley. It can be reached from either direction by a faint path along the fenceline at the top of the woods.

Foster's Stone (also known as the Cuckoo Stone) is thought to be named after Reverend John Foster, a Baptist minister who was born in the Manor House on Wadsworth Lane, Hebden Bridge. He became a well-known essayist, writing of the valley 'the solemnity and silence of these valleys, with almost all their romantic and ghostly influences, have since vanished at the invasion of agriculture and the manufacturing establishments'.

The name **Callis** is recorded in 1375 and may be a corruption of Calais, possibly derived from its time on the edge of the Norman deer park. There is a later cottage called Dover on the opposite side of the river. Tradition links Robin Hood with Callis, where like so many places he is said to have stayed a while.

CONTINUATION ON p130

MAP 35: JUMBLE HOLE CLOUGH

Jumble Hole Clough is one of the most attractive ravines leading out of the Upper Calder Valley. It used to be known as Blackshaw Clough, the stream draining Bride Stones Moor and the area around Blackshaw Head before becoming densely wooded in its lower course. Though it is a small woodland, covering less than a square kilometre, it is so steep and riven by such a maze of paths that it often seems far bigger and can take most of a day to explore properly. Lost in the trees are the ruins of its five mills, most notably the elegant walls of Staups Mill, as well as a series of waterfalls, delfs and crags. The name may derive from *dumbles*, a dialect word for a steep narrow valley, or be similar to Jumps and Jumples, referring to the way the water jumps down the clough.

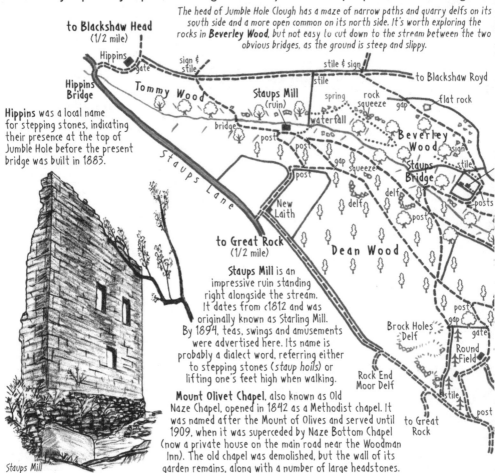

The head of Jumble Hole Clough has a maze of narrow paths and quarry delfs on its south side and a more open common on its north side. It's worth exploring the rocks in **Beverley Wood**, but not easy to cut down to the stream between the two obvious bridges, as the ground is steep and slippy.

to Blackshaw Head
(1/2 mile)

Hippins

Hippins Bridge

Hippins was a local name for stepping stones, indicating their presence at the top of Jumble Hole before the present bridge was built in 1883.

gate

sign & stile

Tommy Wood

Staups Mill (ruin)

bridge

post

Staups Lane

to Great Rock (1/2 mile)

New Laith

stile & sign

stile

to Blackshaw Royd

spring

rock squeeze

gap

flat rock

waterfall

post

gap

squeeze

post

Beverley Wood

sign

Staups Bridge

stile

delf

posts

delf

post

Dean Wood

Staups Mill is an impressive ruin standing right alongside the stream. It dates from c1812 and was originally known as Starling Mill. By 1894, teas, swings and amusements were advertised here. Its name is probably a dialect word, referring either to stepping stones (*staup hoils*) or to lifting one's feet high when walking.

post

gap

gate

Round Field

Brock Holes Delf

Rock End Moor Delf

stile

post

to Great Rock

Mount Olivet Chapel, also known as Old Naze Chapel, opened in 1842 as a Methodist chapel. It was named after the Mount of Olives and served until 1909, when it was superceded by Naze Bottom Chapel (now a private house on the main road near the Woodman Inn). The old chapel was demolished, but the wall of its garden remains, along with a number of large headstones.

Staups Mill

Of the four mills that stood in Jumble Hole Clough, only **Jumble Hole Mill** still functions as a building. In the 19th century it served as Underbank Dyeworks, where silk was dyed in large sheds until the building was destroyed by fire on August 11th 1899. A smaller version was rebuilt and is used as workshops to this day. The walls of five-storey **Spa Mill** clamber up the hillside on the next bend; it is often referred to as Spoil Mill as it is thought spa is a shortening of spoil rather than a reference to a spring. Originally a water mill, it was used to spin cotton and later for manufacturing fustian. The dam above is completely silted up and across the stream stood Spa Hall, a barely traceable terrace that was built to house up to fifty of the workers. Another five-storey mill, **Cow Bridge Mill**, stood over the stream by Cow Bridge, with a row of five cottages opposite. Little remains of the buildings, but its small dam above is intact, thanks in large part to a hydro-electric enthusiast who used it to generate power for his house at Broad Dean. The shed above stands on the site of **King's Chair**, a dwelling used by the dam keeper; the ruins of a similar structure, known as **Queen's Seat**, can still be seen by the north-west corner of Spa Mill Dam.

The ruins of **Beverley End** contain an interesting array of outbuildings and walls tiered up the steep hillside. Some of the hollows in these walls were used as bee boles, which date from the 18th century and housed wicker skeps, a portable form of beehive. *Bee bole* is originally a Scottish term and others are found at Swan Bank Farm, Jumps, and Lumb Bank, where they have recently been renovated. It is also possible Beestones and Beestonley in Stainland are named after these stone bee boles. The wooden beehives with which we are more familiar were not introduced in Britain until 1862.

Staups Bridge, an example of a clam bridge, a type of packhorse bridge formed from a single great slab clamped in place

Scout Delf is an eerie quarry with a massive overhanging rock face in its back corner, with trees reaching out of its cracks for the light above. It is known as The Roost to climbers, for whom it is a home to a number of testing routes. **Dove Scout** above used to be known as Dew Scout; like the Dove Stones on Boulsworth Hill, it is likely to have come from the gaelic *dubh*, meaning black.

The obvious track up Jumble Hole Clough splits by **Cow Bridge** and a path appears to continue up the stream beyond. Though a Right of Way, this doesn't get far and it is an awkward scramble up the stream. The best paths up the clough are reached by following the track either way. Heading left, a path follows the left bank from the next bend all the way up to **Staups Mill**. Heading right, a narrow path doubles back from the junction by Mount Olivet Chapel, winding across the slope to the waterfall in the middle of the clough before continuing up to **Staups Bridge**. Another delightful path further up the slope follows a terrace from the **Naze** viewpoint past Scout Delf.

The fifth of the Jumble Hole mills, **Winters Mill**, actually stands on Dale Clough. The stream emerges from beneath part of the old structure that was known as the **cludgie**, a dialect word for toilet. The name Winters refers to its use as a place where cattle were kept for wintering, as there was winter feed here that was not available elsewhere.

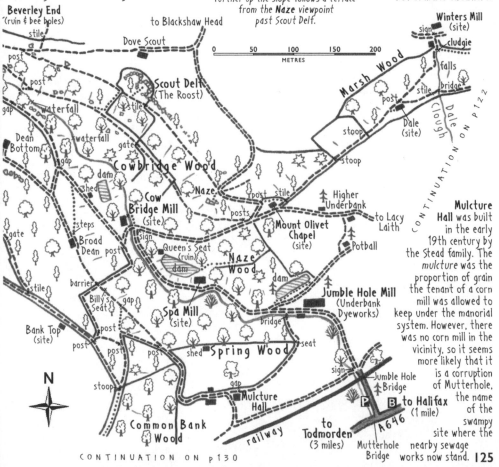

Beverley End
(ruin & bee boles)
stile
post
to Blackshaw Head
Dove Scout
post
gap
waterfall
Dean Bottom
waterfall
gap
shed
dam
steps
Broad Dean
gate
stile
barrier
Billy's Seat
gap
Bank Top (site)
post
post
post
stoop
Scout Delf
(The Roost)
stile
gate
Cowbridge Wood
Cow Bridge Mill (site)
Naze
sign
Queen's Seat (ruin)
dam
Spa Mill (site)
shed
Spring Wood
Mulcture Hall
N
Common Bank Wood
CONTINUATION ON p130

0   50   100   150   200
METRES

post stile
posts
Mount Olivet Chapel (site)
Naze Wood
dam
stoop
Higher Underbank
to Lacy Laith
Potball
bridge
seat
Jumble Hole **Jumble Hole Mill** (Underbank Dyeworks)
stoop
stoop
Marsh Wood
post
stile
Dale (site)
sign
Winters Mill (site)
cludgie
falls
bridge
Dale Clough
CONTINUATION ON p122

sign
Jumble Hole Bridge
P B to Halifax (1 mile)
to Todmorden (3 miles)
railway
A646
Mutterhole Bridge

Mulcture Hall was built in the early 19th century by the Stead family. The *mulcture* was the proportion of grain the tenant of a corn mill was allowed to keep under the manorial system. However, there was no corn mill in the vicinity, so it seems more likely that it is a corruption of Mutterhole, the name of the swampy site where the nearby sewage works now stand. **125**

ROUTE 17: JUMBLE HOLE, RAWTONSTALL WOOD

Distance: 6 miles (9km)

Ascent: 440m

Parking: Various pay & display car parks and street parking in Hebden Bridge.

Public Transport: Hebden Bridge is on the main Caldervale train & bus routes.

Character: The delightful wooded clough of Jumble Hole is easily reached from Hebden Bridge via an exploration of some of the Upper Calder Valley's most beautiful oak woodland in both Rawtonstall and Callis Wood. The route also takes in Horsehold Scout, Staups Mill and Parrock Clough, and is generally reasonably easy to follow. However, care is needed on a couple of narrow paths in Rawtonstall Wood and Jumble Hole, and after heavy rain the streams in Parrock and Beaumont Cloughs can be awkward to ford.

❹ Beyond the waterfall, climb up to a larger path, where you turn right around the ruined enclosure of **Beverley End**, home to a number of 17th-century bee boles. Keep left here to climb to a stile and on to the rock-strewn common above **Beverley Wood**. Reaching a fence, turn left alongside it as far as a prominent sign. Turn back to the left here to drop down to a bridge above **Staups Mill**. Beyond the elegant ruins, climb briefly to a waymarked path leading left high above the stream.

William Dearden (see p117) wrote of **Old Neddy**, a charcoal burner in Rawtonstall Wood and 'real lover of the marvellous', who spoke of the Turret-Faeries that visited him by moonlight. One of his hearths is passed through on the path below Turret crags.

❸ Follow the track down to the next bend, where a path leads on out of the wood. At the far side of the field beyond, turn right up the steps, then left above the ruins of Higgins House. At a junction beyond Dale Clough, go left again to descend to the site of **Mount Olivet Chapel**. Join the track briefly, only to bear right off it at a waymark post on the junction. A narrow path leads across the steep slope through the oaks of Cowbridge Wood, nearing Jumble Hole Clough by its most impressive waterfall.

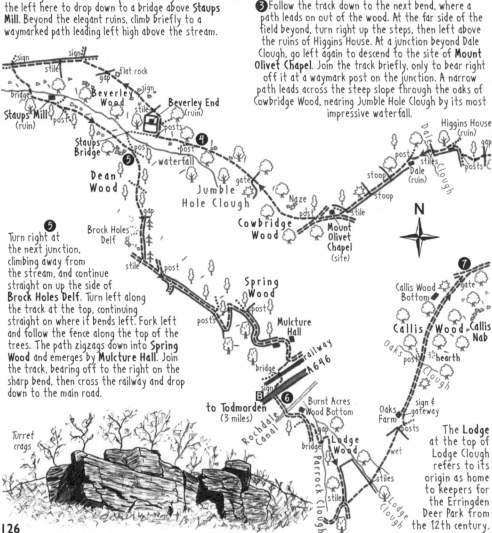

❺ Turn right at the next junction, climbing away from the stream, and continue straight on up the side of **Brock Holes Delf**. Turn left along the track at the top, continuing straight on where it bends left. Fork left and follow the fence along the top of the trees. The path zigzags down into **Spring Wood** and emerges by **Mulcture Hall**. Join the track, bearing off to the right on the sharp bend, then cross the railway and drop down to the main road.

The **Lodge** at the top of Lodge Clough refers to its origin as home to keepers for the Erringden Deer Park from the 12th century.

126

& HORSEHOLD SCOUT FROM HEBDEN BRIDGE

Knott Wood has been managed by a cooperative, Knott Wood Coppicers, since 1994. Hazel coppice and orchards have been planted and areas opened up to improve biodiversity and provide educational opportunities, as well as encourage woodland crafts, with hurdle-making taking place in the delfs below Castle Hill.

2 The path through **Rawtonstall Wood** is lovely but not always obvious; it bends round to the left to cross a small stream. Bear right beyond to climb slightly above Savile Bowling Club. Keep straight on at two separate waymark posts and join a faint path climbing up through landslipped boulders below the **Turret** crags. This emerges by a small wooden toilet and crosses the birch-covered former fields to reach a path up the wall on the edge of **Knott Wood**. You may need to head down to the left to find a gap, from which a path leads on to Turret Hall Road.

Rawtonstall was a sub-division of the township of Stansfield, a steward of which lived at one of the houses at Lower Rawtonstall, which may have been known as the Manor House.

1 From the traffic lights in the centre of **Hebden Bridge**, go down Holme Street, passing the post office to reach the canal. Follow this right, passing below the first bridge, and then turn right off it just beyond Stubbing Upper Lock. Head straight on at the bottom, crossing the river to reach the main road again. Go straight across into **Church Lane** and follow the road as it winds up the steep hillside. There is a shortcut up some steps to the left, shortly beyond which you turn left just before Glen View. A few yards along the track, duck down a path to the left, following the waymark posts into **Rawtonstall Wood**.

[Map illustration showing route from Hebden Bridge through Rawtonstall Wood, Knott Wood, Turret, Horsehold Scout, Horsehold Wood, Crow Nest Wood, with labels: Mytholm Steeps, steps, St James' Church, Glen View, Church Lane, post, posts, HEBDEN BRIDGE, post office, A646, steps, bridge, River Calder, Rawtonstall Wood, hearth, post, Savile Bowling Club, Rochdale Canal, railway, sign, Weasel Hall, workshops, gate, Turret, toilet, gap, Fernley Cottages, gap, Horsehold Scout, seat, gate, sign, stile, New Road, Crow Nest Wood, Horsehold Delf, to Horsehold, Knott Wood, sign, METRES scale 0 200 400 600, Horsehold Wood, gate, sign, gap, Beaumont Clough]

8 Turn left down **Horsehold Road** as far as the next sign, then bear right along the foot of the wood. Turn left down the next track and, at the bend, carry straight on past **Weasel Hall** and down the slope beyond. Turn left at the bottom, then join Palace House Road to cross the railway. Soon after, turn sharply to the right and follow a path back down to the canal bridge at the end of Holme Street.

7 Bear right at the bottom of **Callis Wood**, following the track up to the first sharp bend, where you ignore the sign pointing up the hill and bear left instead through the heart of **Horsehold Wood**. The path crosses Beaumont Clough via an awkward rocky ford, then climbs steadily up to the first of a series of rocky nabs overlooking the Calder Valley. The finest vantage point is the last of these, where a bench crowns **Horsehold Scout**.

6 Head straight across the road into Burnt Acres Lane, crossing both river and canal. Beyond **Burnt Acres Wood Bottom**, bear left on a path parallel to the track to reach a bridge over Parrock Clough. The path winds up through **Lodge Wood** to emerge on the track again *(if the bridge is out, you can follow the track all the way)*. Turn immediately left across the open field to a pair of stiles in Lodge Clough and on towards **Oaks Farm**. Pass through a gateway above the farm and join the track heading down through **Callis Wood**.

a bee bole in the wall above Beverley End

Horsehold takes its name from its role in the Erringden Deer Park, when it served as a stables and later a hunting lodge. William Dearden mentioned a pillar of rock that once projected from **Horsehold Scout** which he called the Watcher. Though long since fallen, it may have inspired folklore of a tower on the crag. **127**

THE OAK

The venerable oak is England's national tree, its great age and slow growth provoking a deep reverence that dates back to the earliest inhabitants. The name *druid* is thought to derive from a Celtic word meaning 'oak-knower' and many rituals were performed in oak groves because mistletoe (literally 'all heal', regarded as the most sacred plant) grew mostly in oak trees. Many churches were built in or near these sacred groves, and it was reflected in the name of some, like St Anne's in the Grove in Southowram. Oaks were seen as giving protection, were sheltered under during storms, and were danced around by newly married couples, echoing earlier pagan marriage ceremonies. It is hard not to feel some of that same connection to the sturdy oaks whose twisted boughs provide endless variation to the woodland cloak on our hillsides today.

Britain has two native species of oak; the sessile oak (also known as the Durmast or Cornish oak) and the pedunculate oak (often known as the English oak). The sessile oak prefers the stony ground of the uplands of north and west Britain, and can most easily be identified by its stalked leaves and unstalked acorns (sessile meaning stalkless). The south and east of Britain is dominated by the pedunculate oak, which conversely has unstalked leaves and stalked acorns. The sessile oak tends to have the more upright and straighter trunk, but the shape is also dependent on a number of environmental factors. However, the two types readily hybridise, meaning that much of the oak woodland in the middle of the country is a mix of both and their various hybrids. In the Calder Valley, there are few pure pedunculate oaks, plenty of pure sessile, and a whole range of hybrids in between, hence the very varied feel of the oak trees here.

The oak is a pioneering species that tolerates poor soils but needs plenty of light and doesn't respond well to being shaded by canopies of beech or sycamore. Oaks don't self-seed beneath other oaks, but instead rely on jays and other animals to carry their acorns out of the wood and plant them on new ground. An oak tree won't produce acorns until it is at least forty years old, and then only every few years, but when it does it can produce as many as 5000 acorns. The leaves of the oak come late, sprouting from tiny clusters of buds and growing slowly, so it seems like the oak woods are still stuck in winter while all around other trees have moved moved into spring. Oak trees provide a unique habitat that

sessile oak leaves and acorns

supports hundreds of species of beetle, moth, aphid, fungi and bird, and the light they allow through their leaves enables a rich carpet of ground flora to grow beneath, providing a richer ecosystem than any other native tree.

Along with birch and rowan, oak is the natural climax vegetation for much of the Calder Valley, yet it doesn't grow particularly well in the steeper valleys, as it generally needs more light. In spite of this, for many years it remained the most valued coppice tree because it had so many uses and responded well to pollarding

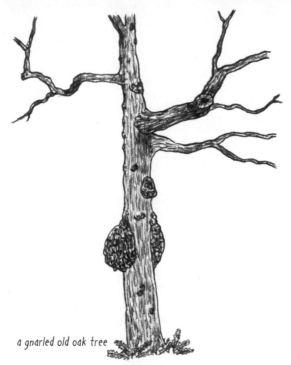

a gnarled old oak tree

and coppicing. For centuries it was the most expensive wood and carried the highest penalties for illegal use. Oak was used in window frames, rails, casks, furniture, carts, barrels, wheels and the frames of most buildings. Buildings like those at Shibden Hall and Binn Royd were made with crucks using two halves of a curved tree fastened together with oak pegs, the tree having been worked while still green to allow the joints to tighten as it dried. Oak palings also surrounded the Erringden Deer Park. Most famously, the pedunculate oak built the British Navy, cementing its place as our national tree. As many as 3000 oaks were needed to make a single Napoleonic war ship, though these would not always be the tallest trees. In fact some of the smallest crooked trees were of most use and knee-timbers were often marked up to be saved for the joints in the ship.

In this area, oak became as valued for its bark as its timber, because of the high tannin content that made it prized in leather tanning. The miles of leather straps (including picker straps) that ran around the mills relied on a good supply of oak bark, usually priced up and imported separately from the timber to be processed at in-house tanpits. There were large independent tanneries at Stone Mill in Sowerby Bridge, White Lee in Mytholmroyd, Bridge Royd in Eastwood, Crown Works in Northowram, and Hipperholme (after which the Tannery Bar is named).

The acorn itself had many further uses, whether for feeding pigs during the autumn (pannage), or for grinding to make traditional flour for bread before wheat became so widely grown. During World War II it is said coffee was also made from ground acorns. The oak apple is an apple-like gall (or growth) that houses the larvae of a tiny wasp and is found on oak twigs in early summer. It was used to make ink until the 20th century, and Oak Apple Day (or Royal Oak Day) took place on May 29th to celebrate the Restoration of Charles II to the throne in 1664. Following the Battle of Worcester, the King had hidden in a tree in Boscobel Wood, Shropshire, which became celebrated as the Royal Oak.

MAP 36: STOODLEY GLEN, EASTWOOD & BURNT ACRES

Stoodley Glen is a long, narrow clough that snakes up to the edge of the moor beneath the Pike, forming the boundary of the historical Sowerby Ramble. There are some beautiful woods in this part of the valley, particularly Burnt Acres and Height Woods, which overhang the canal delightfully and are always worth a visit.

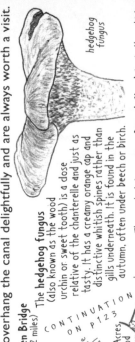

hedgehog fungus

Wood Mill was originally an 18th-century corn mill, later used for making fustian and as a saw mill. It is not the large brick building closer to Burnt Acres Bridge, which was first built in 1854 by Martin Holt. **Perseverance Mill** (often known as Holts Mill) was a picker works that tanned its own buffalo hides for use in the picker straps.

An old track runs up through **Common Bank Wood**, whose open beech spaces are scattered with lumps of rock. It is possible to bear off and skirt along the hillside to join the track up through **Eastwood Wood**: this is more easily done lower down than at the top of the slope. There is also a faint route along the top of the wood, joining a walled corridor to reach the paths into Jumble Hole above Mulcture Hall.

Cockden Mill was a dyeworks known as Dan Crabtree's that had a large pond for storing the urine used in the dyeing process. This was said to be collected in Todmorden with the cry any old lant'. An arch leads under the railway to the site of the mill.

The hedgehog fungus

(also known as the wood urchin or sweet tooth) is a close relative of the chanterelle and just as tasty. It has a creamy orange cap and distinctive whitish spines rather than gills underneath. It is found in the autumn, often under beech or birch.

The most obvious way up **Parrock Clough** is via the vehicle track up to Lodge, but a path bears off left soon after Burnt Acres Wood Bottom and climbs pleasingly through **Lodge Wood**. Another, towards Oaks Farm, is less appealing; it crosses the garden below Burnt Acres Wood Bottom to a gate, then follows the muddy stream up before doubling back on the line of an old track to the left.

The name **Burnt Acres Wood** refers to charcoal production, which is evident in a series of finely preserved charcoal hearths along the bottom of the wood (mostly just above the path), as well as in adjacent Height Wood. It is likely to have been associated with iron smelting, though perhaps it provided for the substantial bloomery nearby in Beaumont Clough.

In the early 19th century, William Dearden recalled someone he called **'the wild man of the woods'**, a madman who intimidated people in the woods. Though largely harmless, he had to be restrained on occasion. He worked as a hodman (a mason's labourer), but could barely speak and ended up killing his brother in rage with a rock near Burnt Acres. After a time in York prison, he lived out his days in an asylum.

to Hebden Bridge (1 1/2 miles)

CONTINUATION ON P123

CONTINUATION ON P125

to Oaks Farm

Burnt Acres Wood Bottom

Rochdale (canal)

River (Calder)

A646

Burnt Acres Bridge

Perseverance Mill

Mulcture Hall

Common Bank Wood

Wood Mill (site)

Burnt Acres Wood

hearth

Eastwood Station (site)

Burnt Acres Lane

to Oaks Farm

Lodge Wood

Lodge Clough

to Lodge

Parrock

Burnt Acres (ruins)

Dyke Lane

EASTWOOD

Eastwood Wood

Eastwood Lane

Cockden Mill (site)

Sowerby Ramble was a narrow strip of land running along the south bank of the Calder from Mytholmroyd to Stoodley Glen, then up Stoodley Clough to the corner of the plantation near Stoodley Pike. It belonged to the township of Sowerby but entirely surrounded Erringden township. It has its roots in the paling of Erringden Deer Park in the 14th century, when it provided access to the township of Sowerby and the commons of Langfield for animals outside the deer park. Those within watered in the Elphin Brook on the other side of the hill. Even after the deer park was dispaled, the Ramble remained as a strip of land 50 to 100m wide, marked out by a series of boundary stones. Few of the original medieval stones remain, but there are still 'S's carved in to numerous stoops, walls and bridges. There are two stones just above Stoodley Glen, one in the open area carved clearly with an SB for Sowerby Boundary, and another in the old wall above.

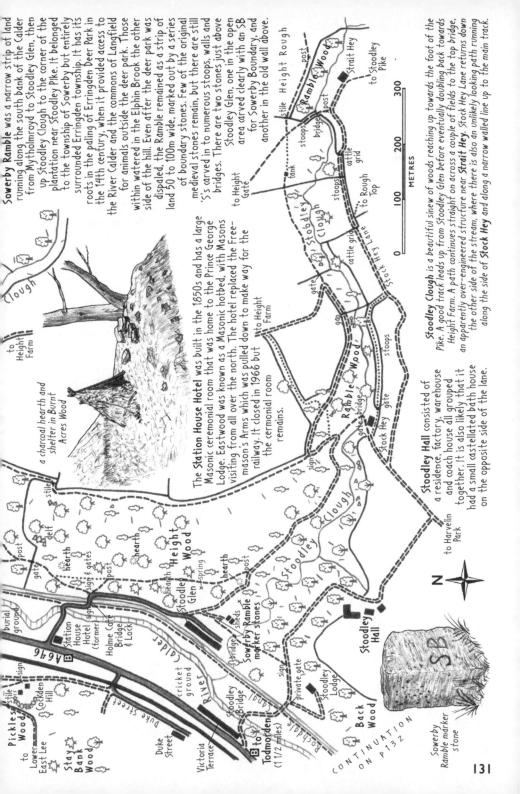

a charcoal hearth and shelter in Burnt Acres Wood

The **Station House Hotel** was built in the 1850s and has a large Masonic ceremonial room that was home to the Prince George Lodge. Eastwood was known as a Masonic hotbed, with Masons visiting from all over the north. The hotel replaced the Free-mason's Arms which was pulled down to make way for the railway. It closed in 1966 but the cermonial room remains.

Stoodley Hall consisted of a residence, factory, warehouse and coach house all grouped together. It is also likely that it had a small castellated bath house on the opposite side of the lane.

Stoodley Clough is a beautiful sinew of woods reaching up towards the foot of the Pike. A good track leads up from Stoodley Glen before eventually doubling back towards Height Farm. A path continues straight on across a couple of fields to the top bridge, an apparently over-engineered structure near *Strait Hey*. Stock Hey Lane returns down the other side of the stream, where there is also an unlikely looking path running along the side of *Stock Hey* and along a narrow walled line up to the main track.

METRES

0   100   200   300

N

Sowerby Ramble marker stone

CONTINUATION ON P.132

131

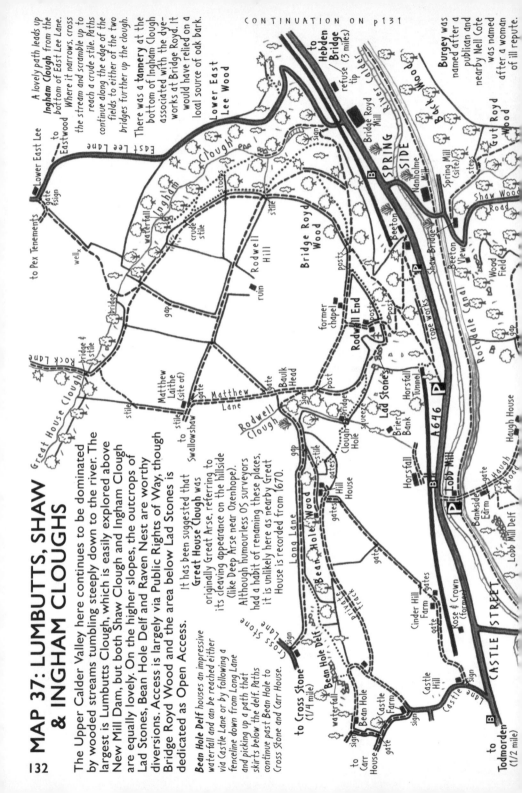

MAP 37: LUMBUTTS, SHAW & INGHAM CLOUGHS

The Upper Calder Valley here continues to be dominated by wooded streams tumbling steeply down to the river. The largest is Lumbutts Clough, which is easily explored above New Mill Dam, but both Shaw Clough and Ingham Clough are equally lovely. On the higher slopes, the outcrops of Lad Stones, Bean Hole Delf and Raven Nest are worthy diversions. Access is largely via Public Rights of Way, though Bridge Royd Wood and the area below Lad Stones is dedicated as Open Access.

Bean Hole Delf houses an impressive waterfall and can be reached either via Castle Lane or by following a fenceline down from Long Lane and picking up a path that skirts below the delf. Paths continue past Bean Hole to Cross Stone and Carr House.

It has been suggested that **Great House Clough** was originally Great Arse, referring to its cleaving appearance on the hillside (like Deep Arse near Oxenhope). Although humourless OS surveyors had a habit of renaming these places, it is unlikely here as nearby Great House is recorded from 1670.

A lovely path leads up *Ingham Clough* from the bottom of East Lee Lane. Where it narrows, cross the stream and scramble up to reach a crude stile. Paths continue along the edge of the two fields to either of the two bridges further up the clough.

There was a **tannery** at the bottom of Ingham Clough associated with the dye-works at Bridge Royd. It would have relied on a local source of oak bark.

Burgey was named after a publican and nearby Nell Cote was named after a woman of ill repute.

132

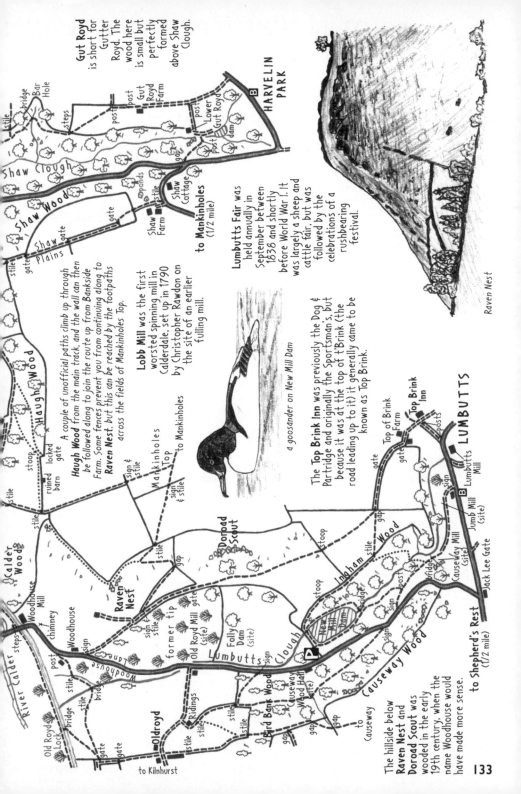

Gut Royd is short for Gutter Royd. The wood here is small but perfectly formed above Shaw Clough.

HARVELIN PARK

Shaw Clough

Shaw Wood

Bar Hole

Gut Royd Farm

Lower Gut Royd

Shaw Cottage

Shaw Farm

Shaw Plains

to Mankinholes (1/2 mile)

Lumbutts Fair was held annually in September between 1838 and shortly before World War I. It was largely a sheep and cattle fair, but was followed by the celebrations of a rushbearing festival.

Lobb Mill was the first worsted spinning mill in Calderdale, set up in 1790 by Christopher Rawdon on the site of an earlier fulling mill.

Haugh Wood from the main track, and the wall can then be followed along to join the route up from Bankside Farm. Some fences prevent you from continuing along to Raven Nest but this can be reached by the footpaths across the fields of Mankinholes Top.

A couple of unofficial paths climb up through

Haugh Wood

Mankinholes Top

to Mankinholes

Calder Wood

Doroad Scout

a goosander on New Mill Dam

The **Top Brink Inn** was previously the Dog & Partridge and originally the Sportsman's, but because it was at the top of t'Brink (the road leading up to it) it generally came to be known as Top Brink.

Top of Brink Farm

Top Brink Inn

LUMBUTTS

Lumbutts Mill

Jumb Mill (site)

Jack Lee Gate

Ingham Wood

New Mill Dam

Causeway Mill (site)

Raven Nest

former tip

Old Royd Mill (site)

Folly Dam (site)

Lumbutts Clough

Woodhouse Mill

chimney

Woodhouse

Woodhouse Lane

River Calder

Old Royd Lock

Oldroyd

Ridings

Bird Bank Wood

Causeway Wood Hall

to Causeway

Causeway Wood

to Shepherd's Rest (1/2 mile)

to Kilnhurst

The hillside below **Raven Nest** and **Doroad Scout** was wooded in the early 19th century, when the name Woodhouse would have made more sense.

Raven Nest

133

Distance: 6 miles (9.5km)

Ascent: 400m

Parking: Various pay & display car parks in Todmorden. Limited free parking in Lumbutts Clough and at Spring Side.

Public Transport: Todmorden is on the main Caldervale train & bus routes.

Character: A lovely exploration of the steep wooded cloughs that form this part of the Calder Valley just outside Todmorden, as well as the craggy hillsides of Lad Stones, Raven Nest and Bean Hole Delf. A couple of short rougher sections in Ingham and Lumbutts Cloughs can easily be by-passed if it is wet, but most of the route is easy-going and simple to follow.

❶ From the centre of **Todmorden**, follow the A646 towards Burnley. Just before the viaduct and bus station, turn right and cross the river, following a path along its far bank. This joins Hall Bank Crescent, from which you can cut through to the main road by a mini Stoodley Pike memorial. Head left up the hill and take the second left up Cross Stone Lane. Turn right into Broadstone Street, then left up a path between houses that emerges on **Carr House Lane**.

The name **Kilnhurst** suggests the existence of an ancient wood where charcoal was burned, but there is little left of Kilnhurst Wood on the slopes above the hamlet.

❷ Continue past whitewashed **Carr House**, then fork right along the hillside. At the first gate on the left, climb up beside Bean Hole, then turn right above the house and join the track leading round to **Bean Hole Delf** and its often impressive waterfall. Just beyond the waterfall, bear left up a narrow path that picks its way along the rough slope into **Bean Hole Wood**. A fenceline guides you up to the the top of the wood, where you turn right along the clearer path of Long Lane.

❽ Emerging from **Bird Bank Wood** at a stile, follow the field edge along to join a track by the sheds of the Oldroyd Ridings. Turn left and continue through the hamlet of **Oldroyd**. Halfway to Kilnhurst, a gate on the right leads to **Trigger's Grave**, but the route continues to Kilnhurst Old Hall. Head straight across the road, following a footpath down between the houses. At the bottom, turn left then right to reach the Rochdale Canal, which can be followed back into the centre of **Todmorden**. Continuing straight on to Stansfield Bridge allows the centre of town to be missed out if starting the route elsewhere.

Billy Holt was one of Todmorden's great characters, a self-educated adventurer and writer who lived at **Kilnhurst Old Hall**. His works, which he sold door to door from a wheelbarrow, included *I Haven't Unpacked* (which sold 250,000 copies), *I Was A Prisoner* (about his imprisonment in Wakefield with the Todmorden Communists in 1932) and *Trigger In Europe* (about his 9000-mile journey around Europe with his loyal white horse). He regularly rode **Trigger** around town and the horse is buried in a grave along the track nearby.

❼ The shortest way through **Ingham Wood** bears immediately left beyond the stile, descending to cross **Lumbutts Clough** near the site of Causeway Mill and turning right up to the road. However, after heavy rain the stream can be difficult to ford, so an alternative follows the main path down to **New Mill Dam**, then keeps left to rejoin the other route as it ascends right to the road. Having rejoined, follow the road briefly right, then ascend some steps and join the lovely path through the beech trees of **Causeway Wood**.

TRIGGER

MAY 11th 1980

Much loved, Noble and Faithfull Companion of WILLIAM HOLT

CLOUGHS FROM TODMORDEN

4 All paths lead to a stile, from which you continue along the edge of the fields until you reach a crude (step-less) stile on the right. Double back into the wood here and fork left immediately to descend gradually through the thick beech masts into **Ingham Clough**. The last section is steep, but a good path the other side of the stream leads down to the road. Beyond the railway tunnel, turn right along the main road, then first left towards Mankinholes.

3 Follow Long Lane all the way round the top of **Rodwell Clough** to join a vehicle track. Keep right along the top of the wood to emerge on the heath by **Lad Stones**, which offers great views of this part of the Calder Valley. Continue along a path by the wall and head straight across a larger path below Rodwell End, following a faint path along the top of the slope (ducking the occasional low bough). Turn right by a post at the far end, then bear almost immediately left and follow one of the paths through the top of **Bridge Royd Wood**.

6 Descend through **Haugh Wood**, joining a track by Haugh House. Just before the buildings of Bankside Farm, turn left through a gate and zigzag up the hillside. Follow the side of a wall across fields to a stile at the top. Bear right here to another obvious stile, from where a path leads down to the steep scarp above Lumbutts Clough. Zigzag down below the rocks of **Raven Nest** and double back left on the path at the bottom. This skirts the hillside below Doroad Scout and ascends slightly to an old wall. Bear right here towards a stile at the top of **Ingham Wood**.

5 Follow the road over the Rochdale Canal, then turn left on an unsigned path immediately in front of the buildings of Shaw Bridge and follow the stream into **Gut Royd Wood**. The path climbs to the top of the pleasant oak wood and continues to a second set of steps, before crossing the field to Gut Royd. 100m beyond the farm, turn right off the track and descend to Lower Gut Royd, where the onward path is sometimes obscured. In the trees the other side of the parking area, an overgrown waymark post directs up some steps to the road. Head straight on up New Road and turn right over a stone stile just before **Shaw Farm**. A path skirts around the farm then follows a fenced line across the fields towards the top of the trees. **135**

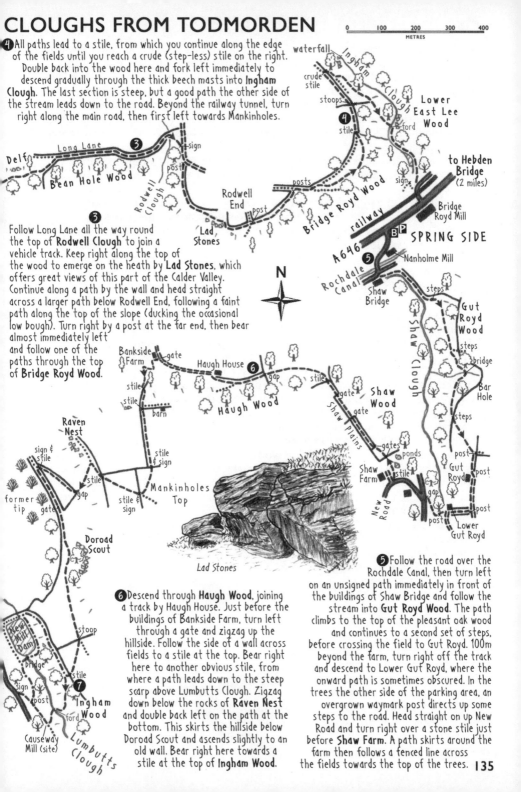

Lad Stones

THE ALDER

The alder tree has numerous variations on its name: eller, oller, owler, and even whistle-wood (because children made whistles out of the hollowed branches). The common alder is a pioneering deciduous tree that likes to grow with its roots in water or wet ground. It is therefore ideally suited to the Calder Valley and is prevalent in wet hollows and along riverbanks, often serving to protect them from erosion. It is found in carr (or wet) woodland like that in Broadhead Clough and is often associated with birds such as the redpoll and siskin, which both love its seed. Alder is nitrogen-fixing and so is a good pioneer species and subsequently nourishes the soil around where it grows. But it does not tolerate shade well and is a relatively short-lived tree, soon giving way to others.

Its gnarled wood can look like that of a young oak, but its leaves emerge far earlier in spring and it bears both male and female catkins. The latter are distinctive in winter as the false cones that look like they belong on a conifer. The leaves are racquet shaped, thick and a particularly rich green. The reddish colour of its timber also means it has been referred to as Scotch mahogany. Fender Stratocaster guitars have been made from alder since 1956 and, because it doesn't rot when constantly wet, Venice is built on alder piles.

The alder was discovered to be a good charcoal wood in the Bronze Age, and is likely to have been widely cut down for that use in this area at a time when it would have been far more populous. Alder charcoal grew to be particularly useful for making gunpowder as it burned quickly at high temperatures. Although alder was thought to make poor firewood as it needs to be very dry to burn and tends to spit, it was still valued for carpentry in the Middle Ages before conifers became widespread. Therefore alder coppices were common; when coppiced it grew quickly, straight and was easy to cut. It was worked locally to produce dishes, pipes and troughs and, despite being a very soft wood, was sometimes used in the timber frames of cottages simply because it was so prevalent. Its most common use in the area, though, was for making clog soles and it was sometimes known as 'clog wood'.

As charcoal-burning declined so too did many of the coppices that supplied the industry. Alder trees were replaced by other ornamental and fashionable species like beech and sycamore, and now they are found only in areas where they would naturally compete and where they are not completely shaded out. The remnants of alder coppices may be identifiable by many stems of a similar size and lots of growth around the base of the tree, and can be seen in Beaumont Clough and Broadhead Clough.

Sadly, alder trees are being attacked by a relatively new disease phytopthera, which arrived in 1993 but is already threatening to wipe out the species across the whole of the UK.

alder cones
and catkins

CHAPTER 11 - TODMORDEN & WALSDEN

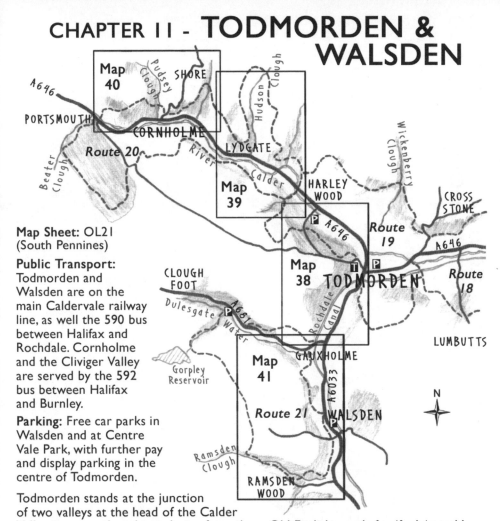

Map Sheet: OL21 (South Pennines)

Public Transport: Todmorden and Walsden are on the main Caldervale railway line, as well the 590 bus between Halifax and Rochdale. Cornholme and the Cliviger Valley are served by the 592 bus between Halifax and Burnley.

Parking: Free car parks in Walsden and at Centre Vale Park, with further pay and display parking in the centre of Todmorden.

Todmorden stands at the junction of two valleys at the head of the Calder Valley, its name thought to derive from three Old English words for 'fox', 'marsh' and 'valley'. It originally referred only to the western hillside towards Sourhall, with Stansfield (to the north), Langfield (to the south-east) and Walsden (to the south-west) on the other hills around the present town. Though not as wooded as Hebden Bridge, trees cling to the steep slopes all the way up the Cliviger and Walsden Valleys to the county boundary. Just behind the town centre, Centre Vale Park and Dobroyd Castle are fringed by fine woodland, and further out you find the densely wooded ravines of Gorpley, Wittonstall, Pudsey and Ramsden Cloughs. But the bleak moors of Inchfield, Todmorden and Walsden hem these valleys in tightly and the trees at this end of the valley are of the most hardy and upland sort. For example, high rainfall and acid soil mean that silver birches are largely replaced by downy birch.

The Cliviger Valley is particularly dramatic, with rocky parapets cresting its steep hillsides. Sadly many of its woods are little more than memories, a few thin oaks where once there was a whole woodland (e.g. Barewise Wood, Robin Wood, Knotts Wood, New Ley Wood and Windy Bank Wood), while others like Thorns Wood and Tower Wood are nothing but names on old maps. Meanwhile the Walsden hillsides are more wooded than the OS map lets on, with newly planted sites and scrub woodland reasserting itself on otherwise barren slopes.

137

Centre Vale Park extends up onto the steep flanks of Buckley Wood and Ewood Wood, and most of its area is woodland rather than open parkland. The woodland continues beyond the Ridge into Hall Wood (high above the arc of the railway) and then into Dobroyd Wood, which shrouds the castle from view. While Centre Vale Park is publicly owned and all Open Access, most of Hall Wood and Dobroyd Wood is privately owned. Consequently there is little access here, while the park is a warren of paths and nooks to explore.

The flatter scrub area at the top of The Ridge that was previously used for allotments is known as Chimney Fields. Until the 1930s a chimney stood on the high ground with a flue leading up from Ridgefoot Mill (located alongside the railway viaduct). The Doghouse was a local lock-up in one of the houses on The Ridge, and gives its name to the lane leading up towards Sourhall.

An old path across the bottom of Ewood Wood is accessible as far as a small stream which marks the end of the Open Access woodland. The overgrown track beyond continues above the houses only to peter out at the back of the grounds of Saltcliffe Hall.

Siggett Lane and **Stickett Gate** (referred to in old literature and postcards) are probably names for the same track through the woods, a sigg being a stick.

Centre Vale Park was mostly laid out in the 1840s by Honest John Fielden, who had the house at Centre Vale built in 1820. The land was later bought by Edward Lord for £10,000 in 1911 and given to the council to create the park. The house became the Todmorden Historical Rooms museum between the wars, but was demolished in 1953 due to dry rot; nothing but its outline and out-houses remains.

The adjoining **Buckley Wood** was given to the people of Todmorden by Mrs Greenwood of Glen View (a former mansion on Stoney Royd Lane).

Now deconsecrated, **Christ Church** (along with St Paul's, Cross Stone and St James', Mytholm) was one of the million pound churches designed by Lewis Vulliamy in the 1830s to support the booming population in industrial areas after the Napoleonic Wars.

There are a number of **wells** scattered throughout Centre Vale Park, the most obvious being in the wall of Lovers' Walk near Platts House (which dates from the 17th century). This used to have iron gates across the front, but others are simple stone troughs. The **holy well** above Christ Church has recently been excavated to reveal a stone-flagged well still full of water. It would have been surrounded by railings and had a hand pump. It is reached by an old path from the end of Well Lane (which used to be Holy Well Lane). People are said to have left small offerings in the well, which were known in Yorkshire as memaws.

Rise Lane, which runs through the only publicly accessible part of Hall Wood, has collapsed into the gaping quarry delf below. A diversion leads through the beech trees above, before the path branches off across the fields. Rise Lane used to continue straight down the hill through where the station is and link up with the other part of Rise Lane, which leads up to it from the main road.

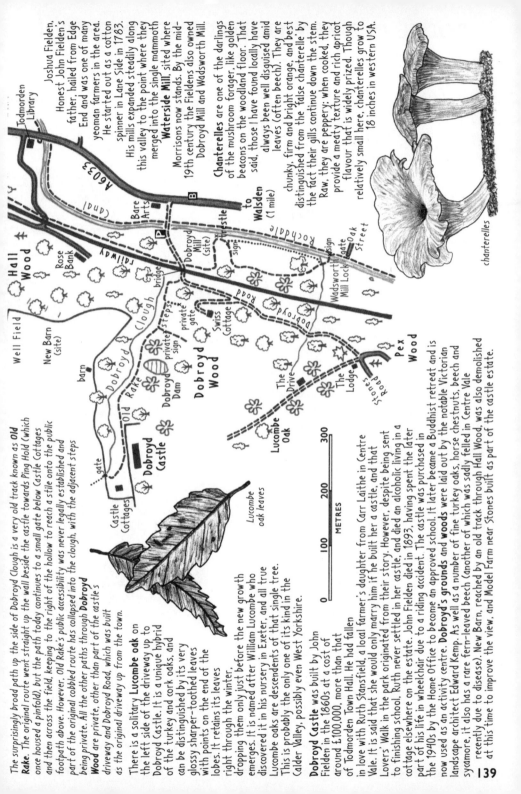

Joshua Fielden, Honest John Fielden's father, hailed from Edge End and was one of many yeoman farmers in the area. He started out as a cotton spinner in Lane Side in 1783. His mills expanded steadily along this valley to the point where they merged into the single mammoth **Waterside Mill**, sited where Morrisons now stands. By the mid-19th century the Fieldens also owned Dobroyd Mill and Wadsworth Mill.

Chanterelles are one of the darlings of the mushroom forager, like golden beacons on the woodland floor. That said, those I have found locally have always been well disguised amid leaves (often beech). They are chunky, firm and bright orange, and best distinguished from the 'false chanterelle' by the fact their gills continue down the stem. Raw, they are peppery; when cooked, they provide a meaty texture and rich apricot flavour that is widely prized. Though relatively small here, chanterelles grow to 18 inches in western USA.

chanterelles

The surprisingly broad path up the side of Dobroyd Clough is a very old track known as **Old Rake**. The original route went straight up the wall beside the castle towards Ping Hold (which once housed a pinfold), but the path today continues to a small gate below Castle Cottages and then across the field, keeping to the right of the hollow to reach a stile onto the public footpath above. Old Rake's public accessibility was never legally established and part of the original cobbled route has collapsed into the clough, with the adjacent steps being private. All the other paths through **Dobroyd Wood** are private, other than part of the castle's driveway and Dobroyd Road, which was built as the original driveway up from the town.

There is a solitary **Lucombe oak** on the left side of the driveway up to Dobroyd Castle. It is a unique hybrid of the turkey and cork oaks, and can be distinguished by its very glossy sharper-toothed leaves with points on the end of the lobes. It retains its leaves right through the winter, dropping them only just before the new growth emerges. It is named after William Lucombe who discovered it in his nursery in Exeter, and all true Lucombe oaks are descendents of that single tree. This is probably the only one of its kind in the Calder Valley, possibly even West Yorkshire.

Lucombe oak leaves

Dobroyd Castle was built by John Fielden in the 1860s at a cost of around £100,000, more than that of Todmorden Town Hall. He had fallen in love with Ruth Stansfield, a local farmer's daughter from Carr Laithe in Centre Vale. It is said that she would only marry him if he built her a castle, and that Lovers' Walk in the park originated from their story. However, despite being sent to finishing school, Ruth never settled in her castle, and died an alcoholic living in a cottage elsewhere on the estate. John Fielden died in 1893, having spent the later part of his life in wheelchair due to a riding accident. The castle was purchased in the 1940s by the Home Office to become an approved school. It later became a Buddhist retreat and is now used as an activity centre. **Dobroyd's grounds and woods** were laid out by the notable Victorian landscape architect Edward Kemp. As well as a number of fine turkey oaks, horse chestnuts, beech and sycamore, it also has a rare fern-leaved beech (another of which was sadly felled in Centre Vale recently due to disease). New Barn, reached by an old track through Hall Wood, was also demolished at this time to improve the view, and Model Farm near Stones built as part of the castle estate.

METRES 0 100 200 300

ROUTE 19: THE WOODS OF TODMORDEN

3 Descend steeply to the foot of **Scaitcliffe Clough** and follow the track right to reach the main road. Head straight across into Stoney Royd Lane and turn right at a sign, following a narrow walled path over the railway. Emerging at Cross Lee, turn left and follow the track all the way up to Bank House. Just beyond the buildings, turn right through a couple of scruffy gates and skirt along the bottom of the slope to a gate. A path continues along the top of the scrub woodland beyond and soon reaches the top of Ashenhurst Road.

John Nowell, who was born at Springs above Harley Wood in 1802, co-founded the Todmorden Botanical Society. He died before his *Flora of Todmorden* was published. It was particularly focused on mosses and was described as being 'as thorough a study as conducted anywhere in the country'.

2 Turn left up Siggett Lane for 100m, then right up some steps to climb steadily through **Buckley** and **Ewood Woods**. At the top, follow the field edge up to Todmorden Edge, where you turn right down the track. Where it forks, head straight on, then descend through an old wooden gate to pass between the buildings of Flail Croft. Head straight on down some steps and follow the walls down into **Scaitcliffe Wood**.

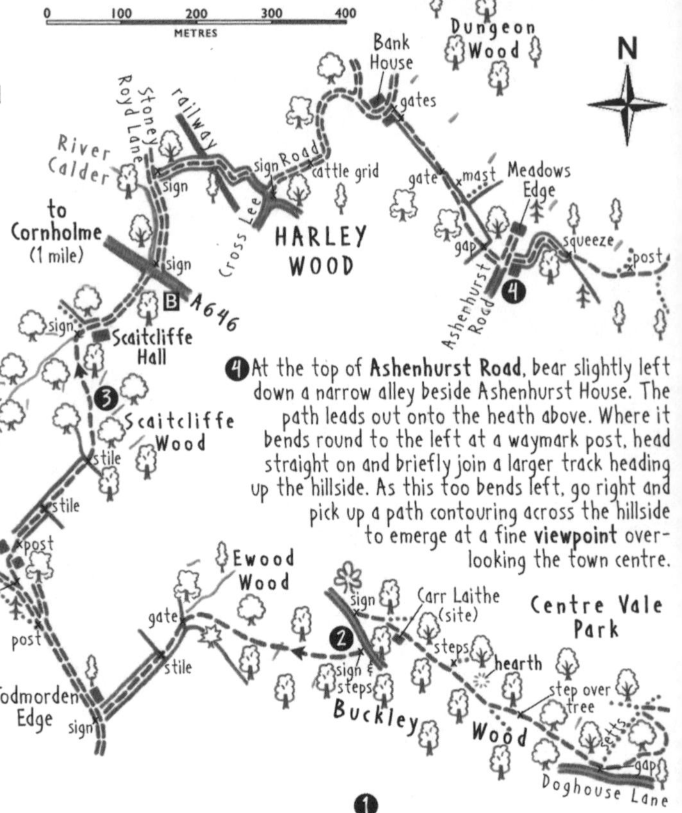

(Map labels: 0 100 200 300 400 METRES · Dungeon Wood · Bank House · gates · N · Stoney Royd Lane · railway · River Calder · Cross Lee · sign · Sign Road · cattle grid · gate · mast · Meadows Edge · to Cornholme (1 mile) · sign · HARLEY WOOD · squeeze · post · gap · Ashenhurst Road · 4 · B A646 · Scaitcliffe Hall · Scaitcliffe Wood · Scaitcliffe Clough · stile · 3 · Flail Croft · post · gate · post · Ewood Wood · gate · sign · Carr Laithe (site) · Centre Vale Park · stile · steps · 2 · sign & steps · hearth · Todmorden Edge · sign · Buckley Wood · step over tree · gap · Doghouse Lane)

4 At the top of **Ashenhurst Road**, bear slightly left down a narrow alley beside Ashenhurst House. The path leads out onto the heath above. Where it bends round to the left at a waymark post, head straight on and briefly join a larger track heading up the hillside. As this too bends left, go right and pick up a path contouring across the hillside to emerge at a fine **viewpoint** overlooking the town centre.

1 From the centre of **Todmorden**, head up the road towards the station from opposite the Town Hall. On the bend, bear right beneath the railway, then head straight on up Ridge Steps and take the higher of two tracks heading right into the wood. At a busy junction, double back to the left and wind up through Chimney Fields. Stay below the road and head straight on through **Buckley Wood**. Ignore a number of paths leading off and continue straight on, passing through the ruins of Carr Laithe to reach the road.

Blackheath Circle

Distance: 5.5 miles (9km)

Ascent: 440m

Parking: Free parking by the railway station and in other places around Todmorden town centre.

Public Transport: Todmorden is on the main Caldervale train and bus routes.

Character: Discover the greener side of Todmorden with this surprising exploration of the three hills around the town centre. Other than Buckley Wood, the area's woods – Scaitcliffe Wood, Ridge Wood, Longfield Wood – are mostly small, but the charming hillsides are still dominated by trees. The walk is completed by a brief diversion to the Butt Stones and Blackheath Circle.

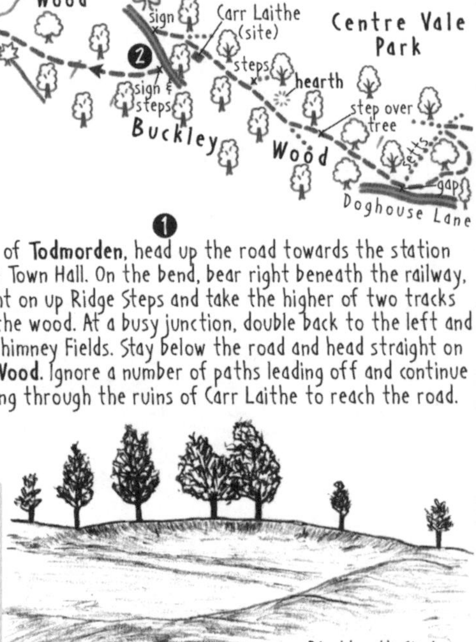

There are hundreds of Quakers buried at **Shewbread Quaker Burial Ground**, including 24 Fieldens, but only a few memorial stones. For a long time, Quakers were not permitted to mark their burial places. Shoebroad and Shewbread are likely corruptions of the Old Testament *showbread*, which was set out for God at all times on a specially prepared table.

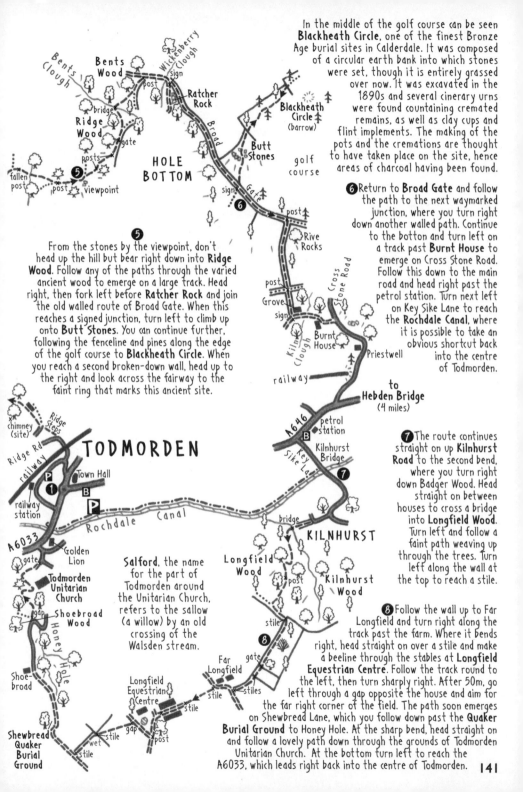

In the middle of the golf course can be seen **Blackheath Circle**, one of the finest Bronze Age burial sites in Calderdale. It was composed of a circular earth bank into which stones were set, though it is entirely grassed over now. It was excavated in the 1890s and several cinerary urns were found containing cremated remains, as well as clay cups and flint implements. The making of the pots and the cremations are thought to have taken place on the site, hence areas of charcoal having been found.

Bents Wood
Bents Clough
Wickenberry Clough
sign
post
Ratcher Rock
bridge
Ridge Wood
gate
posts
HOLE BOTTOM
Broad Gate
Blackheath Circle (barrow)
Butt Stones
golf course
fallen post
post
viewpoint
sign
⑥
post
Rive Rocks

⑤ From the stones by the viewpoint, don't head up the hill but bear right down into **Ridge Wood**. Follow any of the paths through the varied ancient wood to emerge on a large track. Head right, then fork left before **Ratcher Rock** and join the old walled route of Broad Gate. When this reaches a signed junction, turn left to climb up onto **Butt Stones**. You can continue further, following the fenceline and pines along the edge of the golf course to **Blackheath Circle**. When you reach a second broken-down wall, head up to the right and look across the fairway to the faint ring that marks this ancient site.

⑥ Return to **Broad Gate** and follow the path to the next waymarked junction, where you turn right down another walled path. Continue to the bottom and turn left on a track past **Burnt House** to emerge on Cross Stone Road. Follow this down to the main road and head right past the petrol station. Turn next left on Key Sike Lane to reach the **Rochdale Canal**, where it is possible to take an obvious shortcut back into the centre of Todmorden.

post
Grove
sign
Cross Stone Road
Burnt House
Kiln Clough
Priestwell
railway

to Hebden Bridge (4 miles)

Ridge Rd
chimney (site)
Ridge Steps
railway
TODMORDEN
Town Hall
P
①
B
P
railway station
A6033
gate
Golden Lion
Todmorden Unitarian Church
Shoebroad Wood
Rochdale Canal
A646
B
petrol station
Kilnhurst Bridge
⑦
Key Sike La
bridge
KILNHURST

⑦ The route continues straight on up **Kilnhurst Road** to the second bend, where you turn right down Badger Wood. Head straight on between houses to cross a bridge into **Longfield Wood**. Turn left and follow a faint path weaving up through the trees. Turn left along the wall at the top to reach a stile.

Salford, the name for the part of Todmorden around the Unitarian Church, refers to the sallow (a willow) by an old crossing of the Walsden stream.

Longfield Wood
post
Kilnhurst Wood
stile
⑧
Far Longfield
gate
stile
stiles
Longfield Equestrian Centre
stile
gap
post
Shoebroad
Honey Hole
wet stile
stile
Shewbread Quaker Burial Ground

⑧ Follow the wall up to Far Longfield and turn right along the track past the farm. Where it bends right, head straight on over a stile and make a beeline through the stables at **Longfield Equestrian Centre**. Follow the track round to the left, then turn sharply right. After 50m, go left through a gap opposite the house and aim for the far right corner of the field. The path soon emerges on Shewbread Lane, which you follow down past the **Quaker Burial Ground** to Honey Hole. At the sharp bend, head straight on and follow a lovely path down through the grounds of Todmorden Unitarian Church. At the bottom turn left to reach the A6033, which leads right back into the centre of Todmorden. **141**

MAP 39: LOWER CLIVIGER GORGE

The Calder Valley narrows

at Lydgate and is towered over by great tors like Eagle Crag and Orchan Rocks, its slopes riven by steeply cascading streams. These cloughs are the most densely wooded areas, with some of the other ancient woods, like Knotts Wood or Robin Wood, largely lost or much diminished. There are plenty of little paths, with Knotts Wood and Naze a particularly good area to explore from the Staff of Life.

Hudson Clough presents the greatest obstacle on the north side of the valley as no paths cross it between the main road and Hartley Bridge above Hartley Royd. An old path does follow the clough up from the end of Knott Road to Cat Hole Dam, but goes no further. The easiest way into **Cat Hole** (and its carved stone) is probably from the slope above to the west, either side of the Clunters crags.

In 1755, **Cat Hole** was first mined for lead on the site of a drift of lead ore thought to be 3/4 mile deep. It proved largely fruitless as the ore was too expensive to remove, but it didn't stop some independent Welsh miners in 1835 and a company in 1869 trying again. No one ever made a penny from Cat Hole Clough Lead Mine, but there is still a large spoil heap visible at the site below Hudson Moor. A young woman, Ann Clegg, committed suicide in Cat Hole Dam in 1883, as did gardener William Austwick in 1902.

Pennant Clough is one of the few names in Calderdale left with Celtic roots, coming from *pen* (hill) and *nant* (valley). The latter is also found in **Nant Wood** in Cartridge Clough (see p.144).

The paths between **New Ley** and **Hartley Royd** are hard to trace across a largely open hillside scattered with elegant ruins. The only Right of Way follows the fence up the side of **Back Wood** and then bears left across the slope to Mercer Field, from where stiles lead the way.

Clunters is a dialect word that can refer to a clattering walk, huge moorland tufts or a rocky precipice with loose rocks. In this case it likely refers to the craggy knoll overlooking Cat Hole.

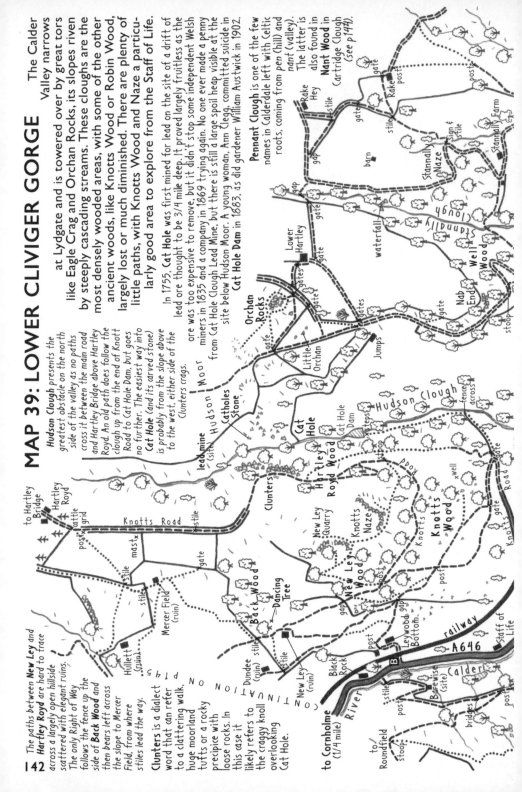

to Hartley Bridge

Hartley Royd

Knotts Road

Hudson Moor

lead mine (site)

Catholes Stone

Cat Hole

Hartley Royd Wood

Clunters

Orchan Rocks

Little Orchan

Jumps

Hudson Clough

Cat Hole Dam

steps

New Ley Quarry

Knotts Naze

Back Wood

Dancing Tree

New Ley Wood

Knotts Wood

Knotts Road

Mercer Field (ruin)

Hullett (ruin)

Dundee (ruin)

New Ley (ruin)

Black Rock

Leywood Bottom

well

Lower Hartley

Stannally Naze

Stannally Clough

Well Wood

Nab End

Stannally Farm

Sign & stile

Rake Hey

Rake

barn

waterfall

(CONTINUATION ON P.145)

Calder

railway

A646

Staff of Life

River

Barewise (site)

bridges

to Cornholme (1/4 mile)

to Roundfield

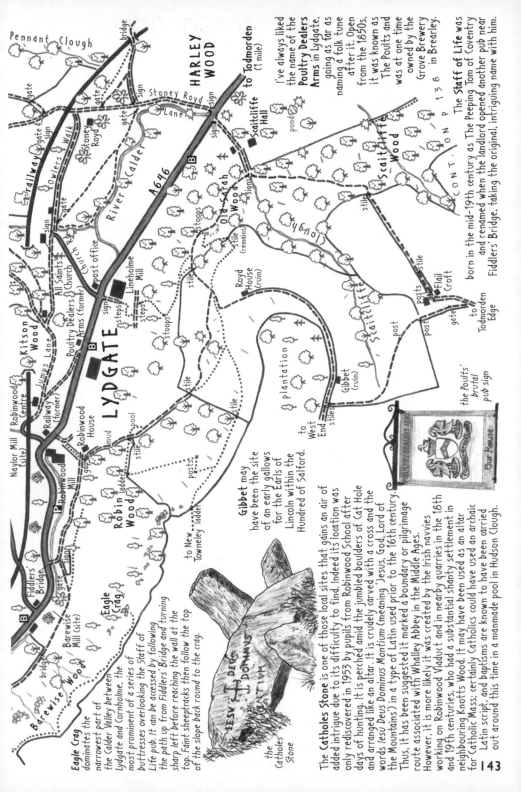

I've always liked the name of the **Poultry Dealers Arms** in Lydgate, going as far as naming a folk tune after it. Open from the 1850s, it was known as The Poults and was at one time owned by the Grove Brewery in Brearley.

The **Staff of Life** was born in the mid-19th century as The Peeping Tom of Coventry and renamed when the landlord opened another pub near Fiddler's Bridge, taking the original, intriguing name with him.

the Poults' brutal pub sign

Eagle Crag dominates the narrowest part of the Calder Valley between Lydgate and Cornholme, the most prominent of a series of buttresses overlooking the Staff of Life pub. It can be accessed by following the path up from Fiddlers' Bridge and turning sharp left before reaching the wall at the top. Faint sheeptracks then follow the top of the slope back round to the crag.

Gibbet may have been the site of an early gallows for the Earls of Lincoln within the Hundred of Salford.

the Catholes Stone

The **Catholes Stone** is one of those local sites that gains an air of added intrigue due to its difficulty to find. Indeed its location was only rediscovered in 1953 by pupils from Robinwood School after days of hunting. It is perched amid the jumbled boulders of Cat Hole and arranged like an altar. It is crudely carved with a cross and the words *Iesu Deus Dominus Montium* (meaning 'Jesus, God, Lord of the Mountains') in a type of Latin used prior to the 16th century. Thus, it has been suggested it marked a boundary or pilgrimage route associated with Whalley Abbey in the Middle Ages. However, it is more likely it was created by the Irish navvies working on Robinwood Viaduct and in nearby quarries in the 18th and 19th centuries, who had a substantial shanty settlement in neighbouring Knotts Wood. It may have been used as an altar for Catholic Mass; certainly Catholics could have used an archaic Latin script, and baptisms are known to have been carried out around this time in a manmade pool in Hudson Clough.

MAP 40: UPPER CLIVIGER GORGE

This is the last hurrah of the Calder Valley right on the Lancashire boundary, by which time the River Calder is a barely traceable channel alongside or under the main road. Instead Redwater Clough dominates the north side of the valley, a deep wooded scar full of waterfalls and crags. Wittonstall Clough is less dramatic but more accessible, with Obadiah Wood being the finest in the area. Elsewhere thin trees cling to the steep slopes and swamp the valley's defining industrial remains.

There was a coal mine over Nant Bridge from Back Rough, whose carr water (rusty-coloured iron oxide run off) is likely to have given **Redwater Clough** its name. There is a large tunnel through the hillside that drained the underground coal workings. It ran beneath Whitaker Naze from Nant Wood to Bankwell Coal Mine adjacent to the old Methodist church.

There are a number of impressive **waterfalls** *in Redwater, Cartridge and Pudsey Cloughs. The latter is a particularly impressive gorge, whose waterfall is most easily accessed from the path up its east bank from Back Rough. Slightly further up and accessed only from the opposite bank is the* **Frying Pan***, a scoured rocky hollow which makes a good bathing spot even if it is too tiny to swim in. A waterfall in Redwater Clough can be accessed via a small gate from the track below Back Rough.*

Whitaker Naze is named after the notable Whitaker family, who built the mansion at The Holme in Holme Chapel. One of their number was among the early settlers in America and performed the baptism of Pocahontas.

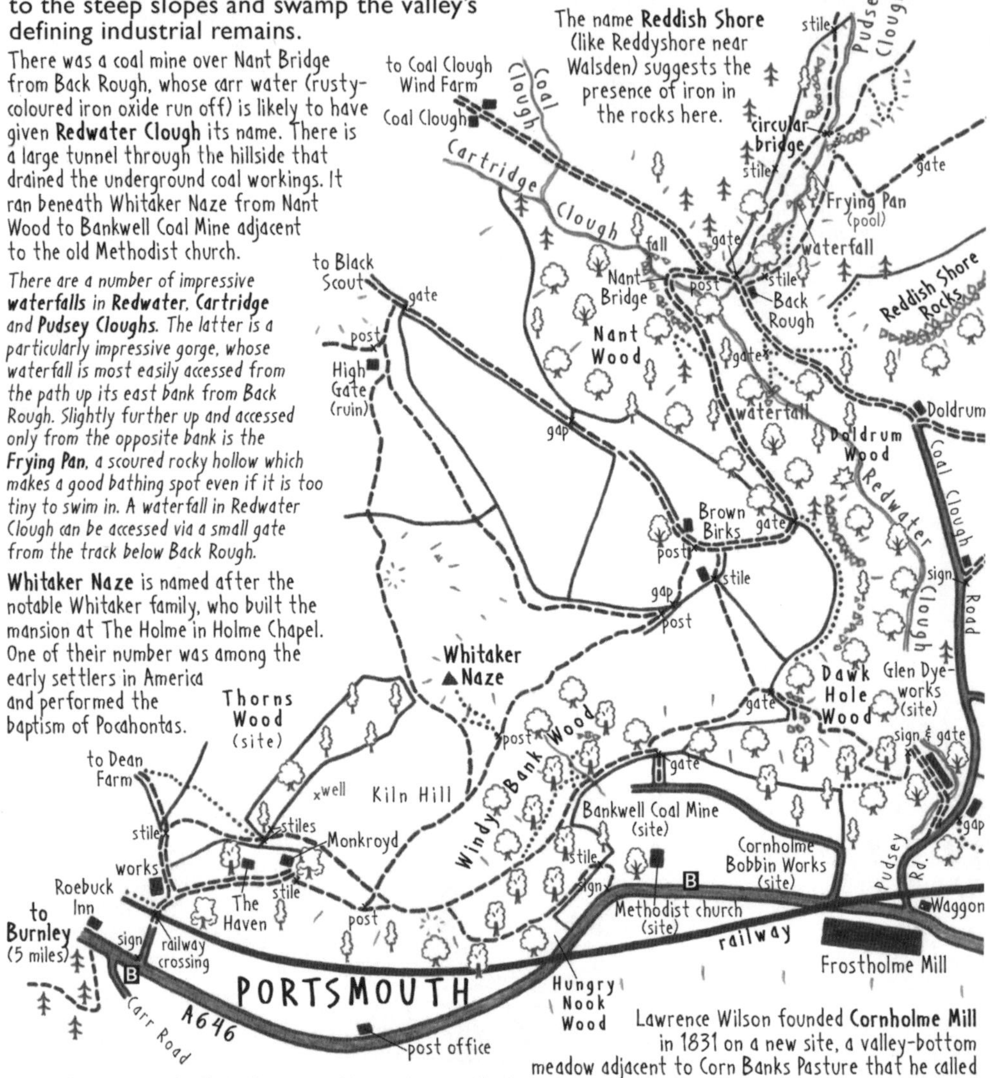

The name **Reddish Shore** (like Reddyshore near Walsden) suggests the presence of iron in the rocks here.

Map labels

Pudsey Clough · stile · Coal Clough · to Coal Clough Wind Farm · Coal Clough · circular bridge · stile · gate · Cartridge Clough · Frying Pan (pool) · stiles · fall · gate · waterfall · Nant Bridge · post · stile · Back Rough · Reddish Shore Rocks · to Black Scout · gate · Nant Wood · gate · post · High Gate (ruin) · gap · waterfall · Doldrum · Doldrum Wood · Brown Birks · gate · post · Redwater Clough · Coal Clough Road · gap · stile · sign · post · Whitaker ▲ Naze · Thorns Wood (site) · x well · Kiln Hill · Windy Bank Wood · post · gate · Dawk Hole Wood · Glen Dye works (site) · sign & gate · gap · Bankwell Coal Mine (site) · Pudsey Rd. · to Dean Farm · stile · stiles · Monkroyd · stile · sign · Cornholme Bobbin Works (site) · works · Roebuck Inn · The Haven · stile · post · B · Methodist church (site) · railway · Waggon · to Burnley (5 miles) · sign · railway crossing · B · **PORTSMOUTH** · Carr Road · A646 · post office · Hungry Nook Wood · railway · Frostholme Mill

Lawrence Wilson founded **Cornholme Mill** in 1831 on a new site, a valley-bottom meadow adjacent to Corn Banks Pasture that he called Cornholme. Prior to that, the only settlements were the hamlets of Pudsey, Vale (the east end of Cornholme) and Shore, but as a large village developed around the mills it took the name of the mill. This became **Cornholme Bobbin Works**, the largest of a number of bobbin firms in Cornholme, making bobbins for the thousands of spindles that needed replacing in the weaving mills every year. There are 'Stansfield turnours' recorded working wood in the area as early as 1379, with timber originally being sourced locally. As demand grew and local sources became diminished, the wood was shipped from Ireland, where Wilsons bought a saw mill. Eventually this led to them relocating to Garston near Liverpool and the mill being used for making shuttles instead. It was eventually replaced by the Bobbin Mill housing estate we see today. The bobbin turning industry declined quickly due to the changing demands of the textile industry, but some bobbins were made by hand from pole lathes until well into the 20th century. Lawrence Wilson is commemorated in an obelisk in the graveyard of the old Mount Zion Methodist Church.

In 1818 Thomas Whitaker referred to a waterfall in **Pudsey Clough** as 'one of singular beauty near the top, overshadowed by a single oak, which might almost be painted of its own dimensions'. There are a few more oaks today, but little has changed. Just upstream is a distinctive circular packhorse bridge, whose parapets have collapsed into the stream.

Cornholme has always struck me as a place lacking pubs, but it is not a new phenomenon as the area was strongly linked to the **Temperance Movement**. Lawrence Wilson, who is said to have brought Methodism to Cornholme, and other large employers encouraged temperance and so there were always more chapels than pubs.

Shore Working Men's Club was opened in 1908 with a concert hall accommodating up to 200 people. It is now a private residence.

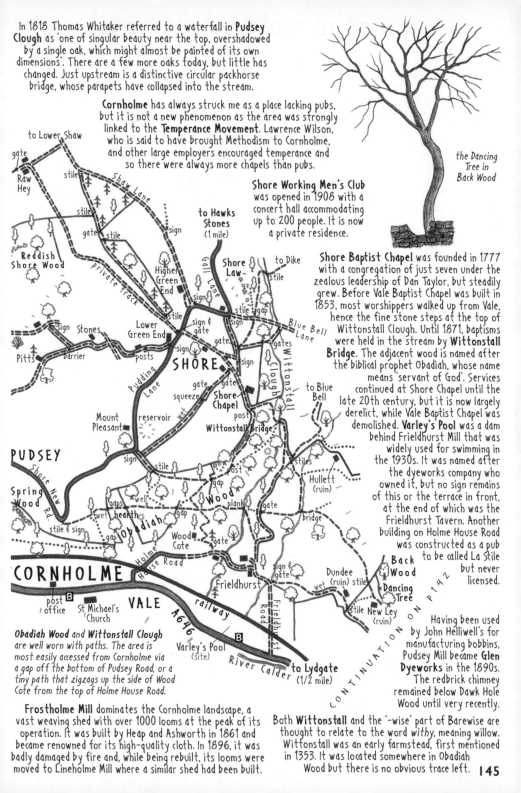

the Dancing Tree in Back Wood

Shore Baptist Chapel was founded in 1777 with a congregation of just seven under the zealous leadership of Dan Taylor, but steadily grew. Before Vale Baptist Chapel was built in 1853, most worshippers walked up from Vale, hence the fine stone steps at the top of Wittonstall Clough. Until 1871, baptisms were held in the stream by **Wittonstall Bridge**. The adjacent wood is named after the biblical prophet Obadiah, whose name means 'servant of God'. Services continued at Shore Chapel until the late 20th century, but it is now largely derelict, while Vale Baptist Chapel was demolished. **Varley's Pool** was a dam behind Frieldhurst Mill that was widely used for swimming in the 1930s. It was named after the dyeworks company who owned it, but no sign remains of this or the terrace in front, at the end of which was the Frieldhurst Tavern. Another building on Holme House Road was constructed as a pub to be called La Stile but never licensed.

Having been used by John Helliwell's for manufacturing bobbins, Pudsey Mill became **Glen Dyeworks** in the 1890s. The redbrick chimney remained below Dawk Hole Wood until very recently.

Obadiah Wood and **Wittonstall Clough** are well worn with paths. The area is most easily accessed from Cornholme via a gap off the bottom of Pudsey Road, or a tiny path that zigzags up the side of Wood Cote from the top of Holme House Road.

Frostholme Mill dominates the Cornholme landscape, a vast weaving shed with over 1000 looms at the peak of its operation. It was built by Heap and Ashworth in 1861 and became renowned for its high-quality cloth. In 1896, it was badly damaged by fire, and while being rebuilt, its looms were moved to Lineholme Mill where a similar shed had been built.

Both **Wittonstall** and the '-wise' part of Barewise are thought to relate to the word *withy*, meaning willow. Wittonstall was an early farmstead, first mentioned in 1353. It was located somewhere in Obadiah Wood but there is no obvious trace left. **145**

ROUTE 20: THE CLIVIGER GORGE FROM

Distance: 7.5 miles (12km)

Ascent: 600m

Parking: Limited offroad parking on A646 near Fiddlers Bridge. Street parking along A646 in Lydgate, Cornholme and Portsmouth.

Public Transport: Lydgate, Cornholme and Portsmouth are on the 517 & 592 bus routes from Halifax to Burnley and the 589 route from Todmorden.

Character: The steep and dramatic Yorkshire part of the Cliviger Valley is only partially wooded, but this walk takes in a great variety of woodland cloughs, dramatic crags, conifer plantations and open moor. It is most satisfyingly started from the bottom of Stoney Royd Lane below Lydgate, but can equally be undertaken from Cornholme or Portsmouth. After meandering necessarily around Hudson Clough, the route soon forms a natural circuit of the head of the valley and the return journey is far quicker.

6 From a gate into the field near the top, bear left and descend beside the wood to pick up a path leading along the wall into **Windy Bank Wood**. A clear path leads on out of the trees. At a waymark post, bear left down to a stile beside Monkroyd. Follow the track down across the railway to emerge on the main road in **Portsmouth**.

5 Keep left through enchanting **Obadiah Wood** to descend to a larger path lower down, which you follow right. Soon after emerging from the wood, fork left down the slope to a gap and a path leading through the remnants of **Spring Wood**. Emerging on Pudsey Road, turn left then immediately right – at this point the main road in **Cornholme** is just 100m ahead. Beyond the far end of Woodbine Terrace, turn left and climb steeply up through **Dawk Hole Wood**; the path weaves up to a fine viewpoint on the crag above.

Dawk Hole Wood

PUDSEY

Windy Bank Wood

Spring Wood

Monkroyd

to Burnley (5 miles)

Roebuck Inn

Portsmouth Mill (site)

7 PORTSMOUTH

A646 railway

Frostholme Mill

CORNHOLME

Beater Clough

Carr Road

falls

The Old Woman

N

Dawk is a dialect word for a hollow, thus **Dawk Hole** is something of a tautology.

Cock Hill Wood

Bearnshaw Tower

Tower Delfs

Height Top

9

Roundfield (ruin)

Lower Moor

Tower Clough

7 In **Portsmouth**, turn right up the A646 then left at a sign opposite the Roebuck Inn. A track climbs steadily up through the older part of **Cock Hill Wood**, continuing up the side of **Beater Clough** and its series of fine waterfalls. At a signpost, turn left up through a delf to reach a stile on the edge of the plantation. Turn right and follow the clear path through the dark conifers, guided by posts to join a vehicle track that leads down through some mountain bike courses.

8 100m after emerging from the plantation, turn right down to a stile and join the road right briefly. Turn left by Bearnshaw Tower and fork right across the field to a stile. Keep right beyond as you pick your way through the delfs on the edge of Lower Moor and join a vehicle track heading left up towards Height Top. Skirt right around the fence here and follow a small path above the wet hollow along the edge of the moor; this soon bends left to descend towards the ruins of Roundfield.

Beater Clough is an ancient boundary and is named after the beating of its waters, an Anglo-Saxon term referring to the whitewater of its many impressive waterfalls.

Portsmouth was named only in the early 19th century. The son of the then owner of the Roebuck Inn, Tommy Clegg, upon returning from duty as a mariner stationed around the coast of England, christened the pub Portsmouth, the joiner's house Chatham, and the milking house Whitehaven. The latter is preserved in the name of The Haven, architect James Green's grand house on the site of the milking house near Monkroyd. He was designer of Stoodley Pike Monument and owner of Portsmouth Mill.

Eagle Crag

146

LYDGATE OR CORNHOLME

❹ At a waymark post where Knotts Lane doubles back sharply, go straight on through **New Ley Wood** and follow the open slope above the ruins of New Ley. Continue over a stile and, after crossing a small stream, turn right, following its line up to a stile on the edge of the wood. Head straight on and cross **Wittonstall Bridge**, before turning left at the foot of the steps.

❸ Reaching **Hudson Bridge**, follow the walled path up the other side and keep left to pass through **Hartley Royd**. Emerging from the conifers, keep left of the mast ahead, following the walled path of **Knotts Lane**. This leads all the way down past the crags above Cat Hole and through the remnants of **Knotts Wood** which houses plenty of coppiced oak. There is a shortcut down the slope half way along, but otherwise it is an easy jaunt.

Hudson Moor was regularly used for illegal gambling schools where men bet on coin-tossing games. It is said turners at Robinwood Mill produced some two-tailed coins by fusing two together.

❷ At the top of **Jumps Lane**, continue straight on through a gate and bear right up the side of the wall. Join a track leading up to the right, then go left over a stile and scramble up onto the crest of **Orchan Rocks** (stay right for the easiest route). At the far side of the rocks, pick up a path that angles down to the wall below (if you hit the quarries you've gone too far right), then turn right and follow the main path across **Hudson Moor**.

❶ Heading away from **Todmorden**, turn right off the A646 opposite the entrance to Scaitcliffe Hall Hotel, following Stoney Royd Lane. Continue under the railway and past **Stannally Farm** then, where the track bends sharply right, head straight on into Well Wood. Continue across **Stannally Clough** and turn sharply right up Jumps Lane, which winds up the beech-covered hillside.

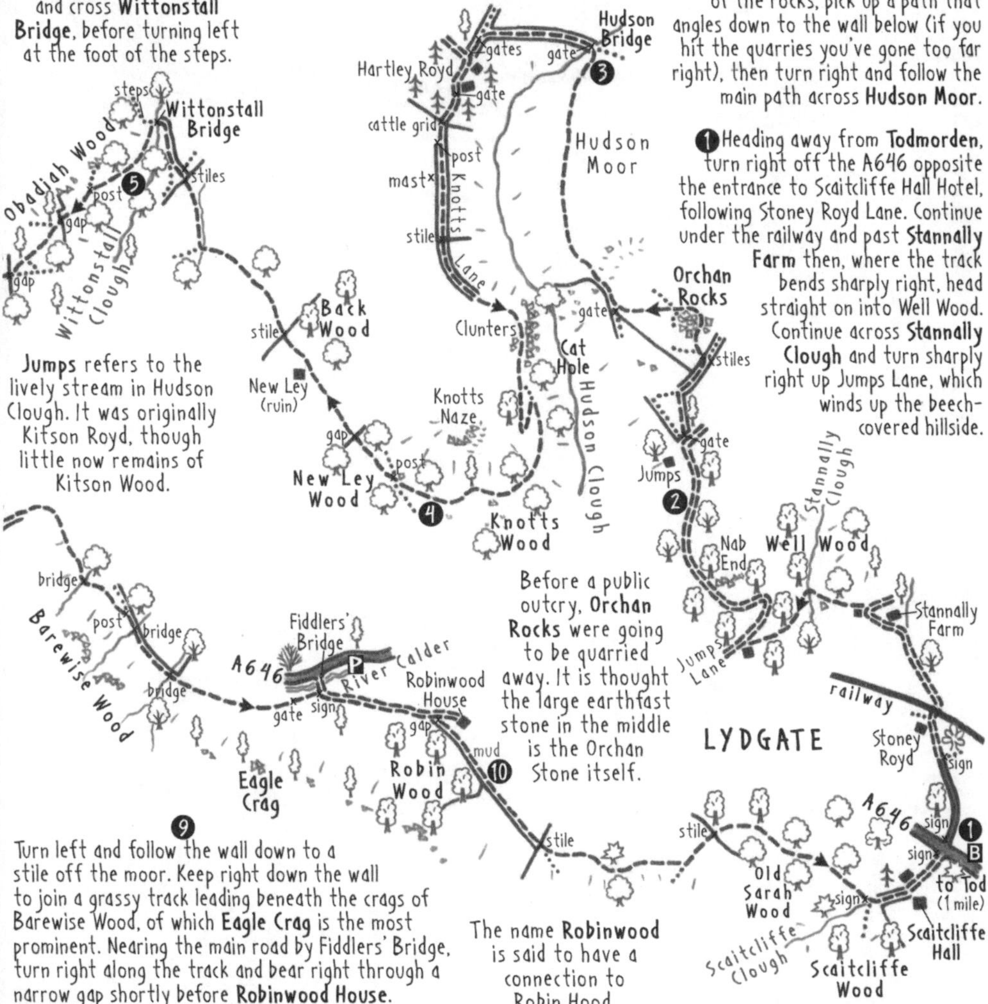

Jumps refers to the lively stream in Hudson Clough. It was originally Kitson Royd, though little now remains of Kitson Wood.

Before a public outcry, Orchan Rocks were going to be quarried away. It is thought the large earthfast stone in the middle is the Orchan Stone itself.

Turn left and follow the wall down to a stile off the moor. Keep right down the wall to join a grassy track leading beneath the crags of Barewise Wood, of which **Eagle Crag** is the most prominent. Nearing the main road by Fiddlers' Bridge, turn right along the track and bear right through a narrow gap shortly before **Robinwood House**.

The name **Robinwood** is said to have a connection to Robin Hood.

❾

The site of **Scaitcliffe Hall** has been occupied since 1411 as home of the Crossley family, Todmorden's original gentry until the 19th century. Having served as a residential care home, it was turned into a country house hotel in the 1980s.

Lydgate is named after the turnpike toll bars built here at the crossing of Hudson Clough in 1768. A *lydgate* was generally a swing gate dividing common from private land.

❿ Follow the muddy path along the wall below **Robin Wood** to a high stile, then bear left across the open slope. Turn left at an obvious track leading down into **Old Sarah Wood** above Lydgate. At the bottom turn, turn left past **Scaitcliffe Hall** to return to the A646.

Map labels: Hudson Bridge, Hartley Royd, gates, gate, cattle grid, post, mast×, stile, Knotts Lane, Hudson Moor, Orchan Rocks, gate, stiles, Clunters, Cat Hole, Hudson Clough, Knotts Naze, gate, Jumps, Stannally Clough, Nab End, Well Wood, Stannally Farm, railway, Stoney Royd, sign, LYDGATE, A646, sign, signs, to Tod (1 mile), Scaitcliffe Hall, Scaitcliffe Wood, Scaitcliffe Clough, Old Sarah Wood, stile, Robin Wood, mud, gap, Robinwood House, River Calder, Fiddlers' Bridge, A646, gate, sign, bridge, Eagle Crag, Barewise Wood, bridge, post, New Ley Wood, New Ley (ruin), gap, post, Knotts Wood, Back Wood, stile, Wittonstall Bridge, steps, stiles, post, gap, Obadiah Wood, Wittonstall Clough

147

MAP 41: WALSDEN & RAMSDEN WOOD

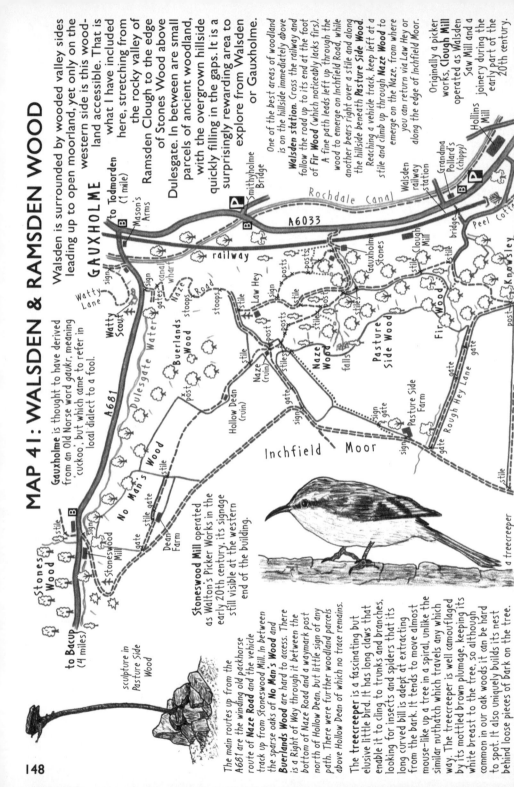

Walsden is surrounded by wooded valley sides leading up to open moorland, yet only on the western side is this woodland accessible. That is what I have included here, stretching from the rocky valley of Ramsden Clough to the edge of Stones Wood above Dulesgate. In between are small parcels of ancient woodland, with the overgrown hillside quickly filling in the gaps. It is a surprisingly rewarding area to explore from Walsden or Gauxholme.

Gauxholme is thought to have derived from an Old Norse word *gaukr*, meaning 'cuckoo', but which came to refer in local dialect to a fool.

One of the best areas of woodland is on the hillside immediately above **Walsden station**. Cross the railway and follow the road up to its end at the foot of **Fir Wood** (which noticeably lacks firs). A fine path leads left up through the wood to emerge on Inchfield Road, while another bears right over a stile and along the hillside beneath **Pasture Side Wood**. Reaching a vehicle track, keep left at a stile and climb up through **Naze Wood** to emerge on the Naze, from where you can return via Law Hey or along the edge of Inchfield Moor.

Originally a picker works, **Clough Mill** operated as Walsden Saw Mill and a joinery during the early part of the 20th century.

Stoneswood Mill operated as Walton's Picker Works in the early 20th century. In between the sparse oaks of **No Man's Wood** and **Buerlands Wood** are hard to access. There is a Right of Way through it between the bottom of Naze Road and a waymark post north of Hollow Dean, but little sign of any path. There were further woodland parcels above Hollow Dean of which no trace remains.

The main routes up from the A681 are the winding old packhorse route of **Naze Road** and the vehicle track up from Stoneswood Mill. In between the sparse oaks of **No Man's Wood** and **Buerlands Wood** are hard to access. There is a Right of Way through it between the bottom of Naze Road and a waymark post north of Hollow Dean, but little sign of any path. There were further woodland parcels above Hollow Dean of which no trace remains.

The **treecreeper** is a fascinating but elusive little bird. It has long claws that enable it to cling to trunks and branches, looking for insects and spiders that its long curved bill is adept at extracting from the bark. It tends to move almost mouse-like up a tree in a spiral, unlike the similar nuthatch which travels any which way. The treecreeper is well camouflaged by its mottled brown plumage, keeping its white breast to the tree, so although common in our oak woods it can be hard to spot. It also uniquely builds its nest behind loose pieces of bark on the tree.

a treecreeper

sculpture in Pasture Side Wood

to **Bacup** (4 miles)

Stones Wood

Stoneswood Mill

Dean Farm

No Man's Wood

A681

Buerlands Wood

Dulesgate Water

Watty Lane

Watty Scout

Hollow Dean (ruin)

Naze (ruin)

Naze Wood

Naze Road

stoops

Law Hey

GAUXHOLME

to **Todmorden** (1 mile)

Mason's Arms

Smithyholme Bridge

canal wharf

railway

A6033

Rochdale Canal

gates

posts

stiles

falls

Pasture Side Wood

Pasture Side Farm

Rough Hey Lane

Inchfield Moor

Fir Wood

Gauxholme Stones

Walsden railway station

Grandma Pollard's (chippy)

Clough Mill

Peel Cotta

Knowsley

Hollins Mill

bridge

148

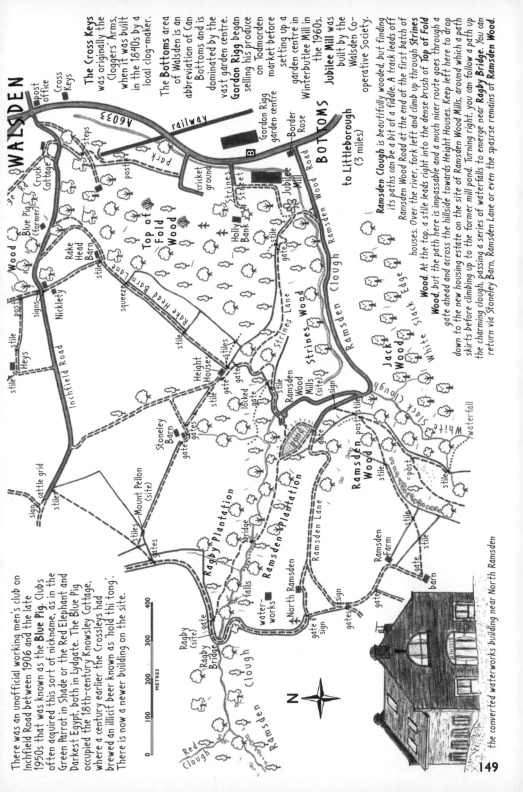

The Cross Keys was originally the Cloggers' Arms, when it was built in the 1840s by a local clog-maker.

The **Bottoms** area of Walsden is an abbreviation of Can Bottoms and is dominated by the vast garden centre. **Gordon Rigg** began selling his produce on Todmorden market before setting up a garden centre in Winterbutlee Mill in the 1960s. **Jubilee Mill** was built by the Walsden Co-operative Society.

There was an unofficial working men's club on Inchfield Road between 1906 and the late 1950s that was known as the **Blue Pig**. Clubs often acquired this sort of nickname, as in the Green Parrot in Shade or the Red Elephant and Darkest Egypt, both in Lydgate. The Blue Pig occupied the 18th-century Knowsley Cottage, where a century earlier the Crossleys had brewed an illicit beer known as 'hold thi' tong'. There is now a newer building on the site.

Ramsden Clough is beautifully wooded, but finding its paths can be a bit of a fiddle. A track leads off Ramsden Wood Road at the end of the first batch of houses. Over the river, fork left and climb up through **Strines Wood**. At the top, a stile leads right into the dense brush of **Top of Fold Wood**, but the path here is impassable and a much nicer route goes through a gate ahead and across the hillside on the site of Ramsden Wood Mills. Keep left here to drop down to the new housing estate on the site of Ramsden Wood Mills, around which a path skirts before climbing up to the former mill pond. Turning right, you can follow a path up the charming clough, passing a series of waterfalls to emerge near **Ragby Bridge**. You can return via Stoneley Barn, Ramsden Lane, Ramsden Lane or even the sparse remains of **Ramsden Wood**.

WALSDEN

BOTTOMS

to Littleborough (3 miles)

the converted waterworks building near North Ramsden

ROUTE 21: GORPLEY & RAMSDEN CLOUGHS FROM WALSDEN

Distance: 5.5 miles (8.5km)

Ascent: 340m

Parking: Free car parks on Vulcan Street in Walsden and the A681 by Gorpley Clough.

Public Transport: Walsden is on the main Caldervale train route and 590 bus service between Halifax and Rochdale.

Character: A fine and varied circuit that combines the rich wooded cloughs of Gorpley and Ramsden with the open pasture of Inchfield Moor. The route also picks its way through the charming backways of Walsden and provides some great views over this attractive part of the valley.

---

③ At the road in **Gauxholme**, turn right then left up Pexwood Road. Double back left on a path climbing past Watty Scout, then bear left through a gap in the wall. The path carries straight on through a gate to the left of one of the houses of **Watty Hole** to emerge near a prominent chimney on the hillside. Follow the concrete track right up past Friths Farm and continue straight on over another walled path to cross the field beyond. A kissing gate leads into **Stones Wood** and the path drops steadily down to the A681.

cairn on Shaw Stone, Inchfield Moor

② Upon reaching a vehicle track at the bottom of **Naze Wood**, turn left immediately over a stile and follow a slightly wet hollow. Turn left where the path forks at a waymark post, then climb out of the wood to emerge at the ruins and fine vantage point of **Naze**. Turn right, following Naze Road as it winds back down to the valley.

④ Follow the A681 up past Stoneswood House to the small car park at the bottom of Gorpley Clough, where you turn left through the gate. An obvious path follows the beautiful stream over a series of bridges and past some lovely waterfalls. It forks near the very top, where the middle path leads up to the works track below Gorpley Reservoir. Follow this round to the left to a gate out onto the open moor.

⑤ On the moor, a path leads straight on, passing to the right of a pylon before bending right and ascending a gentle shoulder. The few waymarkers here will eventually lead you away to the right (a soggy tramp), so keep straight on along the obvious path past some scattered stones. There is a small cairn on **Shaw Stone** at the slight crest on the top of **Inchfield Moor**, from which you descend steadily to reach a line of waymarkers along the **Long Causeway**.

Remnants of slag have been found at a site in **Gorpley Clough**, thought to have been evidence of an early **iron bloomery**. It may have been located on the south-east side of the stream near the head of the clough, or possibly lost beneath the reservoir. There are several other bloomery sites around Walsden, notably at Furnace, near Ramsden Clough Reservoir.

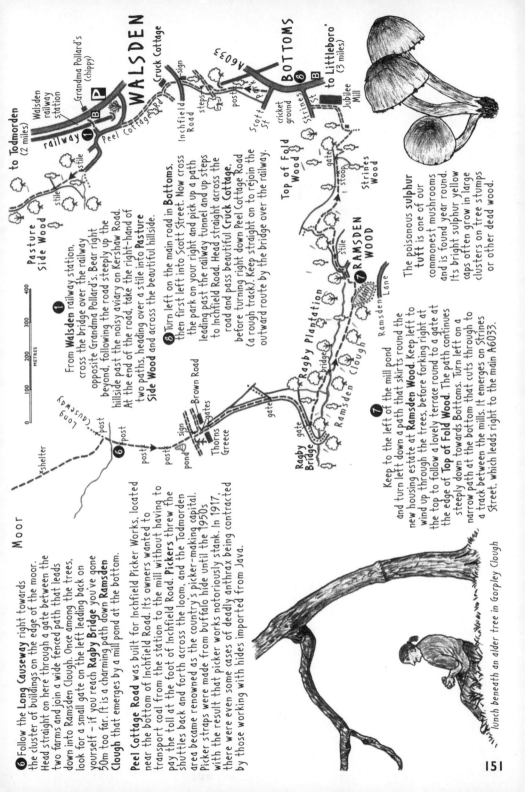

to Todmorden
(2 miles)

railway

Walsden railway station

Grandma Pollard's (chippy)

WALSDEN

Peel Cottage Rd

P

Cruck Cottage

Inchfield Road

Pasture Side Wood

BOTTOMS

A6033

steps

Scott St

Strines St

cricket ground

post

to Littleboro' (3 miles)

Jubilee Mill

Top of Fold Wood

stoop

Strines Wood

gate

Ragby Plantation

bridge

Ramsden Clough

RAMSDEN WOOD

stile

Ramsden Lane

Rugby Bridge

gate

Brown Road

gates

Thorns Greece

pond

sign

post

post

post

Long Causeway

shelter

Moor

METRES
0 100 200 300 400

1 From **Walsden** railway station, cross the bridge over the railway opposite Grandma Pollard's. Bear right beyond, following the road steeply up the hillside past the noisy aviary on Kershaw Road. At the end of the road, take the right-hand of two paths, heading over a stile into **Pasture Side Wood** and across the beautiful hillside.

8 Turn left on the main road in **Bottoms**, then first left into Scott Street. Now cross the park on your right and pick up a path leading past the railway tunnel and up steps to Inchfield Road. Head straight across the road and pass beautiful **Cruck Cottage**, before turning right down Peel Cottage Road (a rough track). Keep straight on to rejoin the outward route by the bridge over the railway.

The poisonous sulphur tuft is one of our commonest mushrooms and is found year round. Its bright sulphur yellow caps often grow in large clusters on tree stumps or other dead wood.

6 Follow the **Long Causeway** right towards the cluster of buildings on the edge of the moor. Head straight on here through a gate between the two farms and join a wide fenced path that leads down into Ramsden Clough. Once among the trees, look for a small gate on the left leading back on yourself – if you reach **Rugby Bridge** you've gone 50m too far. It is a charming path down **Ramsden Clough** that emerges by a mill pond at the bottom.

Peel Cottage Road was built for Inchfield Picker Works, located near the bottom of Inchfield Road. Its owners wanted to transport coal from the station to the mill without having to pay the toll at the foot of Inchfield Road. **Pickers** threw the shuttles back and forth across the loom, and the Todmorden area became renowned as the country's picker-making capital. Picker straps were made from buffalo hide until the 1950s, with the result that picker works notoriously stank. In 1917, there were even some cases of deadly anthrax being contracted by those working with hides imported from Java.

7 Keep to the left of the mill pond and turn left down a path that skirts round the new housing estate at **Ramsden Wood**. Keep left to wind up through the trees, before forking right at the top to follow a lovely terrace round to a gate at the edge of **Top of Fold Wood**. The path continues steeply down towards Bottoms. Turn left on a narrow path at the bottom that cuts through to a track between the mills. It emerges on Strines Street, which leads right to the main A6033.

lunch beneath an alder tree in Gorpley Clough

The **common violet** is also known as the wood
violet or dog violet, and is by far the most
populous violet seen in the wild. It is a bright spring
flower with five bluish-purple petals, and is found
in deciduous woodland, on verges and grassy heath.

The 'dog' part of the name refers to the fact that
it has no scent and was therefore suitable only for
dogs, unlike the fragrant sweet violet, which was
used as a medieval perfume. The violet is
particularly important for butterflies, many of
which lay their eggs on these plants. Violets have
been cultivated since the Ancient Greeks for use in
herbal medicine, as a symbol of fertility in love
potions, and as a traditional cancer treatment.

BIBLIOGRAPHY

Aitken, John – 'On the Discovery of an Ancient Ironmine in Cliviger' in *Transactions of the Manchester Geological Society* (1880)

Armstrong, Lyn – *Woodcolliers and Charcoal Burning* (Sussex, Weald & Downland Open Air Museum, 1978)

Barker, Paul – *Hebden Bridge: A Sense of Belonging* (London: Frances Lincoln, 2012)

Bates, Denise – *Pit Lasses: Women and Girls in Coal Mining c1800-1914* (Barnsley: Wharncliffe Books, 2012)

Beecham, M (ed.) – *Old Northowram Village* (Keighley: Steffprint, 2012)

Billingsley (ed.) – *Aspects of Calderdale: Discovering Local History* (Barnsley: Wharncliffe Books, 2002)

Billingsley, John – *A Laureate's Landscape: Walks around Ted Hughes' Mytholmroyd* (Hebden Bridge: Northern Earth, 2007)

Billingsley, John – *West Yorkshire Folk Tales* (Hebden Bridge: Northern Earth, 2010)

Billingsley, John – *Head, Hood & Hag* (Hebden Bridge: Northern Earth, 2011)

Billingsley, John – *The Last Road* (www.hebdenbridgehistory.org.uk)

Bolton, James – *An History of Fungusses Growing about Halifax* (London: R. White & Son, 1788)

Boswell, Geoff – *On the Tops around Todmorden* (Todmorden: Delta G, 1991)

Boswell, Geoff – *There and Back: Pennine Walks between Hebden Bridge and Todmorden* (Todmorden: Delta G, 2000)

Bottomley, Frank – *Yorkshire's Spiritual Athletes: Hermits and Other Solitaires* (www.zurgy.org/medieval/hermits.pdf)

Bretton, Rowland – 'Colonel Edward Akroyd' in *Transactions of the Halifax Antiquarian Society* (1948)

Bretton, Rowland – 'Wood Hall, Skircoat' in *Transactions of the Halifax Antiquarian Society* (1955)

Bretton, Rowland – 'Coley Hall' in *Transactions of the Halifax Antiquarian Society* (1969)

Clarke, S.R. – *The New Yorkshire Gazetteer* (London: Henry Teesdale & Co., 1828)

Clarkson, L.A. – 'The English Bark Trade 1660-1830' in *The Agricultural History Review Vol 22, No. 2* (1974)

Cliff, David – *Images of England: Ripponden and the Ryburn Valley* (Stroud: Tempus, 2007)

Collins, Herbert C. – *South Pennine Park: A New Recreational Area* (Skipton: Dalesman, 1974)

Comfort, Arthur – *Ancient Halls in and about Halifax* (Halifax Courier, 1912-13)

Crabtree, John – *A Concise History of the Parish and Vicarage of Halifax in the County of York* (Halifax: Hartley & Walker, 1836)

Crossland, Charles – *Pleasant Walks around Halifax* (Halifax: Edward Mortimer, 1910)

Crump, W.B. – *The Flora of the Parish of Halifax* (Halifax Scientific Society, 1904)

Crump, W.B. – *Ancient Highways of the Parish of Halifax* (Halifax Printing Co., 1927)

Crump, W.B. – 'Dialect on the Map: Some Calder Valley Place Names' in Transactions of the Halifax Antiquarian Society (1931)

Crump, W.B. – *Little Hill Farm* (London: Scrivener Press, 1951)

Darke, Mike – *Mytholmroyd Heritage Walk* (Ripponden: Pennine Printing Services, 2004)

Dearden, William (ed.) – *Dearden's Miscellany Volume III* (London: Orm & Co., 1840)

Dearden, William – *The Star-seer* (London: Longman, Rees, Orme, Brown, Green, & Longman, 1837)

Dearden, William – *The Vale of Caldene* (London: Longman & Co., 1844)

Dent, G. – 'Ewood in Midgley' in *Transactions of the Halifax Antiquarian Society* (1939)

Egerton, Vikki – *Luddenden Saga* (Cleckheaton: Amadeus Press, 2002)

Ellwood, Sheena – *At the Foot of the Lud: A History of Luddenden Foot* (Hebden Bridge: Royd Press, 2010)

Faull, M.L. & Moorhouse, S.A. (eds) – *West Yorkshire: An Archaeological Survey to AD1500* (Wakefield: West Yorkshire County Council, 1981)

Field, John – *A History of English Field Names* (London: Longman & Co., 1993)

Forshaw, Charles – *The Wild Boar of Cliffe Wood* (1907)

Gee, Stephen – *Halifax Pubs* (Stroud: History Press, 2008)

Gee, Stephen – *Halifax Pubs Volume Two* (Stroud: Amberley Publishing, 2011)

Gledhill, Barber – 'The Top of a Monstrous Hill: Approaches to Heptonstall' in *Transactions of the Halifax Antiquarian Society* (1995)

Goodall, Armitage – *Place-Names of South-West Yorkshire* (Cambridge: University Press, 1913)

Green, Muriel M. (ed.) – *Miss Lister of Shibden Hall* (Lewes: Book Guild, 1992)

Guide to Hardcastle Crags, Hebden Bridge & Heptonstall, with Historical Notes (Hebden Bridge: Moss Printeries, 1894)

Haigh, Donald – 'At Gretland in the Toppe of an Hill: Four Hundred Years of the Roman Altar, 1597-1997' in *Transactions of the Halifax Antiquarian Society* (1997)

Haigh, Donald – 'The Names Applied to the Road from Halifax to Wakefield through the Middle Ages to Modern Times' in *Transactions of the Halifax Antiquarian Society* (2000)

Hanson, T.W. – 'Ovenden Wood' in *Transactions of the Halifax Antiquarian Society* (1910)

Hanson, T.W. – 'Birks and Brackenbed' in *Transactions of the Halifax Antiquarian Society* (1911)

Hanson, T.W. – 'The Naming of the Hebble' in *Transactions of the Halifax Antiquarian Society* (1914)

Hanson, T.W. – *A Short History of Shibden Hall* (Halifax: Wm Patterson, 1934)

Hanson, T.W. – 'Cattle Ranches of Sowerbyshire' in *Transactions of the Halifax Antiquarian Society* (1949)

Hargreaves, Brian – *Images of England: Elland* (Stroud: Tempus, 2005)

Hargreaves, John A. – *Halifax* (Lancaster: Carnegie, 2003)

Hargreaves, John A. – 'Walking through History: In the Footsteps of E.P. Thompson' in *Transactions of the Halifax Antiquarian Society* (2014)

Harwood, H.W. – 'Hanroyd in Midgley' in *Transactions of the Halifax Antiquarian Society* (1955)

Heginbottom, J.A. – 'The Bee Boles of Calderdale' in *Transactions of the Halifax Antiquarian Society* (1983)

Heginbottom, J.A. – 'The Early Bridges of Calderdale' in *Transactions of the Halifax Antiquarian Society* (1986)

Heginbottom, J.A. – 'Early Christian Sites in Calderdale' in *Transactions of the Halifax Antiquarian Society* (1988)

Heginbottom, J.A. & Gilks, J.A. – 'A Note on the History and Archaeology of Tom Bell's Cave, Hardcastle Crags' in *Transactions of the Halifax Antiquarian Society* (1989)

Heginbottom, J.A. – 'Iron and Wool: Ironworking and the Woollen Textile Industry in Calderdale from the Middle Ages to the Industrial Revolution' in *Transactions of the Halifax Antiquarian Society* (1997)

Heginbottom, Tony & Cant, David – 'An Historical Outline and Architectural History of Hoo Hole in Cragg Vale' in *Transactions of the Halifax Antiquarian Society* (2001)

Hellowell, Sam – *A History of Cragg Vale and in Particular of its Church St John the Baptist in the Wilderness, Volumes I-III* (unpublished)

Helme, Christopher – *Images of England: Brighouse & District* (Stroud: Tempus, 2005)

Helme, Christopher – *Sunny Vale Pleasure Gardens* (Stroud: History Press, 2009)

Holden, Joshua – *A Short History of Todmorden* (Manchester: University Press, 1912)

Horsfall Turner, Joseph – *The History of Brighouse, Rastrick, and Hipperholme* (London: Th. Harrison & Sons, 1893)

Hoyle, James H. – 'The Manchester-Ilkley Roman Road' in *Transactions of the Halifax Antiquarian Society* (1916)

Hughes, Glyn – *Millstone Grit* (London: Gollancz, 1975)

Hughes, Ted – *Difficulties of a Bridegroom* (London: Faber & Faber, 1995)

Ibbetson, Heather Judith – *The Environmental History of a South Pennine Valley: 1284AD to Present* (Belfast: Queen's University, 2012)

James, N.D.G. – *An Historical Dictionary of Forestry and Woodland Terms* (Oxford: Blackwell, 1991)

Jarratt, Jim – *The Fielden Trail: A Ramble through Todmorden's Past* (Otley: Smith Settle, 1988)

Jennings, Bernard (ed.) – *Pennine Valley: A History of Upper Calderdale* (Cleckheaton: Amadeus Press, 1992)

Keighley, Jack – *South Pennine Walks* (Lancaster: Cicerone, 2003)

Kendall, H.P. – 'A Short Paper on Tom Bell's Cave' in *Transactions of the Halifax Antiquarian Society* (1902)

Kendall, H.P. – 'Sowerby Bridge and Stirk Bridge' in *Transactions of the Halifax Antiquarian Society* (1915)

Kendall, H.P. – 'Greenwood Lee, Heptonstall' in *Transactions of the Halifax Antiquarian Society* (1917)

Kendall, H.P. – 'Old Heptonstall: A Chapter in Its History' in *Transactions of the Halifax Antiquarian Society* (1922)

Kendall, H.P. – 'The Forest of Sowerbyshire' in *Transactions of the Halifax Antiquarian Society* (1926)

Kendall, H.P. – 'Halifax Hunts and Huntsmen' in *Transactions of the Halifax Antiquarian Society* (1928)

Kendall, H.P. – 'The Lumb in Soyland' in *Transactions of the Halifax Antiquarian Society* (1933)

Kirker, Anne – 'Walking through History: In the Footsteps of Sam Hill' in *Transactions of the Halifax Antiquarian Society* (2012)

Lee, Glyn – *A Pennine Saunter around Hebden Bridge* (Hebden Bridge: Lee Valley, 2003)

Lee, W.J. – 'The Yorkshire Yeoman' in *Transactions of the Halifax Antiquarian Society* (1940)

Longbotham, A.T. – 'Clay House, Soyland' in *Transactions of the Halifax Antiquarian Society* (1934)

Marshall, William – *The Rural Economy of Yorkshire* (London: Nicol, Robinson & Debrett, 1796)

Marshall, Winnie – *Cornholme: A Border Village* (1932)

Midgley History Group – *Pennine Perspectives: Aspects of the History of Midgley* (Midgley: Midgley Books, 2007)

Muir, Augustus – *The History of Bowers Mills* (Cambridge: W. Heffer & Sons, 1969)

Newell, Abraham – 'Sowerby Ramble and Erringden Deer Park' in *Transactions of the Halifax Antiquarian Society* (1915)

Newell, Abraham – 'Eastwood and the Eastwood Family' in *Transactions of the Halifax Antiquarian Society* (1916)

Newell, Abraham – 'Rottonstall, Stansfield' in *Transactions of the Halifax Antiquarian Society* (1917)

Newell, Abraham – 'Primitive Iron Industry in Upper Calder Dale' in *Transactions of the Halifax Antiquarian Society* (1918)

Newell, Abraham – 'Stoodley in Langfield and its Associations' in *Transactions of the Halifax Antiquarian Society* (1918)

Newell, Abraham – *A Hillside View of History* (Todmorden: Newell, 1925)

Ogden, J.H. – 'An Excursion to Midgley' in *Transactions of the Halifax Antiquarian Society* (1902)

Ogden, J.H. – 'An Excursion to Broadbottom, Fallingroyd and Mayroyd' in *Transactions of the Halifax Antiquarian Society* (1903)

Parker, James – *Illustrated Rambles from Hipperholme to Tong* (Bradford: P. Lund, Humphries & Co., 1904)

Pike, W.T. – *An Illustrated Account of Halifax, Brighouse & District* (Brighton: W.T. Pike & Co., 1895)

Pomeroy, Peter I. – *All O'er t'Parish: A Second Stroll around Cliviger* (Burnley: Lancashire County Council Education Committee, 1983)

Porrit, Arthur – *It Happened Here…* (Halifax: Fawcett, Greenwood & Co., 1955)

Priestley, J.H. – *The History of Ripponden* (Ripponden: Joseph Mellor, 1903)

Priestley, J.H. – 'Mills of the Ryburn Valley' in *Transactions of the Halifax Antiquarian Society* (1933 & 1934)

Priestley, J.H. – 'Brigg Royd and Ripponden Old Bridge' in *Transactions of the Halifax Antiquarian Society* (1935)

Rackham, Oliver – *Ancient Woodland* (London: Castlepoint, 2003)

Redmonds, George – 'Spring Woods 1500-1800' in *Old West Riding, Volume 3* (1983)

Rinder, Albert – *A History of Elland* (Elland: C J W Printers, 1983)

Rinder, Albert & Moody, Albert – *Elland: A Town History Trail* (www.gehs.org.uk)

Robinson, P.W. – 'Commercial, Hydropathic and Private Baths in Calderdale in the 18th and 19th Centuries' in *Transactions of the Halifax Antiquarian Society* (1995)

Rodgers, John – *The English Woodland* (London: Batsford, 1941)

Rotherham, Ian D. – *The Ghosts in Woodlands Past* (www.researchgate.net, 2007)

Royal Society of London – *Obituary Notices of Fellows Deceased* (London: Royal Society of London, 1854-1905)

Rudman, Barbara – *Todmorden: Old Pub Trail* (Littleborough: George Kelsall, 1989)

Smith, Albert Hugh – *The Place-names of the West Riding of Yorkshire* (Cambridge: University Press, 1959)

Smith, Nigel – 'The Medieval Park of Erringden' in *Transactions of the Halifax Antiquarian Society* (2009/2011)

Socialist Medical Association – *Death in the Air! The Menace of Air Pollution* (Richmond: Dimbleby & Sons, 1956)

Spencer, Colin – *The History of Hebden Bridge* (Otley: Smith Settle, 1991)

Stansfield, Abraham & Nowell, John – *Flora of Todmorden* (Manchester: Abraham Stansfield, 1911)

Stansfield, John – *History of the Family of Stansfeld of Stansfield* (Leeds: Goodall & Suddick, 1885)

Stringfellow, Garry – *Rushes and Ale* (Hebden Bridge: Northern Earth, 2010)

Sutcliffe, Glyn – 'Davis, James William: Industrial Dyer, Geologist and Politician' in *Transactions of the Halifax Antiquarian Society* (2004)

Sutcliffe, T. – 'Woodhall and Copley Hall' in *Transactions of the Halifax Antiquarian Society* (1905)

Sutcliffe, Tom – 'Warley Worthies' in *Transactions of the Halifax Antiquarian Society* (1916)

Sutcliffe, Tom – 'The Brearley Halls in Midgley' in *Transactions of the Halifax Antiquarian Society* (1922)

Symonds, Anne – *Slurring Rock Nature Trail* (Todmorden: Waddington & Sons, 1981)

Taylor, Mike – *The Calder and Hebble Navigation* (Stroud: Tempus, 2002)

Thomas, Peter – *Hebden Bridge: A Short History of the Area* (Hebden Bridge: Royd Press, 2008)

Thornber, Titus – *A Pre-Industrial Blast Furnace in the Lancashire Pennines* (Burnley: Rieve Edge, 1994)

Thornber, Titus – *Seen on the Packhorse Trails* (Todmorden: South Pennies Packhorse Trails Trust, 2002)

Thornes, R.C.N. – *West Yorkshire: A Noble Scene of Industry. The Development of the County 1500-1830* (Leeds: West Yorkshire Archaeology Service, 1981)

Trigg, W.B. – 'The Halifax Coalfield' in *Transactions of the Halifax Antiquarian Society* (1930-31)

Trigg, W.B. – 'Scout Hall' in *Transactions of the Halifax Antiquarian Society* (1946)

Turner, Whiteley – *A Spring-time Saunter Round and About Bronte Land* (Wakefield: S.R. Publishers, 1913)

Uttley, Jack – *The Colden Valley and the Early Textile Industry* (Hebden Bridge: 1997)

Vera, F.W.M. – *Grazing Ecology and Forest History* (Wallingford: CABI, 2000)

Walsh, J.F. – 'The Elland Flagstone and the Millstone Grit in the Parish of Halifax' in *Transactions of the Halifax Antiquarian Society* (1948)

Walton, James – 'Some Decadent Local Industries' in *Transactions of the Halifax Antiquarian Society* (1938)

Walton, James – 'Local Woodcrafts' in *Transactions of the Halifax Antiquarian Society* (1940)

Watson, John – *The History and Antiquities of the Parish of Halifax* (London: T. Lowndes, 1775)

Webster, Eric – '19th Century Housing in Halifax and the Growth of the Town' in *Transactions of the Halifax Antiquarian Society* (1986)

Webster, Eric – 'Leisure and Pleasure in 19th Century Halifax' in *Transactions of the Halifax Antiquarian Society* (1989)

Welsh, Stephen – *Cragg Vale: A Pennine Valley* (Mytholmroyd: Pennine Desktop Publishing, 1993)

Whitaker, Thomas Dunham – *Loidis and Elmete* (Leeds: Robinson, Son & Holdsworth, 1816)

Whitaker, Thomas Dunham – *An History of the Original Parish of Whalley* (London, Nichols, Son & Bentley, 1818)

Whiteley, John et al – *About Shelf, An Anthology* (Shelf Parish Church, 1970)

Wilcock, D.T. – *Stories and Folklore from the District Called Hardcastle Crags* (Hebden Bridge: 1927)

Woodhead, T.W. – *History of the Vegetation of the Southern Pennines* (Cambridge: University Press, 1929)

Wray, D.A., Stephens, J.V., Edwards, W.N. & Bromehead, C.E.N. – *The Geology of the Country around Huddersfield and Halifax* (London: HMSO, 1930)

Wyatt, Justine – *The Mills of the Hebden Valley* (Hebden Bridge Alternative Technology Centre, 2011)

INDEX / GAZETTEER

99 Steps, 4, 6
Abel Cote Wood, 100, 102
access, vi
Acorn Wood, 48, 52
Acres Lane, 116
Addersgate, 11
Akroyd House, 98
Akroydon, 41
Albert Promenade, 38
Albion Mills, 36
alder, 136
Alexandra Bridge, 59, 62
Alexandra Lake, 15, 17, 21
Allen's Fireclay Works, 15
Ambler Thorn, 10
amethyst deceivers, 115
ancient woodland, xxix-xxx
Annesley House, 35
Annet Hole, 4, 6
Annet Hole Well, 4
aqueduct bridge (Crimsworth
    Dean), 101, 103
ash, 22
Ash Grove Fireclay Works, 29
Ash Hole, 75
Ashday Hall, 24
Ashday Scout, 24
Asquith Bottom Dyeworks, 66
Atlas Mill, 31
Aufhole, 60, 67
Back Clough, 75
Back Rough, 144
Back Wood (Cornholme), 142,
    145, 147
Back Wood (Eastwood), 132
Back Wood (Holywell Brook), 51
Badger Lane (Shibden Dale), 15
Badger Stone, 83, 92
Bailey Hall Mills, 36
Bairstow End, 36
Baitings Bridge, 68
Baitings Reservoir, 68
Baltimore Bridge, 134
Bank House (Todmorden), 140
Bank House Wood (Copley), 34
Bank Top (Lindwell), 41, 43
Bank Top (Southowram), 20
Bank Top Wood (Cragg Vale),
    86-87, 93
Bankwell Coal Mine, 144
Bank Wood (Holywell Brook), 55
Bare Clough, 74
Bare Head, 11, 18
Bare Head Tunnel, 10, 18
Barewise Wood, 142-143, 147
Bar Hole, 133, 135

barkers, xxiv
Barkisland, 52
Barkisland Hall, 53
Barkisland Mill, 48, 52
Barkisland Stocks, 52-53
Barsey Clough, 48, 52
Bastard service tree, 104
Batting Spot, the, 122
Beacon Hill, 20, 36-37
Beacon House, 36
Bean Hole Delf, 132, 134-135
Bean Hole Wood, 132, 135
Bearnshaw Tower, 146
Beater Clough, 146
Beaumont Clough, 123, 127
Beaumont Clough Bridge, 123
beech, 8
Beech Croft, 48
Beestones, 48, 52
Beestones House, 48, 52
Beestones Mill, 52
Beestones Wood, 48
Beeston Hall Rocks, 64, 68
Beestonley Wood, 48, 52
Bell Bottom Wood, 84
bell pits, 3, 7
Bell Scout, 84
Belvidere, 14, 19, 21
Bents Wood, 141
Berry Bottom, 4
Bethel Chapel (Shelf), 6
Beverley End, 124, 126
Beverley Wood, 124, 126
Bilton Pier, 72, 76
Binn Royd, 40-41
Binns Bottom Colliery, 29
Binns Top, 29, 30
Binns Wood, 29, 30
birch, 107
Birchcliffe, 88
Birchcliffe Baptist Chapel, 96
Birchcliffe Shroggs, 13, 96
birch polypore, 98
Bird Bank Wood, 133, 134
Birdcage Lane & Hill, 39, 42
Birks Hall, 45
Birks Wood (Walsden), xxii
Black Bark, xxxiii
Black Brook, 48-49, 52-53, 54
Blackburn House, 48
Blackheath Circle, 141
Black Rock, 142
Black Scout (Hebden Dale),
    104, 111
Black Scout (Midgley), 81, 91
Blackshaw Beck, 2, 6
Blackwood, xv-xvi

Blake Dean, 108
Bleak Hill, 12
Bloody Row, 10
Bloomer Gate, 80, 91
bloomeries, 110, 123, 150
bluebells, 31
Blue Pig (Walsden), 149
Blue Pig (Midgehole), 98
Bob Mill, 118, 120
Bob Wood, 118, 120
Bod Bridge, 86
bog beacon, 85
Bogden Bridge, 64
Bogden Clough, 64
Boggart House, 24, 29, 30
boggarts, 29, 103
Boggart's Chair, 77
Booth, 73, 76
Booth Dean Clough, 65, 69
Booth Wood (Luddenden), 72
Boston Hill Wood, 99
Bottomley Wood, 48, 52
Bottoms (Walsden), 149, 151
Bottoms Bridge (Siddal), 34
Bowers Mill, 48, 52
Boys Mill (Siddal), 37
Bradley Hall, 49, 54
Bradley Wood (Rastrick), xv
Bradley Wood (Stainland), 49, 54
Branch Road Inn, 48
Brandy Hole Wood, xxx
Break Hole, 108
Brearley, 80-81
Brearley Baptist Church, 80
Brearley Hall, 80-81, 91
Brearley House, 80-81
Brearley Wood, 81, 91
Brian Scholes, 14, 19
Brianscholes, Forest of, 5, 14
Bridge Clough, 98, 100-101, 102-
    103
Bridge Royd Mill, 132
Bridge Royd Wood, 132, 135
Brier Lane, 25
Brigg Royd, 62
Brig Hey, 93
Brighouse, 31
Brighouse Wood, 25
Brink Wood, 85, 92
Broad Bottom, 89
Broad Bottom Wood, 89
Broad Carr House, 55
Broad Dean, 125
Broadfield Clough, 74
Broadhead Clough, xxxiii, 84, 92
Broad Head Plantation, 84, 92
Broadwood Cottages, 86-87

Brock Holes (Mytholmroyd), 84, 92
Brock Holes Delf (Hebden Bridge), 116, 121
Brock Holes Delf (Jumble Hole), 124, 126
Brockwell House, 66
Brookfoot House, 25
Brookfoot Lake, 25, 27
Brook Grains, 63, 65
Brooklands House, 50
Brookroyd Mills, 50
Brotherton Wood, 100
Brow Bridge, 41
Brown Birks, 144
brown roll rim, 88
Buckley Wood, 138, 140
Buerlands Wood, 148
Bullace Trees, 58
Bull Fall Stones, 86
Burgey, 132
Burlees Wood, 89
Burnt Acres Wood, xxi, 130
Burnt Brow, 10
Burnt House, 141
Burnt Wood, xxi, 87
Burr Wood, 49
Butterbowl, 58
Butterworth End Wood, 59, 67
Buttress, The, 116, 121
Butts Clough, 65, 69
Butt Stones, 141
Calder & Hebble Navigation, 34-35
Calder Bank, 114
Calder Bridge (Salterhebble), 35
Calder Coal Mine & Fireclay Works, 26
Calder High School, 80
Calder Holmes Park, 115
Calderside Mill, 122
Calder Valley (name), v
Calder Wood, 133
Callis, 123
Callis Nab, 123, 126
Callis Wood, xxviii, 123, 126
Canal Basin (Halifax), 36
Canal Wharf Saw Mills, 88, 115
Canker Brook, 55
carpentry, xxv
Carr Barn, 138
Carr Hall, 50-51
Carr Hall Castle, 50, 54
Carr Hall Well, 50, 54
Carr House (Mytholmroyd), 115
Carr House (Todmorden), 134
Carr Laithe (Ryburn), 62

Carr Laithe (Todmorden), 138, 140
Cartridge Clough, 144
Castle Carr, 74-75
Castle Carr Reservoir, 75
Castle Hill (Rawtonstall), 122
Castle Hill (Todmorden), 132
Castle Mill (Cragg Vale), 86
Castle Scout, 75
Castle Street, 132
Catherine Slack, 10, 18
Cat Hole, 142, 147
Catholes Stone, 142-143
Cat I'th Well, 73, 76
Cat Rocks, 73, 76
Cat Scout, 114
Caty Well, 73
Caty Wood, 73, 76
Causeway Mill, 133, 135
Causeway Wood, 133, 134
Centre Vale Park, 138, 140
cep, 69
chanterelles, 139
Chapel-le-Briers, 24-25
charcoal hearths, xxi-xxii, 49, 109, 130
Charles Rough, 100, 102
Charlestown Curve, 122
Charlestown, 122
Cheetham Wood, 64, 69
Chelsea House, 14
Chelsea Valley, 14, 21
Cherry Hall, 108
chestnut, 56
Chevinedge, 35
chicken of the woods, 65
Chimney Fields, 138
Christ Church, Todmorden, 138
Cinder Hill Farm, xxiii, 132
Clapgate Lane, 60
Clapper Hill, 75
Clapping Tree, 1
Clay House, 41, 43
Clay Wood, 77
Cliffe Wood (Bradford), xiv
Cliviger Gorge, 142-147
clog sole cutting, xxv
Clough Foot Bridge, 85
Clough Foot Wood, 83
Clough Mill (Walsden), 148
Clough Moor Bridge, 40, 42
Clunters, 142
Coal Clough, 144
Cob Clough, 63
Cockden Mill, 130
Cock Hill Wood, 146
Cock Rock, 101, 105

Colden Water, 118-119, 120-121
Coley Beck, 4-5, 7
Coley Hall, 7
Coley Mill, 5, 7
Colliers Arms, 28, 30
Collin Moor Lane, 41, 43
Common Bank Wood (Eastwood), 125, 130
Common Bank Wood (Hebden Bridge), 88
Common Wood (Hipperholme), vi, xvi, 14, 19, 21
Coneygarth, xix, 82, 92
Coney Wood (Ryburn), xix, 65, 69
Coney Wood (Shibden), see Cunnery Wood
conifers, 70
Copley Bridge Bar, 41, 43
Copley Hall, 39
Copley Viaduct, 39, 42
Copley Village, 39, 40-41, 42
Copley Wood, 34
coppicing, xix-xx
Copriding, 55
Cornholme, 144-145, 146
Cornholme Bobbin Works, xxv, 144
Cow Bridge Mill, 125
Cowbridge Wood, 125, 126
Cragg Brook, 85, 86
Cragg Fair, 93
Cragg Hall Wood, 86, 93
Cragg Mill, 85
Cragg Spa, 85
Cragg Vale, 83, 85, 86
Crimsworth Dean, xxiii, 100-101, 102
Crimsworth Dyeworks, 98
Crimsworth Wood, 98, 101
Cripplegate House, 16
Cromwell Bottom, 26-27, 30
Cromwell Quarries, 24
Cromwell Wood, 24, 31
Cross Keys (Walsden), 149
Cross Lanes Chapel, 116
Crow Nest Wood, 114-115, 127
Crowther Bridge, 26, 29
Crow Wood (Black Brook), 52
Cruck Cottage, 149, 151
Crummock Holme, 39
Cuckoo Rock, 101, 105
Cunnery Wood, xix, 13, 20, 36
Dairy Wood, 27
Dale Clough, 122, 125, 126
Dam Head, 11, 12, 18
Dancing Tree, the, 145

Dark Lane (Shibden), 14-15
Dauber Bridge, 82, 84
Dawk Hole Wood, 144, 146
Deacon Hill Wood, 86, 93
Dean Chapel, 72, 76
Dean Clough Mills, 45
Dean Farm (Walsden), 148
Dean Head Reservoirs, 74
Dean Hey, 83
Dean House (Ryburn), 60
Dean House (Shelf Woods), 4
Dean House Wood
    (Luddenden), 76
Dean Mill (Luddenden), 76
Dean Top Delf, 41
Dean Wood (Jumble Hole),
    124, 126
Dearden, William, 117
Delph Hill, 38, 42
Denton Bridge, 59, 67
Devil's Elbow, 21, 36
dipper, 62
Dill Scout, 118-119, 120
Dill Scout's Wood, 119
Dixon Cliff, 15
Dixon Wood, 58
Dobroyd Castle, 139
Dobroyd Wood, 139
Doctor Wood, 3
Dodd Naze, 88, 96
Dodge Royd Wood, 58, 66
Dodgson Wood, 44
Dog Bottom, 99
Dog Bridge, 87, 93
Doghouse Lane, 138, 140
Dog House Wood, 83
Dog Lane Mill, 52
Doldrum Wood, 144
Domesday Book, xiii
Donkey Pond, 10
Doroad Scout, 133, 135
Dove Scout, 125
Druids, xi
Drumming Wood, 64, 68
Dry Carr, 72
Dry Clough (Cragg Vale), 84
Dud Well, 34-35
Dulesgate Water, 148, 150
Dumb Mill, 14
Dundee, 142, 145
Dungeon Wood, 140
Dunkirk, 82, 92
Eagle Crag, 143, 147
earthballs, 21
Eastwood, 130-131
Eastwood Wood, 130
Eaves, the (Hebden Dale), 98,
    101

Eaves Bottom Mills, 119
Eaves Top Wood, 49, 54
Eaves Wood, xvii, 116, 119, 121
Edge End Moss, 123
Edge End Plantation, 123
Edwards, Joseph Priesley, 74-75
elder, 97
Elland, 28, 30, 35
Elland Cemetery, 35
Elland flags, 35
Elland Hall, 35
Elland Lower Edge, 26
Elland Park Wood, xix, xxvii,
    xxx, 28-29, 30
Elland Power Station, 31
Elland Wood, 35
Ellen Royd, 81
Ellis Bottom, 63
Ellis Memorial Clock Tower, 3,
    5, 6
Ellistones Mill, 49, 53, 54
elm, 112
Elphin Brook, 82, 84-85, 91
Erringden Deer Park, xiv, xvi,
    84, 87
Esther Cliff, 65
Ewood Hall, 80
Ewood Wood, 138, 140
Exley, 34-35
Exley Bank, xxix, 34
Exley Hall, 35
Fairfield, 114-115
Fairy Glen, 24, 30-31
Falling Royd House, 88-89
Falling Royd Tunnel, 89, 115
Fall Spring Wood, 48, 54
Fall Works, 4, 7
Farrar Mill, 34
Fernley Cottages, 122, 127
Fiddle Wood, 60, 67
Fiddlers' Bridge, 143, 147
Fir Wood, 148
Firth House Wood, 52
Fisherman's Hut, 109, 110
Flail Croft, 140, 143
Flathers Pit, 3
Folly (Ryburn), 65, 69
Folly Hall (Halifax), 36
Forest of Sowerbyshire, xiii, xvi
Fort Montague, 24, 31
Foster Clough, 80, 90
Foster Mill Bridge, 99, 103
Foster Wood, 118
Foster's Stone, 123
Foul Hill, 105
Foul Scout Wood, 105, 111
Four Gates End, 86
Four Lane End Colliery, 13
Fox & Goose Inn, 116, 121

Fox Stones, 63
Frank Wood, 72
Freeman's Cut, 27
Freeman's Wood, 25, 31
Frieldhurst, 145
Frost Hole, 84, 92
Frostholme Mill, 144-145, 146
Frying Pan, the, 144
Fulshaw Clough, 74
Galstones Wood, 98-99
Gannerthorpe Wood, 2
Ganny Lock, 31
Gate Head Wood, 48
Gauxholme, 148, 150
giant hogweed, 83
Gibbet, 143
Gibraltar Farm, 102
Gibson Mill, 104, 109, 111
Gibson Wood Cottages, 104, 111
Glen Dyeworks, 144
Glen View, 119, 127
Godley Cutting, 13, 16
Golden Lion (Todmorden), 134,
    141
goosander, 133
Gordon Rigg garden centre, 149
Gorpley Clough, xxii, 150
Gorpley Wood, 150
Gosport Clough, 51, 54
Gough Wood, 60
Granny Wood, 116, 121
Great Dairy, 27
Great Fall, 98, 103
Great House Clough, 132
Great House Wood, 60
Great Jumps, 115
Great Mount Quarry, 100-101
Green Hirst Wood, 100
Green Man, the, xvii
Greenwood Lee, 108
Greenwood Lee Clough, 109, 111
Greenwood Lee Wood, 104
green woodpecker, 49
Greetland Moor, 40
grey squirrel, 40
Griffin Inn, 52
Grove Inn, 81
Gut Royd Wood, 132-133, 135
Hagstock, 12
Haley's Quarries, 12
Halfpenny Can, 24
Halifax, 20, 34, 36, 45
Halifax gibbet, xiv-xv, 37
Halifax Minster, 20, 36
Halifax Zoo, 35
Hall Wood (Elland), 35
Hall Wood (Todmorden), 138-139
Hambleton Hill, 44
Hanging Lee, 64

Hanging Royd (Shibden Dale), 10, 18
Hanging Stones Wood, 62, 67
Han Heys, 49, 53
Han Royd Bank Wood, 80, 91
Hanson Wood, 64, 68
Hardcastle Crags Estate, xxvii-xxviii, 104-109
Hardcastle Crags Railway, 109
Hardcastle Hills, 109, 110
Hard Hippens Bridge, 115
Hareshaw Wood, 99
Harley Wood, 140, 143
Harrow Clough, 55
Harry Castle Hill, 26, 31
Harry Wood, 84, 92
Hartley Royd (Cornholme), 142, 147
Hartley Royd (Luddenden), 77
Harvelin Park, 133
Hathershelf Scout, 82-83, 91
Haugh House, 132, 135
Haugh Wood, 133, 135
Haven, The (Portsmouth), 144, 146
Haven Lane, 114-115
Haven Wood, 115
Hawden Hall Holiday Camp & Tea Gardens, 105
Hawden Hole Wood, 105, 111
Hawksclough Mill, 88-89
hawthorn, 97
hazel, 97
Hazel Hirst, 10
Hazelhurst Clough, 10, 18
Heathwood House, 4, 6
Hebble Brook, 34, 36-37, 44-45
Hebble End, 114
Hebble End Wood, 114
Hebble Hole, 118, 120
Hebden Bridge, 96, 103, 114-115, 116, 121, 127
Hebden Grove, 99
Hebden Hey, 104, 111
Hebden Water, 98-111
Hebden Wood, 105, 111
heck cart, 59
hedgehog fungus, 130
Height Clough, 72
Height Houses, 149
Height Lodge, 75
Height Wood (Eastwood), 131
Helen Hill Farm, 50
Hell Hole, 116, 119, 121
Hell Holes, 108
Helliwell Wood, 100
Henacre Wood, 10
Henchman, The, 40-41, 43
Hepton Hippins, 104

Heptonstall, 98-99, 116, 121
Heptonstall Eaves, 116, 119, 121
Heptonstall Methodist Chapel, 99
Heptonstall Stocks, 98
Hey Edge, 84, 92
Higgins House, 122, 126
Higher House Wood, 87, 93
High Field Coal Pit, 20
High Greenwood Wood, 108, 110
Highlee Clough, 59, 67
Highlee Knowl, 59, 62
Highlee Wood, 59, 62, 67
Hill House Clough, 89, 90
Hill House Wood, 89, 90
Hinchliffe Arms, 86, 93
Hipperholme, 14, 21
Hipperholme Brickworks, 15, 21
Hippins Bridge, 124
Hirst Bridge, 96
Hob Lane Top, 82, 91
Hock Cliff, 73, 76
Holderness Wood, 83
Hole Bottom, 141
Hole int' Wall, 121
Hollas Lane, 40, 42
Hollin Hall, 101, 105
Hollin Hall Wood (Warley), 101
Hollin Hey Bank (Mytholmroyd), 82, 92
Hollin Hey Wood, 83, 92
Hollings, The (Hebden Bridge), 99, 103
Hollins Hey Pit, 55
Hollins Mill (Ryburn), 63
Hollins Mill (Walsden), 148
Hollins Wood (Luddenden), 77
Hollin Well, 84
Hollow Dean, 148
holly, 94
Holly Bank, 149
Hollyleigh, 11, 12
Holme House (Ryburn), 65
Holroyd's Wood, 50, 54
Holt, Billy, 134
Holywell Brook, 50-51, 55
Holywell Green, 50
holy wells, 36, 50-51, 138
Honey Hole, 141
Hoo Hole, 84
Hoo Hole Dye Works, 82
Horley Green Spa, 13
Horse Bridge, 98, 101
Horse Hey Wood, 100, 102
Horsehold, 123, 127
Horsehold Scout, 122, 127
Horsehold Wood, xxii, 122-123, 127
Horse Pasture Clough, 74
Horseshoe Cascade, 108

Horse Wood, 88
Horsfall, 132
Hove Edge, 25
Hove Yard Wood, 87
Howcans Wood, 12, 19
Howroyde, 52-53
Hudson Bridge, 147
Hudson Clough, 142, 147
Hudson Mill, 118
Hudson Moor, 142, 147
Hullen Edge, 55
Hullet, The (Luddenden), 72
Hullett (Cornholme), 142, 145
Hungry Nook Wood, 144
Hungry Wood Arch, 144
Hut Booth Wood, 98
Ibbot Royd Clough, 96
Inchfield Moor, 148, 150-151
industrial revolution, xxvi-xxvii
Ingham Clough, 132, 135
Ingham Wood (Hebden Dale), 109, 110
Ingham Wood (Lumbutts), 133, 135
Intake Wood, 12-13
iron bloomeries, xxii-xxiii
Jack Wood (Walsden), 149
Jagger Green, 50, 55
Jagger Park Wood, 2, 6
Jagger Wood, 14, 19
Jaque Royd, 4
jay, 91
Jay Nest, 77
Jerusalem Farm, 73, 76
Jew's ear, 34
Jockey Gate, 98, 101
John Wood (Hebden Bridge), 96
John Wood (Judy Woods), 3, 7
Jowler Mill, 73
Jubilee Mill (Walsden), 149, 151
judd walls, 18
Judy Brig, 2-3, 7
Judy Wood, 2-3
Jumb Mill, 133
Jum Hole Beck, 14, 19, 21
Jumble Hole Mill, 125
Jumble Hole, 124-125, 126
Jumm Falls, 87
Jumm Wood, 87
Jumples Court, 44
Jumps (Lydgate), 142, 147
Kebroyd, 59, 60, 62, 67
Kebroyd Mills, 60, 67
Kell Brook, 73, 76
Kell Lane, 13, 19
Keppit Holme Dam, 105
kersey, 59
Kester Hole, 4-5, 7

Kiln Clough, 141
Kiln House Wood, 76
Kilnhurst, 134, 141
Kilnhurst Old Hall, 134
Kilnhurst Wood, 141
King Cross, 38
Kings Dean, 41
Kitling Bridge, 98, 102-105
Kitling Clough, 98, 102-103
Kitson Wood, 143
Knotts Naze, 142, 147
Knotts Wood (Cornholme), xx, 142, 147
Knott Wood (Charlestown), xxxiii, 122, 127
Knowl Wood, 87
Knowsley Wood, 148-149
Lad's Law (Heptonstall), 116, 118-119, 121
Ladstone House, 59
Lad Stones, 132, 135
Lady Royd, 109
Lake Calderdale, ix
larch, 70
Larch Close Wood, 45
Lark Hall Wood, 87
Law Hey, 148, 150
Law Wood (Lumbutts), see Ingham Wood
Lee Bank, 98
Lee Hill, 51
Lee Mills, 99
Lee Wood (Hebden Dale), iv, vi, 99, 103
Lee Wood (Holywell Brook), 51
Lillands, The, 27, 31
Lilly Bridge, 20, 36
Lilyhall, 99, 116
lime, 56
Lime House, 11, 18
Lindwell, 41
Lineholme Mill, 143
Lister, Anne, 16, 36
Little Bradley, 49
Little Haven, 59, 62
Load Clough, 77
Lobb Mill, xxix, 132
Lodge Clough, 126, 130
Lodge Wood, 126, 130
Long Causeway (Hebden Bridge), 119
Long Causeway (Walsden), 151
Long Chimney, 58
Long Royds, 89
Long Wood (Copley), xx, 39, 42
Longfield Wood, 141
Longley Wood, 59
Lord Nelson, 77

Lord Wood, 85, 92
Lovers' Walk, 138
Lower Dyson Lane Mill, 63
Lower East Lee Wood, 132, 135
Lower Shibden Hall, 11
Low Lodge (Luddenden), 75
Low Moor Iron Company, 3
Low Wood (Judy Woods), 3, 7
Lucombe oak, 139
Luddenden, 77
Luddenden Brook, 71-79
Luddenden Foot, 77
Luddenden Spa, 72, 76
Lumb Bank, 119, 120-121
Lumb Bridge, 102
Lumb Clough, 60, 67
Lumb Hole, 102
Lumb Mills, 118-119, 120
Lumbutts, 133
Lumbutts Clough, 133, 135
Lumbutts Fair, 133
Lydgate, 143, 147
Machpelah, 88, 115
Mackintosh's Toffee, 36
Madam Wood, 5
Making Place Hall, 67
Mankinholes Top, 135
Maple Dean Clough, 40, 42
Marshalls Works, 24-25
Marshaw Bridge, 86-87
Marsh Wood, 125
Martin Mill, 96
Martin Wood, 84, 92
Masons Arms, 148
Matthew Laithe, 132
May Royd Wood, 88
May Royd, 88-89
Meg Scar Wood, 65
melancholy thistle, 51
Mercer Field, 142
Mere, the, 13, 19, 20
Middle Dean Wood, 98, 101
Middlewood Farm, 25
Midgehole, 98, 101, 103, 105, 111
Midgley, 81
Milking Bridge, 119, 121
Mill Bank, 60
Millhouse Dyeworks, 58, 66
Mill Wood (Judy Woods), 2
Milner Wood, 48
Mirken Delf, 115
Mirken Wood, 115
Miss Lister's Road, 36
Mixenden, 44-45
Mixenden Reservoir, 44
Mixenden Stone, 44
monkey puzzle, 75

Monkroyd, 142, 146
Mould Grain Wood, 104, 111
Mount Olivet Chapel, 125, 126
Mount Pellon, 149
Mount Tabor, 44
Mulcture Hall, 125, 126, 130
Mutterhole Bridge, 125
Myrtle Grove, 62
Mytholm (Hebden Bridge), 119, 122
Mytholm (Luddenden), 72, 76
Mytholme House (Shibden), 14
Mytholm Mill, 122
Mytholmroyd, 80, 82, 84, 89, 90, 92
Mytholmroyd Farm, 90, 92
Mytholm Steeps, 119, 120, 127
Nab Wood (Ryburn), 64, 69
Nanholme Mill, 132, 135
Nant Wood, 142, 144
Naylor Mill, 143
Nazebottom Baptist Chapel, 123
Naze Road, 148, 150
Naze Wood (Jumble Hole), 125
Naze Wood (Walsden), 148, 150
Nether End Beck, 66
New Bridge (Luddenden), 72, 76
New Bridge (Midgehole), 98, 105
New Cragg Hall, 86, 93
New Ley Wood, 142, 147
New Mill (Cragg Vale), 86
New Mill (Wainstalls), 73, 76
New Mill Dam (Lumbutts), 133, 135
New Zealand, 64
Niagara Weir, 62
Nibble and Clink Dam, 73
Nicklety, 149
No Man's Wood, 148
Norcliffe, 15
Norman Forests, xii-xvi
North Brow Wood, 2
North Dean Delf, 40, 42
North Dean Station, 35, 41
North Dean Wood, 40-41, 42-43
North Dean Wood Charity, 40
northern hairy wood ant, 110
Northowram, 13, 14, 19
Northowram Hill, 13
North Ramsden, 149
North Well, 99
North Wood (Greetland), 49, 54
North Wood (Shelf Woods), 5, 7
North Wood (Shibden Dale), 13, 20
Norwood Green, 3, 5, 7
Nowell, John, 140
Nunnery, 72
Nursery Nook, 99

Nutclough Mill, 96
Nutclough Woods, 13, 96
oak, 128-129
Oaken Royd, 58
Oaklea Manor, 48, 52
Oaks Clough, 123, 126
Obadiah Wood, 145, 146-147
Ogden, 33
Old Bank, 20, 36
Old Bridge Inn, 63, 67
Old Castle, 90
Old Chamber, 115
Old Cragg Hall, 86
Old Dan Lane, 55
Old Field Stone, 101
Old Gate (Hebden Bridge), 119, 121
Old Hanna Wood, 3
Old House Bridge, 58
Old House Wood, 84
Old Rake, 139
Oldroyd, 133, 134
Old Royd Mill, 133
Old Salem Mill Pond, 99
Old Sarah Wood, 143
Old White Beare, 3
Old Woman, the, 146
Only House Wood, 14, 19
Orchan Rocks, 142, 147
Ousel Hall, 11, 12, 18
Outlane, 51
Outram's Valley, 49
Ovenden Wood, 44-45
Over Wood, xxii, 108
Owler Bank House, 99
Owler Cote, 80
Owlers Walk, 143
Owl Hill, 86
Ox Heys Wood, 5
Palace House, xiv, 114
Paper Mill, 85, 86
Paper Mill Wood, 85
Parish Wood (Judy Woods), 2, 6
Park Nook, 28
Park Wood Crematorium, 28, 30
Parrock Clough (Cragg Vale), 84-85
Parrock Clough (Eastwood), 126, 130-131
Pasture Side Wood, 148, 151
Peacock House, 76
Pecket Well Clough, 98
Peel Cottage Road, 151
Pen, The, 122
Pennant Clough, 142-143
penny bun, 69
Penny Hill, 52
Perseverance Mill, 130
Pex Wood, 139

pickers, 151
Pickle Bridge, 3
Pisser Clough, 109
Pitts, 145
Plains Lane, 28
Plane Tree, 84
Platts House, 138
Plod Well, 86
pollarding, xix-xx
pollution, vii, xxvii
porcelain fungus, 93
Portsmouth, 144, 146
Poultry Dealers Arms, 143
praying hole (Colden), 118, 120
praying hole (Crimsworth Dean), 101
Pretoria Bridge, 63
Priestley Green ,7
Priestley Ing Wood, 87
Priestwell, 134, 141
Psalm Rock, 105
Pudsey, 144-145, 146
Pudsey Clough, 144
Pule Nick, 12
Purprise, 102
Purprise Wood, 101
Q-pits, xxiii
Quebec, 63
Queensbury, 10
Queen's Seat, 124-125
Rabbit Hole, 105, 111
rabbits, xix
Ragby Bridge, 149, 151
Ragby Plantation, 149, 151
Ragley Delfs, 118, 120
Rake Holes Well, 4
Ramble Wood, 131
Ramsden Clough, 149, 151
Ramsden Plantation, 149
Ramsden Wood (Halifax), 44
Ramsden Wood (Walsden), 149, 151
Ramsden Wood Reservoir, 44
ramsons, 80
Rastrick, 27, 31
Ratcher Rock, 141
Raven Nest, 133, 135
Ravenstone Wood, 55
Raw Hey, 145
Raw Hole, 104
Raw Holme 98-99, 103
Rawroyds Viaduct, 55
Rawroyd Wood, 55
Rawson Wood, 66
Rawtonstall, 122, 127
Rawtonstall Bank, 119, 122
Rawtonstall Wood, xxii, 122, 127
Ray Gate (Castle Carr), 75
Ray Gate (Hebden Dale), 98

Redacre House, 89, 90
Redacre Wood, 89, 90
Red Beck, 14-15, 21, 24-25
Red Clough, 149
red deer, xiv, 50-51
Reddish Shore Rocks, 144
Reddish Shore Wood, 145
redpoll, 27
Redwater Clough, 144
Reins Wood, 27, 31
Ridge, the, 138
Ridge Wood, 141
Riding Hall Bridge, 2, 6
Ridings (Luddenden), 72-73
Ripponden, 62-63, 67, 69
Ripponden Bank Top, 63
Ripponden Co-operative Society, 63
Ripponden Wood, 60, 62
Rise Lane, 138
Rishworth, 65, 69
Rishworth Hall, 65
Rishworth Hall Wood, 64-67, 69
Rishworth Mill, 65, 68-69
Rishworth School, 65
Rishworth Station, 63
Rive Rocks, 141
Robin Hood, xiii
Robin Hood Inn, 85, 86
Robin Hood Rocks, xiii, 83, 92
Robin Hood's Hotel, 38, 42
Robin Hood's Scar, 28, 30
Robin Wood, 143, 147
Robinwood Mill, 143
Rodwell Clough, 132, 135
Rodwell End, 132, 135
Roebuck Inn, 144, 146
Roebucks Wood, 77
roe deer, xiv, 100
Rom Folly, 105
Rom Hole, 109, 110
Rom Hole Stone, 109, 110
Rookes Hall, 7
Rookes Wood, 5, 7
Rough Hey Wood, xxxiv, 58-59, 66
Rough Wood, 86
Roundfield, 146
rowan, 97
Rowshaw Clough, 108, 110
Royds Hall, 2
Royds Hall Beck, 2-3, 6-7
Royds Hall Great Wood, 2, 6
Rud Clough, 86
Rud Clough Wood, 86
Ruddle Scout, xxiii
Rudstoops Clough, 86
rushbearing festival, 58

163

russulas, 6-7
Ryburndale Paper Mills, 65, 69
Ryburn House, 62
Ryburn Reservoir, 64, 69
Ryburn Valley Branch Line, 63
Salford, 141
Salterhebble Basin, 34-35
Salterlee House, 12
Saltonstall, 72-73, 76
Sammy Wood, 14, 21
Sandal House, 119, 121
Sandyfoot Clough, 48, 52
Sandy Gate, 96
Sandy Pickle, 85, 92
Sandy Pickle Wood, 85
Savile Bowling Club, 122, 127
Savile Park, 38
Saw Hill, 66
Sawood House, 14
Scaitcliffe Clough, 140, 143, 147
Scaitcliffe Hall, 140, 143, 147
Scaitcliffe Wood, 140, 143, 147
Scarr Wood, xx, xxvii, 38-39, 42
Scar Wood (Black Brook), 48, 52
Scar Wood, Wheatley (see Larch Close Wood)
Scotsman's mixture, xxviii
Scots pine, 70
Scout Delf, 125
Scout Hall, 11, 18
Scout Head (Midgley), 81
Scout Plantation (Luddenden), 74
Scout Wood (Mytholmroyd), 82
Scout Wood (Shibden Dale), 11
Severhills Clough, 60
Severhills Mill, 60
Shackleton Wood, 104, 109, 111
Shavey Clough, 55
Shaw Clough, 132-133, 135
Shaw Edge Wood, 60
Shaw Lodge Mills, 37
Shaw Park, 50
Shaw Wood, 132-133, 135
Shears Inn, 37
Sheffield Royd, 35
Shelf, 4, 6
Shelf New Hall, 4
Shewbread Quaker Burial Ground, 141
Shibden Brook, 10-11, 12-13, 18-19
Shibden Fold, 13, 19
Shibden Hall, 13, 16, 20
Shibden Head, 10
Shibden Mill, 12
Shibden Mill Inn, 12, 19

Shibden Park, 13, 16, 19, 20
Shibden Spa, 13
Shoebroad Wood, 141
Shore, 145
Shore Baptist Chapel, 145
Shore End Wood, 75
Shore Law, 145
Shore Working Men's Club, 145
Shots Scar, 41, 43
Shrogg House (Copley), 34
Shroggs (Hebden Bridge), 115
Shroggs Park, 33, 45
Shroggs Wood (Halifax), 45
Shroggs Wood (Northowram), 12-13, 19
Siddal, 34, 37
Siddal Top, 28
Siddle Wood, 64, 69
Siggett Lane, 138
Siling Brink, 119
Simm Carr Colliery, 11, 18
Simm Carr Spa, 11
Skircoat Common, 38
Skircoat Green, 34
Slater Bank, 99
Slater Bank Wood, vi
Slead Sike Wood, 25
Slitheroe Mills, 63, 65, 69
Slurring Rock, 105
Small Shaw Wood, 100, 102
Smeekin Hill War Memorial, 98, 101, 103
Snake Hill Wood, 45
snigging, 105
Snoddy Mountain, 2, 6
snowdrops, 18
Snow Hill, 64-65, 69
Snydal Farm, 20, 37
South Holme Wood, 25
Southowram, 21, 24
Southowram Bank, xxix, 20
Sowerby Bridge, 58, 66
Sowerby Parsonage, 66
Sowerby Wood, xv
Sowood, 51
Sowood Hill, 51
Soyland Mill, 60
Soyland Town, 67
Spa Mill (Jumble Hole), 125
spas, 11, 13, 72, 85
Spa Wood (Cragg Vale), 85
Spa Wood (Luddenden), xxviii, 72, 76
Spewing Spring, 64, 68
Springfield Mines, 12, 19
Spring Mill (Eastwood), 132
Spring Side, 132, 135
Spring Wood (Cornholme), 145, 146

Spring Wood (Cragg Vale), 84, 92
Spring Wood (Hebden Dale), 99, 103
Spring Wood (Jumble Hole), 125, 126
Spring Wood (Skircoat Woods), 39
spruce, 70
St Andrew's Church (Stainland), 50, 54
St Anne's in the Grove, 24
St Bartholomew's Church, 63, 67
St Helen's Well, 50-51
St James' Church (Hebden Bridge), 116, 119, 127
St John's Church (Rishworth), 69
St John's Church (Triangle), 59
St John's in the Wilderness Church (Cragg Vale), 86-87
St John's Well, 7
St Mary's Church (Elland), 30
St Mary's Church (Luddenden), 77
St Stephen's Church (Copley), 41, 43
Staff of Life Inn, 142
Stainland Cross, 50, 54
Stainland Rec, 48-49, 54
Stainland Well, 51
Stainland, 50, 54
Stake Lane, 82, 91, 92
standing stones, 110
Stannally Clough, 142, 147
Stannally Naze, 142
Stansfield Bridge, 134
Stansfield Mill Bridge, 58
Station House Hotel, 131
Staups Bridge, 124-125, 126
Staups Common, 13, 19
Staups Mill, 124, 126
Stay Bank Wood, 131
Stephenson House Wood, 89
Sterne Mill, 39, 42
Stirk Bridge, 66
Stock Hey, 131
Stoneley Barn, 149
Stones Mill (Ryburn), 65
Stones Wood, 148, 150
Stoneswood Mill, 148
Stoney Royd (Lydgate), 147
Stoney Royd Cemetery, 20, 37
Stoney Royd Farm, 80, 91
Stony Spot Plantation, 75
Stoodley Clough, 131
Stoodley Glen, 131
Stoodley Hall, 131
Stoodley Ramble, 131
Stoodley Wood (see Back Wood)

Strait Hey, 131
Strangstry Bridge, 26
Strangstry Wood, 26, 31
Strines Wood, 149
Stubb Clough, 115
Stubbing Wharf, 122-123
Stubbing Wood (Black Brook), 48, 53
Stump Cross, 13, 19
suede bolete, 29
sulphur tuft, 151
Sunny Bank (Cragg Vale), 86, 93
Sunny Bank Pit, 15
Sunny Bank Wood (Hipperholme), 15, 21
Sunny Vale Pleasure Gardens, 15, 17, 21
Sun Wood (Shelf Woods), 4-5, 7
Sutcliffe Wood (Cragg Vale), xxviii, 83, 92
Sutcliffe Wood, xv, 15, 21, 25
Sutton Dam, 73
Swan Bank, 86
Swan Bank Colliery, 37
Swardy Hill Plantation, 86
Swift Place, 64
sycamore, 61
Tag Cut and Lock, 26-27
tanneries, 132
tanning, xxiv-xxv
tarpan, xi
Temperance Movement, 145
tenter posts, 24-25
Tenter Wood, 86, 93
Thompson, Edward Palmer, 37
Thorns Greece, 151
Thorns Wood, 144
Thorpe Mills, 59
Throstle Bower (Luddenden), 72, 76
Throstle Bower (Mytholmroyd), 80
Thrush Hole Wood, 115
Thunnerley Wood, 50-51, 55
Tinker Bank Wood, iii-iv, vi, 99
Tinker Hey, 40
Tinker's Trail, 2
Toad Rock, 119, 121
Toby's Cave, xvii, 119
Tod Bottom, xxix, 13
Todmorden, 134, 138, 141
Todmorden Edge, 138, 140
Todmorden Town Hall, 134, 138, 141
Todmorden Unitarian Church, 141
Tom Bell's Cave, 104, 106, 111
Tommy Wood, 124
Top Land Business Park, 82, 91

Top Bradley Mill, 49, 55
Top Brink Inn, 133
Top of Fold Wood, 149, 151
Top o'th Delf, 12
Tower Clough, 146
Tower Hill, 84
treecreeper, 148
Treesponsibility, xxix
Triangle, 58
Trigger's Grave, 134
Trooper Hill, 75
Troughabolland Wood, 13
Tudor House, 19, 21
Turf Stone, 105, 111
Turley Holes, 86
Turner Wood, 65, 69
Turret, 122, 127
Turret Hall, 122
Turvin Brook, 85, 86-87
Turvin Mill, 87
Twelve Apostles, 83
Twist Clough, 83, 85
Twist Wood, 10
Tythe Barn, 88
Underbank, 122
Upper Heys Wood, 72
Upper Lumb Wood, 86
Upper Shibden Hall, 10-11, 18
Vale Mill (Cragg Vale), 86
Valley Dyeworks (Brighouse), 25
Varley's Pool, 145
Vicarman Clough, 72
Victoria Lake, 15, 17
Victoria Mill (Cragg Vale), 87, 93
Victoria Mill (Hebden Bridge), 115
violet, xxix, 152
Wade Bridge, 73, 76
Wade Wood, 72-73, 76
Wadsworth Bank Fields, 89
Wainhouse Tower, 38, 42, 46
Wainstalls, 73, 76
Wakefield Gate, 20, 38, 42
Walker Pit, 13, 20, 36
Walkley Clogs, xxv, 115
Walsden, 148-149, 151
Walshaw, 108
Walshaw Wood, xxii, 108-109, 110
Walterclough Hall, 15
Walterclough Pit, 15
Walterclough Valley, 14-15, 17
Warley Wood, xv
Wash Falls, 87
Waterside Mill, 139
Water Scout, 11
Watson Mills, 58
Watty Hole, 150
Watty Scout, 148, 150
Weasel Hall, 114, 127
Weather Hill Wood, 83

Well Holme Park, xx
Well Wood, 142, 147
West Vale, 41, 43
Whams Wood, 85
Wheat Ing Bridge, 100, 102
Wheatley, 45
Wheatley Viaduct, 44
Whin Hill Wood, 45
Whins, 116, 121
Whiskam Dandy, 20
Whiskers Wood, 11
Whitaker Naze, 144
White Hill Nook, 98, 105
Whiteley Arches, 122
Whiteley Wood, 50
White Lion (Hebden Bridge), 103
White Slack Clough, 149
Whittle Wood, 48
Who Could a' Thowt It, 15, 21
Wickenberry Clough, 141
Widdop Gate, 108
wild boar, xi, xiv
wildwood, ix-xii
Will Clough, 87
willow, 32
Willow Gate Rock, 105
Wilson, Lawrence, 144
Windy Bank Wood, 144, 146
Winter Well, 101, 105
Winters Mill, 122, 125
Wittonstall Bridge, 145, 147
Wittonstall Clough, 145, 147
Wodewose, xvii
wolves, xiv
wood anemone, 53
Wood Fall, 4-5, 6
Wood Hall, 39
Woodhead Park, 14
Wood Hey Clough, 115
Woodhouse Mill, 133
Wood House Scar, 38, 42
woodland pasture, x
Woodman Inn, 123
Wood Mill (Eastwood), 130
Wood Nook, 28
wood sorrel, 39
Wood Top (Cragg Vale), 92
Wood Top (Hebden Bridge), 115
Wood Top Scout, 83
Wormald (Barkisland), 52
Wormald (Ryburn), 64, 68
Wriggles Bottom, 84
yew, 78
Yorkshire pudding fungus, 88
Zachariah Wood, 48-49, 53

Other woods in Calderdale

(still in existence but not included in this book due to
being of small size or having limited public access)

Ainley Long Wood, Elland
Ainley Round Wood, Elland
Alegar Bank Wood, Brighouse
Allen Wood, Sowerby Bridge
Bank Wood, Walsden
Birks Wood, Walsden
Black Cam, Todmorden
Brandy Hole Wood, Greetland
Chadwick Wood, Elland
Charles Wood, Mill Bank
Clifton Wood, Brighouse
Clock Face Wood, Ringstone Edge
Clough Head Wood, Rishworth
Clunter Wood, Walsden
Cock Walk Wood, Brighouse
Cold Acre Edge Plantation, Outlane
Corner Bank Plantation, Rishworth
Crawstone Hall Wood, Greetland
Dixon Scar Wood, Sowerby
Gallows Pole Hill Plantation, Barkisland
Grey Stones Wood, Warley
Harper Cliff Wood, Hipperholme
Henshaw Wood, Walsden
Hey Head Wood, Booth Wood
Hey Wood, Outlane
High Royd Wood, Warley
Hollins Hey Wood, Holywell Green
Lower Birk Hey Wood, Bailiff Bridge
Magson House Wood, Warley
Malverly Wood, Walsden
Mellings Wood, Todmorden
Oak Hill Bank Wood, Brighouse
Park Purse Wood, Elland
Red Lane Dike Plantation, Outlane
Seoul Wood, Walsden
Spring Wood, Walsden
Storth Wood, Elland
Sun Wood, Walsden
Sunderland Plantation, Cragg Vale
Upper Hathershelf Wood, Mytholmroyd
West Royd Wood, Warley
Whin Hill Wood, Pellon
Whitaker Pits Wood, Bailiff Bridge
Willow Wood, Luddenden Foot

Lost woods of Calderdale

(those to which reference has been made on old maps or documents but are no longer in existence - grid references provided where known)

Birks Wood, Halifax (GR 078261)
Black Hill Wood, Cragg Vale (GR 998233)
Black Wood, Sowerby (unknown)
Brackenbed Wood, Ovenden (GR 077263)
Burnt Wood, Cragg Vale (GR 997233)
Burr Wood, Holywell Green (GR 087203)
City Wood, Hebden Bridge (unknown)
Cliffscar Wood, Rastrick (unknown)
Common Wood, Northowram (unknown)
Crow Wood, Ovenden (unknown)
Crow Wood, Sowerby Bridge (GR 068241)
Culpin Wood, Sowerby (unknown)
Dairy Wood, Rastrick (GR 139226)
Daisy Bank Wood, Warley (GR 044242)
Dry Hey Wood, Greetland (GR 091212)
Ell Wood, Brighouse (GR 144239)
Ellen Royd Wood, Rastrick (GR 147211)
Elm Wood, Halifax (GR 097241)
Grimescar Wood, Rastrick (unknown)
Harley (or Hareley) Wood, Todmorden (unknown)
Heeley (or Hilly) Wood, Rastrick (GR 145222)
Hollin Bar Wood, Mytholmroyd (GR 027247)
Holme Wood, Cragg Vale (unknown)
Jagger Wood, Greetland (unknown)
King Wood, Luddenden (unknown)
Kitson Wood, Lydgate (GR 922256)
Knowl Wood, Todmorden (GR 932228)
Linland Royd Wood, Rastrick (GR 138228)
North Wood, Southowram (unknown)
Pickman Wood, Rastrick (GR 151213)
Quarry Wood, Sowerby (GR 047233)
Raven Nest Wood, Todmorden (GR 952242)
Rawson's Wood, Sowerby (GR 041228)
Round Wood, Greetland (GR 090210)
Round Wood, Rastrick (GR 149223)
Rows Wood, Stainland (unknown)
Sage Wood, Soyland (unknown)
Snipes Wood, Walsden (GR 926227)
Sowerby Wood, Sowerby (unknown)
Spring Wood, Norland Green
Spring Wood, West Vale (unknown)
Steps Wood, Warley (unknown)
Still (or Stile) Wood, Triangle (unknown)
Toad Holes Wood, Triangle (unknown)
Tower Wood, Cornholme (GR 906262)
Upper Birk Hey Wood, Bailiff Bridge (GR 153250)
Warley Wood, Warley (unknown)
Wham Wood, Heptonstall (unknown)
Willow Hall Wood, Skircoat (GR 063245)

Now available from the same author:

THE CALDER WOODLAND WAY

A beautiful fold-out map of this newly devised
23 1/2-mile route, which runs the length of Calderdale
from Brighouse to Walsden and takes in many of the
Calder Valley's finest woodlands

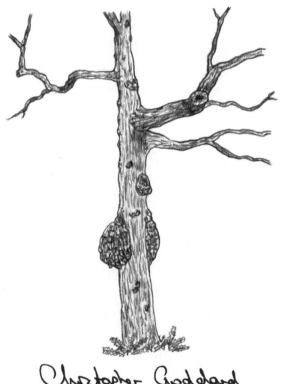

Christopher Goddard

The Calder Woodland Way map is now available for £4.99 at my
website below. I would also welcome your feedback, queries and
any suggestions or corrections you may have.

www.christophergoddard.net